D1020667

The Making
of an American
Psychologist

An Autobiography

Seymour B. Sarason

The Making
of an American
Psychologist

An Autobiography

Jossey-Bass Publishers

San Francisco • London • 1988

THE MAKING OF AN AMERICAN PSYCHOLOGIST
An Autobiography
by Seymour B. Sarason

Copyright © 1988 by: Jossey-Bass Inc., Publishers
350 Sansome Street
San Francisco, California 94104
&
Jossey-Bass Limited
28 Banner Street
London EC1Y 8QE

Library of Congress Cataloging-in-Publication Data

Sarason, Seymour Bernard, date.
   The making of an American psychologist.

   (The Jossey-Bass social and behavioral science
series)
      Bibliography: p.
      Includes index.
      1. Sarason, Seymour Bernard.
2. Psychologists—United States—Biography.
3. Psychology—United States—History.   I. Title.
II. Series.
BF109.S27A3   1988   150'.92'4   [B]   88-42798
ISBN 1-55542-110-5 (alk. paper)

Manufactured in the United States of America

The paper in this book meets the guidelines for
permanence and durability of the Committee on
Production Guidelines for Book Longevity of the
Council on Library Resources.

JACKET DESIGN BY WILLI BAUM

FIRST EDITION

Code 8841

The Jossey-Bass
Social and Behavioral Science Series

For Esther and Julie
By Way of Explanation

Contents

Preface

Although I found writing my professional autobiography to be interesting—in some strange way even fun, the tortures of writing notwithstanding—I found no less interesting what I left out in the total experience. I do not refer to the contents of my professional career but to the welter of impressions and issues that intrude into your thinking as you try to decide what to include in and how to organize the story. Someone said that you write an autobiography to find out who you were and are. That is a wise observation. It is also a humbling one, especially for a psychologist, because it confronts and challenges you with every important question about the substance, processes, and development of human behavior. More correctly, it forces you to realize that there is quite a gulf between our elegant theories and Williams James's "stuff of experience."

The human capacity to abstract and conceptualize has changed the world and eveyone in it, but it is a capacity that seems to have diverted us from recognizing the concreteness of human experience. The word is not the thing, the label is not the product, the abstraction is not the concrete, language is a dull reflection of the cloud-chamber quality of the human mind. Don't ever confuse the language of autobiography with the lived life. At its best, autobiography is a static organization of out-croppings that give you glimpses of an organism that was and is never at rest, always becoming, always arriving but never arrived, a mature adult concerned with how it will be when he or she "grows up," a mortal wanting immortality. Why climb Mount Everest? One of the climbers said, "Because it is there." You do not write an autobiography because it is "there" to be written. You may start out as if it is "there," but you soon realize that you have a lot of learning and unlearning to do and that there is no peak. You are constantly ascending and descending a psychological mountain that has no peak.

Perhaps the strangest part of the experience for me was the recognition that phenomenologically there is no separation among past, present, and future, but that we are always living in an amalgam of the three (as William James well knew). As soon as we have identified the present, it becomes the past and part of a purposed future. So, for example, while at the end of Chapter Five I relate that I was on my way to begin graduate school at Clark University, at the moment when I was writing, there were no boundaries among past, present, and future. Although I tell about a historically verifiable event, neither then nor when I was writing was there a separation between past, present, and future. That separation comes about for the purpose of communication through an acquired language containing the concepts of past, present, and future, in the process of which we attribute characteristics to our phenomenology (then and now) that it never had. Psychologically axiomatic in the writing was that the "I" in that far past and today were the same. That axiom is, of course, invalid. But what permits me to adhere to that axiom? Part of the answer is that the stuff of raw experience—before labeling and categorization—has an immediacy in which there are no boundaries among past (near or far), present, and future, no past "I" that contrasts with the "I" of the moment. It is an omnipresent "I," a seemingly silent constant in a stream of action and change.

In beginning to write, I was aware that my overarching purpose was to tell the story of how in the post–World War II era the field of psychology and the larger society had undergone transformations undreamed of before that war. And I wanted to do that by describing my career, which started before that war. It would be an autobiography of a career in which the truly private and personal would intrude only occasionally, just enough to make the career comprehensible but not to the point where it diverted me and the reader from the transformations in the field and the society. I was prepared to look inward and outward, but the latter far more than the former. What I was not prepared for, what kept intruding, was the question of how I had changed and the annoying thought that the "I" who was writing was not the "I" about whom I was writing. I assumed a constancy that on reflection I felt could not be true. I came to see the wisdom in the statement that autobiography is a way of finding out who you *were* and *are*. I would only add, again to counter the implications of language, that neither was a referent to a static point.

Given my tendency to rivet on the "I" of my future, I find it ironically amusing that over the course of my career, and with increasing emphasis, a dominant theme in my thinking and writing has been the significance of seeing one's field and the problems one studies in a social-historical context. Psychology, I have argued, was not born yesterday, and if one wants to understand its assets, deficits, and culture, one has to deal with a history that is the opposite of parochial, an endeavor that permits us to see how transformations in the field always involve perceptible change side by side with unexamined stasis. It was not until I began to write this autobiography, and began to ruminate about the constancy of my "I," that I realized that it represented a culmination of my rebellion against a field that instilled in its contributors to the literature a fear, and/or an antipathy toward or obedience to, an unwritten rule against the use of the "I" in writing. I am not, I should hasten to add, an advocate of personal expression for the sake of expression. And I am quite aware that many times, perhaps most of the time, the impersonal "we" or "one" is sufficient and efficient as long as the writer feels that truly personal but relevant opinions are adequately reflected in the writing.

What I have found impressive over the years is the frequency with which my colleagues have said that the impersonal style of writing was an obstacle to saying what they wanted to say in the way they felt it. Distancing my "I" from what I was writing was always a source of irritation and frustration. It took years for me to screw up the courage to say, "For me to say what I want to say, I have to write in the first person. The form will be dictated by the substance, and that substance is how I see the field and the world." As I realize now, when I said that and began to act in accord with it, my "I" had undergone a transformation. And not long after that, I began to entertain the thought that some day I would write my autobiography. If it took fifteen years to begin to write it, it was because I intuitively knew two conflicting things: that I wanted to find out who I was and am, and that facing and digging up the past would confront me with personal and conceptual problems that would bewilder me. And not the least of those problems would be distinguishing between historical fact and phenomenological truth, between the "I" of today and the "I" of yesterday, between the personal sense of agency and the constant bombardment from my social surround.

   Conceptually bewildering to me is the sense of agency, the sense that I propel myself in the maze of my surround, that I am acting on rather than being acted on, that I am, therefore, what I am because of what I think and do. In some abstract way, I know that my sense of agency is too one-sided, that I am constantly being acted on, that the relationship between the internal and external is transactional, that my psychological oxygen is not explainable only in terms of my psychological chemistry. I explain myself through myself, using various concepts that identify external people and events that have influenced me. The explanations seem to work until you take on the autobiographical task of explaining yourself to yourself and others, especially if, as in my case, I had to take seriously a particular point of view that I considered fundamental and on the basis of which I had been critical of psychology. And that point of view was eloquently, incisively, and compellingly expressed by John Dollard in 1935 in *Criteria for the Life History* (New Haven, Conn.: Yale University Press), long out of print and scandalously forgotten.

This is not the place to present or summarize his argument except to say that a life or professional history is not comprehensible only in terms of an individual psychology that rivets on the individual sense of agency. That sense is terribly important, of course, but it is, so to speak, the eye of the hurricane. Far more went on and is going on than the individual is aware of. It is not, Dollard said, a problem of culture *and* personality but culture *in* personality; that is, how culture in its silent and nonsilent ways transactionally shapes and is shaped by the individual. It is easy to nod assent to that position, but Dollard makes it clear that psychology has yet to take seriously the consequences of that assent. Dollard was writing about the conceptual obligations you take on when you seek to reconstruct the life history of someone other than yourself, obligations extraordinarily difficult to discharge well. The task, I have learned, is exponentially more difficult when you are both subject and object, when your narrow sense of agency gets in the way of seeing the larger picture, when indeed that sense is the obstacle to be overcome, when it can become overcome, at best, only partially. As I write this autobiography, it is as if John, a long-term colleague of mine at Yale, is peering over my shoulder and saying, "Come off it, Seymour, you know damned well that trying to see and convey yourself in the larger picture earns you a grade of honors for motivation, but a pass plus for the adequacy of the final product." John would have been pleased at the emphasis I place on American culture, if only because it alerts the reader to the implications of the obvious fact that I and psychology bear the imprint of a distinctive and historically atypical society, and that even in that culturally diverse society, I bear the influences of its eastern, urban, New York segment.

On the very day that I finished the chapter on my years at Dana College, the front page of the *New York Times* contained a summary of a report of The Carnegie Foundation for the Improvement of Teaching highly critical of undergraduate education. The major criticism contained in that report is that colleges have become credentialing institutions at the expense of their avowed purpose to provide a general education. I needed no convincing on that score. I treasured my undergraduate education precisely because it allowed and required me to venture

into areas of knowledge and history that forever put their stamp
on and in me. It has been only in the past decade that I have
come clearly to see how colleges have become semiprofessional
settings, vocational settings, appendages to graduate and professional schools. But what about the years between when I
finished college and now? How and why did I get caught up
in a changing society so that not only was I insensitive to the
ongoing transformation, but in many ways I colluded in it? The
answer, simple to state but difficult to explain, is that I got caught
up in the American conception of progress, that is, a confusion
between change and progress. I shall elaborate on this in later
chapters, but I mention it here as an example of how embeddedness in the larger picture can prevent you from seeing the force
and direction of that larger picture. And that, I have found,
is the bedeviling aspect of writing one's autobiography. How
did the "I" transact with the "it" (the larger society)?

Why foist these musings on the reader? My answer is that
writing an autobiography is not a summing up or an exercise
in memory. Nor is it an attempt to solve a personal jigsaw puzzle that when completed is a comprehensive picture. It is all
of these things and more. And the more is that the more you
know and find out and put into words, the more you need to
know and find out, and that it is an endless process. This is
not to tell the reader that the story is incomplete but rather to
indicate that the process of doing it is incapable of completion.
It is not a problem-solving process that has a once-and-forever
solution. These reflections are not intended to engender more
skepticism in the reader than he or she already has, or should
have. They are intended to alert the reader that the written autobiography is a product of a largely unreported process that is
as illuminating of the writer as he or she hopes the final product will be.

There is more of the personal in this book than I expected.
Initially, I thought that I would begin with my introduction to
psychology in college and go on from there. But I soon saw that
the kind of psychologist I became (and at age sixty-nine am still
becoming) would make no sense apart from some discussion
of the America in which I grew up, how that America put its

stamp on our family, how illness literally paralyzed and galvanized me, how being Jewish in metropolitan New York City was so much a feature of my makeup. And I found that the aim of describing the fantastic transformations psychology has undergone in my lifetime required that I explain some of my own transformations, especially how I came to feel marginal to mainstream psychology.

I must tell the reader that when in this book I use the term *American psychology,* I am referring to those parts of it that explicitly deal with individuals in social contexts. It has always been the case, more today than ever before, that a significant and important segment of the field borders on physiology, biochemistry, and what is today called the neurosciences. About this segment I say very little except when its participants fall into the trap of biological reductionism. How does one explain the extreme pendulum swings in explanation of human behavior from a riveting on the intrapsychic to a no less narrow concentration on central nervous system processes? That question does get raised in later pages, because I have lived through two of those pendulum swings, making me somewhat knowledgeable about tunnel vision. Those pendulum swings are not explainable only in terms of what has happened in an intellectual-scientific sense in these fields. In ways we do not study, those pendulum swings reflect, in part at least, changes in the societal atmosphere. Social history is always a potent variable. American psychology has yet to take it seriously. So, this book is about me, America, and American psychology. And if I have done justice to none of them, it is not for want of trying.

I have been fortunate in the people I have known and with whom I have worked. To name them here would be an indulgence of my gratitude and a burden on the reader. I am one of those rare academics in mobile America who has taught in only one university. I am fortunate that I have been at Yale all of these years because, despite all of its craziness and stuffiness, its somewhat irritating (to me) sense of preciousness and mission, it allowed me to do what I wanted to do and it surrounded me with colleagues whom, despite our obvious differences, I respected for their extraordinary talents. In the more than four decades I have been at Yale, there were several people who were of great help to me in ways I need not detail: Carl Hovland, Claude Buxton, John Dollard, Frank Beach, and Wendell "Tex" Garner. Tex Garner has been more than a colleague; he has been a dear friend. Each of these people had a range of intellectual interests, an awareness of the social world, that was the opposite of parochial. Each fit the mold of the ambitious, hardworking Yale professor, but each was also a gentleman, a term that, however antique it sounds to the modern ear, says it all.

One of the most troubling issues in writing this book was in restraining myself from expressing appreciation of individuals who enriched my personal and professional lives in myriad ways. Nowhere was this more difficult than when I had to mention the role of my wife, Esther, in my professional development. I panic when I think what my professional career would have been without her. She expanded my horizons in regard to clinical psychology, especially in psychotherapy. Without her participation the Psycho-Educational Clinic would never have been created. And without her involvement, my work in "work and aging" would not have been possible. It was her study on the introduction of the new math that stimulated me to conceptualize the culture of schools. I mention Esther in a number of places in the following pages. I keep it at "mentions," all factual. The truth is not there. I trust the reader to intuit the truth.

Dodie Allen is more than a secretary. She read, typed, and helped edit the first two-thirds of this book. When she became ill, I had an anxiety attack. (She has returned!) Betty Faison then came on the scene, and I realized immediately that I was indeed a lucky guy. Dodie and Betty are models of patience, understanding, forbearance, and graciousness. Occasionally one's cup of good fortune does run over.

New Haven, Connecticut   Seymour B. Sarason
June 1988

Other Books by Seymour B. Sarason

Psychological Problems in Mental Deficiency

Truk: Man in Paradise, with T. Gladwin

The Clinical Interaction

Mental Subnormality, with R. Masland and T. Gladwin

Anxiety in Elementary School Children, with K. Davidson, R. Waite, F. Lighthall, and B. Ruebush

The Preparation of Teachers: An Unstudied Problem in Education, with K. Davidson and B. Blatt

Psychology in Community Settings: Clinical, Educational, Vocational, Social Aspects, with M. Levine, I. Goldenberg, D. Cherlin, and E. Bennett

The Culture of the School and the Problem of Change

The Creation of a Community Setting, with F. Grossman and G. Zitnay

The Creation of Settings and the Future Societies

The Psychological Sense of Community: Prospects for a Community Psychology

Work, Aging, and Social Change: Professionals and the One Life–One Career Imperative

Human Services and Resource Networks: Rationale, Possibilities, and Public Policy, with C. Carroll, K. Maton, S. Cohen, and E. Lorentz

Educational Handicap, Public Policy, and Social History: A Broadened Perspective on Mental Retardation, with J. Doris

The Challenge of the Resource Exchange Network: From Concept to Action, with E. Lorentz

Psychology Misdirected

Psychology and Social Action

Schooling in America: Scapegoat and Salvation

Psychology and Mental Retardation

Caring and Compassion in Clinical Practice: Issues in the Selection, Training, and Behavior of Helping Professionals

The Making
of an American
Psychologist

An Autobiography

1

Why Write
One's Own Biography?

If mentally constructing or writing your autobiography requires neither defense nor explanation, seeking to publish it does. During World War II when gasoline rationing was necessary, one of the most frequent signs posted here and there said: ''Is this trip necessary?'' In regard to publishing an autobiography, it is apparent that many individuals think it is necessary for the world, or a segment of it, to know the story of their lives. So, for example, if you are seeking high political office, the published autobiography is explicitly justified as a necessary means for informing the public of your accomplishments, view of the future, and personal integrity. It is more personal advertising than it is searching reflection, more information giving than it is a summing up, more about a promised future than a candid introspective account of a complex life. Some would say that it is hardly autobiography, although they, I think, would understand the function the document serves. It is a form of personal-political advertising intended to create interest in and support for the writer—there is an agenda for the future. The author (not infrequently with the help of a ghost writer) has made the assumption that by virtue of his or her public role, there are people who would be interested in the story to be told. This document, call it what you will, requires some degree of personal revelation. The author knows this, the public expects this, although the author—far more than the general public—knows well how restricted an account it is.

At best, this type of semiautobiography is very different from that written by public officials (for example, presidents) who have left public life. They know they will be in the history books (as footnote or chapter), that the public is interested in them, that the published record of their lives and roles contains gaps and distortions, and that much of the private thoughts and relationships that governed their actions remains private and must to some extent be made public. Of the many factors that spur them to publish the stories of their lives, one of the more frequent is the desire to defend themselves, that is, to cast past decisions or behavior that were controversial in a new light, in a more complicated context of the private and the public self. That is why upon publication this type of autobiography arouses curiosity in the reading public: how much of the inside story, how much "inside" him- or herself and the office, will be revealed? What will we "really" learn about person and office? The public wants to know, and what it expects to get is a somewhat different and complex picture of the relation between appearance and reality.

The bulk of autobiographies is written by people who are household names: high public officials, corporate executives, movie stars and others from the performing arts. Far fewer in number are autobiographies written by scientists, but here too they are usually individuals whose names, if not their accomplishments, are so to speak in the public domain. Historically, however, a sizable number of autobiographies have been written by writers (poets, essayists, novelists), many of whom are or were not well known. For example, Coe located 600 instances of the autobiography of a childhood, "the majority of them well outside the canons of recognized 'literary classics,' but not, for that reason, without literary merit. Many of them, in fact, might be acknowledged as 'classics' were it not for the fact that the genre to which they belong has hitherto been perceived as anomalous" (R. C. Coe. *When the Grass Was Taller: Autobiography and the Experience of Childhood.* New Haven, Conn.: Yale University Press, 1985, p. xiii).

The serious autobiography is begun not because the writer already possesses clarity about "truths" but because he or she intuitively knows that that clarity will be achieved only by the most searching analysis and reanalysis, shaping and reshaping, of a past. The truth undergoes change, not from truth to falsehood, not so much because of the constant dialogue between writer and an imagined future reader (the intent and emphases of the former and the receptivity and understanding of the latter), as because of the colliding and abundance of memories that make the achievement of a focus agonizingly difficult. Just as no artist can reproduce a tree in all of its details, the autobiographer cannot reproduce in words the complexity of memories. The artist, visual or literary, must confront the problem of selection at the same time that it complicates the rendering of a perceived truth. What we expect of the autobiographer is a constant struggle between fidelity to a past and to the perceived truth. And, of course, different individuals vary considerably in how they control the struggle. If as readers we are not informed about the details of the struggle, we implicitly assume that the struggle was not treated lightly.

If the autobiography is powered by a pursuit of a truth, why seek to make it public? Obviously, the reasons are many, as I have suggested, but one of the most basic is the assumption that the truths you have arrived at should be made public: what you have to say the world needs to hear. That assumption is taken for granted in the case of individuals who are generally well known. In the case of less well-known people, that assumption poses difficulty, if not for the public then for the writer, who knows that there is no built-in receptivity for his or her account. But even here the belief that what one has learned should be made public spurs the autobiographer to seek publication. Self-confidence, tinged with arrogance, is a ubiquitous factor.

On the surface, it would appear that the truths contained in an autobiography are of a very different order from those in a report of research in a scientific journal. There are, however, notable similarities. Just as there are autobiographies that clearly play fast and loose with the truth, there are scientific reports about which the same can be said, sometimes to a degree that makes the front pages of our newspapers. And just as the autobiography reflects a selective reporting process, that is also the case with the scientific report, if only because the demands of brevity are so great. The scientist, like the autobiographer, decides what the reader needs to know to make a critical judgment about believing or not believing the central truth in the report. And, let us not forget, the scientific report contains a final section in which the researcher interprets his or her results, a process that can open the floodgates of bias, narrowness, and self-contradiction.

The published scientific report—which can vary considerably in believability and comprehensibility—is, like the published autobiography, not the outcome of a cold, programmed, rational process. And like the autobiography, the scientific report is intended to instruct, convince, and persuade. It says to its audience: I have uncovered a truth you need to, or should, know. But, it could be argued, the scientific report differs most dramatically from the autobiography in that its underlying message to the reader is: if you repeat what I did, you will get the same results and you will be driven to similar interpretations. (As often as not, I believe, replication gives different results and, therefore, different interpretations.) In the case of the autobiographer, the underlying message is only somewhat different: I have truths to tell that, if I have shaped and articulated them well, will allow you to conclude that you understand me in the sense that what I have recounted is not foreign to your own life despite the fact that we are different people. You can identify with and verify my truths. We have not lived in completely different worlds.

There are differences between the scientific report and the autobiography, and if I have emphasized some similarities, it was to make the point that conveying truths through language, regardless of genre, involves comparable problems and interpersonal dynamics. By *interpersonal dynamics,* I refer to the fact that the writer, if he or she is writing for publication, has a reader or readers (real or imaginary ones) in mind. Writing may be quintessentially a private activity, but it is a privacy replete with an audience and, therefore, governed by the dynamics of interpersonal exchange. And that exchange determines in part how the truths will be shaped and articulated.

The above is by way of prologue to explanation for my autobiography. The first facet of the explanation goes back a long way in time. I have always been interested in (really fascinated by) history in general, and my personal history in particular. I am less than an amateur historian. If a history book on the library shelf strikes my eye, I am likely to peruse it and then take it home. It would be fair to say that I am indiscriminate in my choices. When I came to Yale in 1945 for my first teaching position, I became aware that the graduate students in my seminars not only did not share my fascination with history, but in fact tended to regard history as a kind of museum of relics to which one went on Sunday if there was nothing better to do.

One example will suffice. A visitor to our department in 1947 interviewed one of our students and asked what he had read of the work and writings of Wolfgang Köhler. The student, the visitor later told me, replied, "Köhler? That's old hat. No one reads him any more!" The visitor, like me, was taken aback. To me, at least, what the student said was equivalent to a physics student saying that Rutherford or Einstein was old hat, or a student in physiology saying that Sherrington and Cannon were no longer important.

But let me give another example, from 1986. It was a seminar for all first-year graduate students. How many students, I asked, had heard of Roger Barker, someone I regard as an older and major figure in the field and a man who had been given the highest scientific award by the American Psychological Association? Only two of the sixteen students had *heard* of Barker, and none had read anything by him. In addition, no one in the 1986 class had read anything by John Dewey, let alone his groundbreaking paper in the previous century: "The Reflex Arc Concept in Psychology."

As the years went by, the ahistorical stance of American psychology increasingly troubled me, as did my relatively ineffective efforts to instill in students an interest in history. How,

I would ask myself, can I get them to see that their present contains a past, that their world of psychology was not born yesterday? It took me a long time to perceive a pattern: their interest in the past correlated rather well with use of my own history to illustrate a point. Whenever I used personal history to make a point (and to them my personal history was a form of ancient history), they seemed more alive and interested.

Sometime in the 1960s I began to entertain the thought of writing my professional autobiography as a way of making history more interesting. Like so much entertainment, the thought had little staying power. But as that decade drew to a close, I found myself giving more thought to writing my professional autobiography. Psychology as an academic discipline as well as a field of everyday professional practice had undergone fantastic transformations in size, diversity, and influence. And one of the consequences of these transformations was that the historical context out of which they emerged played little or no role in the forging of a sense of identity among the thousands seeking credentials as psychologists. The future of the field seemed limitless and glorious precisely, it seemed to be assumed, because it had finally emerged from a parochial past.

In the 1960s we were used to hearing from young people that you could not trust anyone over thirty. In psychology, it was less a matter of not trusting its past and more that its past was seen as largely irrelevant to the wondrous breakthroughs that seemed at hand. From my perspective, I was fortunate to have lived through the transformations in psychology. I entered the field before World War II, when psychology was a small, university-based field that prepared its students primarily for a career in the university. And it was a field that held its annual convention on a university campus, occupying only a small part of it. Today, there are only a handful of cities that have the facilities to accommodate the convention needs of the American Psychological Association.

But, as later chapters will indicate, I was no less fortunate to have acquired early on an abiding interest in the nature and workings of American society, and, therefore, I have always sought to interrelate societal transformations with those in psychology. Psychology, like Topsy, did not just grow in a vacuum. Its traditions, thrusts, substantive theories, organizational vehicles, and relation to public policy and the corridors of power all bear the imprint of American society.

To understand American psychology and its transformations, one has to understand America and its transformations, and to understand psychology in America, one inevitably has to see America in a changing international arena. So, for example, psychology today is not comprehensible unless one grasps the consequences of Hitler Germany in the 1930s. These consequences continue to pervade American psychology, a past very much in the present. And that is the point that spurred the writing of this autobiography: to describe and discuss my professional career in a way that would illuminate both psychology and America. And in thinking about and writing it, I knew (rightly, it turned out) that I would be rediscovering the country in which I was born and reared. I knew something about America, but there is nothing like writing—any serious writing—to set the dynamics of rediscovery in motion. Needless to say, I rediscovered much about myself.

Although very few psychologists have published their autobiographies, I have to assume that far more have seriously considered doing so. It may be reticence, or the belief that one's published works stand on their own and there is no need to place them in a completely lived life—that is, that relating those works to time, place, and private self would add little of significance to the works or the field. It is very likely that the autobiography is a literary form very uncongenial to those who for years have written journal articles or books that are explicitly impersonal. It is not fortuitous that over the centuries most autobiographies have been written by literary figures.

Psychologists spend little time trying to disabuse the general public of the belief that psychologists are experts in the springs of behavior and the significance of actions. After all, psychologists do not spend years of education and training to obtain empty credentials. They do learn a good deal about human behavior, and we expect them to have a refined sensitivity to the porosity of the boundaries between their ideas and works, on the one hand, and what we call the self, on the other hand. It is, therefore, precisely because of that sensitivity that I find it puzzling that so few psychologists have sought to write and publish their autobiographies, have been tempted to make public what they well know: that their published papers and books are a highly selected account of the "real" story, an account that inadequately explains where ideas come from, why one chose to study them in this way and not that way, and the diverse implications of these works that the psychologist felt constrained to omit.

I am reminded here of the report by a number of eminent psychologists on the training of researchers. It is a revealing document in that its major point is that the picture of the research process conveyed in journal articles bears little resemblance to the phenomenology of the researcher as he or she formulates, carries out, and writes up a study. As in any creative process, the research process is clearly not an impersonal one in which fantasy, ambition, personal style, and needs are alien factors. That, of course, has long been known and documented; it is a part, albeit a small one, of the history of Western science. Some may regard it as the gossipy side of the history, interesting, even titillating, but in some ultimate sense of secondary value in understanding the march of science.

To others, like myself, the scientific endeavor (or any other endeavor) is both a personal and an institutional one embedded in a society and, therefore, revealing of that society's major features. It is not understandable in narrow terms. Who studies what and in which ways is not explainable only in terms of personal esthetics or scientific tradition. And that, of course, is doubly true for the way in which research affects the society. The researcher is first a product of his or her society and then a product of his or her education and training. But he or she is always one product, the literary conventions of scientific publishing to the contrary notwithstanding. In all fields of science, we are used to hearing the phrase "contribution to the literature." From the standpoint of illuminating the psychology of the scientist, that use of the phrase is quite misleading.

In post–World War II America, no field has been more transformed than psychology. If it always (and inevitably) had the imprint of American society, and if that fact rarely was given importance, the postwar era has brought that fact to the fore as never before. That is a major reason I undertook to write my professional autobiography. I was both witness to and participant in those transformations, but it took decades for me to begin to see that the equation "American psychology = psychology" (an equation I had unreflectively accepted) tested the limits of parochialism; indeed, exceeded them. I am not referring to the fact that psychology in America is not the same as psychology in other countries around the world. That is obvious. What is less obvious is that American psychology, like rock and roll and McDonalds, has steadily come to dominate the international scene. We are the Romans of the modern era, building roads of psychology literally across the earth.

I say that not as criticism but simply as a warning that we cannot afford to gloss over the relationships between these transformations and American society. When the president of General Motors said that what was good for General Motors was good for America, it elicited sneers and derision, although in another era there was more muted criticism of President Coolidge's statement that the business of America was business. If that kind of identity did not sit well with the intellectual community, it was not because of rampant antibusiness or anticapitalist sentiment, but rather because ours was a complex society composed of groups with competing and even contradictory self-interests differentially enamored with growth and power. To give priority in value to the traditions and "philosophy" of the marketplace was regarded as an egregious misinterpretation of what America stood for. And yet, one not unfair way of describing American psychology in the post–World War II era is that it has incorporated the features of the marketplace as never before.

As members of university departments, as private practitioners, as staff in public agencies, as staff in corporations, as part of private consulting and research companies, as textbook writers, as active members in state and national professional organizations, as radio and television celebrities—in these and other roles, psychologists have become entrepreneurs to a degree unimaginable before World War II. Here again, I say this not in a spirit of criticism but as description that should suggest that growth and change have unintended consequences to which we are insensitive because our socialization into our society was so successful. To become sensitive requires that we become more reflective about ourselves as products of our society. To become autobiographical is not, should not be, an indulgence. To anyone interested in how he or she became what he or she became, the autobiography is a necessity.

Why publish this autobiography? Although I have some status in American psychology, I am far from being a household name in the field, like Carl Rogers, B. F. Skinner, Jerome Bruner. With one exception, I have worked in several areas (mental retardation, education, community psychology) none of which is in the mainstream of American psychology. The exception is clinical psychology, which did not exist in the university before World War II but now is the largest subspecialty in psychology, a transformation incomprehensible apart from changes in American society. Although I entertain the hope that my past writings will have staying power, I realize that the odds are against that happening.

Candor requires that I say that I regard some of my work as important—very important—not, however, because I did or wrote something that nobody else thought of (perhaps with one exception) but because that work carried on a tradition of criticism of the field, a tradition that by its nature gave me minority status. I regard what I describe and discuss in this professional autobiography to be important: what I have to say I think others, in and outside of psychology, should know. What I say will not be unfamiliar to many readers, but I hope that it will be said with a personal concreteness that will add something to their knowledge of themselves, their fields, and America. I have always regarded myself as a representative sample of one, and felt that what was true in and about me would strike responsive chords in many other people.

2

The Sense of Place: Brooklyn–New York–Newark

If few people write their autobiographies, I nevertheless assume that most, if not all, people engage in the process of mentally outlining and revising the "story" of their lives: trying to make sense of a past varying in its crazy-quilt qualities. Who has not heard people say what the anti-hero in *Pal Joey* sings: "If they asked me, I could write a book"? Writing that book is an intimidating affair, and for the bulk of people an impossibility, because intuitively they know and respect the fact that it is far easier (but still difficult!) to say what one has learned from living than to explain it meaningfully to oneself or others. To attempt to explain immediately confronts you with an array of memories, events, feelings, people, and places that bewilder and overwhelm, that make a mockery of concepts such as beginnings and ends, causes and effects, and even explanation itself. And, of course, there is the additional obstacle that because explanation requires searching, constructing, and reconstructing, we quickly realize that telling our "truths" will require exposing ourselves and others to possible scorn, ridicule, and certainly misunderstanding. If the autobiographies we construct over our lifetimes rarely get written, it has as much to do with our respect for the awesome task of explanation, of "put-

ting it all together,'' as with our respect for the difficulty of using language as a medium for the translation of experience. If
language is a wondrous and unique human attribute, let us not
confuse wondrousness with perfection, or even adequacy for certain purposes of which the written autobiography is one. It is
the best medium we have, but its inadequacies for the translation of experience should not be glossed over.

When do people begin mentally to construct their autobiographies? The word *begin* is misleading, because it suggests
a point in clock-calendar time when an individual ''decides''
to begin interrelating his or her past and present for the purpose of making personal sense of them. The kind of reflection
the word *begin* suggests is something that already characterizes
young children. If anything characterizes them, it is curiosity
about themselves and their worlds, and it is curiosity powered
by a need to understand and explain what we would term universal problems: how children are ''made,'' why boys and girls
differ anatomically, the nature of time and space, how our bodies
''work,'' why ''big people'' do what they do, and so on. These
are not idle questions, they are problems to be solved, and the
answers have to do with an emerging ''I'' and ''me'' in an interrelated past and present. In short, young children are auto-
biographers. The construction of our personal history begins
early in life. That personal history is constructed around the
need to solve problems that are emotionally powerful. And
children will differ markedly not only in the substance and structure of their personal history but in their proclivity in subsequent years to pursue and elaborate that history.

Like the word *begin,* the word *construct* is misleading, because it can be interpreted to mean a witting, deliberate action
or decision. A more felicitous description would be the phrase
''acquiring a past,'' because it is like so many other features
in development that we acquire without labeling or trying to
explain them. We acquire them, we have them, they are there
in our story, and we do not take distance from them—they do
not become an object to be scrutinized—unless events conspire
to make us take distance.

Children, no less or more than adults, vary tremendously
in what I can only term their interest in pursuing their personal

histories. How many children keep journals or diaries? When does such activity start? How frequently do children ask questions indicating an interest in their autobiographies, and to whom are they directed? I raise these questions not only because I believe they deserve study but in order to express the caution that it is too easy to think about the development and vicissitudes of the substance and form of the personal history primarily in terms of individual dynamics, as if the substance and structure of the individual's external world were backdrop, occasionally intruding into the story. Of course they intrude, but that wording egregiously glosses over the pervasiveness and ubiquity of that external world as it gets absorbed into our picture of our selves and their histories.

These introductory thoughts were stimulated by the difficulty I encountered in setting limits to this book that I labeled as my professional autobiography. I knew from the outset, of course, that the limits were arbitrary, that the adult me contained converging tributaries from the preceding years. What I was unprepared for when I began to reflect was precisely the kind of reflections others have so well described: the role of place and all that connotes about individuals, groups, physical structures, and the organization of space. As an adult on my analyst's couch, I talked endlessly about my mother, father, siblings, sex, lurid fantasies (pleasurable and otherwise), and recurring dreams, all having a very long history. And they were quite relevant to the reasons that spurred me to the analytical couch. But it was precisely the focus those reasons required that left in the background what I shall call the culture of place, which I felt as a whole but which now as an adult I feel or can describe in a more differentiated way—a way that illuminates continuities crucial to my understanding of myself today as a person and psychologist (a distinction that, in my case, literally makes no sense).

For example, I was born in the Brownsville section of Brooklyn and lived in an apartment house there for the first six years of my life. My mother's grandparents lived nearby for some of those years, as did half of her married siblings. I have no memories of the apartment, but I do have (and have always had) a rather clear picture of the neighborhood and that of my Brooklyn relatives: tall apartment houses; rows of two-story houses; many grocery, candy, and other types of stores; horse-drawn "vans" filled with fruits and vegetables and led by vendors shouting their wares in strange accents; Italian men pushing two-wheeled ovens and proclaiming the tastiness of their sweet potatoes and chestnuts; other Italian men delivering huge cakes of ice for our iceboxes from their horse-drawn wagons; and finally, people, lots of people, strolling or sitting on their stoops, or children older than I playing one or another game in the streets. The picture has a Breughel-like quality: lots of people doing lots of different things in a relatively small place, with a sound (not noise!) level that was loud and musical. It was a "peopled" place. I did not know what Italian meant, but those who were called Italian I saw—rather, I was taught to see by my Jewish parents—as strange, powerful, and dangerous, although a part of me saw them as interesting and friendly.

I felt it all as a whole, but in a narrow cognitive sense it was composed of unrelated knowledge, perceptions, and attitudes. The whole was indeed more (much more) than the sum of its parts. It was a whole that, in William James's sense, existed on the fringes of consciousness. But it existed, it was powerful, and for the most part it was very positively toned. What I did not know then—and rarely discussed on the analytical couch—was that I was a Jewish New Yorker of the Brownsville-Brooklyn species. More generally, I was already an urban character from head to toe. What that means is that in those early years it was as natural as breathing—which is to say you never noted it, indeed you could not put it into words—that you lived closely with and among an assortment of people, lots of people, where you belonged, where you were part of a scene that was physically-architecturally distinctive. There was no other world. There was no reason, for me at least, to think there was another world. I had not yet acquired a past.

The picture I have described is not intended to convey a Garden of Eden from which at some point I was to be catapulted. If I were to attempt to make the picture more complete—to make it more a large mural than a single picture—it would contain scenes, memories, and relationships containing many upsetting features. My nuclear and extended families were very conflict ridden, as hours on the analytical couch well documented. But, reflection forces me to conclude, that unrepresentative picture played a significant role in my professional-intellectual development. What that role was I shall discuss shortly, but let me first describe when I began to acquire a past.

We moved from Brooklyn across the river to Newark when I was six. The move was spurred by my mother's desire to be near her parents, who had gone there to be nearer four of their children, all of whom had pressured my grandparents to join them and, not incidentally, were financially far more secure than their three siblings in Brooklyn. So I moved into a familiar and dense extended family; we took an apartment in a building where my aunt, uncle, and their three sons lived and which they owned. One of their sons was a year older than I. It was a family network at the center of which were my grandparents. It was around and through them that social relationships and "happenings" took place. Those relationships, I must emphasize, were conflict ridden—or, to put a gloss over them, you could say they were ambivalent—but to a very young child they defined identity and obligations. You *belonged,* and in ways that required neither questioning nor articulation.

The past I acquired had a specific and general content, like orbiting pictures and attitudes that would from time to time enter my stream of consciousness and suffuse it with diverse feelings. The specific content had to do with Brownsville-Brooklyn: where I had lived, the school I had gone to, the large apartment houses, the street vendors, the noise and activity, and my aunts, uncles, and cousins who were so different from my Newark relatives and with whom I felt unaccountably (then) more kinship. The general factor, and the influential one for my present purposes, I can only label as New York, a label easy to apply and extraordinarily difficult to explain. Any adult living outside of New York City but in its metropolitan area does not have to be told that "the city" is always *there* geographically and psychologically. It may attract or repel, or both, but it is never without significance for what one is, how one thinks, and what one thinks about. It is, I contend, no different for young children.

I have plumbed the recesses of my memory to determine whether I had the concept of New York City when we lived in Brooklyn, and nothing surfaced. But as soon as we moved across the river, words such as *Brooklyn, Brownsville, New York,* and *Newark* began to take on discrete meanings. For one thing, my father continued to work in New York, which meant that he and the rest of us would be up at an ungodly hour so that he could get the trolley to the Hudson Tubes (now the Path trains) to his work site in the garment district in Manhattan. Papa was going to work in New York, and that was not the same as Brooklyn. And Brooklyn was not Newark, at least in physical-architecture appearance. In the Hawthorne Avenue–Clinton Hill neighborhood of Newark, there were no large apartment houses but many more single, shingled, one- and two-storied houses painted white, few street vendors, trolleys that I had never seen before, and populated *hills* that simply had not existed in my Brooklyn. How, I wondered, did the trolley (like the engine that could) get up the Hawthorne Avenue hill? Newark was in relation to Brooklyn as "the country" was to Newark: less populated (so it seemed), less visually crowded (so it seemed), and more fresh looking. In our family, "the country" was where there were discernible space between one-family houses, gardens and trees, no stores, and it was adjacent to a forest. My feelings about "the country" (the equivalent of "Gunsmoke" territory) were mixed: attractive in the ways the unknown and the unfamiliar can be attractive but, at the same time, a source of fear that it was a place bereft of all that is wrapped in the phrase "my neighborhood." "The country" was strange and dangerous. I was becoming increasingly an urban character. Life was with people, not with open spaces, trees, forests, rivers, and panoramic skies. We lived on Hawthorne Avenue at that point, where for several blocks there seemed myriad stores: Jewish bakeries, Kosher meat markets, what seemed to be countless candy stores, Jewish fish stores (one owned by my grandparents), Jewish, Jewish, Jewish. Compared to the smells, sights, and excitement of those stores, "the country" had few attractions. How I would stand riveted and enthralled by Mr. Dobbins's surgical genius in disemboweling a chicken or deboning a piece of flanken!

And how I would admire and be embarrassed by my mother's bargaining colloquy with him: "Take this fat off before you weigh it, let me see again how much it weighs, is that really a fresh pullet?"

Soon after the move, New York, as distinguished from Brooklyn, completed the triad of places that suffused my being, unreflectively but powerfully. The New York Yankees, Yankee Stadium, the ticker-tape parade for Lindbergh, the *New York Times*, the *New York Daily Mirror* (the *Journal-American,* the *Daily News,* the *World Telegram,* the *Herald-Tribune*), skyscrapers, the Empire State Building, Broadway, Grand Central and Penn Station—these and countless other words standing for people, events, and places became part of my language and fantasies. The fact is that we rarely visited Manhattan; when we visited across the river, it was to Brooklyn. Once a year my father, who was a cutter of children's clothes, would take me to "his place"—that was the only way his site of employment was described—to be outfitted. He would deposit me with the owner of one of those little and narrow eateries, and I would sit there through the morning, be outfitted during the lunch hour, and then we would take the Hudson Tubes back to Newark. Those excursions took place on Saturdays because my father worked on Saturday morning. The forty-hour week in 1927 or so was still in the future. I would sit in that eatery—the food, smells, accents, and people were not strange to me—gazing, watching, ruminating about the hustle and bustle of Manhattan's garment district. Where did all of these people come from? What were they doing, why were they doing it? There was excitement in the air and in me, tinged with a vague anxiety, but exciting nevertheless. New York–Manhattan was a frightening, wonderful place, populated by people who moved fast and talked loud as if they had to make sure they would be heard above the din. And those buildings! So tall that at street level you could not tell whether the sun was shining.

What I felt as a child of seven or eight sitting alone in that eatery (occasionally being given a malted milk or some other goody according to a schedule of reinforcement I could never fathom) is not dissimilar from what I experience today, sixty years later, when I get off the train from New Haven, walk through Grand Central, and exit on Forty-second Street. Thousands of people, most of whom seem to ooze purpose; the pulse quickens, I walk faster, the height of the buildings matched only by an air of heightened excitement, there is much that has to be accomplished, fascinating things are going on, important decisions are being made—there is a world to be conquered, and *this* is the place where conquests are made and paraded. And I want to be part of the parade.

The significance of what I have related from those early years truly became known to me only when I began to think about my professional autobiography. I began to see connections (*not* causes) with many facets of my experience as a psychologist or, more accurately, a particular kind of psychologist. For one thing, the substantive problems that came to interest me, and the roles and attitudes I had in relation to them, were unreflectively grounded in an urban phenomenology. So, for example, my first position after leaving graduate school in 1942 was in a new state institution for the mentally retarded (Southbury) in a rural, semi-inaccessible area of Connecticut. It was a beautiful area in "the country." Although I came to love it in an esthetic sense, I never felt at home there. Home meant Manhattan, Brooklyn, and Newark, where we had family and where (in Manhattan) we (my wife and I) took courses and sought intellectual-cultural nourishment. From the time we went to our offices on Monday morning, a background theme in our lives was thinking about and preparing for our departure to "the city" on the 4:45 P.M. Flying Eagle Bus to New York on Friday. We truly lived in two worlds, and there was never a doubt about which was the tail that was wagging the dog or, to choose another metaphor, which was the sun and which was the planet. When we got off the bus at the Forty-second Street terminal in the now nonexistent Dixie Hotel, we were intellectually and personally at home. We would scoot up to Teachers College to take a clinically related course, decide whether we had the time or money for a play or a concert, and take the subway to Brooklyn where my in-laws lived; I would get up the next morning to return to Manhattan for an analytical hour, at some point squeeze in a visit to my family in Newark, and then scoot back to the Dixie Hotel to take the last bus back to rural nowhere.

I shall have much to say about Southbury later, in Chapter Seven. But for my present purposes, several features of that institution have to be noted. The first is its innovative (indeed unique) rationale: children (they were called that regardless of chronological age) would come there, be trained and educated, and then return to home and community. Southbury was not to be, as all other such institutions were, custodial, that is, a human warehouse. That was an astonishing rationale in those days. I took that rationale seriously not because it was institutional policy but because it was a part of my being that people belonged only in their home and community. That was no less true for the residents at Southbury than it was for me. I never had to put that into words. They, I, and their parents needed and wanted the same things. But where did the bulk of the residents come from? The answer was cities: Bridgeport, Waterbury, New Haven, Torrington, Meriden, and so on. And what were some of the frequent characteristics of these residents? The answer was impoverished economic background, race (black), brushes with the law, and upsetting behavior in the public schools.

It would be true but misleading to say that I quickly came to see Southbury as largely a reflection of urban living. It is misleading in the sense that the elements constituting that knowledge were already known to me by virtue of the fact that I was an urban character. I had gone to public schools in cities, I went to college and graduate school in cities, and my political development was quintessentially urban in substance and outlook. What Southbury did for me was to cohere those elements, to deepen and broaden my understanding of cities, so that I began to see why Southbury was doomed to fail. Daily, on an hour-to-hour basis, I was dealing with *individuals* in their adjustment to an institution at the same time that I was aware that the reason they were at Southbury reflected the nature, structure, culture, and traditions of urban living in America. It was at Southbury that I began to conceptualize what I intuitively already knew: without the psychological sense of community, the individual is adrift, searching for meaning, alone and lonely. Southbury was testimony to the ever increasing dilution of the sense of community in our cities, a historical development that began several centuries ago. In addition, Southbury was one of society's modes of dealing at one level with what appeared to be, and what was sincerely believed to be, a humane approach to a frequent problem in cities at the same time that that mode weakened the bonds of community. Almost from the day it opened its doors, it was apparent that returning the residents to home and community would be infrequent, and in many cases impossible. Despite its rationale, and an architecture consistent with it, the dynamic of warehousing began.

Take but one example. Given the background of most of the residents in relation to the fact that Southbury was in the middle of rural nowhere, how would one maintain the desired ties between resident and family, as well as other segments of his or her neighborhood and community? The scandalous (at best, incomprehensible) fact was (and still is) that there was no public transportation between the institution and any city in the region. And in those days, far fewer of these impoverished families owned cars than would be the case today. The grief this caused resident and family is hard to comprehend. Over time, that grief transmuted to memories and longings for people and places both of which were no longer what they had been when the resident had been admitted to Southbury. Everything and everyone had changed, and that included the resident. The pain and sense of loss that accompany the "you can't go home again" experience is one thing; to experience "home no longer needs or wants me" is quite another thing. That is saying it from the standpoint of the child; to say it from the standpoint of the family would require different wording but not a different thought.

Was not mental retardation also a rural phenomenon? Of course it was, and a part of me knew it. Did not the principles of human behavior and those of community organization apply to rural areas? If my world was divided into cities and "everything else," did I not have an obligation as a psychologist to understand that everything else? If early on in my career

I applauded and was fascinated by anthropological accounts of foreign cultures, what made me so blind to my ignorance about a part of my own society? If I spent countless hours reading, talking, arguing, and writing about America, why did I know so little about why was I so uninterested in life outside of cities? The answer is a complex one that goes far beyond me and the purposes of this book, but part of that answer would be that we are products of place. For me, concepts such as culture, environment, and ecology incompletely capture what I mean by place—more correctly, what I feel about place. They are cold abstractions that, however concretized, seem to fail to convey, especially for our early years, how place—its sights, sounds, smells, architecture, boundaries—becomes part of, gives shape to, and emotionally colors and suffuses the sense of self. It literally is part of the *picture* we have of ourselves and the world. It becomes background in that picture, remaining unnoted but powerful, until "something happens" to startle us to recognize that it has been silently playing a role. And that is what happened when I began to think about my professional autobiography. It was easy to decide that this would be an autobiography of my career as a psychologist. Early in that career, I learned that in writing a book the first question you had to ask and clearly answer is what you are *not* going to write about. You set limits and you stay within them if only because everything is—or seems to be or can be related to—everything else, and your knowledge is pathetically miniscule for such a grandiose task. But when I began to reflect and ruminate about my professional life, starting with my college years, a place (for brevity I shall call it New York) began to invade the stream of consciousness. Needless to say, the invasion included particular individuals, relationships, and events and all else to which our developmental theories and studies sensitize us. But independent of all of that, there was New York as an atmosphere, an ambience, a sea of imagery, a place of wonder and awe, a magnet that attracted and a kind of meteor that illuminated and exploded, a place to be in and conquer, a whorish Babylon and a Periclean Athens. That is an attempt at description by an adult, but it does capture for me the features of place I experienced as a young child. I was caught up, sucked up, and shaped by New York, never fully realizing how much it was in my psychological bloodstream and, equally important, how having that factor in my bloodstream made me allergic to so many aspects of non–New York.

Let me give another example, which is more dramatic if only because it involves a particular time, place, and person. The person was Henry Schaefer-Simmern: artist, art historian, and art theorist. He opened up the world of art to me. (I shall have much to say about him and his influence on me as a psychologist in Chapter Eight.) The place was the Metropolitan Museum of Art. Schaefer stood me in front of a large painting of a farm scene by Poussin, with the instruction: "Examine the painting and tell me what you can change in it and where— color, line, shape, and so on—without having to change anything else." I told him that I did not cotton to farm scenes, to which he replied: "Your job is not to say whether you like the content or not but to understand the problem the artist was faced with and how he solved it."

So I studied the painting and came to two conclusions. First, I understood in a way I never had before what a gestalt is, because if I changed this or that color or line, however small and apparently unimportant the change, I would have to change a lot of other things. Everything in the painting was wondrously interdependent, nothing was random. The second, and in many ways more upsettingly instructive, conclusion was how set I was to ignore and dismiss something the contents of which were "uninteresting," that is, strange and unfamiliar to my urban world view. I was about twenty-six years old at the time, but I continued to see the world much as I had as a young child of the New York type.

Over the course of our lives, different places influence us, they become part of us, and each succeeding place is influenced by earlier places and determines how we will experience subsequent ones. A place is not a scene or a geographical setting. It is not a way of life, because that suggests a degree of conceptualization that occurs only after we have settled in a new place. In mobile America, many people experience what to me is an astonishing number of places. I have experienced relatively few places, and all of them have had New York as a magnet.

Place plays a significant role in the pasts we acquire. But, obviously, those pasts are shaped by many other factors. When I look back over my childhood—again because of what this book stirred up in me—I am struck by two things. The first is that important aspects of my psychological past were acquired informally and casually in the context of nuclear and extended family. For example, my grandparents, parents, aunts, and uncles were born in Russia. On countless occasions, I heard in their conversations words and phrases such as *pogroms, the czar, Kulaks, drunken soldiers, hiding in cellars, crossing the ocean, Castle Gardens–Ellis Island, sweatshops,* and *the Lower East Side.* It would be wrong to say that I *listened* to those conversations; rather, I heard these words that became associated with danger and threats to life. More correctly, the word *Russia* came to stand for all that one should avoid in life. I cannot remember when I knew I was Jewish, just as I cannot remember when I first learned to swim (which was quite early). But at some point I knew that being Jewish meant that there was a place called Russia that hated Jews. There were other people, called Christians—goyim—who did not like Jews, but those words did not call up the concrete imagery I associated with Russia. The point is that I heard these conversations; nothing was explained to me. Indeed, I cannot remember a single occasion when it was explained to me what being Jewish meant. There were, of course, the Jewish holidays, but they were more mystifying than illuminating. At Passover, for example, I heard about pharaohs, Moses, and unleavened bread, and I knew that the holiday ritual began by one of the male children asking the four questions about why the celebration was taking place. The answers always came in Hebrew, which I did not comprehend. Aside from strengthening an inarticulate feeling that I belonged to a disliked and persecuted group, I was never provided with explanations either at or above my level of understanding.

At seven years of age, I began to attend Hebrew school several late afternoons a week as well as on Sunday mornings. I learned to read and write Hebrew—but I never understood Hebrew. I could translate this or that word, and that was it. I learned what I was supposed to learn, and, as in the case of public school, satisfaction had two sources: being with and mak-

ing friends, and successfully competing—that is, being as good
as or better than they were in performance. School was never
intellectually interesting. Learning to add, multiply, subtract,
divide, and deal with fractions—this was something you did by
rote, and the goal was to get the right answer. You learned
arithmetic for the same reason you ate three "good meals" a
day: it was "good" for you, you needed it, you would not
"grow" well if you lacked it. I understood numbers as well as
I understood nutrition, which is to say that I understood nothing.

When I look back at those days of childhood, I see myself
in two distinct and contradictory ways: first as an ambitious per-
former and second as someone always asking myself (*not* anyone
else) why, why, why, why? I cannot recall any "why" ever being answered. In later chapters, I shall discuss my immersion
in the field of education. Suffice it to say here that a central theme
(perhaps *the* central theme around which all my thinking revolved)
in that immersion is that schooling is (but does not have to be)
a boring, intellectually unchallenging, uninteresting experience
in which the curiosity of children goes unrecognized or unheeded.
If that theme became increasingly focal to my thinking, its origins
were in my public and Hebrew school experience. Of course,
I accumulated a wealth of facts and rote skills in classrooms.
With just a little provocation, I could reel off the capitals of the
then forty-eight states, add a long column of figures with what
to others was amazing speed, give the dates of historic events,
and list the presidents of these United States. But all of that and
much more was encapsulated knowledge unrelated to the world
around me. I was an achiever, not an understander. What kept
airplanes in the air? Why did lights go on when you flicked a
switch? Why did voices come through the radio or telephone?
What was electricity? Why was Saturday special for Jews and
Sunday for Christians? What was a cold? Why was my father's
work seasonal? What did it mean that he was a cutter of children's dresses? Why didn't we have a telephone or a car like
my aunts and uncles? The questions were endless, unarticulated
publicly, and unanswered.

I do not want to convey the impression that I was obsessively concerned with these kinds of questions, because I was

not. In some inchoate way, I knew that I understood little about myself and the world around me, although I saw everyone—child and adult—as sure of what they were doing and why. It was not until I was an adult and a psychologist that I realized that making sense of my past was what most interested me. In the most literal sense, the substantive content of *everything* I have ever done and written has been largely autobiographical. Although I never put it this way until now, it would be descriptively accurate to say that it was as if I found that understanding myself, and applying that understanding to research and writing, was far more fascinating than any other "problem" in my field. When I became a psychologist—and I, like everybody else, was a psychologist before I "became" one—I was truly fated to be a "personal" psychologist. If asked (or even if I were not asked), I would say that I was going into psychology because I wanted to understand human behavior and to help people.

There was truth in that kind of conventional utterance, but the more motivating truth was that I had to make sense of me and my past. Not "had to" really, but I wanted to. And, as can be intuited from some of the things I have already said, I wanted to parade what I learned before the world because it was important. If I have never underestimated my ignorance, it surprisingly did not interfere with my ambition, if not grandiosity. I was an achiever, and that meant recognition by others. Strangely, I had few doubts that what I learned and said would receive some recognition.

The second conclusion I came to from reviewing my childhood can best be adumbrated by this question: Why was so little done by my family formally to anchor me in their pasts? Why was so much of it informal, albeit powerful? Some could argue, I suppose, that I am being somewhat ungrateful because, within the limits of their knowledge and means, they did whatever they could to further my development according to conventional values and standards of American society. If the relationship between my mother and father was a very troubled one, leaving many scars I still deal with today, if they were quite the opposite of being worldly-wise, I never doubted their love for me. Indeed, I have always had difficulty comprehending in others the feeling that they were unsure of the love and support of their parents. It is simply a feeling foreign to my experience.

But as my adult years proceeded and my quarrel with the alienating features of social living took on substance and shape, I keenly felt the lack of an identification with a historical past. I refer specifically to a profound ignorance about religion in general, Judaism in particular: its historical and theological contents. I had absolutely no doubt that I was Jewish, nor did I ever wish to be anything else. But I was not Jewish in the same sense in which I was an American: knowledgeable about and rooted in a long past that pervasively determined so much of my world view. My Jewishness was largely ahistorical. Hebrew was taught to me in a mindless fashion, and Yiddish—that musical, expressive language of warmth and mystery—was never taught to me, although it was used between my grandparents and their children as a language of conversation, as well as for those occasions when adults did not want children to understand what they were saying.

I still love to hear Yiddish and will never forget the first time the young woman who later became my wife took me to her parents' home (in Brooklyn, of course), and I heard Esther speak with them in a marvelously fluent Yiddish. I was envious and delighted. The envy was not only because I loved to hear Yiddish (of which on my own I had acquired a little comprehension) but because it reflected, and obviously so in the Kroop family, far less of a division between Jewishness and Americanness. To me, that relative lack of division was something that I had been missing in my life. My parents wanted to be Americans, to be part of this land of opportunity, and if they were aware (as they were) that they would only approximate that goal, there was no question that their children should and would be fully Americanized. And that meant that I was cut off from their near and historical pasts. To resort to jargon: my parents were upwardly mobile, and there was no point in rooting their children in a past useless in American society. Sending me to Hebrew school was something a bit more than a token gesture to their pasts; it was to "remind" me that I was Jewish, a reminding that I did not need and that engendered in me no sense of continuity with Jewish thought and history.

The above is prologue to this question: When and why did I come to have an interest in that abstraction we call history, an interest that shows up in some of the different lives I have lived in my fifty years in psychology? That interest was there before I went to college, but it was in my first year in college that it hit me with great force—especially in courses on English literature and European history—that lacking a knowledge of the Old and New Testaments was a hindrance to comprehending Western literature. Here I was, Jewish, reading essays, novels, and plays written by Christians who used the names, imagery, and events of the *Jewish* bible, about most of which I knew next to nothing. I knew Christians had their own Bible, but the relation between the two bibles was a complete mystery to me. Literally, I had never read the Old Testament in English (or in Hebrew for that matter). If before college I had had the occasion to read the New Testament, I would have considered it as sinful as eating ham, and, I can assure you, I *knew* that was sinful. If I knew that eating ham was sinful, I also knew that I did not know why it was a betrayal of my parents, "my people," and God.

In any event, what college exposed for me was, first, my ignorance of Jewish history and theology and, second, how in countless ways these subjects entered—directly or indirectly— into Western thought and literature, now and in the past. For example, I remember having to read a certain novel and coming across a reference to the Book of Job. Of course I did not understand the meaning of the reference, but I assumed from the context that the Book of Job was in the New Testament. I didn't know any Jew whose name was Job—it had a very Christian sound to me. How amazed and even a little angry I was when I learned otherwise! I came from a historical past to which I had never been exposed. My Jewishness was in an intellectual sense amazingly unsubstantial, like froth on the ocean waves. And like Job, but for my own parochial purposes, I found myself asking why, why, why? There was nothing dramatic in all this, no obsessing, just the sense that I had been made part of a historical past that went back thousands of years and that for many people, Jewish and Christians (Islam came much later for me), that story was still in their living present.

In 1966 we went abroad for the first time and spent most of six weeks in Italy. I bought a tour book on Italy, the first sentence of which leapt off the page, almost preventing me from reading on. The sentence was: "Remember, every Italian is at least two thousand years old!" Now I knew what it meant to live in a country, or any of its subregions, and to have history stare you in the face. Again, I felt envious, a sense of regret that in 1966 I could say I was forty-seven years of age, not three or four or five thousand plus years of age.

To say that I regret that my parents did little or nothing deliberately to merge their pasts into the one I was acquiring is an egregious instance of blaming the victim. They had been severed from their pasts, near and long term, religious and otherwise. My mother had come to this country as a young child, and she regarded herself (and was regarded by others) as "Americanized." It never would have occurred to her that transmitting a past was important. Family ties were important, but the basis for these ties was emotional, not cultural or religious. She met many of the stereotypes of the Jewish mother: loving, overprotective, guilt producing, and ambitious. The past was something to be overcome, not to be passed on. She wanted "the best" for her children, and that best was in all respects in the American present and future. The thought that the fires heating the American melting pot should be less hot—perhaps even put out—could never occur to her. If she felt as an outsider in American society, her children would not, must not. As with so many immigrants, the unverbalized axiom undergirding her thoughts and actions was "my children must have a better life than I have had." That "better" meant "different" and would be a mighty challenge to maintaining continuity between generations, that the contents of and adherence to millennia-old traditions might go by the boards—these were possibilities or issues that never complicated her thinking. My guess is that if these issues had been presented to her, she would have said that "maybe it is a good thing that these traditions should go by the boards.'' That these issues came to be central to my personal and intellectual development would have been mystifying to her.

I am amused by my fantasy that I am trying to explain this to her and when I am through, she replies, "What did I do wrong?" That I frequently feel like an outsider, that I am not sure how I should judge the significance of my life, that a sense of historical rootlessness bothers me, that I am not sure "what it is all about and what it adds up to," the sense of and need for ultimate purpose and transcendence—these thoughts and feelings would, I am certain, have been familiar to my mother, because she, like me and many other children of immigrants, was part of the American experience. She, of course, never heard of de Tocqueville, and I myself did not read him until relatively late in my career. If he did not say and understand it all, he did say and understand the guts of these thoughts and issues to an amazing extent (before the middle of the nineteenth century, no less). If my mother were alive today, she would seek to understand me, as many today will, in narrow psychological terms—that is, in terms of personality and family dynamics. That understanding has some validity (Freud was no fool or fraud), but it would be a limited understanding. America is a variable!

My father was a different cup of tea. He came to this country as a young adult. Unlike my mother, he spoke with a slight accent, and was much more Jewish in a religious sense, but he was no match for my mother in deciding what was best for their children. I always knew that he was religious and would have been more so if not for demands of work and my mother's objections. After my parents met my wife's parents (preparatory to our wedding), my father-in-law-to-be (an Orthodox Jew) told me that I should be very proud that my father had been extensively schooled in historical and theological Judaism. Indeed, my father-in-law said, my father's knowledge and training far exceeded his. This came as a complete surprise to me, because nothing of this knowledge was ever transmitted to me. When he had me accompany him to the synagogue on holy days, I was impressed by two things: his seriousness in prayer and what appeared to be his complete memorization of what was in the books of prayer. The book would be open, he would flick pages, his lips would be moving at an incalculable clip, and he seemed never to look at the open pages. I understood nothing, and he explained nothing. I was envious, angry, and bored—seemingly at the same time.

If the prayer books were a mystery, so was the fact that my father religiously read the *New York Times*. In fact, he was the only adult I knew in my childhood who read that paper, and that was a source of irritation to me, because the *New York Times* did not have comics. Also, sitting on a table in one of the rooms in our apartment was a Webster's unabridged dictionary that I lacked the strength to pick up until I was about seven or eight years of age. My father had bought it a year after he came to this country. Why? The answer, which I got only years later, was that he had visions of a high school education, maybe more. That answer saddened me, because it told me how little I understood or knew about him. In our extended family, my father was liked but not respected. I said earlier that he was not worldly-wise, which was how my aunts and uncles regarded him. He did not have a business, he worked in a factory—that is, he was not ambitious in the way they were. And, unlike them, he tried to sustain his religious heritage. In a conventional American sense, he was not worldly-wise. I knew he did not fit in with my more affluent, socially striving relatives. I resented the friendly derision my ears would pick up from what they said to and about him. I wished my father would be more like them, and yet I resented their attitude of superiority toward him. These relatives wanted to be at home in America (they were not then or ever); my father was still at home in his cultural and religious past. Today I know that he knew the importance of learning and scholarship in Judaism. The *New York Times* and the dictionary were to him derivatives of a past in which he felt most at home.

I know that my ambitiousness came to me through my mother. I have never been clear about what came to me through my father. Why, I have long asked myself, have the *New York Times* and that dictionary stuck in my mind? Of all the memories of my childhood that come back to me, why should those two stand out? And why is one of my oldest memories in the form of a picture and an associated feeling? The picture is that of myself (at age eight or nine, no more than ten) walking the dozen blocks to the neighborhood library, alone but happy, wondering what books I would find to take home. The feeling is that after walking into the library and scanning from the doorway shelf after shelf of books, I am saddened by the realization that I will never know everything that is in each of those books. Today, when I walk into Yale's awesome, Gothic Sterling Library, I have the same feeling, but it is tinged with wry amusement that the grandiosity of childhood does not die easily—although it must have for my father.

I have no interest here in fathoming the dynamics of my relationship to and ambivalent identification with my father. My mother and father are both in me as individual personalities, and as very contrasting and conflicting representatives of the immigrant experience in America. If I am more clear about the influence of my mother, it is no doubt because she was more dominant and directing. Her approval meant almost everything to me. And yet today when I am looking in the mirror and shaving (I used to admire my father shaving with that long, dangerous straight razor), and reflecting on who I was, and became, and why, I sense a kinship with my father that I cannot recall having with him as a child.

I cannot resist relating the following story, because it says much about how my father regarded his two sons, his father, and himself. My father had surgery for a prostate condition. My brother Irwin, now a professor of psychology at the University of Washington in Seattle, visited him on one day, and I came to see him on the next. During my visit, a nurse came in to see how my father was doing. She was a very friendly soul who continued to talk aloud regardless of what she was doing. My father had introduced me to her, telling her that I was a professor at Yale. A few minutes later, out of nowhere, she looked at my father, smiled, and with a sincere, childlike expression of curiosity said, "Mr. Sarason, how come a man like *you* has two sons like *them?*" To which, with practically no interval between question and answer, he replied with the most uncomplicated sincerity imaginable, "Didn't you know that intelligence skips generations?" My father revered and respected his father's learning and scholarly status in the Jewish community in the old country. My father aspired to but never achieved intellectually what his father had achieved. His two sons, however, were carrying on in the American way the traditions of learning so central to historic Judaism. I used to find this story very funny. I no longer do because of what it says about faded dreams.

There is one other anecdote I must relate, because it captures so well how the attitudes and experiences of childhood elicit and suffuse an adult experience. It starts in 1972 with a telephone call from a faculty member of the Jewish Theological Seminary in New York. He was a rabbi and a fully trained psychologist. He told me that the seminary had a special fellowship program for individuals who headed Hebrew schools around the country, some of these schools being full-day parochial settings and others after-school programs. A couple of times a year, these teacher-administrators are brought to the seminary for two-day meetings to discuss common problems, ideas, and future plans. And, I was told, there were problems. Would I, in light of my writings about experience in schools, come to their next meeting several months hence? My immediate silent reaction had several components: ironic laughter (nothing had changed from the time I was in Hebrew school), and in the land of the blind, the one-eyed astigmatic man is king!

I told him that I had to decline for several reasons: I had had no professional experience in parochial schools, I did not understand Hebrew, I was too ignorant of Judaism, and I had no basis for believing that I could be helpful. I assumed, I said, that nothing had changed from the time I had been in Hebrew school (which had been a kind of disaster for me), but that was no warrant to accept their invitation. But he persisted and finally asked whether he and another faculty member could come to New Haven to talk. I said yes, first because I go by a standard rule that I will see anybody who wants to see me. In addition, I was Jewish, and that meant to me that I had a special obligation to any other Jew who sought my help about a Jewish issue.

I knew that the meeting would be interesting and instructive, to me at least. Finally and perhaps most influentially, my respect for and envy of people steeped in and at home with their religion and its long history immediately came to the fore. These people knew an area of human thought, behavior, and history about which I knew almost nothing. They were truly scholars, I was not. And that reflected realistic modesty on my part. If they viewed me as an expert, that was their problem, about which I had forewarned them.

They did come to New Haven, and we talked for a couple of hours. The theme that pervaded our talk was their concern (to indulge in understatement) that generations of young Jews were growing up ignorant of and unrelated to Judaism except in the most superficial ways. Assimilation and mixed marriages were rampant. In regard to the world of action, they raised two questions: how can the Hebrew school experience be made more interesting and substantively attractive to students, and how can parents be made more involved in the significance of religious education? For too many parents, a Hebrew education for their children was more a balm to their conscience than a desire to instill in them a commitment to Judaism as a religion and, therefore, a way of life. As one of them said (paraphrased), "Must we rely on a Hitler or a Seven-Day War to remind Jews that they are Jews, rooted in history, not rootless people adrift in a materialistic world?"

They probably were unaware that their questions touched conflicts within me as a person and a psychologist. From childhood on, I knew that the religious person lived his or her days according to rules and obligations that not only gave structure to those days but infused them with purpose and direction in relation to past and future. Observing and being with my grandparents, I knew that they lived their days with a kind of serenity and purpose that no one else in the family seemed to manifest. Those are the words of an adult, but they do reflect the contrasting perceptions of me as a child. To me as a growing child, being religious meant you knew what you were doing and why. With my grandparents, I felt a warmth and stability that I felt with no one else, an oasis of conflict-free living. My childhood was a troubled one, and so it is not surprising that I can recall but two places where I felt that people knew exactly what they were doing and why, and with a strange (to me as a child) combination of seriousness and pleasure: the home of my grandparents and my father's "shul." To me, a synagogue or temple was (and still is) an imposing, modern structure in which silence reigns among a well-dressed, passive congregation, the men all beardless and the women sitting with them smartly dressed. I went to Hebrew school and was bar mitzvahed and confirmed in Temple B'Nai Abraham. The temple reflected my mother's aspirations. My father, however, belonged to a shul (which I always associate with orthodoxy) that was small, where women sat upstairs, many of the men had beards, there were distinctive odors, and the decibel level during prayer was wondrously high. When they prayed, they *prayed,* and I never doubted that God heard their prayers. If I understood nothing, if I resented the long walk from our house to the shul, I nevertheless felt a kind of warmth, the memory of which floods me with nostalgia today. In those two places, I belonged in a way that I experienced but one other time in my life.

The seminarians had read what I had written in the field of education. They were unaware that in the previous decade I had begun to write extensively about the psychological sense of community—more specifically, that a central problem in American society was the frequency and destructiveness with which people experienced the lack of belonging, the absence of the feeling that one was embedded in a stable, predictable, mutually supportive network of relationships that defined identity because that network was grounded on an agreed set of rules and obligations. The "long day's journey into night" did not have to be, should not have to be, so troubled and lonely. And if that problem had become so widespread, it was not understandable apart from the fact that several centuries ago, socially centripetal religion began to compete unsuccessfully with the socially centrifugal industrial revolution. What plagued me as a person and occupied me as a psychologist was truly a seamless web of feeling and thought. I knew precisely what the seminarians were fighting for and against. I felt kinship with them, less because we were Jews and more because we were struggling in different ways to put life-sustaining meaning into living. They had a better anchor than I, yet I was unable to use it.

By the time the visit was over, there was not a doubt that I would be at the meeting. I was aware of the feeling that I was "going home." I was amused but not surprised by the fact that the meeting would be on December 23 and 24. To Jewish but secular me—precisely the kind of Jew who sent these seminarians up the wall—those dates required changing our plans for the *Christmas* holiday.

If I had ever had to give serious thought to Jewish education, I would have quickly concluded that the educational problems (teacher preparation, quality, and style and, of course, student attitude and motivation) in Hebrew schools were no different from those in the public schools. The cultures of schools are remarkably similar, because they derive from unarticulated axioms that give rise to predictable institutional and classroom structures and dynamics—but more of that later. Suffice it here to say that the discussion over these two days confirmed this point, although making this clear to them did not make them feel any better.

There were about fifteen teachers sitting around the table. The leader and moderator was Rabbi Roth. (Of course, consistent with the concept of "quality" in Jewish culture, we sat around the table drinking coffee or tea and eating the most delectable little pastries—which in number could have fed a convention—confirming to dispassionate me that only in New York can you get the best of anything. I *was* home.) For the first hour, in a rather nonlinear kind of way, the discussion centered around what seemed to me to be theological issues. What impressed me, however, was the individuals spoke in English until they invoked authority, and then they would quote the authorities in Hebrew. And quotations were not one-liners! I felt increasingly humble (and irrelevant) and viewed these young scholars with undiluted admiration. The image of my father, who seemed to know the entire prayer book by heart, returned. And so did the image of my grandfather return (in that they, like he, seemed to know how to live and why), and I was envious.

Let me describe one interchange. In making his point, one of the teachers referred (in English) to a Hebrew sage as supporting evidence. When he finished, the young man on my left said somewhat caustically that that sage was being inaccurately quoted, and he then proceeded for what seemed to be thirty seconds to quote in Hebrew what that sage had said, accompanying his ending with an expression of triumph. There was silence, broken after a few seconds by Rabbi Roth, who quietly and sensitively said to the young man on my left, ''You left out a sentence in that quotation that would change the meaning of what you said,'' and he quoted the sentence in Hebrew, of course.

There are at least two ways that one could react to that meeting. There are some who would see these teachers (many if not all of whom had rabbinical training) as young people who, if not pedants, had narrow intellectual scope and interests, operating in a rather closed system of values, beliefs, and knowledge. It is not germane here to discuss that reaction. More germane is my reaction that these were people secure in a past that structured a present that did not threaten them as persons but would plunge others into a search for meaning that would end in failure. These teachers were not searching for meaning. Their millennia-old past was not for display in a museum of relics, it was in their everyday lives. If they thought they possessed truths, they were not intent on recreating the past from which those truths had emerged. They were intent on suffusing the present with those truths. If the world had changed, it said nothing about the need to infuse those changes with these truths; indeed, it spoke volumes about the relevance of those truths. They were believers, not fanatics. They were too quintessentially American to believe that they could or should foist their truths on others. And, again typically American, they saw formal education as the vehicle to accomplish their purposes despite the fact that that vehicle was ineffective, as that two-day meeting confirmed in spades.

If I felt at home in that meeting, it was not only because they ''accepted'' me, or because we were Jews *and* Americans and, therefore, shared many outlooks and attitudes that did not have to be put into words. I was "at home" because we struggled with the problem of how to justify our existence. That they had a far more comprehensive answer than I—an answer I wanted to (but could not) assimilate—was less important to me than the fact that they were asking the right questions. But the truth is that from early childhood, "believing and belonging" occupied my thinking, again not obsessively but with a poignant transiency, infrequent but stabbing thoughts that seemed to come from and go to nowhere. As adults we talk about the meaning of life; as children we think in terms of the fact and meaning of death. The nature and meaning of death were always sources of worry (*anxiety* is too strong a word) to me. To a clinically inclined person, that statement is no doubt food for thought about me as a person, or even as a "case." I would not disparage such interpretations, but I would emphasize that that kind of worry has also to be seen in relation to the frequency and strength of a child's need to believe and belong. Was it Samuel Johnson who said that nothing concentrates the mind more today than knowledge of the fact that one will be executed tomorrow? And that concentration in the mind of a child inevitably takes place, as it does for adults, in the context of "believing and belonging."

When I was in my late teens, I read a poem that contained a line that absolutely gripped me (one of those "a *ha*" experiences) because it encapsulated so well a theme from my past and my present, and one that I knew would be in my future. The line was: "Life takes its final meaning in chosen death." What should I believe in, with whom do I belong, how do I or should I decide to understand and choose? It was a line that illuminated the past me to my present me.

A caveat is in order here, for the general reader but for psychologists in particular. What I have related in this chapter is in no way intended to suggest that the child is the father of the man, that what came to occupy me as an adult and a psychologist is largely explainable by certain themes and experiences in childhood. That these themes and experiences explain fully how and why I became a psychologist is nonsense, as will become clear in a later chapter. That they bear similarity to what came to be central to my work and writing is *not* nonsense only if one takes into account continuities in social living that sustained or reinforced those themes and early experiences. So, for example, the "New York factor" that loomed large in my childhood continued to loom large, less because I planned it that way and much more because of factors beyond my control, such as World War II, being Jewish, the characteristics of the job market, and chance (as later chapters will confirm). And, I must emphasize, the theme of believing and belonging that increasingly became central to my work and writing has roots in my childhood and was continuously exacerbated and reinforced by the complex consequences of the simple fact that I grew up in America. You do not have to know anything about me to know that it is highly likely that believing and belonging would be problems I struggle with in American society—where the contents of the melting pot did not melt, where the yo-yo features of its economic system can drastically alter outlooks and lives, where upward social and economic mobility separates people from their pasts, where competitive struggle shapes and alters social relationships, where change is confused with progress and facts with truths, where generation gaps are fostered and feared, where the values of individualism are on a collision course with strivings for social cohesion.

You do not have to be a sophisticated psychologist or social scientist to know that this wondrous society has the defects of its many virtues. And those defects ensure that most if not all of its citizens find believing and belonging unsettling affairs. If each year we are treated to a plethora of books about how to think, what to believe, how to rear children, how to be assertive, how to do your own thing, and so on, and if these books continue to sell well, it says a good deal about what many people feel they need. If each person is a unique organism, it is in large measure due to the transaction, beginning with birth, between organism and a distinctive larger society. As a body of theory, research, and practice, American psychology in its quest for universal laws or generalizations has taken a very narrow view of the organism. The irony is that in such a quest American psychology has ignored America. Women, blacks especially, and other minorities, like the waves of immigrants in our national past, need little instruction on this point.

3

Becoming Aware of America: Growing Up in the Great Depression

When, preparatory to writing, I had decided that I would restrict my autobiography to my professional career, I felt a sense of relief because I would not have to describe and explain my childhood and adolescence, a task of translation to which I did not feel adequate and, more importantly, that would not be all that interesting to readers. Far from containing horror stories or noteworthy events or anything remarkable in a social-historical sense, my childhood and adolescence were normally neurotic. It is to Freud's enduring credit that he was crystal clear that it was wrong to proceed as if there were two psychologies: one for the analyst and one for the patient. There was, or should be, one psychology illuminating of and applicable to all of us. Whatever the psychology to which you adhere, it speaks to commonalities of process and context assumed to be at play in our lives. If people differ widely (and wildly), it is because of the seemingly infinite permutations and combinations between process and context. I could not justify foisting on the reader the minutiae of the permutations and combinations of those early years. To do so would be an unnecessary indulgence, which, at best, would demonstrate that those years were marked by the usual intrapsychic, interpersonal conflicts of developing males. I could write about those years in ways that would make

me appear appropriate for presentation at a clinical case conference. But, I knew, the world needed that like it needed another
underarm deodorant. If I had anything that I thought the world
needed to know, it had to do with how my professional career
was inextricably related to the nature of our society and the
transformations it had undergone. More correctly, it would be
a way of saying to younger people, regardless of the career they
have chosen or will choose, that they, like me, will be products
of their time and place in a distinctive society. Riveted as they
are on the future—to a degree that is distinctively American—
young people see themselves as products of an imagined future,
not of a present containing their individual and societal pasts.

The decision to restrict the scope of this autobiography
is an example, adumbrated in the previous chapter, of famous
last words. And the present chapter underlines the naiveté of
that decision, because I take up (really, hoisted by my own
petard) some strands of my adolescence that got woven into the
fabric of my career. That these events forever suffused my private
world is less important here than how they became part of my
professional outlook and actions. These events played no role
in my becoming a psychologist; that is, I intend no cause and
effect. They stamped in and on me a view of the world that
guaranteed that once I decided on a career in psychology, they
would give substance and direction to it. The belief that the child
is the father of the man is valid only if one assumes that society
remains constant. That assumption, of course, is literal nonsense, a denial of the obvious, of which many otherwise thinking people are surprisingly capable.

As a way of introducing these strands, let me start with
a question: How would teenagers of the last fifteen years describe
the world they have lived in? I restrict what I have to say to
teenagers whose objective includes a college education, a group
with which I have had extensive contact. I shall make no attempt to be comprehensive, but rather will focus on a few formulations derived from these contacts that have received confirmation in the popular and professional literature. One could,
I am sure, quarrel with this or that aspect of a particular formulation, but in the main each of them describes an attitude

or outlook or assessment that teenagers, at least, have verbalized in my talks with them. I have never directly asked them to describe the world they have lived in. The formulations I came to grew out of discussions centering around career planning and choice, personal problems, peer relationships, and work experiences of diverse and transient sorts. Here are six formulations:

1. Educational experience consists of a seemingly interminable series of rites of passage, many of which are empty of personal significance. To the extent that they are, so to speak, union cards that permit one later to enter the world of work, you have to obtain them.

2. The world of work contains myriad options, so many, in fact, that thinking about, let alone deciding on, a future career is akin to gambling, in the sense that you are far from secure that the choices will be appropriate to your abilities, talents, and interests. The lucky person is one who knows early on what he or she wants "to be" in life.

3. The world of work can be a trap. Work should be interesting and fulfilling, allowing for self-expression and providing the material means for recreation, travel, and comfortable living. Too many people are unhappy in their work and, therefore, in their private lives. No one expects that this fulfillment occurs when one is through with formal education, but one has a right to expect that personal enjoyments will not be sacrificed to stultifying or financially unrewarding work.

4. This is an unpredictable world, one that can change rather quickly. Planning for the long term can be an exercise in futility. You plan, plan, plan—delay, delay, delay—and suddenly something happens in the world that exposes the fragility of your plans. To give up satisfactions in the here and now for those to come at a later time can lead to disillusionment and disappointment.

5. This is not a moral world, and certainly not one we control. Yes, it is a world of opportunities, but in seizing them we run the risk of becoming other than the kinds of people we want to be. You have to stay loose and play it cool.

6. You can be many things in life. But the way things are set
    up, you have to decide on *one* thing. You can be *A* or *B,*
    but you cannot be both. You have to decide, but how do
    we know *now* what that decision should be?

These formulations rest on several axiomlike beliefs. The
first is encapsulated in the motto of my travel agent: ''See the
world before you leave it.'' There is a world to see and experience, and that world *should be* available to you. The second is
that there is a place for you in the world of work. You may not
like that place, it may lack features you expected it to have, *but
there is a place.* You may change places, albeit with some difficulty.
The third is as obvious as it is articulated: You may have many
things to worry about, but they do not include worry about
eating and lodging.

None of these axiomlike beliefs undergirded my thinking and actions as a teenager. I became a teenager three years
after the stock market crash of 1929 and within weeks of Franklin
Roosevelt's ascendancy to the presidency in 1932. The Great
Depression was picking up steam. It was not only an economic
depression but a psychological one as well. The memories are
still vivid. I heard about people throwing themselves off buildings
in New York. Why did my uncle's brother commit suicide that
way? Why was my father not working? Why did we have to
move to a cheaper apartment? I cannot erase the scene of people standing silently and anxiously outside the local bank, which
like all others had been closed by presidential decree. The only
scene comparable to it in gloom and mourning was the time
I happened to spend in Dallas and Austin two days after the
assassination of President Kennedy. (I flew to Dallas on a DC-9
with one other passenger!) I was aware of a change in the quantity and quality of the food my mother prepared, as I was of
the fact that there was less on her plate than on ours. Nor can
I ever forget the day I went to school without a brown bag for
lunch because there was nothing to put in the bag, and later
that morning my father appeared at the door of my classroom,
giving the teacher a bag with a sandwich in it. And then there
was the time when, standing next to my father, I heard him

ask my uncle to lend him two dollars to be repaid when he went back to work, and my uncle (who could afford it) said no. And I became a "salesman." Beginning at age fourteen, in the summertime, I would be given (by someone somewhere) a box with a shoulder strap containing dry ice, ices, and ice cream Popsicles. I would roam the streets proclaiming my wares, choosing neighborhoods by criteria indicating that I had more than a nascent sense of social class. The box was heavy, but it was no burden, because I knew that the couple of dollars I would give to my mother were needed and would be deeply appreciated. I felt no shame selling ice cream on the streets, but I did feel shame selling handkerchiefs. My father was able to get packaged handkerchiefs "on consignment," and I would go house to house selling them. I think I felt shame because I knew that people liked and wanted ice cream (usually for their children). But handkerchiefs? I felt like a beggar. And I made sure that I did not begin my house-to-house routine until I was at least a mile away from where we lived, in what to me was the beginning of the "country." Those were the days when adult men were selling apples on street corners for a nickel apiece.

To me this was not an unpredictable world, but rather one where the major goals of living, to have enough to eat and to be able to pay the monthly rent, were daily predictable problems. That's the way it is, and that's the way it will be! There was no reason to expect that that world would change. I never thought about what I wanted to be in life, let alone being aware that I had options, that I could choose. Options? No concept could be more foreign to my personal world. When in the ninth grade I entered Madison Junior High, I was enrolled in the commercial program, which meant that I took "junior business training" and typing. I also took Latin and ancient history because they were required of everyone. It was my parents' hope that when I finished high school, I would (with God's help) find a job "in an office," a phrase that to them meant that although I would be using my hands, I would also be using my head. The point is that for me the future was tonight and tomorrow. There was no stimulus for, no basis in reality to, a more distant future. I cannot remember a single instance when I or my

parents used the word *college* as something in the future. I knew
that my older cousins were going to college, but their parents
were, by our standards, "well off." Their future was not mine.
I respected and envied my older cousins, especially Leo and
Oscar Schneider, not only because they were in college, but also
because they were smart and they were football players who
made the first team. Contrary to what I said above, I have to
assume two things: I wanted to be like my cousins and go to
college and play football, and I knew that my fantasies had no
basis in reality. College required money, and my family flunked
that requirement with a resounding *F*. To expect that college
would be a topic of conversation in a family worried about eating
and housing is to compound ignorance with stupidity and insensitivity, a feat of which many people (now and then) are quite
capable. Hope and ambition require a hospitable soil. Poverty
is an antifertilizer.

It was not until I entered high school in the eleventh grade
that I became aware that there were people who, like myself,
were poor but, unlike myself, saw it primarily as a social disaster,
not as a family one. Take, for example, Isadore Polton, who
daily seemed to challenge our history teacher's explanation of
the United States' present and past. Concepts and words such
as *imperialism, class struggle, robber barons, capitalism,* and *socialism*
were new, mystifying, and exciting to me. I admired the way
Izzy said what he did and stood his ground. I was bothered by
his criticism of America, because it sounded unpatriotic and I
did not know where his arguments led. But I also admired the
patience and respect Mr. Coleman and Miss Stephenson showed
in listening to Izzy and asking him pointed questions. If I thought
Izzy was unjustly critical of our country, I was wise enough to
know that I had no basis for partaking in those discussions. What
I took away from those discussions was that Mr. Coleman and
Miss Stephenson agreed with Izzy that there were features of
our society about which one should be critical and that one
should seek to change but that his approach was not the answer.
There was one facet of those discussions that had special mean-
ing for me and that made it impossible for me to agree with
Izzy. When he would compare America unfavorably with Russia,

what would come to mind were all the stories I had heard from my parents and relatives about the persecution of Jews in Russia. How could a Jew like Izzy speak so favorably about Russia? It took a few more years for me to understand that many people, Jews and non-Jews, saw Russia as a model to emulate, a country where money was not a determinant of opportunity and status, where prejudice was nonexistent, and where justice (*true* justice) reigned supreme. If I could not accept that argument then, it said much about how the experiences and memories of the adults in my extended family had been absorbed by me. I have always felt indebted to Izzy and a few other like-minded students for demonstrating that there were different ways to look at America. The concept and facts of a depression began to take on new meanings. It was the beginning of my rediscovery of America.

What I have related is in no way an explanation of my becoming a psychologist, directly or indirectly. Its significance resides in the fact that when I became a psychologist, the odds were very high that "my psychology" would be focused on the individual in his or her societal setting. More specifically, I would be drawn to the ways in which socialization into society works for and against optimal development. It would be a psychology of the underdog: how and why the status of underdog becomes permanent or is overcome. Indeed, appearances to the contrary notwithstanding, everything I have ever done in psychology has been about one problem: how does one account for variation in discrepancy between potential and performance? And if that problem took on a somewhat obsessional feature in my thinking, I explain it largely by what the Great Depression did for and against me; that is, by the fact that an internal world is incomprehensible apart from the larger society into which we are born and reared, that however wondrously complex and mystifying "mind" is, it is no more so than society is. And the process whereby we discover or rediscover who we are is the process whereby we discover or rediscover our society. The discovery-rediscovery process has or should always have a Janus-like feature.

What I have related had two purposes. The first was to give the reader a glimpse of what one teenager encountered and how the consequences of that encounter became a lifelong feature of his phenomenology, in later years entering into his professional interests. Countless others who grew up in the thirties have written (or could write) similar accounts. Mine is not grossly atypical, if atypical at all. I did not know then, as I do now, that what was truly atypical of the thirties, and fateful for the societal future, was not only the unprecedented rate of unemployment, or the suddenness with which the direction of lives changed, but the beginning of a sea-swell change in governmental responsibility for its citizens. That government is best that governs least—that was a guiding value of the citizen-government relationship before the Depression. With 20 percent unemployment; a frightening escalation of business bankruptcies; unemployed World War I veterans bitter, angry, and increasingly militant in regard to denial of their request for congressional approval of a bonus; a socialist candidate receiving nearly a million votes in the 1932 presidential campaign; soup kitchens for the starving and seemingly endless lines of people waiting in line for public welfare, which was more public than it was welfare—in the face of these facts and events, government had no choice but to take an active role, quite a departure from tradition and ideology. It was explicitly stated that this new role was a temporary one, another example of famous last words.

If the role was not temporary, neither were the ideological controversies surrounding it. Indeed, with the election of President Reagan in 1980, that controversy reappeared with the sharpness and force it had in the first of President Roosevelt's terms. Young people today may view this as a new development, unaware that it speaks to issues and outlooks that go back to the founding of the republic, unaware that the issues are legitimate and horribly complex. If as a teenager in the thirties I did not know what it was all about, and mouthed oversimplifications utterly insensitive to the possibility of unintended consequences, I can argue today that the severity of the Depression made looking to history a mammoth irrelevancy. But that is a narrow psychological argument. What it obscures, in my opinion, is that America has always been a society in which its citizens view the present as a way station on the road of progress to a better future. The past is something to overcome, perhaps to be respected the way young people are asked to respect older people: a kind of superficial courtesy to those with whom one feels little or no kinship. And that brings me to the second purpose in writing about America in the thirties: to emphasize that the controversies that marked that decade are very much alive today. For example, it is not hyperbole to assert that there is no psychologist today who does not feel that his or her career is not in some way, in small or large part, dependent on or affected by governmental policy. And many of them, precisely because of the dynamics of dependency, are markedly ambivalent about the relationship. Few of them are aware that what they are experiencing, the perspectives they adopt, reflect far more general issues that came to the fore in the early thirties and are still with us. Psychologists tend to think that what they do *as psychologists* rests, among other things, on a history of their field. That is true, but no more true than the statement that what they do rests on the nature and history of America. I am amazed (and disheartened) at the number of psychologists who do not comprehend why the Depression marked the beginning of a societal drama that would in a relatively short period of time transform American psychology.

Within a few hours of writing the above, I got in the mail the June 1986 issue of the *New Criterion,* the lead article in which is Hilton Kramer's "Writing the History of the New York Intellectuals" (pp. 1-6). Why, he asks, is so much attention being paid to that group who came on the scene in the thirties?

The issues that were of primary concern to the New York intellectuals from the Thirties onward—namely, Marxism in politics and modernism in culture—are still, in one form or another, the central political and cultural issues of the present day, and they affect a larger part of our society than ever before. The way these issues were argued thirty or forty or fifty years ago; the divisions they caused, the loyalties they engendered, and the positions that resulted from them; above all, the fate that this movement met with in the upheavals of the Sixties, and the changes which followed from that—the whole intellectual dynamic of this complicated history has turned out, for better or for worse, to have played a considerable role in shaping our institutions and setting the agenda for a great deal that remains under intense debate today. On many matters that are now of urgent concern in the Eighties there is simply no way of grasping their rudiments without some knowledge of this antecedent history. There is no way, for example, that one can intelligently read the intellectual press today—or, for that matter, follow the part of the popular media which concerns itself with matters of intellectual debate—in isolation from this history. On subjects as diverse as Nicaragua, the Museum of Modern Art, the fate of contemporary music, or the studies of the humanities in the universities, what is now being thought and implemented as policy is likely to have its roots in this particular aspect of the past.

Those intellectuals and that scene became influential in my life, as later chapters will show. At this point in my story, I quote the following words of Kramer as a way of italicizing what I have said.

For many people, of course, it is extremely irksome—if not something worse—to be reminded that these and many other current issues have an intellectual history which bears directly on the ideas we now hold (whatever our position) and even on the language with which these ideas are expressed. They would much prefer to forget the past—most especially (need one add?) the mistakes of the past. The amnesiac impulse, though always selective, exerts a tremendous appeal, allowing those so inclined to deny or erase all traces of the old arguments or, what comes to the same thing, to rewrite them in a way that conforms to current orthodoxies. To be told that these orthodoxies are themselves, more often than not, a reconstructed residue of the old arguments is, understandably, an affront to intellectual dignity and a blow to the pride many take in representing a generation that is unencumbered (as it pleases them to believe) by the burden of history. But to ignore or deny the past is not, finally, a viable option for a serious mind. The past must be faced if the present is understood, and except for those who prefer to dwell in the realm of fantasy—no small number, alas, in today's intellectual world—there is no escaping the fact. Many try, of course. But theirs is the fate of those who are condemned to repeat what they have forgotten or denied.

The human animal is unique in two ways. It is incapable of avoiding dealing with the past, present, and future at the same time. It has many ways—subtle and blatant, witting and unwitting—of dealing with that incapability.

I now turn to an event that forever changed my life in almost every respect, a personal disaster that had, or led to, serendipitous consequences. The Great Depression put a stamp on me, but neither directly nor indirectly does it throw light on why I became a psychologist. The same cannot be said for the nature and consequences of the personal catastrophe, although here again I intend no simple cause-and-effect explanation.

My sister, three years older than I, contracted polio shortly before I was born. She was left with a spinal weakness that drastically limited free and flexible use of her arms. She looked physically normal, but she was mightily handicapped. I cannot remember ever being aware of her handicap. But I was aware, with dread, that there was a sickness called infantile paralysis, and woe to the person who got it—really to the child, because it was believed that it was a disease of childhood. And you were likely to get it in the summer months. Some readers will remember the anxiety that pervaded our society in regard to a possible severe flu epidemic. If that was anxiety, then it is utterly inadequate as description of what people felt in regard to polio, epidemics of which seemed to come in cycles. If children looked forward to summer as an escape from school, for their parents it was cause for sleepless nights.

In the fall of my junior year in high school, I came down with polio. What I remember of those few days was running a high fever, being taken by ambulance several miles to an isolation hospital, seeing my parents watching me from outside my glass-enclosed room, being held by several nurses while my spine was being tapped, unable to move my right arm, moving my left arm with difficulty, and having some difficulty breathing because my nose and throat were involved. I was in the hospital for several weeks. Memories of those weeks are cloudy. When I got off the bed, my right arm was a dead weight, and because my left arm was weak, I needed assistance. If my right arm was not in a sling, I could not stand erect for very long. My breathing returned to normal, but I had difficulty swallowing food, requiring that I roll my head this way and that to get the food down (true, but to a far lesser degree, today, unnoticeable to others). When I returned home, it was in an airplane splint: my upper body was corseted, with both arms positioned out to the sides at shoulder height. I looked as if I were pronouncing a benediction on the world. After several months, my left arm had recovered sufficiently so that a new one-arm brace-splint was made. The right arm remained a dead weight. The splint was taken off when I went to bed at night, and for two or three periods of time during the day. The itching was excruciating; scratching was a delight.

Those are the bare facts of those early weeks and months. You have only to be capable of a modicum of insight to intuit what it meant for a fifteen-year-old male to become a "cripple," which is how a neighbor, in my presence, described me to my sister. And if you are a sophisticated psychologist, regardless of theoretical persuasion, you should be able to describe in detail the personal and family dimensions of the disaster. I did not, a decade later, go into psychoanalysis for the hell of it.

Let me add some more bare facts before I draw conclusions that may be as surprising to the reader as they are to me, surprising to me because I *now* understand why, despite my later politically radical activities, and they were radical, my criticisms of American society were not powered by the vehemence and even venom my political affiliation seemed to require.

Within a few weeks after returning home from the hospital, I was provided a teacher who visited me a couple of days a week, as a result of which I was able to finish the academic year. By the time my senior year began, I was able to return to school in the one-arm, raised splint. During this time I was in the care of an orthopedic surgeon, Dr. Henry Kessler. I would see him in a hospital clinic because we could not afford his five-dollar fee for a home visit. He was a genial individual already regarded as the top orthopedic surgeon in the area. (Only later did I learn that he was a pioneer in the reattachment of severed limbs. During World War II, he was chief orthopedic surgeon for the navy in the southeast Pacific theater of operations. Following the war, he created his own institute, which exists today and bears his name.) In the early spring of my senior year, Dr. Kessler told us what we already knew: without surgery, my right arm, which already had begun noticeably to atrophy, would always be a dead weight. An operation could give me some use of the arm. I could not understand how that arm could be "fixed up" to give me some use of it. In fact, I had privately concluded that I would be better off if the arm were amputated; at least I would be able to be on my feet without in minutes feeling tired. Dr. Kessler left no doubt in our minds that I would be better off with the operation.

How much would the operation cost? The answer was two hundred dollars. It would have been no less disheartening if he had said a million dollars. We could, he said, have his assistant for much less. We went home from that clinic visit anxious and gloomy. I began to adjust to the permanency of my handicap. I did not count on my mother's desperation and, therefore, boldness. What I should do, she said, was to write a letter to President Roosevelt, who was a polio victim and who had started the March of Dimes to support research and rehabilitation. Explain to him my condition and economic predicament. What have we got to lose? The letter was sent, and a few weeks later I received a reply from Marguerite Le Hand, the president's secretary, saying that the matter would be brought to his attention. A few weeks after that, we heard from Dr. Kessler: he would do the operation gratis, and all hospital costs would be covered! I was also told that "my case" would be under the egis of the New Jersey State Rehabilitation Commission, a fact that later had a good deal of significance.

The operation took place on the Friday before the July 4th weekend, which, as luck would have it, was a scorcher. If I remember that meteorological fact, it is because when the effects of the ether began to wear off, I found myself in another one-armed affair, but this time made of plaster of paris, which because of the heat was not solidifying, especially the part on my back. I was immobilized, as much because of the weight of the cast as because of anxiety about moving. (To this day I am psychologically unable to tolerate heat, another instance of knowledge of origins having no therapeutic consequences.) I lived in that cast for three and a half months. If I had had difficulty coping with an arm that was a dead weight, it was nothing compared to the weight of the cast. Precisely because it was such a hot summer, the itching was somewhat intolerable. Necessity being the mother of invention (sometimes), I unwound a clothes hanger, made a couple of holes in strategic places in the cast, and could reach the itching points.

Came the day when the cast was to be removed. It seemed as if all the doctors and nurses in the clinic were there to observe. Dr. Kessler began, using something that looked like a hedge cutter, by removing that part of the cast on top of my upraised, extended arm. He then said to me, "Now raise your arm." I looked at him with strong disbelief, but an order is an order, and so, looking at the atrophied arm, I gave it the message. I was able to raise it a few inches! I did it again, and again, amidst applause from the onlookers. Then the rest of the cast was removed. What the operation had done was to attach muscles from the top of my arm to my neck muscles. I could now raise my arm forty-five degrees to my shoulder, though when my arm was at my side, I could not flex the elbow. My hand and fingers had never been affected. Now, objectively, I had very limited use of my arm. Phenomenologically, I was cured, whole again.

Before I got polio, my fantasies about my future were, for all practical purposes, nonexistent or, more correctly, only for the short term. After I got polio, my fantasies centered on ambition and accomplishment in a very specific way: I was going to be a writer, more specifically, a dramatist. Anything in the newspapers or on the radio that was about Broadway and the New York theater interested me (to indulge in understatement). You could say that writing was the one thing I could do with my deadweight right arm, when the splint was off. And I should add that as soon as the double airplane splint was removed, and my left arm was free, I learned to write "lefty" within a week. That says more to me about the strength of my motivation and burgeoning fantasies of ambition than anything else. (When I was out of the splint, I could write with either hand. Today, when I have to write on a blackboard, I can do so only with my left arm.) The only clue to my writing fantasies that I find interesting is that *I*, with the splint off, wrote the letter to President Roosevelt. Why did my mother ask me to write it? She was perfectly able to do so. Had I demonstrated before I got polio any interest in a talent for writing? For my purposes here, my intrapsychic dynamics and their history are unimportant. What is important is that becoming a dramatist, a famous one no less, became a goal.

When you have to be physically inactive and passive, you are left with fantasy as a major form of pleasure and expression. Fantasy, of course, is a double-edged sword: it can become an end in itself or it can lead to action, or it can do both, as I think it did in my case. At some point I did begin to write plays, about which, fortunately, I have absolutely no memory. What I do remember is that I enjoyed the process of writing: thinking, imagining, writing, agonizing, creating my world and shutting out the real one, which was suffused with despair and the struggle for survival. Only in later years did I come to understand that what I experienced was as nothing compared to what my parents experienced. They gave me love and unconditional acceptance. What, in their straits and with a second handicapped child, could I give them?

My writing fantasies made it likely that when I took my first psychology course I would be drawn to that field. They also made it likely that I would be attracted to that part of psychology concerned with motivation and conflict: within the individual and between the individual and an obstacle-laden social world. And because writing never held any terror for me, quite the contrary, psychology would be a most appropriate vehicle through which I could express myself in words. Then, as now, writing as a form of personal expression was primary. Psychology became a means to an end, which makes it sound far more rational and planned than it was. Up until the moment I knew I was going to college, I had not the faintest idea of what I could or would do. In 1935, the Depression was at its highest point. Where does a handicapped high school graduate get a job? I went to college only because the New Jersey State Rehabilitation Commission arranged for me to obtain a scholarship loan from Dana College in downtown Newark, payable after I was graduated from there. New Jersey then had no state college, and, needless to say, in those days there were no free community or junior colleges. There was no free anything in higher education. As for millions of other youths, being graduated from high school was the terminal point in formal education. And we were graduated to a jobless society.

The Depression forced me to become aware that there was much wrong—economically, politically, morally—about America. That awareness, however, through my high school years was superficial, indeed inchoate. If there was a lot wrong, it was also true that our political leaders were trying to fix it. I did not understand that they, like me and my family, did not know, so to speak, what had hit them. It is hard to convey to young people today the inspiring, morale-sustaining role of President Roosevelt. The nation would sit huddled around their radios to hear his "fireside chats," his patrician, Harvard-inflected voice conveying compassion and reassurance that there was light at the end of the nightmarish tunnel. To the adults, at least, the name Roosevelt had been associated with an earlier president who was an activist, crusading person who took on the economic oligarchy in his quest for justice. Theodore Roosevelt was a fighter, and Franklin Roosevelt was living up to that reputation. When in his inaugural address he said that we have nothing to fear but fear itself, it had the same electrifying, attention-getting effect as when a later president said that we should ask not what our country could do for us, but rather what we could do for our country. The impact of Franklin Roosevelt is not explainable in terms of his voice, bearing, personal style, or rhetoric of hope. These were major factors, of course, but they led to action: things were being done and tried, the government was not being passive. If in our daily existence we were not benefiting from these actions, if our daily existence was suffused with despair, that was no warrant for criticizing the president and giving up on America. And if he was not righting the situation, it said more about the power of the Wall Street "moneybags" than anything else. I had a Manichean view of America: there were the good guys and the bad guys, and you should take the money from the latter and distribute it to the former. It made no difference how you did it, but you should do it now, today. It was not until my second year in college that that Manichean view got reflected in a formal political ideology in which the abstraction capitalism was substituted for the bad guys.

These comments are prologue to a conclusion that brings together a personal characteristic and some objective facts. The personal characteristic is hard for me to explain and write about because it can be interpreted as either a self-serving form of self-deception or, worse yet, a witting distortion in the service of a false saintliness. I do know something about the human capacity to distort and to be self-serving! It is a somewhat bottomless capacity. The personal characteristic is that I have never been able to hate people. I can get very angry at people, there are people I dislike intensely, but neither the anger nor the dislike has depth. As a child and prehandicapped teenager, I could never physically or verbally retaliate against a perceived personal injustice or insult. I would fear anger within myself and fear even more anger expressed by others, whether toward me or not. I have always wanted to be liked, to be close, to patch things up, to avoid anger and conflict, for my relationships to have features other than those present in the relationship between my parents. I am capable of anger, incapable of sustaining it, and too disposed to explain away or to excuse actions of others that have hurt me. I know how this is going to sound: it is prepotent in me to want to like people and for them to like me. I avoid like the plague their strong negative feelings and my own. My friends sometimes find it incomprehensible that I will say I like someone who, I must admit, could never benefit from a hundred Dale Carnegie courses.

These prehandicap characteristics became even stronger as a result of my getting polio. Extreme dependency is not calculated to make it easy to express strong negative feelings, and, equally obvious in my case, the inability to be physically aggressive and the fear of physical retaliation took on new depths. Of crucial significance, however, is the fact that as a direct consequence of contracting polio I received a good deal of help and support from a variety of individuals and agencies. If America, like me, was in an unenviable condition—there was something very wrong with both of us—it was nevertheless true that there were people, agencies, and services that were caring and compassionate. Hospital and clinic personnel, visiting teachers and high school staff, the March of Dimes and social agencies, the New Jersey Rehabilitation Commission—they and others strove to be and were helpful. Coming as it did at the high point of the Depression, it could be argued that I was "lucky" to have gotten polio—otherwise I never would have gone to college; I would have been in the armed services in World War II, with a fair chance of being maimed, or killed, or otherwise scarred. Luck is in the eye of the beholder. The fact remains, and it was something I was quite aware of, that ours was a society that saw me as an obligation it should discharge. So, when later in college I became a political radical (not a liberal) adhering to a political ideology that had little good to say about America; that saw certain social classes composed of greedy, heartless people; that saw the underdog as virtuous, naturally kindly, and possessed of folk wisdom; that required that I see the future in Armageddon terms; that also required that I see certain groups and classes as enemies toward whom I should feel, if not hatred, then disdain and vitriol—I was never capable of the passion and emotionally expressive militancy the politically radical ideology required. By temperament, personal style, and life experience, it was extraordinarily difficult, in practice impossible, to see people or the world in Manichean terms. I shall have more to say about this in a later chapter, but here I wish only to describe something I saw countless times within and among rival left-wing political parties. There were endless debates on fine points regarding ideology and action. Not only did these debates seem endless, but the participants on both sides were capable of invective and derogation that were personal and deep, bordering and oftentimes spilling over to personal attack. I listened with fascination, with admiration of the Talmudic hairsplitting, with envy of the level of knowledge and verbal facility, but shrank from the display of personal venom and what I would call hatred. And most mystifying and upsetting to me were those occasions when two good friends found themselves on opposite sides of a theoretical dispute and ended up as personal enemies, no longer speaking to each other and seeking to excommunicate each other from the party. I was not built for interpersonal warfare.

It has been said numerous times that the autobiography is unique in that the writer and subject are one and the same person. That assertion can be made only by someone who has not attempted his or her autobiography. In my case, at least, the assertion has to be qualified. When I reflect on my childhood and early teens, I am flooded with memories of people, places, and occasions. And it is as if in those years it was more a flood than a well-laid-out scene or, better yet, a stage on which a cast of characters act out their purposes and feelings in relation to each other. It is a flood from within and without; I am carried by it here and there, not knowing where I am being carried and why. To change the metaphor: I see myself in those years in a cloud that obscures horizons, that literally restricts what I can see, but occasionally beams of sunlight break through, giving me, if not a glimpse of another world, a new view of my little world. I cannot control either the clouds or the flood. I am not the captain of my fate and the master of my soul. I see myself not as lost but rather as without purpose, accommodating to the purposes of others in a dutiful way.

The me of today has trouble identifying with the me of those years. Before starting this autobiography, I had, like every other adult, ready explanations for perceived continuities between my childhood and my adulthood. As a psychologist, I knew those explanations were composed of fact and myth. What I did not know, what this writing forced me to confront, is how faulty and incomplete these explanations are in regard to context. I tried to illustrate this in Chapter Two when I discussed the significance of the Brooklyn–Newark–New York "place factor," a factor I was only faintly aware of until I began to write this autobiography. But context goes far beyond the factor of place. So, for example, how did I become an American? The answer is the same as the one I gave to the question how did I become a Jew? I do not know, I cannot remember, and yet if anything is indisputable, if anything is psychologically continuous over my lifetime, it is that I am quintessentially American and Jewish, more so than I am a male. An Israeli friend,

Dr. Michael Klaber, once said to me that he could imagine himself as a Frenchman or Englishman, or as a female, or as a homosexual, but not as other than a Jew. If he can see himself as an Englishman or Frenchman, it probably is because his family had to leave Austria to escape from Hitler, he became an Israeli before Israel became a country, and he saw himself as a *European*. I cannot see myself other than as an American. I ask how I became an American not for the narrow purpose of understanding myself, but rather because that question will occupy later chapters where I try to understand psychology in America. It has been said that psychoanalysis could not have been born in America, that William James's pragmatism is typically American, that John Watson's behaviorism could not have been developed elsewhere, that the difference between Lewis Terman and Alfred Binet is the difference between America and France (or Europe), and that Gestalt psychology was typically and historically German. Clearly, where you become a psychologist is a difference that makes a difference. How I became an American is the opposite of an idle question for comprehending psychology in our society.

Child and developmental psychologists have done scores of thousands of studies of American children. Very few bear directly on how children come to have an American world view. If you peruse the anthropological literature on so-called primitive cultures (it has taken a long time for the adjective *so-called* to precede the word primitive, an instance of the point I am making), a ubiquitous feature of the ethnographies is an attempt to answer the question: how does an individual *become* an Alorese, a Kalahari Bushman, a Trukese, and so on? How did these people come to absorb and possess a world view distinctive for their contexts? We know more about the process for them than we do about ourselves.

How does one come to have an American world view? In what ways does that world view differ from those in other societies? How do that world view and its underlying axioms get reflected in our language, our attitudes toward self and others, our view of the future, our response to crisis, our use of resources, our sense of national and world history, our sense of and response to perceived differences in regard to race, religion, gender, and ethnicity? Having to write my professional autobiography, and justifying it for what light it sheds on a particular era in American psychology, I could not avoid the question of how my childhood and adolescence put the stamp of America in and on me. (I say "on" because from the first time I went to a foreign country in 1966, I was surprised how many people said they knew I was American without my saying a word, and I did not carry a camera. I should not have been surprised, because in my own geographical bailiwick I can spot "foreigners," and I am right far more often than not. It may be clothes, hair style, bearing, or facial expression, but something "tells me" the person is not a native American. Such diagnosis may become more problematic if the Americanization of the world continues its present course.) If I could not avoid that question, I have to admit that I can adduce little concrete evidence to explain how I came to be the American I am. In my years in public schools—and the observance of national holidays such as Independence Day, Armistice (now Veterans') Day, Thanksgiving, Labor Day—I absorbed distinctive attitudes toward and knowledge (albeit selective) of America. But the deep feelings of pride and even joy that make up what we call patriotism, and that get absorbed even by children belonging to groups to which America has not been kindly, are but one facet of the American world view, a facet of the world view of every child in every other country on this earth.

There is one distinctive feature of the American world view that I can say was a part of my phenomenology in those early years, and that later pervaded my personal and professional lives for much but not all of my adult years. That was the bedrock belief in *progress,* the national equivalent of "every day in every way I am getting better and better, smarter and smarter, wiser and wiser." Even in the depths of the Depression, when the country seemed to be enveloped in clouds of anxiety and gloom, there was a part of us that believed that for us *as a nation* the Depression was a temporary and surmountable pothole on the road to a better and bigger future. It was a belief encapsulated a few years later in the title of a World War II song: "We Did It Before and We Can Do It Again." We were special on this earth, an attitude that goes back to the belief of the pilgrims that this land was a Garden of Eden.

There was one other belief that had long been a feature of the American world view and in which I was a firm believer in my high school years: the fulfillment of the American dream of inevitable progress required that we have as little to do as possible with the conflicts and upheavals of the rest of the world, Europe in particular. If that belief is less strong today, if we have gone from an extreme stance of isolationism to an ambivalent internationalism, it appears still to be true that we tend to see ourselves as basically moral and virtuous, as much in need of protecting the dream as ever. I mention this here because in my college years (1935–1939) I slowly, very slowly and inchoately, began to see and feel a relationship between the stance of isolationism—a nation alone among nations—and an ideology of individualism within the nation that, for me, at least, made for the feeling of aloneness. If I was drawn to a collectivist political ideology, it said as much about my need for community as it did about my assessment of the causes and consequences of the Great Depression. It was not fortuitous that the theme of community came to be central to my career as a psychologist. That it did not become central until mid-career says a good deal, as later pages will reveal, about the nature and strength of my socialization into American psychology. I learned a lot in the process of that socialization; it took years to unlearn it.

Thinking about and writing one's autobiography is, I quickly learned, a process of selection and reconstruction in the service of painting a personal picture. You do not begin with a picture but rather with a torrent of sketches, trying literally to see what goes with what, to change this or that—deliberately to distort—in order for a perceived truth to emerge as clearly as possible. The dangers, of course, are many, not the least of which is that preoccupation with self over a lifetime makes it extraordinarily difficult to see the larger context within which that self emerged. We know ourselves in a way that we cannot know that larger context. Phenomenologically, the self is not an abstraction the way context is. We literally see our self. We cannot see contexts. Contexts are abstractions or inventions. My mother, father, sister, and brother are real to me, but as soon as I say *family*, it refers to something more than is given when I think of each separately. So, when we hear someone say that he or she is in large measure a reflection of his or her family, we nod assent, even though we have no idea what that term means or has meant to the person. Ordinarily that does not bother or mystify us. But it is a mammoth problem for the biographer seeking to comprehend another person's phenomenology, or the autobiographer seeking to understand a self of the past. The problem may be somewhat less problematic for the biographer who knows from the beginning that his or her subject from the moment of birth exists, so to speak, in a series of concentric circles: the mother, the family, the neighborhood, town, or city, state and nation. But the task is to describe how these circles set the stage for and impinge upon the subject of the biography, a task made complex by the fact that each of the circles is itself a function of time and era. So, for example, if the subject of the biography is born into an immigrant family, the serious biographer seeks to understand how features of the "old country" stamped on and in the parents are affected by and in turn affect their response to the new country and, therefore, become salient for the young child. If this task is somewhat less thorny for the biographer than for the autobiographer, it is because the latter is both subject and object. It is one thing to see yourself in those concentric circles, and quite another for someone else to see you in them. Either can do it poorly or well, and a major criterion for judgment is how compellingly the boundaries of those concentric circles are dissolved by the writer.

What does it mean to be an American? We do not ask that question unless events conspire to force us to ask it. Travel to a foreign land (better yet, living in it), a civil or world war, a Supreme Court decision in 1954, an assassination of a president, a women's liberation movement, racial riots, the centennial celebration of the Statue of Liberty, a Sacco-Vanzetti trial and aftermath, the Great Depression—these and other events remind us (often shock us) that this abstraction called America is palpably in each of us, albeit in diverse ways. For me, the

Great Depression was the beginning of my interest in what it meant to say that I was an American. It is a beginning that has had no end. And my vague, unsatisfactory answers were enormously complicated by the question of what it meant to be Jewish. Of one thing I am certain: a psychology that does not deliberately and centrally concern itself with these kinds of questions will never be able to comprehend the sources, nature, and vicissitudes of the behavior of Americans. And that psychology hardly exists today. At its core, American psychology has aimed to discern processes and generalizations applicable to people anywhere, any place, any time. Be it learning, perceptual, Gestalt, psychological, or developmental theory, the goal has been the formulation of universal laws. That is, it should go without saying, a legitimate and laudable quest, and real strides have been made. But that is no warrant for ignoring another question, no less universal: how are we shaped by the nation into which we are born? We take for granted—I would say we know as we know few other things—that being an American has made and makes a difference in acquiring a world view. We are not French, Afghans, or Iranians. That we know, and in saying that, we refer to something quite personal, not given by a description, however detailed, of the institutions constituting the country, let alone the rhetoric articulated by political figures.

As concrete example, it has been noted that only in the last two decades have Americans of Italian background begun to make their mark in public office, the corporate world, academia, and literature. Indeed, if you go back over the early history of American psychology—especially that part concerned with the nature and measurement of intelligence, school performance, and mental retardation—you cannot avoid gaining the impression that Italian-Americans, as a group, were intellectually inferior and ethnically, religiously, and socially insular. Study after study on IQ in different ethnic and racial groups "demonstrated" that Italians were near the bottom of the list. Why is the picture so different today? A good part of the answer is given in R. Gambino's *Blood of My Blood* (New York: Anchor Books, 1974), a fascinating analysis and account of the Italian experience in America. If it has taken long for the Italians as a group to take their places in all spheres of societal activity, it has taken American social science, especially psychology, an unconscionably long time to recognize what it means to be born and reared in America, to be the product of two cultures, each of which becomes part of our psychological bloodstream from the moment of birth. As a Jew, I have known this, just as every Italian does. If my life is at all representative, I know more (albeit still superficially) about how I became a Jew than about how I became an American. Is it because we have come to feel, have been made to feel, that the Jewish or Italian part of us is somehow alien to us, something we can examine, something we never lose sight of, without truly comprehending the nonalien part of us? It is not fortuitous that early in my career I was mightily influenced by two books that were never assigned in any of my psychology courses. The first was William I. Thomas and Florian Znaniecki's *The Polish Peasant in Europe and America* (New York: Knopf, 1927), and the second was John Dollard's *Criteria for the Life History* (New Haven, Conn.: Yale University Press, 1935). Before I became a psychologist, I had a nascent interest in what it means to be an American (not how I *became* an American). During the process of becoming a psychologist, that interest received absolutely no nurture. If you were interested in what it meant to be an American, you could look up *American* in the dictionary or start reading outside of psychology. I started to read.

4

Themes from Childhood
and Adolescence

You do not expect children and adolescents to take distance from their social scene, let alone from the society at large, and to identify on some level of generality the factors impinging on them or the sources of those factors. If we do not hold such expectations, it should not be assumed that teenagers, at least, are incapable at some level of such abstractions. We like to believe that young people, tied to concrete and immediate experience, and absorbed with an emerging self, have no interest in or capability for generalization about their social worlds; that is, whatever generalizations they make are so superficial as to cause one to question the use of the term *generalization*. That conclusion receives a jolt during times of social upheaval, when we hear youth discuss and pass judgment on features of the society they view as inimical to their roles as individuals and citizens. The clearest examples come from periods of re-evaluation in Third World countries when young people, eschewing an old ideology for a new one, identify features of the society that they seek to change. We label the ideology political, tending to forget that such an ideology at its core calls for basic changes in the nature of social relationships and in the content and use of means of communication. The ideology defines what is good and bad for the individual and the collectivity. Whether or not we accept the ideology does not permit us to gloss over the fact that its young adherents, and they can be young, possess interrelated generalizations about society as it is and should be. But we do not have to use Third World examples. As I pointed out earlier, during the Great Depression there were many youths of high school age who adopted a political ideology that allowed them to say that this or that feature of the society was a baleful influence that needed to be altered. And then, of course, there was the decade of the sixties. That was a decade during which I spent a great deal of time in the public schools, and it was a constant source of amazement to me how many children— white and black, male and female, rich and poor—identified and criticized features of their local and larger society. I do not want to exaggerate the level of sophistication of their critiques but rather to emphasize their articulate sensitivity to features of their society they saw as adverse to their futures. If their critiques had a deeply personal significance, they nevertheless directed attention to the nature of American society.

Up until I went to college, my interest in and understanding of our society were virtually nonexistent. I confirmed the stereotype of the self-absorbed adolescent for whom yesterday did not exist, today was all-important, and sports the be-all and end-all of masculine existence. Why was I whatever I was? How would I explain myself to myself? To others? These questions could not occur to me. They are questions that preoccupied me in later years but in a very unsystematic way. Writing this autobiography literally forced me to confront these questions. Like everybody else, I think I know the major characteristics of my "personality": the internal "stuff" of my mind and its relationship to overt behavior and action. Let us leave aside the inescapable fact that we are capable of mammoth self-deception and that there are inevitable discrepancies between how we see ourselves and how others see us. What we cannot leave aside is a consequence of the obligation of autobiography not merely to describe a complex life, but to explain it from the changing vantage points of different times in that life. Autobiography is a constructing and reconstructing process, a kind of jigsaw puzzle in response to which you seek organizing principles to give order to what you see, chastened by false perceptions and moves and humbled by your ability to ignore the obvious. And if you do not complete the puzzle, or it takes a long time to do so, the prepotent tendency is to blame yourself and to ignore the fact that the maker of the puzzle did not intend to make life easy for you. We are far more aware of our internal workings than of the nature of externals. A case in point is my ambitiousness. How to explain it?

I have always seen myself as ambitious but not competitive. That is to say, if anybody had asked me when I was a youngster whether I was ambitious—whether I wanted to achieve "great things" in life—I would have said yes, however unrealistic the realization of those ambitions might have then seemed. To *want* to achieve seemed natural, right, and proper. You could explain the strength of my ambitiousness by family tradition, structure, and dynamics. Such an explanation would certainly be in order, but only if it included the interaction between the Jewish immigrant experience and American culture; more correctly, the interaction of the tradition of learning and intellectual achievement with a culture that prized and glorified individual striving and achievement. If you did not have to be Jewish to like lox, cream cheese, and bagels, you did not have to be Jewish in America to take to ambitiousness. The more I have plumbed my experience in the public schools, the more aware I have become of how in myriad ways we were taught to want to be ambitious, to achieve, to climb the ladder of success. There was a world to conquer, and our success would depend on individual motivation. If the social reality often made a mockery of the ideological message, the fact is that the message did not lack validity, and, it goes without saying, we were given example after example of what was valid in the message. Edison, Lindbergh, Ford, Lincoln, Franklin, Booker Washington, Babe Ruth, Paul Robeson, paralyzed Franklin Roosevelt—the names were legion, and each had by virtue of unrelenting striving and ambitiousness overcome the obstacle of mean beginnings, racial prejudice, or other handicap. Those were names we heard in school or read about on the sports page. That Babe Ruth grew

up in an orphanage, that Paul Robeson and Jim Thorpe over-
came racial prejudice to become pre-eminent athletes, was heady
stuff for me. And if what I heard in school about ambitiousness
needed reinforcement, I heard at home from parents about Al
Jolson, Eddie Cantor, George Jessel, Douglas Fairbanks (Jewish
and from Brooklyn, I think), and scores of others who had reached
the pinnacles of success in the movies, theater, or radio. America
was the success story of the world, and if you wanted to participate in that success, you could, but only if you were truly
ambitious. My ambitiousness is inexplicable unless the variable
of America is part of the explanation. Focusing on my intrapsychic dynamics in the context of a Jewish family is very incomplete and misleading, and for a long time that kind of explanation is how I explained myself to myself and to others, on
and off the analytical couch.

Nothing better illustrates the point I am making than a
radio program of the thirties to which the bulk of adolescents
listened every weekday in the early evening. It was ''Jack Arm-
strong, the All-American Boy.'' (Wheaties explained only a
small part of Jack!) He encapsulated the virtues of perseverance,
obstacle surmounting, and achievement-ambitiousness. And so
did the Hardy Boys and Tom Swift and Horatio Alger. America
made them, and they made America. They gave in their ways
as one-sided a picture as that which rivets on family tradition
and intrapsychic dynamics. American psychology has yet to integrate meaningfully those two pictures.

If I saw myself as ambitious, and was encouraged to be
so, why was I (and do I continue to be) reluctant unequivocally
to accept it in myself and to admit it to others? For one thing,
as I indicated in the previous chapter, social-economic factors
and the realities of physical handicap gave little basis for hop-
ing that my fantasies could be realized. But, I have learned,
there was another set of factors, which I then hardly understood,
another example of emphasizing the internal over the external,
the personal over the cultural. If there was anything I knew in
my public school years, it was the crucial importance of being
smart or intelligent—more correctly, the crucial importance of
being regarded as intelligent. And being intelligent meant that

you were not in the crowd, but above it. One way of describing the culture of schools is that it defines and rewards intelligence, which, I repeat, meant that if you were not in a class by yourself, you were in a very small, select group of individuals. In practice, intelligence was more than doing well, it was doing better than the others on all tests in all subjects. No pupil was ever in doubt about who was regarded as intelligent, or bright, or smart. To be intelligent meant that you were successful, and if you were successful, it meant that you were intelligent. That is quintessentially American and therefore such a pervasive feature of our schools. What has stuck in my memory are those few classmates who could draw well—far better than anyone else—but who were not regarded as intelligent. Their classmates were awed by their drawings and paintings, as were their teachers, but that did not mean they were ''intelligent.''

And it was no different outside of schools. If someone was rich, it meant they were intelligent. If most of my aunts and uncles were far more affluent than we were, it meant that my father, a lowly cutter of children's clothing, was less intelligent than they were. To me, to possess the garments of success—a car, a telephone, your own house, or an apartment in a ''nice'' neighborhood, or to be sent by your parents to a summer camp, or to eat in a restaurant—meant that you were smarter than someone like my father. None of this will be comprehensible to the adult reader who cannot comprehend how well children are made sensitive in countless ways, formal and informal, to messages from the culture, a process of absorption as powerful as it is subtle. I am saying nothing that in principle is not contained in the societal diagnosis by the women's liberation movement and by blacks and other minorities.

I did not regard myself as intelligent. I knew I was not ''dumb,'' but that did not mean I was intelligent. I could list a couple of scores of names of classmates whom I believed teachers regarded as intelligent. I am not on that list. As I go over that list today, I am struck, truly struck, by how many on that list were perceived by me as coming from ''well-off'' families. I saw them as more self-assured and more assertive than I. I did not see myself as impressing anybody, least of all me. How I envied those classmates who seemed so quick to get the right answer, who seemed to have such a good opinion of themselves, who in terms of all-round performance were Jack Armstrongs or the female equivalent, and who lived in the best neighborhoods. It is true but facile to explain my opinion of myself in terms of family, identification with father, and that abstraction "social class" that obscures as much as it illuminates. If your explanation leaves out the diverse and pervasive ways by which children are judged in terms of intelligence, and how those judgments become part of the self-picture, with enormous consequences for motivation, aspiration, and the forging of a future perspective, you are leaving out a significant factor shaping the lives of American children.

Now for some objective facts that will complicate what I have said and cast it in a new light. I finished the eighth grade at the age of twelve, two years earlier than is usual. That came about in two ways. First, three times I found I had been skipped a grade. Second, one summer I went to school and got high enough grades to be advanced a year when school reopened. Clearly, I was regarded as intelligent as I defined it earlier. I must have been doing something right! And yet, I judged myself in a way discrepant with those facts. Here again, one can resort to an explanation involving the dynamics of my "personality," and that explanation would be valid but incomplete. It would be incomplete to the extent that it ignores some stultifying, mind-destroying features of the American classroom and school. Obviously, I met whatever academic standards that were set: I could answer questions teachers asked, I did my homework, and I did well on tests. But it was equally obvious to me that, despite knowing the right answers, I did not *understand* why they were right answers. That was especially true in arithmetic. I could perform the operations (multiplication, division, fractions)— more correctly, I memorized the operations—but I did not understand why they worked and how they related to anything on this earth with which I was familiar. But I was a nice, dutiful, conforming pupil who learned what he was supposed to learn, even though it made no personal sense. From my vantage point, my *really* intelligent classmates understood what it was all about

and why. I was a fraud. This came to a head in high school
when I took algebra and geometry, which literally had no meaning for me. My job was to *do* algebra and geometry, not to
understand them. That I had a strong need to understand (I
know now) was very much a reflection of something deeply personal. But that is no warrant for ignoring how the American
classroom is unwittingly geared to the production of ''right
answers'' at the expense of understanding. Schoolteachers teach
the way they were taught. They are victims no less than their
pupils. They are not villains.

The discrepancy between how I judged myself and how
others judged me was fateful for my career in psychology. By
the time I entered graduate school, I was already convinced in
the most personal and concrete ways that the concept of intelligence—its definition, measurement, and function in American
society, and schools in particular—was at best nonsense and at
worst symptomatic of abysmal ignorance about the transactions
between organism and social contexts. To understand that concept, one had to understand it in light of American history and
society, within which the worship of the technological and methodological is such a prominent feature. And it goes without saying that once I entered psychology, I was predisposed to be
drawn to what goes on in schools. Becoming a psychologist
meant not only that I wanted to understand myself better but
that I wanted to change American psychology. Grandiosity
aside, I entered psychology with an agenda.

Relevant here is my initial reaction (somewhere, sometime
in college) to the assertion that women as a group were not as
intelligent as men. It was an assertion buttressed by ''studies,''
scores of studies. I was flabbergasted. That assertion made as
much sense to me as geometry and algebra, except that, unlike
the case with geometry and algebra, I had a wealth of personal
experience that rendered that assertion dead wrong. It had never
occurred to me that anyone could judge girls less intelligent than
boys. And when in graduate school I pored over studies (and
memorized their hypotheses, methods, and findings) demonstrating female inferiority, I responded precisely the way I did to
algebra and geometry: it made no sense. So, when the women's

liberation movement picked up steam in the post–World War II era, zeroing in on, among other things, the issue of intelligence, I needed neither instruction nor convincing. And if a century from now our world still exists, I have no doubt that the assertion of intellectual differences will be seen as another instance of how era and culture can imprison us.

There was another discrepancy, and that had to do with maleness. I saw myself as cowardly, a sissy, fearing any display of hostility by myself or other boys that might lead to a fight. I can remember only one time that I fought another boy, but that only confirmed my opinion of myself, because Harry Geiger, I knew, was more of a coward than I was. I lived with or near three cousins who were brothers, one whom I envied and two whom I worshiped. I envied Artie, a year older than I, because I saw him as bigger, stronger, and fearing nothing and nobody. I worshiped his older brothers, Oscar and Leo, because each had been on the first squad of Barringer High's football team. Leo went on to play for Cornell, and Oscar played for Brown, where he was on their famous Iron Man team. It is impossible for me to exaggerate how puny and inadequate I felt in relation to them. I never felt the way I thought a boy should feel. Matters were not helped any by the fact that I knew that everyone in our extended family said that Leo and Oscar were very intelligent, as indeed they were. Artie was not described in that way. He was the terror of the family, and to me he was lucky because he was a "real" boy. So I was a double fraud: I was not intelligent, and I was a coward. And I never saw myself as being an athlete. I lacked the physical agility and strength a real boy needs to play baseball, football, and basketball.

But writing this autobiography made me realize I was a good athlete if you go by conventional standards. We lived very close to a school that had a large playground, and during the summers there was a playground director who organized teams for intra- and interplayground tournaments. During any one summer, there must have been upwards of a couple of hundred boys and girls organized into teams. Something was always going on, even at night, because the playground had floodlights. The fact is that I was always on the first team. In baseball I was *the* pitcher, and I was a good switch hitter. And I was no slouch in the other sports. But the clincher in this picture is what happened when a spanking new high school was built in the neighborhood. I was in the first class to enter the school. How can you have a high school and not have a football team? Not in America! So when Weequahic High School opened in September, one of the first announcements was a call for candidates for the football team. I not only wanted to be on the team but I wanted to play center like Oscar and Leo. How I imagined myself in that football uniform! I need not detail the struggle with my mother to get permission to go out for the team. I won. Bear in mind that I was two or more years younger than any other candidate. I was shorter than anyone else. I weighed around 140 pounds, which was really puny because I wanted to play center, a position calculated to satisfy one's masochistic needs, which obviously were strong in me. It is a position from which one can give punishment, but that was not an aspect I relished; indeed, it bothered me. I felt like a child among giants. I still find it somewhat incomprehensible that I became the backup center to someone who looked to me to be ten feet tall, with weight appropriate to height. In practice scrimmages, I played against him. Why I did it is a little more clear to me than how I did it. I see myself as running here and there, looking *up* to try to see where the action is, where the play is going, avoiding direct contact, but ending up at the bottom of the pile. And what a pile it was! I feared injury, but I feared any display of unmasculinity far more.

Practice began early in September. Because it was a new team in a new school, no game was scheduled with a rival high school until mid-fall. Within a period of weeks, I had lost about twenty pounds, a loss not noted or picked up by the coaching staff. It was then that I came down with polio. I had won the battle with my mother. I had lost a larger war within myself. The fact is that after I contracted polio, there was a part of me—a part I would allow myself to recognize fleetingly and with guilt— that was relieved that I was removed from an arena in which I had to prove that I was a real male. And that was when fantasies about literary-theatrical achievement started to take over.

The playing fields would be different; the ultimate goals remained the same.

The psychoanalytically inclined person would have a field day explaining the discrepancy between the way I saw myself as a young male and actual performance. But why a field day? More likely, a person would ask: So what else is new? An over-protective, Jewish mother, the oedipal triangle, the castration complex, a strong counterphobic tendency, the internal battle between activity and passivity, the self-protective nature of the process of sublimation—these and more can be employed to make me a textbook case of the content and processes of the young, developing male child. I do not question the validity of that clinical assessment. But it is not the whole story. What it leaves out is the strength of the myriad ways in which the young American male is literally bombarded with messages defining the nature of masculinity. Newspapers, radio, movies, peer groups, pulp magazines (especially westerns)—these were the major conveyors of the message of what a male should be: out-ward going, assertive (if not fearless), tolerant of pain, coura-geous, attractive to girls, unanxious, and capable of standing up for his rights even if that meant fighting. It was all right if a girl was a tomboy; it was shameful if a boy was a sissy. It was all right, indeed it was laudable, if you were courteous and respectful, but something was wrong if you were a Mama's boy. You should want to compete, to test and demonstrate your physical prowesses, not to shrink from or avoid competition. It was a message to and about the *individual* male child: his responsibility to *himself* and to the American ideal of the mas-culine child. All else was backdrop.

Parents and the family context are conveyors of societal messages, but only in part. By virtue of their socialization into American society, they have absorbed aspects of the picture of American maleness, but again only in part, especially if they were Jewish immigrants. What a source of surprise and pride it was to me that Barney Ross, a Jew, was a world champion fighter! Even *my* parents took pride in that. I am reminded here of the time when I was in my late fifties and found myself in Israel talking with an Israeli who was a commander of a tank corps. He was dressed like a commander, looked like one, talked like one, and, by God, he was one—and a Jew, to boot! And I met scores of other Israelis, an experience that forced me to understand in the concrete what I knew in the abstract: to be a Jew in Israel was a different cup of psychological tea from what being Jewish in America was for me as a child. I am not explicable in terms of a psychology that leaves out the America my family coped with. In my case, the clear and loud messages I was getting about masculinity were always on a collision course with family values and context. My Jewish family and America are in my psychological bloodstream. Yes, different Jewish families "produced" different kinds of males in America. And America was not the Eastern European *shtetl*, or what was then a Palestine kibbutz. If this is a glimpse of the obvious, it is one that American psychology (indeed, Western psychology, including that of Freud) has not confronted squarely. It took me a long time to understand it in a truly personal way.

At the beginning of this chapter, I said that I saw myself (and still see myself) as ambitious but not competitive. If that is valid as "seeing," it may be invalid by the criteria others used to describe me. To me, competitiveness has always meant that you vie with others for some reward (symbolic or material) and that, therefore, there are winners and losers. You strive to win, and if you lose it is a defeat. And at no time is a defeat more poignant, less easy to rationalize away, less easy to compensate for than in the preadult years. When Vince Lombardi said about pro football that winning is what it is all about, he could also have said that about what the American boy was expected to feel. And no one in all of American sports, past or present, has been revered (or quoted) as much as Vince Lombardi. The name of the game *is* winning! And writing this autobiography has told me that it is most unlikely that I escaped the consequences of the virulent American virus of competitiveness and winning. I offer a few examples. Each year in Hebrew school, two religious plays were staged for parents. You tried out for a part, and usually there was a handful of boys vying for the "big" part. I competed, and very successfully. Indeed, I always won. A more compelling example is from my senior year in high school, when I still had my right arm in an airplane splint. It was announced that a teacher was organizing a radio production of Dickens's *Great Expectations,* and that it was going to be broadcast on WNBC in Radio City in New York. You can well imagine the flock of students who wanted to be in the cast. It was like the scene in the movie *42nd Street* when, before the opening curtain, the director says to the chorus girl who will fill in for the inebriated star something like: "You are going out there a nobody, but when the show is over tonight you will be a star and your name will be in lights." Airplane splint and all, I competed against the others, and I got the lead part. I achieved local stardom, helped no end by a photograph of the show's cast around the microphone of a studio in Radio City.

These and other instances force me to the conclusion that I was literally an actor—that is, I could act as if I were competitive even though I saw myself as otherwise. If anything is clear about the me of those years, it is that I had a fear of failing and losing, never really being clear about what would happen if I failed. Indeed, winning presented a problem, because I knew how a loser would feel, and that decreased the strength of the satisfaction derived from winning. I felt as sorry for the loser as I would for myself in his position. So, when I came up for tenure at Yale, I perceived the department as having to choose between me and a colleague. I had absolutely no doubt that he would be chosen, and that would be understandable to me: he was very "intelligent" and productive and, to me, he looked as a Yale professor should look. When I was informed of the decision, my immediate reaction was less one of surprise than of pity for my colleague. I sought him out to tell him how bad *I* felt! This speaks volumes about my "psychodynamics," but here, too, I do not think it is the whole story. If engaging in competition, tournament style, is encouraged and rewarded, it is also true in America that we are taught that it is unseemly to parade one's competitiveness, and we cloak it in a variety of garments that hide from us and others how much we want to be better than everyone else, how deeply we want to stand on the mountain of success. We are supposed to appear modest, as if what we have achieved is simply a recognition of objective performance relatively independent of the strength and content of our private fantasies. It is my impression that in no other country are people as sensitive to the concept of "public image" as we are in America. And that concept bespeaks a cleavage between public and private image, the former possessing none of the unseemliness of the latter.

I have in this and previous chapters described aspects of my world of childhood and adolescence. I did not do this because I thought it was intrinsically interesting, let alone distinctive. Put in another way, I am not a "great man" who wants to explain to the world how greatness was achieved, requiring that its origins in early life be plumbed and the threads of continuity carefully traced, making it all seem near inevitable. However interesting the autobiographical accounts of such people have been, I have long been dissatisfied with the ways they locate and weight the influence of the culture of their countries on their development. For example, in the past decade a spate of books has been written by those who were part of what has been called the New York Intellectuals of the 1930s. Their impact nationally was far out of proportion to their numbers. Unlike me, they are household names in academia and beyond. Without exception, they try to portray, and usually do it well, how their childhood and adolescence bore the imprint of the fact that they had lived in the Bronx, or Brooklyn, or Manhattan. They were New Yorkers from head to toe. But as they bring their stories to their later years, a new theme emerges: how *American* they were (and are) but did not recognize or want to recognize, and it was more the latter than the former. That recognition did not arise *sui generis* but as a result of events in the world posed by Hitler Germany, Stalinist Russia, and World War II. If that recognition came to the fore in midlife, it is not a recognition the substance of which is made clear to a reader like me. And if I felt that way, it was because in the middle of my career in psychology I found myself engrossed with the relationships between America and American psychology, and, therefore, when I would be reading an autobiography, I found myself judging it in terms of how directly the writer confronted the fact that he or she was born into, reared in, and socialized in a particular country in a particular period of its history. Geographically, intellectually, and politically, I was on a distant periphery of a circle in the center of which were the New York Intellectuals of the thirties and subsequent decades. I met some of them, I read what they wrote, and I felt kinship with them. But there was always a part of me—what some of my friends said was the "bourgeois" part of me—that could not accept the readiness with which this influential group disparaged American culture and society. I shall elaborate on this in the next chapter. Here I wish to emphasize that my developing interest in this problem increasingly had little or nothing to do with political ideology, let alone patriotism, which so often is "the refuge of scoundrels." It was at the same time both far more simple and far more complex than that. How does one become an American? That is a simple question. The answer is fantastically complex, no less so than the answer to the question of what is an atom. For example, it takes a good part of one's life to begin to appreciate how America is composed of regions geographically distinct, each of which has a distinctive ambience that becomes reflected in a distinctive world view. And yet, despite these differences, there is a common core that leaves no doubt in the minds of foreigners that we are American. The issue has a pressing urgency, because we are well into a unique phase of human history in which all nations and their cultures are struggling with the consequences of the fact that they do and must interact with each other. The vicissitudes of that struggle in the past are warning enough that we have to better understand radically different outlooks, a significant part of which remain, at best, unarticulated and, at worst, beyond the fringes of awareness.

What I have recounted about my childhood and adolescence may strike some as coming from another world or an era no longer with us. The world has changed in terms of appearance, problems, knowledge, expectations, and feats of human creativity and stupidity. We like to believe that we learn from the past, that we have overcome it, and that the future is ours to shape. Those beliefs do not reckon with the strength with which our socialization into our society implants in us unarticulated attitudes and outlooks that ensure that the past will be part of our present and, therefore, influential for our futures. Of course the world has changed, but it is a non sequitur to conclude that those changes are completely or largely independent of continuities (the cultural DNAs) that derive from our social-psychological heritage. As we shall see, American psychology was and continues to be *American* in very distinctive ways, an obvious fact to foreign psychologists. When Freud, rightly or wrongly, feared what would happen to psychoanalysis in America, he was reflecting a perception of America quite different from that of American psychology and medicine. Freud, the European pessimist, did not look kindly on American optimism. For somewhat different reasons, Piaget feared what would happen to his work when American psychology "discovered" what he learned by talking to children.

5

Dana College
and Radical Politics

I entered Dana College in Newark in 1935 at age sixteen. Dana was an old red-brick building a few blocks away from the downtown center, near the muddy Passaic River. I was told that it was the former Feigenspan Brewery. Those were the days when a moderate-sized city had several breweries. Obviously, it had been extensively renovated when it housed the Newark Institute of Arts and Sciences, which had a cooperative arrangement with New York University. That relationship was severed when it became Dana College. After World War II, it was taken over by Rutgers University as the Newark campus of the new state university. Dana was a commuter college, with far more evening than day students. It had (for it) an extensive curriculum in accounting and business, and the former New Jersey Law School had been absorbed by the college. Shortly after I entered, Dana College became the University of Newark. I always think of it as Dana College, and with boundless fondness and gratitude.

If anybody had asked me what a college was, I would not have been able to reply except to say that it was a place where you learned. Learned what? And the answer would have been: what college teachers—the words *professor* and *faculty* were just words to me—wanted you to learn. I had read the catalogue and learned that there were departments, chairmen (no women, of course), deans, and a president. And I found out that for the first year or so I had no decisions to make. There were required survey courses in English literature, Western history, political institutions, economics, and at least one other I cannot recall. It may have been psychology, because I know that all freshmen took the introductory course. If I did not know what college was, it was largely because I did not need to know. Going to college was a privilege, a door opener to a new world of ideas, and that was enough. Besides, it was infinitely better than looking for a job that did not exist. The truest statement I can make about my perspective when I entered college is that I had four years before I would be walking the streets looking for employment. I was on vacation, and I would enjoy it, although I had only the foggiest notion what "it" might be.

You did not go to college—at least to Dana College—as preparation for graduate school. Indeed, I did not know what graduate school was or meant. I knew that if you wanted to be a physician or lawyer, you spent three or four years after college in a law or medical school. Some students wanted to be lawyers, but none said they were going into medicine. If you wanted to go into medicine, you did not go to the likes of Dana College. In the hierarchy of colleges, Dana clearly would have been (and was, I learned by the time I finished) considered bush league, the college equivalent of the one-room schoolhouse.

For most of us, going to college was an end in itself, the last time in our lives we would be exposed to and live in the world of knowledge and ideas. It was not, except for the business students, a preparation for the world of work. We hoped that when we were through, the fact that we had a college degree would give us an edge over those less educated, but, given the hope-destroying Depression, our hopes were not high. A significant percentage of the students were Jewish. There was a smattering of blacks. The student body was evenly divided in terms of gender. Within days of beginning college, it was apparent to me that the blacks and I came from the most economically impoverished homes. That judgment was based on several criteria. First, I brought my lunch, while the others ate in the local eatery. Second, I came from home by bus (cost, a nickel), while a fair number of others came by car or train. Occasionally, I walked the five or so miles to school to save the nickel for a soda in the eatery, which I experienced as no hardship at all. Third, students had money to go to the movies in the nearby downtown, where ticket prices were higher than in neighborhood movie houses. They had "spending money," an allowance, proof positive to me that they came from another world. If you read some of Philip Roth's early novels and short stories about the Newark-Maplewood-Orange Jewish communities, you get a picture of the backgrounds of a fair number of the students at Dana College, although Roth's picture is more from the post– than the pre–World War II period.

The dominant impression I got from my early months at Dana was that, as a group, the students were serious, bright, and intellectually curious. Dana was a microcosm of urban, Northeast America. It had a vibrant atmosphere lit up by numerous clubs and informal groups concerned with the political-social issues of the day, year, and era. For example, I quickly learned about Mayor Frank Hague of Jersey City, a national figure in the Democratic Party, whose views on civil liberties were somewhat Hitlerian. Unions were anathema to him, and, of course, socialists and Communists did the work of the devil. (Socialists and Communists were people who formed unions, practiced free speech, and criticized Hague.) Hague proclaimed—clearly, loudly, publicly—"I am the law." America, I quickly came to learn, had always had its Frank Hagues. Within a few months of beginning college, I became aware of the political-social world. If my head was not swimming, it certainly was expanding. The adjective *liberal* in *liberal arts* explicitly refers to a process of liberation from ignorance and prejudice. I had begun my liberal arts education.

Those who remember the sixties well have a good idea of what Dana was like. Issues surrounding race, unemployment, poverty, the Italian-Ethiopian war, the Japanese Manchurian invasion, and (of course) Hitler—these became the daily fare for discussion and proclamations. I became an avid reader of newspapers, especially the *New York Times*. Those were the days when New York seemed to have scads of newspapers. It was important to read the *Herald-Tribune*, because it represented so well the conservative view of the world, and, in addition, it was even more important to read Hearst's *Journal-American*, because if we adopted the opposite of its superpatriotic, reactionary position, we would obviously be right and on the side of the angels.

What you absorb and what you become in your college years have several sources, but none is more important than the students with whom you develop relationships of varying intensities. Precisely because Dana was small—and had none of the trappings of a campus college—it was possible to observe, if not get to know, most of the other students. I had the good fortune to become part of a group that stimulated, nurtured, and matured me. It was a relatively well-knit core group of friends through each of whom a new part of the world opened to me. One of the students was Melvin Tumin (with whom I had gone to Hebrew school), who is now professor of sociology at Princeton. Another was Herbert McClosky, who is professor of political science at Berkeley. The third was Samuel Lerner, who is head of a large social agency in Detroit. And then there were two secretaries. One was Rose Kohn Goldsen, who is professor of sociology at Cornell. The other was Shirley Strauch, with whom I fell in love. Shirley was somewhat older than I, infinitely more mature, and as bright and knowledgeable as they come.

If someone had nothing better to do than to determine how many Dana students of the years 1935–1939 achieved important academic positions, it would not surprise me if, relative to the size of its student body, Dana would be first in the country. Such studies have been carried out, and it is understandable if they saw no reason to include the likes of Dana College. Harold Garfinckel, professor of sociology at UCLA, was a student at Dana. Eli Chinoy became professor of sociology at Smith and, before his untimely death, had made his mark on the field. There are more, and if one included those who by conventional standards were "successful"—in law, public service, and business—it is an impressive record. It is true but terribly incomplete to explain this record by the characteristics of individual students.

On average, as a group they were, to understate it, very highly motivated, prepared to absorb whatever they were asked to learn. So, for example, if it had been required of me to take a course in Goethe's use of the umlaut, I would have plunged in with interest and curiosity. But equally important to an explanation is that what was characteristic of me was no less so of many other students. My years at Dana constituted one of the two times when I encountered such a passion for learning in students. The other time was during the years 1945–1950, when, by virtue of the GI Bill of Rights, young (and old) veterans, many of whom had only dreamed about an undergraduate and graduate education, flocked into our colleges and universities. They, like others in the prewar years, hungered for a wider intellectual horizon. To explain individual performance independent of all that is implied by the concept of zeitgeist is grossly misleading, albeit it contains a kernel of truth.

If the students and the zeitgeist were important, the faculty was, perhaps, more so. They were, as individuals and as representatives of their disciplines, serious, stimulating, supportive, and even electrifying. Their intellectual fervor and scholarly range were contagious. Jewell and Flink in economics, Zabriskie in history, Fuhlbruegge in political science, Bebout in government, Bates and Stephens in English literature, Woodward in geology and the history of science, Killian in sociology, Gaudet and Watson in psychology, Keosian in biology, Abarbanel in German, Kingdon (president) in philosophy, and Henry in mathematics—each in his own way held your attention and respect. After half a century past graduation, how many people can quickly name the instructors of every course they took and recall them with affection and gratitude? Their influence was less in how they made subject matter alive and more in helping us adapt a sympathetic but critical attitude to the rules of evidence and the pitfalls in the interpretation of texts. That may strike some as somewhat high-blown and abstract, so let me put it this way: what those instructors did was to make me *want* to be part of the world of ideas and to *recognize* that ideas have antecedents and consequences in action. In short, for me and others, these instructors—without ever putting it into words—got us to understand why the academic life could be fascinating and fulfilling. When I started at Dana, college was a place where teachers taught and students learned. It did not take long for me to realize that colleges were forums for the presentation and discussion of how the human mind tried and continues to try to understand its place in the physical and social world. At the time, I had no reason to believe, no basis for believing, that Dana might have been atypical in how well it was serving the function of providing the ingredients that make for productive forums. With the passage of years, I had to conclude that if Dana was not literally unique, it was certainly atypical. Only yards away from the muddy, industry-lined Passaic River there existed an amazing oasis of intellectual ferment.

In the history of higher education in this century, the City College of New York is legendary in at least two ways. The first has to do with the number of its graduates who achieved eminence in medicine, law, and science. The second has to do with the decade of the thirties, when CCNY was a social-political cauldron kept heated by a collection of student activists who, shortly after World War II, began to put their imprint on— indeed, give direction to—the social sciences, literature and literary criticism, and political theory and action. Those of us at Dana who were involved in radical politics either knew or heard about some of these individuals who not only held positions of "power" in this or that radical party but who wrote for their party's publications. If only because of our respect for the printed word, we looked up to these individuals as minor leaguers do to major leaguers. Within the past decade, a number of these CCNY activists have published memoirs or autobiographical fragments in which are contained descriptions of their student days. In all respects, with one exception, the picture they paint is identical to the one I have sketched for Dana and which I will fill in later in this chapter. The one exception is that their accounts say very little about the influence of the faculty in shaping their thinking. The only faculty member I can recall whom several of them mention is Morris Cohen, the legendary philosopher who was temperamentally and intellectually allergic to superficial thinking. I am not alone among my Dana cohorts in giving the faculty a far more important role in our personal and intellectual development. If that faculty did not contain a Morris Cohen, it was on average far above the norm of any college faculty I have known in terms of "turning on" students to the intellectual world.

How can one account for such a collection of sterling teachers and thinkers? It took me years to realize that the question required a social and not a psychological answer. In the days of the Great Depression, college teaching positions were scarce, to put it mildly. Even at the most prestigious universities, those who received their doctorates had low expectations for securing a teaching position, any position, anywhere. This meant, of course, that colleges that had openings could pick from the cream of the doctoral crop. And, obviously, Dana–University of Newark attracted some unusual individuals, many of them from Columbia, Harvard, Yale. What was also in Dana's favor was that it was across the river from New York, not in the prairies or some isolated college town. If Dana had a minimally adequate library, for example, Manhattan had all that a scholar needed. Some of the faculty lived in Manhattan. I have suggested that as a group the Dana students were "hungry" for learning. The faculty were hungry for the opportunity to pass on to students their knowledge and wisdom. If their hunger was satisfied, so was ours.

In my freshman year, I took the introductory psychology course taught by Frederick J. Gaudet, who had recently obtained his doctorate at Columbia. With his thick, black hair, manicured goatee, erect posture that made him look taller than he was (and he was not short), and deep, throaty voice, he fit two stereotypes: college professor and magician. On first seeing him, you did not notice that one of his eyes was disfigured; that head of hair and goatee were too prominent. He was handsome, the women swooned, the gossip mill had it that he was a gay blade, and it was a fact that he had a problem with alcohol. He was a serious, inspiring, interesting teacher. To us he was an icon and myth destroyer. I have never taught an introductory psychology course, but I have been told that it is hard to make it uninteresting, although some have been able to do so. Students come to that course with all kinds of questions about themselves, especially sexual ones, and they expect to obtain illumination, if not answers. The main feature of introductory texts is that they present the field as a scientific endeavor, and to the extent that the instructor follows the text in his or her lectures, he or she dampens the interest of the students. Dr. Gaudet did not, could not, follow the text slavishly, although we were required to know it well. He had the knack of making principles and theories relevant to our lives. I am tempted to say that he tried to engender in us the attitude that you take data and theories with more than a few grains of salt. That sounds somewhat nihilistic, or at least hypercritical, and it was the case that by the end of the course there were few things about psychology and human behavior for which we felt we had a secure scientific explanation. Far from lowering our respect for psychology as a field of inquiry, it increased both our interest and respect.

There was one conviction, some would call it a bias, that Dr. Gaudet possessed that mightily influenced me, as much because of the way he posed the issues and presented the data as because of the readiness with which I wanted to agree with him. It concerns a problem that is truly basic to psychology (but not only psychology), because where you stand in regard to it illuminates your understanding of "human nature" in its transactions with the social fabric. We call it the "nature-nurture" or "heredity-environment" problem: What limitations do genetic factors place on human ability in its developmental aspects? What is the role of social contexts in restricting or facilitating intellectual growth? It has been an enduring problem and controversy in the history of psychology, and for at least one very important, indeed fateful, reason: where you stand in regard to it has practical consequences for social policy and action. It is not a problem to which society is indifferent. In fact, it becomes a scientific issue precisely because the society, clearly or inchoately, has identified it as an issue. So it is not happenstance that the problem becomes a "hot" one scientifically when society is bothered, puzzled, and upset by the perceived failure of certain groups to meet customary standards of intellectual performance. The waves of immigration in the nineteenth and early twentieth centuries, the rejection rates and test scores of recruits in World War I, disappointment in the results of compensatory educational programs in the 1960s and '70s—those are the kinds of societal contexts in which the roles of heredity and environment appear on the national agenda and spur and increase the interest of the scientists in diverse fields who by their data and explanations further feed the fires of public discussion, controversy, and proposals for action. Where you stand on the issue is a difference that makes a practical difference, both within and without the scientific arena.

Dr. Gaudet was unabashedly a partisan of the environmentalists. It perhaps would be more correct to say that he enjoyed exposing the methodological flaws of the nurture-favoring studies and presenting explanations alternative to those advanced by these researchers. What has stuck in my mind is the detail with which he presented and discussed Goddard's studies of a New Jersey family, the Kallikaks. Bear in mind that in 1935, when I took the introductory course, Goddard's studies were not ancient history. They had been done somewhat more than two decades earlier, Goddard was still alive and well, and his work was truly in the public domain. Whether it was Goddard's, or Cyril Burt's, or the scores of studies on the intelligence of blacks, Dr. Gaudet left no doubt in our minds that on purely scientific grounds the claims for the decisive role of heredity were, at best, unsubstantial and, at worst, instances of unrecognized prejudice distorting the canons of logic. Fifty years after taking that course, I wrote a foreword to J. D. Smith's *Minds Made Feeble* (Rockville, Md.: Aspen, 1985), a Perry Mason kind of book because Smith had uncovered the real name of the Kallikak family, which, according to Goddard, had two lines of descent: one that from the time of the American Revolution had produced eminent, upstanding citizens and the other a line of dependent, immoral, mostly feebleminded individuals who lived in a kind of Tobacco Road culture. Having uncovered the real name of the family, Smith was able to demonstrate that every criticism ever made of Goddard's studies was valid. A few years before Smith's book, S. J. Gould, a biologist-paleontologist, in his *The Mismeasure of Man* (New York: Norton, 1981), had taken dead aim at Goddard's work. Smith hammered the final nail into the coffin containing Goddard's data and explanations.

I cannot assert that Dr. Gaudet denied a role to heredity in intelligence. What I can assert is that he held two convictions, and passionately. The first was that evidence for a major role of heredity was so shaky that it was scientifically and socially irresponsible to use that evidence as a basis for societal action. The second was that our understanding of the developmental relationships between social contexts and intellectual performance was superficial. He viewed John B. Watson's extreme environmentalism as both arrogant and illusory, as oversimplification run rampant. Freud, he pointed out, was a very different cup of tea, because he had begun to plumb the complexity of early development in its intellectual-motivational-affective-family aspects. If he was critical of Freud, it did not prevent him from recognizing that Freud had realistically complicated how we had to think of those aspects. The more I reflect on that introductory course, and on all the others I took from Dr. Gaudet, the clearer it becomes that he was a thoroughgoing skeptic, temperamentally incapable of committing himself to a "truth," too knowledgeable about the myriad ways in which people, in science and elsewhere, allow bias, willingly or unwillingly, to pervade their perception and logic. It is not happenstance that his doctoral dissertation may have been the first by a psychologist to demonstrate the variations in the sentencing tendencies of judges dealing with very similar kinds of defendants. The law is the law, and we treasure the belief that we are a society based on the rule of law and not the passions of individuals. I can hear Dr. Gaudet saying, "a likely story!"

Dr. Gaudet's view of psychology and the world was tailor-made for young people relatively open to new ideas and unwilling to believe that they could not overcome the limitations of background and even personal inadequacy. With the passage of years, I came to see that his impact on me and others stemmed less from the substance of what he taught or his skeptical attitude to conventional wisdom, and more from their implications for another issue, which psychology considered off limits: free will. He said little or nothing about free will, but everything

about him underscored the importance he attached to two interrelated factors: what you believe about yourself and what others
believe about you. It was not until years later, when I read
William James, that I understood that Dr. Gaudet, without ever
saying it or perhaps even knowing it, agreed with James that
the issue was not how in the abstract you regarded the logical-
scientific status of the concept of free will, but rather the strength
of your belief that you were "free" to choose and act. As James
emphasized, it makes a world of difference whether you have
or do not have such a belief. Today in psychology the issue is
implied by such concepts as locus of control, the self-fulfilling
prophecy, the dynamics of "blaming the victim," and learned
helplessness.

It has always seemed puzzling to me that the Jamesian-
Gaudet view of free will has played very little role in the cyclical
nature-nurture controversies, even though it seems obvious that
just as it is legitimate to assume some kind of relationship between heredity and development, it is no less legitimate to assume a relationship between development and the strength of
one's belief that one is free to choose and act. How that belief
arises and how to account for its variations are questions that
go far beyond psychology as a discipline, involving as they do
the culture and history of local and societal contexts. If anything
is clear in human history, it is the frequency with which dominant groups underestimated the capacities of other groups, a
fact to which as a Jew I was quite sensitive. I did not need to
be persuaded how easy it was (and is) for a derogated group—
be it the Kallikaks, Jews, blacks, Italians, or scores of others—to
view themselves as others viewed them, to feel impotent to hope,
to choose, and to act. I learned a great deal from Dr. Gaudet,
and if I emphasize his frequent discussions of the nature-nurture
issue, it is because they made clear to me that how you stood
on these issues, as citizen or scientist, influenced the social actions you advocated. More than that, your stance indicated your
respect for the "data" of human history. And it was not long
after I came to Dana that history came to fascinate me, albeit
in a very partisan, amateurish, confining, but enormously productive way.

If Dr. Gaudet could not proclaim "the truth" in regard to the nature-nurture controversy, it did not stop me from proclaiming it, at first to myself and soon to those populating my world. I became a political radical enamored with the Marxian view of human history. The verb *became* obscures far more than it illuminates. I cannot explain how I "became" a Marxist in the way I can explain how I "became" a Yale faculty member. It does not help matters much to say it was a process. Many people were politically radicalized by the events of the thirties and were sympathetic to the Marxian view of things. Few of them, however, formally joined the Communist or Socialist parties. Before coming to Dana, I had never heard of Marx or, if I had, it had no significance for me. I had heard of communism and communists, both of which were associated in my mind with Russia and, in light of family history and blood-curdling stories, were bad. Why did I join the radical segment of the Socialist Party and not the Communist Party? Family history and terror stories predisposed me to the Socialist Party, which viewed the Russian Revolution and its consequences as a gross distortion of Marx's vision and held the Communist Party responsible. No less and perhaps more important was the fact that my closest friends at Dana also wanted to join the Socialist Party, and I saw them as far more politically knowledgeable and astute than I was. They appeared to know Marx far better than I did; they knew far more about the Russian Revolution than I did; and they seemed to manifest a degree of passionate conviction that I envied. I assumed that they had read and digested Marx's *Das Kapital.* I never got beyond the first fifty or so pages without falling asleep. I sincerely wanted to be and become a radical socialist, but my commitment lacked intellectual substance and security. An analogy may be helpful here. I was like the psychology student who finds psychoanalytical theory *the* way of understanding self and the world, learns the jargon, talks with assurance, and tries to convince you and everyone else to think the way he or she does. That Freud (like Marx) speaks to crucial issues, that what he says is far from nonsense, that he has thrown light on what heretofore received little or no illumination, that he has to be taken most seriously, that (in John Dollard's words) he has given us some pearls to be strung on the necklace of human wisdom—with these statements the student would fully agree. But what the passion and word mongering prevent the student from recognizing is that Freud (like Marx) was, among other things, a critic: someone incapable of accepting conventional wisdom, someone who treasured independence of mind, someone who knew the dangers of words, labels, and sloganeering. To that part of Freud, as in my case with Marx and socialism, the student is utterly insensitive; it is a part with which he or she cannot identify. This is not explainable by attributing it to the enthusiasms of youth, because there are some, a minority to be sure, who can take critical distance from what others proclaim as the truth, the whole truth, now and forever. If I was one who could proclaim the truth in the arena of political theory and action—albeit with a conscious sense of superficiality—it would not be the last time I did so. As I shall indicate in later pages, several years later I was broadcasting the completeness and eternality of psychoanalysis. Indeed, already at Dana, I began to regard Freud and Marx as the latter-day saints in the new church of the Truth.

Entering and becoming immersed in the world of radical, left-wing politics had an enormous impact on me as a person, citizen, and psychologist. It was literally an educational experience in the best sense of the root meaning of *education:* it elicited from me thoughts, attitudes, and values that slowly coalesced to give me a sense of personal and intellectual security, a sense of an internally derived identity that was not a reflection of what others thought, but something forged within me. Put in another way, I became a person relatively capable of thinking for myself, unable to tolerate the conflicts engendered between what in my heart of hearts I believed and what my commitment to a particular ideology said I should believe.

Let me start with the language of radical, left-wing movements. Central to the language and, therefore, imagery of radical parties and sects—and I went from the Socialist Party to the Socialist Workers Party to the Workers Party—are Russia and the Russian Revolution. Just as American politicians invoke the language and imagery of our revolution and the "founding fathers,'' the radical left is steeped in the origins of the Russian Revolution and its founding fathers: Marx, Engels, Lenin, Trotsky, and Stalin. And to be steeped meant not only knowledge of events but the use of concepts and labels that had descriptive and explanatory value. Peasants, proletariat, lumpen proletariat, bourgeois, class conflict, soviets, commissars, lackeys, Thermidor—these are but a small sample of concepts and labels that are foreign to the American ear but that come to have for someone who becomes a party member a reality or conceptual meaning embedded in a complicated political theory and history. If it is complicated, it is also fascinating, instructive, and relevant to anyone who seeks to understand the modern world. But the fact remains that the theory and history are European in site and imagery, and so is the language. As a party member, you were expected and motivated to be familiar with that theory and history. But as a party member you were also a missionary: to proselytize for new recruits and circulate the party publications, which meant, among other things, going to poor neighborhoods, knocking on doors, explaining why you were there, and leaving the party newspaper for them to read. We were like the Jehovah's Witnesses who two or three times a year ring our doorbell, introduce themselves, explain their mission, and leave us with the *Watchtower*. And that is the point: in all the times I talked to people, I met with polite incomprehension or the promise to read what I left with them. And when I would return, they said either that they were not interested or that they did not understand what they had read and did not want to pursue the matter further. That did not surprise me, because from the start it seemed obvious to me that I, and the readings I gave them, spoke in a language truly foreign to them. But that was also true when I would seek to get other college students to listen to my message. When I articulated my concerns to party officials, I received the stock answer that we had to expect that people would not easily overcome their indoctrination into an American way of thinking that blinded them to the needs and interests of their class if they were workers or, if they were ''bourgeois,'' to a protection of their class interests. That answer, of course, is not without merit, but it is an answer that implies that there is a distinctive American culture reflected in a unique history, language, and self-imagery to which an essentially "foreign" message has to adapt. We could talk with each other, but that ensured that we would remain a sect. The fact is that in practice we channeled our thoughts and energies into criticizing and undercutting other radical left-wing parties, especially the Communist Party, which had departed from the truth as we saw it. All of these parties had common ancestry; they shared the same language and imagery. I was aware that the problem I raised was not one that would be noticeably ameliorated by simply changing language and imagery, as if employing colloquial language would act as a kind of lubricant that would dissolve incomprehension and elicit acceptance. But the problem was a symptom of something more basic: a misreading of America and the American experience. I shall present two examples of what I mean, and I ask the reader to bear in mind that this book is a professional autobiography and not a political discourse.

When you become familiar with the history of czarist Russia, you, as an American, will be struck by the strength, pervasiveness, and effectiveness of the regime's restrictions on what we call individual rights. "Restrictions" is a mild characterization, because it does not convey the persecutory actions that dissenters experienced. "To go underground" (then as now) was a matter of survival and not choice. Counterintelligence breeds counterintelligence; secrecy of information and activity is one of the sine qua nons for the pursuer and the pursued, the persecutor and the persecuted. For a revolutionary party in Russia to see itself, Custer style, surrounded by enemies with guns loaded and raised was good reality testing.

When I joined the Young Peoples Socialist League and became a "Ypsl," I did not realize the extent to which it was disdainfully regarded by the Communist Party and sects that had broken away from that party. *Disdain* is too weak a word. *Seething derogation* would be more appropriate, because the Socialist Party was seen at its theoretical-value core as "bourgeois" because not only was it critical of the Russian Communist regime but it eschewed violence as a means of societal change. Further-

more, it espoused within the party and the larger society freedom
of discussion and dissent that robbed it of that kind of discipline
and militancy required of a vanguard revolutionary party or
movement. It is fair to say that it viewed the Socialist Party as
too "American," too committed to the Bill of Rights, in a society
that made a mockery of those rights. As I heard a Communist
orator say with a sneering smile, "The Socialist Party is a debating and educational society that would be more at home on the
Chautauqua circuit than it is in the class struggle." And a few
minutes later, he described Norman Thomas, for years the leader
of the Socialist Party, as someone who never should have left
the ministry to subvert the true interests of the workers of the
world. Norman Thomas was, more than any other left-wing
leader I have ever known or heard, quintessentially American
in several respects. At the same time that he was incisively critical
of injustice and its sources in American society—criticisms informed by facts and history, leavened with humor, and based
on a commitment to certain basic principles—he also believed
that there was an American ethos that could be adapted to, or
would not be in conflict with, the transformations that a socialist
program would require. He saw merit in certain of the values
on which the society was based. He was not prepared to write
America off and substitute wholesale the Russian Communist
ideology that regarded America as an "evil empire" that needed
to be changed, root and branch, as if there were nothing of moral
value to be salvaged. The fact that Norman Thomas was truly
a public figure who gained the respect of thousands who disagreed
with him politically was viewed by the other left-wing parties
as proof positive that he was politically naive and incapable of
understanding the nature of American capitalist society. He
simply could not grasp the "truth" as Lenin, Trotsky, or Stalin
had proclaimed it. He was, they argued, a clear example of someone who could not unimprison himself from his middle-class
origins. If anything is apparent to me with the passage of the
years, it is that Norman Thomas understood America better
than anyone else, its failings and its accomplishments. And no
one understood better the lessons to be learned from the totalitarian movements. Under his leadership, the Socialist Party did

lack "revolutionary" militancy and internal discipline. It did have some of the features of an educational and debating society. It did reflect the characteristic American optimism that reason, morality, and goodwill will ultimately triumph. But for several decades it and Norman Thomas were articulate voices pricking the American conscience. If America did not buy socialism, it ultimately bought many of its specific social welfare proposals.

What I have said about Norman Thomas and the Socialist Party contains judgments influenced by the passage of the years. In those earlier days, I saw the Socialist Party as insufficiently radical, and so when my friends decided to leave the party and become members of the far more radical Socialist Workers Party, I went along with them. That party, I should emphasize, considered itself (and was) to the left of the Communist Party— that is, it considered itself the true believer and proclaimer of the Marx-Engels-Lenin-Trotsky tradition. Trotsky was alive in exile, the fountainhead of what was right in Marxian theory and political action, the most knowledgeable critic of how Stalin, in his climb to power, had brought about a "distorted, degraded" workers' state. Trotsky was our hero.

Perhaps the first eye-opener of what it meant to be a member of a truly revolutionary party was that you were given a party name, on the assumption that you and the party needed to be protected against governmental agencies seeking to ferret out subversives plotting a revolution. There was also the practical consideration that if your employer or others found that you were a member of such an organization, you could be fired or discriminated against. I responded in two ways to this practice of secret names. The first was that the practice made sense because there was a long history in America of local, state, and federal authorities who sought to uncover or destroy or incriminate political groups that advocated the violent overthrow of the government. And, frequently, they could not discriminate between those who advocated violence and those who did not. J. Edgar Hoover, who for years was head of the FBI, had a classically paranoid view of political dissenters; that is, they were guilty until they proved themselves innocent of subversion, constitutional guarantees for the right to advocate notwithstanding.

And Hoover's self-righteousness in his self-appointed role of judge of the public welfare permitted him to commit the Stalinist-Communist fallacy: the means, any means, justify the ends.

If I understood the rationale for adopting a party name, I found it hard to believe the party view that America was far along on the road to a fascist restriction of civil liberties or that authorities saw our minuscule party as a threat to societal stability. That these authorities were mindful of our existence I had no doubt, but that they feared us seemed to me a grossly unrealistic evaluation of our influence. If anything was clear to me, it was that America tolerated a fantastic diversity of people, actions, and attitudes and, very importantly, that there were numerous individuals and groups who devoted their energies to the protection of the civil liberties of those with whom they sharply disagreed. America was not Russia, an obvious fact that our party, an offshoot historically of the Russian Communist Party, could not perceive. Ours was a party that psychologically "lived" in Russia as much as it did in America and, as a consequence, misread a complex America. And when I say "lived," I refer to what seemed like continuous, torturous, detailed discussions of how Stalin had managed to subvert the direction of the Russian Revolution. Was Russia *still* a workers' state to be protected at all costs from its capitalist enemies? That question seemed to be argued and debated interminably, and there were those who, disagreeing with Trotsky's affirmative answer, either left the party or were excommunicated. I would watch with unease how close friends would become bitter enemies because they disagreed on some important theoretical point. I came to see that the party's conception of discipline was authoritarian at its core. Once the party adopted a position, it became your position. It *had* to be your public position, or else. Although the party rhetoric supported internal debate and "democracy," the atmosphere was not, for me at least, conducive to either. What I believed in a "gut" sense, I could not bring myself to say out loud. And the clearest example of that involved the party position that Hitler Germany represented the inevitable degradation of war-making capitalism aimed at the destruction of Russia, and that it was in the interest of capitalist America to support such destruction, that is, the capitalist world was ganging up on the workers' state. However unsophisticated I was in the orthodox Marxian analysis of the contemporary world, in my heart of hearts I could not accept that view of America, Germany, and Russia, a view discredited by subsequent events. To label America as capitalist was true, but horribly incomplete and misleading. To see Russia as a bastion of virtue, albeit misled, was an illusion. And to see Hitler Germany only in terms of capitalist dynamics—as if its anti-Semitism and Wagnerian mythology of racial purity, memory, and history were explainable in economic-materialistic terms—was an irresponsible indulgence of reductionism.

I derived numerous benefits from my experience in radical parties. As I said earlier, one of the most lasting benefits was in the form of a requirement: you had to know political theory and history. Our world was not born yesterday, and it is incapable of being understood in simple terms. Granted that as individuals and collectivities we are, among other things, expressions of time, place, and era, but they in turn are inexplicable in terms of the present and near past. If I learned a great deal about Russian and European history—albeit on the level of a rank amateur—I also learned a great deal of American history. Perhaps the best way of putting it is that I gained a healthy respect for what I did not know, I became more humble about my knowledge and capabilities and more fearful of all that is implied in the saying "we have met the enemy, and it is us," or the variant about the college student who went to Europe to find himself except that he wasn't there. But in one respect I did find, or begin to find, myself, and that was the attitude that in whatever I chose as my career, I would (must) see it and me on as broad a societal stage as possible. My ambitiousness, bordering on grandiosity, remained undiluted side by side with a realistic modesty, a strange but by no means unusual combination. I continued to want to save the world. I knew I would not, but the fantasy was too pleasurable to give up. If I could not be a Trotsky, perhaps I could be a Freud! Psychology became increasingly attractive. And yet, to add another contradiction, the economic realities of family and the Great Depres-

sion forced me to adapt to the brute fact that I was essentially
going nowhere after I left the paradise of Dana College.

Another benefit from my political experience may sound
strange to some, but I can assure the reader that it became influential in my thinking as a psychologist. In its specific form
it is: beware of leaders who lack a sense of humor. In its general
form it is: beware of people who take themselves so seriously
that they cannot entertain the possibility that their theories and
actions may be wrong in whole or in part. With a couple of exceptions, every party leader I knew or observed was a humorless
individual who viewed members as existing for him (= the
party), unable to be or talk with them without conveying superiority of knowledge, or status, or power. They were deadly serious
people who possessed the truth and could not brook dissent.
The two exceptions were Norman Thomas (Socialist Party)
and Max Schactman (Workers Party). I do not like the adjective
warm to describe people except that it does convey an interpersonal receptivity, a kind of reaching out, or a kind of spontane-
ous reciprocity. Thomas and Schactman were warm people
for whom I gained an immediate liking and respect, although
my interactions with them were very fleeting. I observed and
listened to them on numerous occasions. They had an exquisite
capacity for satire leavened with a sense of the absurd. They
could be very funny in the stand-up comic tradition. It was fun-
niness in the service of serious matters, but not a hostile fun-
niness that made you think twice about trusting them not to
make you feel like an inconsequential worm. Let me give an
example that will have meaning for those who saw or heard the
recording by Danny Kaye singing that song in *Lady In The Dark*
in which, for what seems to be an eternity, he recites in rapid
fire two or three score tongue-twisting Russian names all ending in "off." You hold your breath waiting for Danny Kaye
to catch his breath. And when he pulls off that feat, you relax
and explode in both laughter and respect. On several occasions,
I heard Max Schactman perform a similar feat in the course
of making the point that Stalin had literally wiped out almost
every Communist leader and general who had played a role in
the Russian Revolution. It was a long, long list that Schactman

delivered in a Danny Kaye style that made you want to laugh and weep at the same time. While he was delivering the names, laughter welled up within you, it got expressed, but when he was through, the enormity of Stalin's pathology overwhelmed you. When I read Schactman's brief obituary in the *New York Times* a few years ago, it was with sadness, because it said nothing about his sterling personal qualities, so unusual among leaders in radical movements. Although it would be very wrong to say that I knew him, he nevertheless was someone the memory of whose style has always remained with me, especially when I became engrossed in the nature of leadership in new settings.

A third benefit that I derived from my days in radical politics—a reinforcement of what I had vaguely known—became a dominant theme in my thinking as a psychologist. It was what I later called the psychological sense of community, the sense that you are part of a dependable network of relationships that dilutes feelings of loneliness. I was part of such a network during college. Indeed, there was almost a complete overlap between my party and college networks. We were a group and tended to move as a group. I have already described my unease at seeing how party politics sundered friendships and put party "purity" at the pinnacle of personal values and actions. The obligations of purity produced the problem that there were a couple of students who were members of the Communist Party, and many more who were fellow travelers, whom I liked a good deal, and who liked me, but from whom I kept a social distance even though I wanted to know them better and to be with them. I felt that I was robbing myself of relationships that I needed and wanted. The obligations of political purity directed social purity, mightily restricting my community of friends. I was learning that I was the kind of person who wanted (needed) to be with people I liked, however different from me they might be. Differences of opinion, almost regardless of substance, should not prevent seeking a basis for friendship. What was percolating very inchoately in my mind was something I could articulate only in midlife: the larger the network of satisfying reciprocal friendships, the better your chances that you will be able to tolerate a world seemingly calculated to make you feel lonely, that is, to be able to dilute the insidious consequences of being locked up in an inevitably private world. At the same time that my party affiliations helped me cope with that problem via three marvelous friends, it prevented me more than I wished from enlarging my circle of relationships.

By the time I was a senior, in the fall of 1938, I knew that I wanted to be a psychologist, and that meant going to graduate school. I also knew that unless I received a fellowship, I would be walking the streets looking for work. With Dr. Gaudet's encouragement, I applied to at least fifteen graduate schools. Applying to graduate schools was for me the equivalent of buying a lottery ticket. Maybe lady luck would get me in somewhere. I applied to Yale, the Harvard Graduate School of Education (where Dr. Gaudet knew Walter Dearborn), Columbia, Wisconsin, Clark, and other reputable places. The letters of rejection were monotonously similar except for those from Harvard and Clark. Harvard admitted me "on probation," but I would have to pay my own way, and if I did well I might later get some financial support. Clark admitted me with a tuition scholarship ($200) and a room in a graduate student house. If I could forgo eating, I had it made! What I did not count on was that I would be a beneficiary of lady luck, the Great Depression, and the gods of war. My sister had dropped out of high school to get some low-paying job to help out our family, and my father was called back to work as a consequence of the eruption of war in Europe and the stimulus to our economy by the enlarging and rearming of our military. How the family managed it I truly do not know, but I went off to Clark University with a trunk of clothes, a bus ticket to Worcester, Massachusetts, a paper bag of sandwiches, and fifteen dollars, which would (in those days) allow me to eat for a month without putting on weight. In some abstract, nonaffective way, I knew that my leaving was an emotional calamity for my family. How much of a calamity it was I did not fully comprehend until decades later, when my wife and I deposited our daughter to start college at Clark. Fifteen minutes after we began the return trip to New Haven, we both started to cry.

6

Clark University
and Becoming a Psychologist

I did not know it then, but taking off in 1939 for graduate school at Clark University in Worcester, Massachusetts, was the beginning of my interest in anthropology and commmunity psychology, if not my discovery of American cultural diversity. When my "I" of today looks at the film of the bus trip to Worcester and the early weeks there, I see myself as a kind of Tevye from *Fiddler on the Roof,* leaving home for a new, strange world. I was not fleeing persecution, although I knew I was starting a liberation process. Having read all of Thomas Wolfe's novels, I intuitively knew that you can't go home again. I was leaving New York and Jewish ambience for a gentile city housing the College of the Holy Cross (which then had football teams as intimidating to opponents as the Catholic Church was to Tevye, like me). I had a New Yorker's conception of the rest of the world, so artfully conveyed in Steinberg's hilarious *New Yorker* cartoon. To me the word *travel* meant going from Newark to New York. Going to Worcester required the outlook of a Tevye and Columbus. When I meet incoming graduate students today, I can validly assume that they have been around the country and that most of them have crossed several oceans. I can also assume that they have little or no appreciation of what it means—to blacks and other minorities—to be plunged into a strange culture for which your background has ill prepared you.

Starting graduate school, like starting college, is the beginning of a socialization process intended to change you. You are supposed to become something you were not before. It is not only that something will be "added" to what you are and were, but that something will be subtracted, and you are far more aware of the former than of the latter. And by *subtraction*, I refer to the sense of origin and predictability, the sense that you are in a familiar world that will remain familiar, the sense that your future will not require you to be other than what you are or wish to become. The beginning graduate student willingly and enthusiastically seizes the future—he or she wants to feel growth by addition—unaware that one may be giving up something, or that one is highly likely to have a future in which the sense of embeddedness will encounter one disruption after another, one move after another—a series of adaptations that engender nostalgia for the good old days (which may not have been all that good, except for the fact of dependability). America, we are used to hearing, is a highly mobile society, perhaps the most mobile the world has known. And that is usually said with amusement and pride. But you pay a price, small for some but large for others, and the price is that we are always losing or forgetting or rejecting a part of us. The phrase "going to graduate school" refers to a geographical and psychological disruption not captured by the concept of transition. What the beginning graduate student is usually unaware of is that the disruption is one of a series that he or she will likely encounter in the course of a professional career in mobile America. It is in the cards of an American game, a kind of floating crap game in which one cannot count on site and composition of the group.

I am one of those rare academics who have taught at only one university. That is not happenstance, nor is it a fact about which I have no regrets. But it is a fact reflective of a deep reluctance to sever ties with site (New York–Brooklyn–Newark) and family. It was a reluctance compounded with fear about straying far from one's origins. Going to Clark was in contemporary jargon a "growth experience," but it also was in part an alienation from a past from which I both did and did not want to depart.

Worcester, in central Massachusetts, is an old mill-factory city, composed largely of two- or three-story wooden houses, each level having open porches. And it seemed to possess more churches than there were people on the streets. It had a genteel quality of working-class "oldness." Old, quiet, and lonely— those are the adjectives that the thought of Worcester still conjures up in me. Those adjectives refer to appearance, because Worcester became for me a "warm" city once I understood and became related to its ethnic groups: Swedes, Finns, Irish, "old" Americans, and Jews. I had never known Swedes or Finns as individuals or as bearers of a cultural tradition, but through two fellow graduate students (Carl Frost and Jorma Iltanen Niven) who became lifelong friends, I soon became exposed to a culture still resistant to American cultural homogenization. Jorma was a Finn and a Worcester boy, proud of both, and he became my "informant" about Worcester history and culture. Carl was Swedish and religious, and through him and his wife, Evelyn, I came to see and vicariously experience the socially centripetal force of culture and religion. What I learned about myself was that I was (and am) most at home with people who are self-consciously ethnic. Perhaps it would be more correct to say that it takes me a longer time to feel interpersonally secure with people who by name, behavior, or site of origin are not obviously ethnic. This reminds me that when I spoke of my Dana College years, I spoke only of a group of friends who were Jewish and socialist. I did not mention an exception: Patrick San Giacomo was as Italian as I was Jewish. I could not feel more at home and secure than when I was with Pat and his family. Our friendship did not extend beyond college, because I never really returned to the Newark area where he lived. I was told that he changed his name to Patrick St. James, which, although a correct Anglicization of his name, speaks volumes about the pressures that many children of immigrant parents experienced in America. To explain America, then or now, to explain an American without mentioning his or her cultural and religious origins is, I would maintain, as egregiously incomplete (to characterize it dispassionately) as to ignore sex or race or age. American psychology has managed to be egregiously incomplete and, therefore, misleading.

In light of the above, I must mention two other fellow graduate students: Harry Older and Ivan Birrer. They were very different from each other, but they had two things in common: they were both from Kansas, and they had both graduated from Fort Hays State College, where they had been students of George Kelly (who after World War II went to Ohio State, where he became an influential figure in American psychology). I had, *of course,* never known anyone from Kansas, and I had never heard of Fort Hays. To me, they were Americans, which meant that they were devoid of any manifestation of ethnicity. Their speech, what they talked about, and their outlook were strange and unfamiliar to New Yorker me. It took a while for me to feel at home with them, but I always knew that our relationships lacked the element of similarity, based on a shared feeling of cultural marginality. I can best put it in this way: Jewish me had little or no worry about how Swedish Carl, Finnish Jorma, or Greek Bill Betinis would look on my Jewishness. I did worry about how two Kansans would look at a New York Jew. Ivan was a reserved Kansan and more intimidating than Harry, who was as open and socially smooth a person as I have ever met. What made for some initial suspiciousness about Harry was that he was a golf enthusiast, which to me was proof positive that we came from and lived in two wildly different worlds. But he was also a New York Yankees fan, which suggested to me that he could not be all bad.

We were an ecumenical collection of culturally diverse graduate students. As I look back over four decades of cohorts of Yale graduate students, that degree of diversity stands out today. Indeed, the diversity seems to have increased with the years. What is noteworthy (on reflection) is that never during my days and years at Yale was this diversity ever made relevant to graduate education in psychology. Whatever was learned and discussed in seminars, whatever was presented to us, would not have changed even if we were Martians and not a diverse group of Americans. I could understand this if the subject matter had been chemistry, physiology, or neuroanatomy. But when the subject matter is human behavior in any of its major aspects, and a goal is the honing of observational and/or helping skills, should one studiously and completely ignore the experience of students in the academic equivalent of Ellis Island? Is that experience devoid of relevance to the substance of what we teach?

In graduate school I learned far more about America from out-of-class living than from all the seminars I took. And in that living I include my expanding experience in, and knowledge of, Worcester. Those seminars would have been taught in the same way with the same substance if the instructors had been teaching them in Seattle or New Orleans. I did learn in these seminars concepts and information that I could use to explain me to myself, but only a part of me, that part that had to do with what I call the narrowly internal, "psychological" me. That part of me for which one has to resort to such terms as religion, social class, cultural contexts, ideology, zeitgeist, and the American experience—that part of me was barely illuminated, if at all, in graduate school. Of one thing I am certain: why psychology "grew up" the way it did in America was a question I was never asked to think about. It was as if the question had such a self-evident answer that it required neither asking nor answering. We were, of course, made aware that American psychology in general differed from German, French, British, or Soviet psychology. It is only somewhat unfair to say that the differences were explained as being either because "we" were right and "they" were wrong, or because we simply had a grasp of more of the truth than they did. Yes, we were told (or we read) that Freud's psychology bore the stamp of Viennese society, but what that meant remained a mystery. And we were told that Gestalt psychology was typically German-European, but here too it was never made clear why that was so. The fact is that the instructors were not discriminating against foreign psychologists. It is my impression that they said even less about American psychology in relation to America.

I had a lot of spare time in graduate school, and being a reader, I read a lot about psychology and America, no doubt spurred and shaped by the Marxian notion that who you are,

what you work at, and what you can become aware of are not
independent of how the society in which you are formed is organized. So, for example, I never had to put into words that
American psychology was developed and dominated by male
Protestants (a Catholic or a Jew here, a woman there) who were
as American as my Kansas colleagues. Nor did I put into words
the inchoate feeling that American psychology (William James
excepted) was arid and not to my taste. Why was I so attracted
to Freud and the Gestaltists? Was it in part because most of
them were Jews? That Freud seemed to be talking about me?
That the Gestaltists were trying to go from the whole to its parts,
to distinguish between appearance and reality, and to demonstrate the superiority of a Galilean mode of thinking over the
Aristotelian mode in which the properties of something were
inherent in it by nature and captured by its membership in a
category or class? Was I drawn to these approaches because they,
in America, were antiestablishment?

Writing an autobiography is an exercise in self-exploration, to belabor the obvious. But can you become a psychologist
without exploring your past by the criteria John Dollard described
so well? When I say exploring, I in no way mean a course of
psychotherapy or a traditional psychoanalysis. Neither in theory
nor in practice (again, as Dollard showed) does therapy meet—
indeed, it is not intended to meet—Dollard's *Criteria for the Life
History*. How and in what context such self-explanation should
take place I cannot say. I am tempted to say that no less important than doing a dissertation for the doctorate would be to require students to write their autobiographies, with special emphasis on how they became (or are) Americans interested in this
or that problem in American psychology. The autobiography
would have three focuses: historical and cultural America, an
American graduate student, and American psychology. Parochialism is not without its virtues, but only when it is a consciously
deliberate stance for a specific, time-limited purpose. I am reminded here of a study by a student in architecture. He made
a map of the Yale Campus (which is in the Broadway and Forty-
second Street area of New Haven), which he gave to scads of
Yale students with the instruction that they draw lines showing

where on the campus they had been on the previous day and indicate off-campus sites where necessary. With very few exceptions, none of the students left the campus. And what about one of my undergraduate advisees who was a biology major, anxiously complaining to me that the Yale library did not have a book he needed for a term report? I suggested to him that he try the New Haven Public Library, to which he replied with the question, where is that library? I was flabbergasted, because he lived in Berkeley College, which is two blocks from that library!

My comments are not for the purpose of introducing into undergraduate and graduate education a major on cultural America and its communities. They are intended to suggest that anyone interested in the social science aspects of psychology has to be encouraged and helped to overcome parochialism. If at Clark and at Dana my parochialism was less than most students', it was because of my political interests and the kinds of friendships I developed, not because of the substance of psychology to which I was exposed. The situation is not different today. Several years ago, the mass media gave a lot of play to a report that listed the states according to per capita income and also listed the cities having the highest percentage of their population at or below the poverty line. Connecticut was either first or second in terms of per capita income. New Haven, a small city, was seventh on the poverty list (Hartford and Bridgeport were also in the top fifteen). Each year since those findings were made public, I have asked students in my seminar to say what they knew about the economic status of Connecticut and New Haven. At best, they could say that the state was affluent. Without exception, they would register shock when I gave them the New Haven findings. Their knowledge of New Haven was miniscule, and most of it was either erroneous or distorted. What bothers me is not their ignorance but their lack of curiosity about their community surround. If they were chemists or mathematicians, it would be somewhat more understandable and tolerable from an educational standpoint. But to be a psychologist interested in human behavior in contemporary living is a very different cup of tea.

Why did Clark accept me as a graduate student? (Why did they take two students from what Harry Older called "Fart Hays" State College?) In my relief at being accepted in a department that had played a crucial role in American psychology—you cannot write a history of American psychology without devoting many pages to Clark—I never asked why they took me, and no one else did. In those days, there was no Graduate Record Examination or Miller's Analogies Test that you took to establish that you stood out from the pack. If there had been, I would not have been accepted, because I never did well on those kinds of tests. In one of my undergraduate courses, Dr. Gaudet had us take the Henmon-Nelson group test of intelligence, on which my score put me in the eightieth percentile—a score that put me in, not apart from, the pack. That score, plus others I will discuss in a later chapter, were the basis for my early-on personal conclusion that intelligence tests should not be taken seriously and that they stood in relation to overall potential the way in which restaurant menus stand in relation to the quality of food served. There is a relationship, but it is not high. If Clark accepted me, it was less because of a cum laude record from an unknown college and more because of the letters of recommendation.

During my first two decades at Yale, I served on the department's graduate admissions committee. During each of those years, there were one or two applicants who I felt strongly should be admitted but who were not because their scores on the Graduate Record Examination hovered around a cutoff point, and/or they came from colleges with which we were unfamiliar. I kept a list of those rejectees. I am sorry that I no longer have the list, but my memory tells me that at least half of them became eminent people in the field. I am reminded here of one of our students who came perilously close to being terminated after two years because he did not meet a grade of honors in two courses. Just before the meeting that would determine his fate, I had read his final exam in my course and had given him a grade of high pass. When the discussion began and I realized that he would be terminated because he lacked a second course with honors, I reported that I had just read his final exam and that I gave him honors. He is a very eminent person in his area of specialization. I would not have predicted his accomplishments, but I had no doubt whatever that he had the intellectual-conceptual marbles, plus the industry, to be a competent and respectable psychologist.

I do not relate these anecdotes to parade my superior judgment. I have met my quota of errors, some of which derive from my being unduly impressed with scores on the highest end of the continuum. I have related these anecdotes to make the point that, my test scores to the contrary, I never doubted my own ability to make a contribution, the kind of bedrock attitude that tests do not tap. It is as if I was going on the basis of "judge me (as I judge myself) by what I do and can learn to do, not by my test scores. Give me the opportunity, and I will make the most of it." Call it self-confidence or arrogance, or both, I had it in spades (side by side with several areas of functioning in which I felt inadequate). What I have related here directly influenced what I did in the field of mental retardation, and in the most personal way shaped more than a decade of my research in test anxiety. My "I" has always been center stage in all that I have done. I like to call it self-exploration. Others may view it as a euphemism for self-indulgence.

I did not learn the major reason Clark accepted me until a few weeks after I got there. Three years before, the most distinguished members of the psychology department left Clark to go to Brown, Columbia, and Rochester. This came about because of a long series of disagreements between the department and the president of the university (who was a geographer). He had made Clark a world-renowned place in geography, but he had done that at the expense of other departments. He was also a narrow-minded fool whom, by the time I left Clark, I had characterized as the only person I knew who had become senile at the age of two. In one of his early books, Upton Sinclair described Clark as the Academic Tragedy of America, thanks to Wallace Atwood. Although I never checked it out, when I got to Clark I was told that Thorsten Veblen was Atwood's brother-in-law, a contrast between two people that I still find hard to contemplate. In any event, when I got there, the department of psychology was small and undistinguished and had trouble attracting graduate students. There were four full-time faculty, of whom two later became well known: Raymond B. Cattell and Donald Super. Saul Rosenzweig was an adjunct whose full-time position was at Worcester State Hospital. He taught the graduate course in abnormal psychology.

By today's standards, it was a small department, but in those days psychology was a relatively small and narrow field that prepared people primarily for a career in teaching and research. Psychology, with a few notable exceptions, viewed itself as a scientific discipline intent on establishing basic laws of human behavior, and that meant theory building, experimentation, and rigorous methodology. The applications would follow the demonstration of valid laws. You did not go to graduate school to become a clinical, industrial, or educational psychologist. For example, clinical psychology did not exist as a graduate field. You entered graduate school to learn psychology, most if not all of it. Physiological, social, abnormal, personality, and child psychology made up the core curriculum, together with experimental psychology, which was a kind of umbrella under which came animal learning and perception (the eye and the ear). And, of course, there was statistics. Students were left in no doubt that without a thorough grounding in statistics, you could not be a respectable psychologist. If you could not think statistically, you were of inferior quality. And it was hard to avoid the impression that an overarching goal of psychology was to establish the biological basis of human behavior. It was reductionism with a vengeance.

There has always been a tension in psychology in regard to whether it was a social or biological science, and that tension got manifested in different ways and degrees in different departments. If anything was and is characteristic of American psychology, it is that graduate departments differ significantly in what they regard as the core of the field. We are familiar with the fact that in America, unlike most foreign countries, each community determines (within wide limits set by the state department of education) the curriculum for its schools, including the textbooks to be used. The same situation obtains in higher education, where each college and university, and each department in them, decides what will be taught. That independence of choice does not make for dramatic diversity in the teaching and textbooks in biology, comparative anatomy, chemistry, and the like. But it does in psychology. So I quickly learned in my first weeks at Clark that the psychology I learned at Dana College was obviously different from what Harry Older and Ivan Birrer got at Fort Hays, what Helen Feldman got at Connecticut College, and what Jack Bernard got at New York University. But it made little or no difference, because what we got at Clark was substance, orientation, and values new to all of us. Graduate school did not build on what we knew, it welcomed us to a new building—which was different from that at Harvard, which in turn was different from that at Yale, which was different from that at Columbia, or Duke, or Cornell, or Berkeley. Of course, there was (and is) overlapping among graduate programs, but the similarities were less than the differences, and each program took pride in the differences.

The one characteristic the different departments had in common was training in research: theoretically oriented, hypothesis testing, statistically sophisticated, and preferably experimental in design. This emphasis in part explains why animal learning was such an important area in psychology, that is, you could control variables to a degree almost impossible with humans. It may well have been the case that the Norway rat was more frequently used as "subject" in doctoral dissertations than the college sophomore. I doubt that any academic psychologist would have denied that there was a variety of ways of studying a problem and contributing to its understanding. But in graduate education, it was clearly communicated to the student that he or she (very few "shes") would be exercising good judgment if the problem he or she chose would be studied in an experimental design for which appropriate statistical techniques were available. It would be unfair to say that elegance of design and method was considered more important than the chosen problem itself, on the level of rhetoric at least. But in practice it worked out that way. Someone once caricatured the graduate student by saying that he or she was a person who in statistics had learned the Latin square design and was now looking for a problem to adapt to that design. Like all good caricature, it reflected reality.

How was I shaped by my graduate education? I use the word *shaped* advisedly, because I did not come to Clark with formed, specific interests I wanted to pursue. I came with the same stance with which I approached college: I wanted to learn *everything*. Given the size of the Clark faculty, it was possible to take every seminar offered, and most of them were required. And if they were not required, you took them anyway, because in order to be admitted for candidacy for the doctorate, you had to pass "prelims," three-hour essay exams on five consecutive days. From your first day at Clark, you heard about prelims, a rite of passage that grew increasingly formidable as that week approached. If I wanted to learn everything, the department played into my naive grandiosity.

It is, I think, fair to say that in those days graduate schools turned out psychologists who were educated in psychology. Of course, you developed an area of specialization, but that was in a context of a general education. That is infrequently the case today, and for three reasons. The first is that students today come to graduate school with a declared major area of interest, such as clinical psychology, cognitive psychology, social psychology, psychobiology, child development, or community psychology. Indeed, their application for admission requires that they declare their major area of concentration. So if you ask a student why he or she is in graduate school in psychology, the answer will be in terms of a specialty. The second reason is that each specialty encompasses a very wide area of theory, research, and practice, which, if it is to be comprehended, leaves little time for exploration outside that specialty. Generally speaking, the faculty in each specialty take a possessive-protective attitude toward their students and seek to ensure that they are well educated within that specialty. And when that attitude interacts with the declared interests of the student, the rest of psychology takes on the features of foreign territory. The third reason is that all students are required to take time-demanding courses in statistics, which, although intrinsically nonpsychological in substance, are regarded as essential tools for doing research and comprehending the research literature. As a result, we are producing not psychologists but narrow specialists.

What I find most troublesome about this state of affairs is the restricted intellectual curiosity of incoming students. That judgment may sound like a complaint from a senior citizen, nostalgic for the good old days. It could be—and is—argued that the kind of student I prize was always in short supply, the percentage of them today and in the good old days being the same. Although there is no evidence by which the issue can be decided, the "no change" argument requires that one assumes that the dramatic increase in specialties on the undergraduate and graduate levels has had no consequence for those factors determining who chooses to go into psychology. We are used to hearing that we are well into an era of narrow specialization in all fields of science and professional practice. Who has not heard him- or herself saying that we are required to know more and more about less and less? That message is clearly conveyed to undergraduates and is equally clearly reflected in what they say in their applications to graduate school. And what they say is what they know (or have been advised) that a department wants to hear. I can say from years of experience on admission committees that the student who says that he or she has no area of specialization but hopes to develop one in the course of graduate education will not receive a high rating from a committee composed of specialists, all of whom are intent on getting their quota of students for their area.

The character of a field is determined by, among other things, factors of cohort selection and self-selection. To argue that these factors are the same today as they were before World War II is patent nonsense. And to argue that these changes are all for the good is to entitle one to the Dr. Pangloss Chair of Psychology. The Panglossian outlook that every day in every way we and our world are getting better and better implicitly suggests that what "was" is not only inferior but is not worth knowing. It is not only that history is "bunk," as Henry Ford, Sr., put it, but that it is no guide for the present and future. And if anything characterizes psychologists in training today, it is either ignorance of the history of the field or explicit lack of interest in that history, or both. But why blame the victim? I am far from alone in the opinion that in contrast to many foreign countries, American culture tends to produce in its citizens an ahistorical stance, one in which visions of the future render interest in the past an irrelevance. Relatively speaking, America is a new society. It was born, so to speak, as a departure from the past and as an opportunity to create a new future. The "new" world was to be different from the "old" one.

In its beginnings as an academic discipline, the founders of American psychology were far less ahistorical than is the case today, if only because so many of them were quite conscious of the European (largely German) centers in which they had studied. And they were also aware that as Americans they had a distinctive world view that would put a distinctive cast on the development of psychology in this country. As the decades went on, this sense of history got weaker and weaker in two respects: in regard to the history of psychology in general and American psychology in particular, and in regard to the relationships between psychology and American culture.

Autobiography is a form of indulgence that sets (or should set) limits on the degree to which you elaborate on certain themes of conceptual importance to you. The ahistorical-asocial stance of contemporary American psychology is one of those themes that I find I must struggle to contain within acceptable limits. That struggle lessened because in the course of writing this chapter there appeared in the November 1986 issue of the *American Psychologist* an article "Toward a Critical Social History of Developmental Psychology" by four senior people: Urie Bronfenbrenner, Frank Kessel, William Kessen, and Sheldon White. Among its major points are the adverse significance of increased fractionation-specialization in the field and of the ahistorical-asocial stance. They also note that what is true in developmental psychology is no less true in other parts of psychology.

What I found most interesting in that article is the recognition accorded to John Dewey, who, more than any other psychologist, was sensitive to the fact that, as a field, psychology was not comprehensible apart from its emergence from and embeddedness in American society. (One of my recent books, *Psychology Misdirected* (New York: Free Press, 1981), was dedicated to John Dewey.) Psychology has never known how to deal with John Dewey except by dismissing him as a philosopher or educator; that is, he "once" was a psychologist who "became" an educator and philosopher—a use of labels that is the hallmark of the mentality of specialists who gain security by erecting and fortifying boundaries that identify insiders and outsiders, strangers and friends. I consider it the Great Wall feature of American psychology.

Neither in college nor in graduate school was I required to read anything by John Dewey. But I knew about John Dewey (he became one of my heroes) in my college years because he was a member of a commission to investigate Stalin's charges that Trotsky was a traitor, a plotter of the overthrow of the Russian regime. Those were the years when it seemed that every well-known participant in the Bolshevik revolution was put on trial, said their mea culpas, and thanked Stalin in advance for their inevitable execution. To a Trotskyite like me, those trials were neither charade nor farce. They were undiluted tragedy, cruelty, and disaster. Anyone who wants to get a feel for the dimensions of Stalin's crimes should read *The Great Terror* by the historian Robert Conquest (New York: Macmillan, 1968). The fact is that Stalin's charges were generally accepted as true by the general public and the intellectual community. It took several decades before it became crystal clear that the charges belonged in the genre of political and malevolent fiction. So, when I learned about Dewey's participation in a commission to investigate the charges, I got interested in Dewey.

Kessen is absolutely correct in saying that Dewey believed that "only with science as a way of knowing and democracy as a way of life can one really hope to achieve an understanding of the way children learn and grow." And for Dewey, democracy largely meant American democracy, its history, promises, and obligations. It was second nature to Dewey, who never lost his rootedness in his Vermont origins, to develop a psychology consistent with the spirit and letter of the American democratic ethos. And that is why, when he looked at the American classroom and school, he was aghast at how it reflected a psychology more consistent with a totalitarian than with a democratic view of human potentialities. That he became a defender of someone such as Trotsky requires no deep interpretation. Dewey knew well that the substance of a psychology was not independent of the society from which it emerged. In the next chapter, I shall describe how Dewey, thanks to Hitler, came to be a decisive *intellectual* influence in my life, and in a way far more direct than I ever could have imagined.

Inevitably, you are influenced by your teachers, although not always in ways they intended. Through Raymond Cattell, a British psychologist, I was exposed to a non-American psychology, distinctive in two respects: an emphasis on factor analysis as a method for describing and "measuring" personality and an emphasis on instinct and genetics as explanatory concepts of human behavior. Neither emphasis made much sense to me. I regarded factor analysis as the methodological tail wagging the substantive dog. My low opinion of factor analysis was undoubtedly colored by the fact that in those precomputer days, doing a factor analysis (of the tetrad difference variety) was an exercise in boredom. You multiplied, and you multiplied, and you multiplied, and you found yourself cursing those who in the dim recesses of history invented arithmetic. And when you were all through and had isolated general and specific factors, you gave reality to each factor by giving it a name, confusing the label with the "thing." I understood the rationale and goal of factor analysis, but I could not avoid concluding that it was being employed in a "garbage-in and garbage-out" way. You began with the elements of personality, you had at least one "objective" self-report measure of each, and you employed a methodology that stacked the cards in favor of finding the elements you initially assumed to exist. And if it did not come out the way you expected, you tended to blame inadequate measures and not the basic conception of personality dynamics and organization. Indeed, dynamics and organization—the glue and the substance—were simply not in the picture.

Neither then nor now do I consider myself a sophisticated critic of factor analysis as a method grounded in an integration of statistical-mathematical-geometric theory. But it is a method and theory inherently nonpsychological in nature. So when it is employed for the purpose of illuminating human behavior, the initial crucial question is the appropriateness of the method for your theory of human behavior. And Cattell had a theory of human personality tailor-made for that method. That was no ground for criticism. But what was ground for criticism was his view that a theory was invalid, or at least suspect, if it could not be tested by methods of factor analysis. Method was decisive; indeed, the basis for a world view. If Cattell was articulately critical of Freud's emphasis on psychoanalytical *method* as *the* way of comprehending the human personality, he seemed oblivious to his own vulnerability to the same kind of criticism. But I remain grateful to Cattell, because he served as an example of how commitment to a method can put blinders on you. That does not mean that I learned that lesson in a once-and-for-all way. No less than Professor Cattell, I was and probably remain quite capable of narrowness, powered by what I would like to believe is rational and objective thinking but that at its root is omnipresent passion, as I shall now demonstrate.

Where Cattell and brash I tangled was on the nature-nurture problem. It was self-evident to him, and discussed explicitly in his early books, that heredity explained much of human behavior. So in one of the seminars he took the position that salesmen are born, not made. To me that was sheer nonsense. Although I was no longer a Trotskyite, I was enough of a Marxist to regard hereditarian explanations as an unjustified defense of the status quo; that is, what is "natural" is the way things should be, the consequence of a Darwinian-Spencerian view of natural selection. We did not argue about the facts but about the "truth," and two people could not have more divergent conceptions of the truth. What neither of us could see or articulate was that each of us represented very different national outlooks. Cattell came from class-conscious England, still dominated by Galton's work and writings, and I was a product of an immigrant America where "all men are created equal." American culture and ideology have never been hospitable to hereditarian explanations of individual and group behavioral characteristics. It is true that *every* immigrant group that came to America was viewed by the white, Protestant establishment as cultural, intellectual inferiors who could negatively, even drastically, alter the social fabric. But at the same time, that view was countered, controlled, and mitigated by acceptance of a basic constitutional respect for the individual's right to seize opportunities for growth, to forge a new future. You can write the history of America as a catalogue of prejudice and injustice. You can also write it as a catalogue of events in the fight against prejudice and injustice.

No one has understood or described these contrasting histories better than de Tocqueville in his *Democracy in America* (written in the third decade of the nineteenth century). It is amazing and astounding how well he caught the complexity and distinctiveness of the American character. I did not know it in 1939, but his book explained more of my behavior in Professor Cattell's seminars than you could glean from studying me in any other way. I did not realize it then, but Marx's utopian vision of human potentialities bore remarkable similarities to the early view of America as a rediscovery of the Garden of Eden. In any event, I was no less extreme than Professor Cattell. It was probably the case that he was far more gracious toward and tolerant of me than I was toward him. He was a cultured, sophisticated, talented, and imaginative Britisher. I was a brash, loud, arrogant, Brooklyn–New York–Newark American Jew. We locked in a battle about psychology unaware that the larger war was cultural. It would be closer to the truth to say that he was probably far more aware of that larger stage than I was. After all, it would not have been easy for him if he had said what I think he knew and believed: American psychology was misdirected to the extent that it was distinctively American. Graduate students spend a lot of time talking about their instructors. We probably talked more about Raymond Cattell than about any other member of the faculty. We delighted in the fantasy that he and John B. Watson found themselves alone on a desert island. How soon would it be before they agreed not to talk with each other as a way of avoiding mutual destruction?

Each of the Clark faculty broadened my knowledge of psychology. From Robert Brown, I learned more than I wanted to know about vision and audition. What stood out in his seminar was the way he stimulated us to examine each theory in the light of the research literature, requiring us to pinpoint the issues or questions each theory left unresolved, and then to contrast the explanatory power of competing theories. It was in his seminar that I began to understand, albeit dimly, that theories were fictions productive of research intended to contribute to a new fiction that would stimulate further research and, in turn, new fictions. I was not interested in the eye and the ear. It was an area that seemed utterly unrelated to anything in which I was interested. Indeed, if I had not been required to take his seminar, I would not have. But if I had not taken that seminar, I would have robbed myself of a piece of wisdom to which psychologists of subsequent generations are increasingly insensitive. Despite the fact that I was uninterested in the substance of the seminar, it was self-evident to me that these were important problems to some psychologists and that I *respected* them for the seriousness and ingenuity with which they pursued what interested them.

I underline the word *respect* because too frequently today many graduate students study only what is of interest to them, which is bad enough, but also tend to derogate that which is foreign to their interests. *Derogate* may be too strong a term, but I use it as a kind of antonym to the connotations of the word *respect*. It is one thing to seek to become expert in a special field. It is quite another thing to so prize your field that you cannot understand how someone in another specialty can be as passionate about that subject matter as you are about yours. There are too many psychologists, faculty as well as students, who cannot accord respect to those in other parts of the discipline. They would resent being called prejudiced, but that is precisely what they are, and it is prejudice fed by ignorance. I can understand not respecting this or that colleague on personal, intellectual, or moral grounds. I have difficulty understanding not having respect for a field, especially when you are ignorant of the history, structure, and substance of that field. I am not, of course, advocating a live-and-let-live philosophy that rules out criticism, controversy, and out-in-the-open expression of opinion. To rule those out is to rule out the possibility that the ignorance that feeds prejudice will not be lessened. I have developed a short fuse in regard to students who proclaim their interests, take pride in their narrowness, and have no curiosity about the scope of their ignorance. Unfortunately, that basically anti-intellectual attitude gets reinforced, or minimally countered, in graduate education, although psychology is far from alone in this respect.

Through Donald Super I was exposed to what may be termed vocational psychology: career choice, career development, and job satisfaction. Indeed, his was the only course that was directly related to our "real world." It may well have been the case that a psychologist like Donald Super could not have been found in a recognized department of psychology. What he represented sounded much too applied and unrelated to the "basic" issues in psychology. But I knew then and in subsequent years that he was dealing with issues of substance and theory that were quite related to the nature of our society, especially how its changing economic features impinged on youth entering the work force. Decades later, when I got interested in the relationship between the experience of work and the sense of aging (the passage of time), it strengthened a sense of intellectual kinship I always felt with him. He went on to become a leading figure in his field, which today remains of peripheral interest to mainstream psychology. You do not receive recognition in psychology by identifying yourself with a field that has associated with it the adjective *vocational*. It sounds oh, so practical, applied, and narrow, even though the nature of our work so pervasively determines our sense of identity and our sense of the world.

It was through Saul Rosenzweig that I was exposed to the personalities and traditions of "Harvard Psychology," and that meant Gordon Allport and Henry Murray. Allport's book on personality enormously influenced me, primarily because it avoided a portrayal of the individual as a congeries of elements or parts having no integrative glue. That is putting it negatively. Allport was the first academic psychologist to take seriously and compellingly the problem of conceptualizing the uniqueness of the individual in ways that made for a general psychology that was viable and productive. His book and associated writings provided a conceptual foundation for most of the psychologists who after World War II played a role in establishing clinical psychology in graduate education.

Today, the word *holistic* is uttered as a badge of honor, a way of indicating that one is for virtue and against sin, a euphemism truly devoid of substance. I do not think that Allport ever used that term, but his book remains a splendid example of the obligations one has to assume when one uses the adjective *holistic*. Allport was one of the most cultured psychologists of his day, by which I mean that he had a firm knowledge and understanding of European psychology and philosophy (including Freud), which he sought to integrate with American psychology. The word *parochial* would never occur to anyone reading Allport. He was the first psychologist cogently to dispute the psychoanalytical view that adult personality was a direct derivative of the motivational struggles of early childhood, as if all that intervened was of secondary significance. His concept of the functional autonomy of motives stimulated much controversy and was prodromal of later changes in psychoanalytical theory. Was there another American psychologist of his day who was as familiar with European existentialism and phenomenology? I met Allport once through a meeting arranged by Dr. Rosenzweig. I found him somewhat aloof but gracious, very hardnosed, the opposite of mushy, and intimidatingly knowledgeable. I came away with the feeling that I should leave graduate school for a year (at least), get a good eye examination, and start reading. I had the distinct impression that he was an intellectually lonely person. He certainly was an example of what he wrote about: uniqueness.

One of my first publications after graduate school (written with Esther and based on an individual with whom she had worked) was accepted by Allport, who was then editor of the *Journal of Abnormal and Social Psychology*. We submitted it to him, less because we thought it should be published (a case study was not frequent in that journal) than because we knew he was sympathetic to the case study as a way of raising questions of more general import. In the past twenty years, I have not met a student, at Yale or elsewhere, who was familiar with Allport's writings. That is particularly scandalous in the case of clinical students, who are unaware that they are grappling with issues for which a reading of Allport would pay conceptual dividends. If you think of a field in the way Allport thought of the individual, you could say that his concept of the functional autonomy of motives explains a good deal of the unrelatedness of American psychology today to its earlier stages of development. If American psychology has for all practical purposes forgotten Allport, it is because his contribution got transformed by developments endogenous and exogenous to the field. Allport well understood that although the man contains the child, the child is not the father of the man. History is never discontinuous, although we like to believe that it is, and we tend to teach it (when we do) in psychology as if it were the case.

And then there was Henry Murray, with whom Dr. Rosenzweig had worked at Harvard Psychological Clinic. I cannot overestimate the impact on me of Murray's *Explorations in Personality* (New York: Oxford University Press, 1938). Here was a man, a psychiatrist and a psychologist, devoted to a multifaceted study of individuals, employing and inventing psychological tests and observational procedures with the ultimate goal of formulating a theory of personality that embedded psychoanalytical theory into a more general psychological theory. This was not theory building in a vacuum. To me it represented an intellectual wrestling match between thinking and action, between the fictions of theory and the concreteness of experience, between the human mind seeking order and a reality that seemed to keep that order secret. Murray was a man of action and thought. Like Allport, he *enjoyed* thinking. Unlike Allport, he needed to test his thinking in action. Both were interested in the lives of individuals in a way far more creative and clarifying than any other by an American psychologist (except one I shall mention in a later paragraph).* In so characterizing

*In his recent memoir, *Seeking the Shape of Personality*, Robert White briefly and beautifully conveys the intellectually heroic proportions of Henry Murray's leadership and accomplishments while he was head of the clinic.

Allport and Murray, I am conveying how I thought and fantasized about them in my graduate years. I never had reason to alter my judgments in subsequent years. In the case of Murray, it needs to be noted that he attracted around him at the clinic a group of individuals who, after World War II, were major influences in personality research, clinical psychology, and social psychology—a kind of *Who's Who* in American psychology.

Perhaps the greatest influence of the Clark psychology department on my development derived from the virtues of its defects. As I indicated earlier, I came to Clark shortly after its luminaries had left. It was understaffed and chaired by Vernon Jones, an educational psychologist who had written on character and citizenship in the public schools. When I received my acceptance from Clark, I went to the library to find if he had written a book. I read his book with dismay. It was a pedestrian book about which I jotted down several pages of critical notes, with the expectation that I would discuss them with him when I came to Worcester. When I met Dr. Jones, I knew immediately that I could have no intellectual discussions with him. Dr. Jones was a prissy, intellectually insecure individual who deserved to be chair the way I deserved to be chair of a department of astrophysics. That may be too harsh, but he did illustrate the degree to which the Clark department had fallen from its eminent heights. However, he was a gentleman, a characteristic I treasure far more today than I did in 1939. Today I realize the pressures he had to feel, sandwiched as he was between a department with a glorious past and a very problematic future.

I shall never forget the first day I walked into the department's seminar room: a large, tall, cavernous room on one wall of which were the pictures of everyone who had received a doctorate or had taught in the department. The wall contained a

I am of the opinion that Henry Murray (still alive at ninety-five) will turn out to be one of a handful of those whose work truly shaped twentieth-century American psychology. Professor White's memoir, printed in 1987, is privately circulated (Marlborough, N.H.: The Homestead Press, Route 101, 03455).

large fraction of the history of psychology in America. It was on that day, and every subsequent day, an intimidating wall: a reminder of your puniness and ignorance as well as a stimulus for fantasies of greatness (and I oscillated between those extremes). I have no doubt that Vernon Jones had similar Ping-Pong feelings.

The point of all this is that the program at Clark was not very demanding. I had time, and Clark had a marvelous psychology library. And I read—voluminously, with joy, and indiscriminately. For example, one of the pictures on the wall of the conference room was that of Howard Odum, who had received his degree at least two decades before I got there. Who was Howard Odum? So I went to the library and began to read what he had written, and I was amazed that he had "become" a sociologist at the University of North Carolina, and a rural sociologist at that! In fact, I had to conclude that what Odum wrote about said more about what I considered to be the real world than most of what I was exposed to in my graduate courses. Reading Odum stuck with me through the years, an example of someone who reached out beyond the borders of his formal training. What Odum wrote about seemed interesting *and* important, and that was more than I could say about much that I was asked to read in psychology. I need to reiterate that what I read in psychology I knew to be important, but I did not find much of it interesting, let alone engrossing.

I lived in two worlds: psychology at Clark and that other world "out there" in which (in 1939) the Second World War had begun, America was rearming, the Depression was thereby receding somewhat, and a national debate was started about what the stance of our country should be in regard to Hitler Germany, Fascist Italy, and Imperial Japan. It was the latter world that explains my reaction when I found J. F. Brown's 1935 book *Psychology and the Social Order* (New York: McGraw-Hill). Here was a psychologist, from Kansas no less, trying to bring together Marx, Freud, and Kurt Lewin. Its opening pages contain as incisive an indictment of American social psychology as has ever been written. That was heady stuff for me, but what made reading Brown so engrossing was his analysis of the nature of American capitalist society, describing it and its problems (for example, race, lynching, unemployment) in terms of Marx, Freud, and Lewin.

The book was a tour de force. It was not a polemic or a political tract, nor an uncritical acceptance of Marx, but a truly scholarly effort at integration of an individual psychology with a cultural-historical-political-economic conceptualization. Like no other book I read in graduate school, Brown's emphasized for me that I lived in two worlds: parochial psychology and the world of affairs, national and international. To understand the world of affairs, it was necessary to have *a* psychology that would help explain how and why people were both similar and different. If it was necessary, it was egregiously insufficient, and that was the central problem that occupied Brown. It was my problem then, and it remains my problem today. I was not and am not a J. F. Brown, but I have always believed that it will take heroic and creatively conceptual efforts like his to change our accustomed world view of human behavior. Such efforts require what C. Wright Mills called the "sociological imagination," a characteristic all too rare among social scientists. It has been virtually nonexistent in American psychology, which is why I have such unbounded respect for Dollard and J. F. Brown, and feel sadness and regret that what they stood for, what they tried to do, has gone unrecognized.

It is not happenstance that both men transcended the confines of psychology. They were truly social scientists. Neither then nor now does graduate education in psychology foster such transcendence. On the contrary, graduate education has become increasingly molecular in terms of overarching theory, research, and practice. In principle, I have no quarrel with the molecular orientation, and I certainly would not deny that in psychology it has clarified many aspects of human behavior. I am far from being a nihilist. But, as I came dimly to see at Clark, the human organism lives in and is a wondrous product of a society that has a distinctive history, culture, structure, and world view that are mammothly influential for the organism and yet cannot be conceptualized in psychological terms. But when they are conceptualized—when the dynamics of the larger picture are given us—

we quickly see how impoverished and distorted our psychology has been, the price one pays for adherence to a rampantly molecular orientation. Is this not the lesson we should be learning from the women's liberation movement? Or from the struggle for racial equality? Or from the Holocaust?

Can you write the history of American psychology without bringing up "the Jewish question"? Scores of American psychologists have done just that, another instance of a psychology divorced from the social realities. In my three years at Clark, I cannot recall a single instance where I felt discriminated against because I was Jewish. At the same time, I was aware of several things: there was not a recognizably Jewish name under any of the pictures on that seminar wall; there were very few Jewish names in departments of psychology anywhere in the country (except, of course, at the City College of New York, Brooklyn College, and Klineberg at Columbia). But there were a lot of Jews who were psychologists several miles away at the Worcester State Hospital: David Shakow and Saul Rosenzweig from Harvard and Eliot Rodnick from Yale were some who were there. And except for the course that Saul Rosenzweig taught, there was no relationship at all between the Clark psychology department and the state hospital.

It is fair to say that in those days American psychology was aclinical. It would be nearer the truth to say that it was anticlinical, that is, a field of problems and practice more art than science, more applied than basic, and, therefore, less worthy. No one ever said it to me, but from my earliest days at Clark I concluded that if you got your doctorate in psychology and you were Jewish, you became a clinical psychologist, which meant that you administered psychological tests. It was a conclusion based on very hard data! Years later, when I was at Yale and discussing my Clark days with Dr. Jacob Levine (chief psychologist at the Veterans Hospital), who went to Clark as an undergraduate and then to Harvard for his doctorate, he trotted out a letter from Professor Boring informing him that he was being accepted for graduate work. In that letter, Boring said that he felt obliged to tell Jack that he should not come to Harvard with the expectation that he would get a position in a university. Some of Harvard's best students (he mentioned Shakow and Rosenzweig) had been Jewish, Boring wrote, but the department simply had been unable to place them. Why come to Harvard, Boring asked? And the answer was: for intellectual excitement and education. This situation, of course, was not peculiar to psychology. One of my heroes has been Carl Becker, the historian who was at Cornell. About ten years ago, I came across a book containing a selection of his letters. A significant number of these letters were to former Jewish students who had become his friends and for whom he had been seeking university positions appropriate to their high abilities. It makes for sad reading.

Somewhere in the late 1970s, I participated in a symposium sponsored by the Division of the History of Psychology at the annual meeting of the American Psychological Association. I was there not because of credentials as a historian, which I do not possess, but because the president of the division—Dr. David Krantz—was a friend and he needed another participant. My comments were brief and centered around the fact that a history of American psychology that did not confront the role of religion and religious prejudice was at best incomplete and at worst a distortion. I could not escape the feeling that many in the audience felt uncomfortable with my remarks and would have preferred that I had not introduced a sour note into an otherwise informative and pleasant discussion. Throughout my adult years, I have known that religion—like it or not, practice it or not—is a crucial ingredient in American society and, therefore, in the psyche of all of us, albeit in different degrees and ways. It is no less an ingredient than science. Indeed, there are probably far more people for whom religion is more of a direct influence in their daily lives than there are people for whom science is a living factor in their daily lives.

In any event, I hold the opinion that the history of American psychology—as an individual and organized endeavor as well as in its substantive concerns—has very much been influenced, directly and indirectly, by changes in the religious origins of its members. And if you add racial, ethnic, and gender changes, the relationships between the molecular orientations become even more clear. To understand itself, psychology must go beyond its customary boundaries—and we are back to de Tocqueville, Dollard, and Brown.

At the end of my second year at Clark, I had to begin planning seriously what I would be doing when I left Clark a year later. I knew that I would apply for a position in a college or university, but I also knew that would end up as a fruitless endeavor. As a more practical step, and with the help and support of Saul Rosenzweig, I was accepted at Worcester State Hospital as an extern on a three-day-a-week basis. I was the first Clark student ever to have worked out such an arrangement. Worcester State Hospital was probably the best known and respected institution of its kind in the country. It had a large, active research program in the biology and endocrinology of schizophrenia, supported by various research foundations. Its clinical psychology unit was also regarded as the best of its kind in terms of both research and training. Any place that had David Shakow, Eliot Rodnick, and Saul Rosenzweig had to be in a class by itself. If you add to those names the people who interned there, it is a most impressive list of people who became leading figures in American psychology after World War II. And the same was true for its psychiatry and resident staff.

In those days, psychoanalysis as theory and practice got, relatively speaking, short shrift in graduate education. Of course, in seminars on personality theory and abnormal psychology, Freud was read and discussed, but in a very abstract, rote kind of way. Freud received respectful but not serious hearing, if only because he was being discussed by instructors or writers of textbooks who had no personal experience with analysis. That was not true at Clark, because Saul Rosenzweig had been or was being analyzed at the time. But that said more about Worcester State Hospital than it did about Clark, despite the fact that it was at Clark, in 1909, where Freud gave his introductory lectures on psychoanalysis. It seemed as if most of the psychology and psychiatry staff at the hospital were being analyzed by Geza Roheim, who would spend several days a week in Worcester analyzing staff members in a local hotel room. To be at the hospital meant that you would be exposed to psychoanalytical thought in a way and to a degree that you could not avoid, and far from being disposed to avoid it, I ate it up—all of it. I became a true believer, no less and a good deal more so than I had been of Marx, Lenin, and Trotsky. I now lived in three worlds: academic psychology, the world of affairs, and psychoanalysis. Like Caesar's Gaul, it was a tripartite division that was as fascinating as it was problematic, except that at that time I saw no problem at all, especially after having read J. F. Brown.

What I did not know at the time—what made it seem as if Worcester State Hospital was a unique setting in its interest in matters psychoanalytical—were two facts. The first was that some leading academic psychologists (for example, Boring and Landis) had gone into an analysis and were writing up their judgments of the experience for publication. The second fact, ultimately far more fateful for American psychology, concerned what was going on at Yale's department of psychology and Institute of Human Relations (about which much more in later chapters). And what was going on there was truly unique: a serious and systematic attempt to wed academic and psychoanalytical psychologies. It is unfortunate and scandalous that the history of Yale's Institute of Human Relations has never been written, because what was going on there, especially between 1935 and 1940, played a very significant role in American psychology after World War II. Indeed, its influence extended far beyond psychology into anthropology and sociology. And central to that endeavor was the integration of psychoanalytical and learning theory. John Dollard, Leonard Doob, Neal Miller, Robert Sears, and Hobart Mowrer were some of the members of the department engaged in the endeavor.

At that time, half or more of the department had been or were being analyzed, a fact that I still find amazing and that testifies to the intellectual beehive quality of the atmosphere there. On the surface and from a distance, Yale was seen as a place where learning theory was at the top of the agenda, dominated and directed by Clark Hull and his laboratory (containing scores of Norway rats spending most of their days running mazes to get pellets of food). For example, I wrote to Hull requesting a reprint of one of his studies. He not only sent me the reprint but put me on his mailing list, which meant that every two weeks or so I would get mimeographed reports of work and theorizing in progress, most of them having to do with Hull's developing mathematico-deductive theory of rote learning. That I comprehended nothing of what he was up to goes without saying. But what I did comprehend, mistakenly, was that psychology at Yale must be egregiously parochial and a dead end. I could not have been more wrong. The Harvard Psychological Clinic, Worcester State Hospital, and Yale's Institute of Human Relations—in each of these places in the thirties can be found, among other things, the beginning foundations for the emergence of what in the post–World War II era became clinical psychology. None of the people in these centers could foresee how in a few short years their pioneering work would alter and give direction to significant segments of American psychology. If anybody can be called the father of modern clinical psychology, it is David Shakow, but he never envisioned how his efforts and those of his colleagues (there were firm collegial relationships among the three centers) would alter the substance and shape of psychology as a result of the societal dynamics accelerated by our entry into the war. The fact is that Worcester State Hospital was an academic center outside of academia. Research was the major activity of the staff, and the diagnostic testing service was staffed by interns. No less than at the university, it was hard to avoid the impression that clinical work (which meant diagnostic testing) was less worthy than research. If the Jews could not be in the university, they could at least develop their own mini-academy, which David Shakow did.

It is no easy matter to say what one learns from whom during an internship. Initially, you are like a snowflake in a storm, responding to this or that gust of ideas, tasks, and responsibilities. You realistically feel ignorant and insecure, and you strive to appear otherwise. But by the middle of my year there, I had arrived at several firm conclusions: psychological testing was something of a bore; the test reports I wrote seemed to play no role at all in what happened to patients; psychologists were second-class citizens in a medical-psychiatric setting; psychiatric diagnoses, talmudically discussed and sometimes voted on, seemed unrelated to treatment (which then meant a course of electric or insulin or Metrazol shocks); and the food in the cafeteria in which the lowly interns ate was against, not for, life. Those were the negatives. The positives were exposure to a new literature; close contact with a variety of patients; and, toward the end of the year, an introduction to projective techniques for purposes of personality assessment. Psychotherapy, however defined, was off limits for psychologists, whose major tasks were testing and research. Practically speaking, the most significant positive was the credentials I obtained to seek a job in a hospital or clinic.

However inadequate, I must resort to words to convey my reactions to observing patients undergoing shock treatment. They were lined up, assembly-line fashion, and then one by one they would be placed on a bedlike structure and strapped down, the juice would be turned on, the convulsions would begin, they would lose consciousness, the juice would be stopped, and after a time they would be unstrapped and helped off the bed. It was hard for me to watch. I was of two minds. First, this was being done in the interests of patients by professionals who seemed to know what they were doing, and why. Who was I to say otherwise? Besides, fellow graduate students in physiology were doing the same thing to cats in the laboratory, and they assured me that it was the wave of the future. What I was observing at the hospital was not a wave but a tidal flood. My second reaction was encapsulated in that "still, small voice within" that said something was terribly wrong, morally and psychologically wrong.

By the end of the year, I came to a conclusion that got strengthened over the years: it is in the warp and woof of medical education and culture to resort to somatic, body-altering procedures when understanding and interpersonal treatment of psychological disorders are faulty, inadequate, or inefficient because of the numbers involved.* I shall have more to say about this in later chapters, but I need add here that in its long-standing

*My experience at Worcester State Hospital was one of the earliest sources of my most recent book, *Caring and Compassion in Clinical Practice* (San Francisco: Jossey-Bass, 1986).

effort to become a respectable part of the medical community, psychiatry has oscillated between biological reductionism and a pitifully inadequate, superficial attention to family and community factors. And that oscillation is not comprehensible apart from the history of medicine in American society. It would be incorrect to say that I learned this in my externship year. Here was American history and society, there was psychology, and over there was psychiatry—they were separate and distinct areas of interest and experience for me. But in that year of externship, despite my unawareness, the problem of interrelating them was germinating. And one of the fertilizers that nurtured that growth during my graduate days was Freud's book on lay analysis, a book in which Freud sought to explain why the medicalization of psychoanalysis (and he had America in mind) would be an intellectual disaster ("The Question of Lay Analysis." In J. Strachey (ed.), *The Complete Psychological Works of Sigmund Freud*. Vol. 20. London: Hogarth Press, 1959). Unfortunately, Freud was absolutely and prophetically correct.

In the middle of my last year at Clark, when it was apparent that I would receive my doctorate in June 1942, I began to take steps to get a job. Together with Harry Older and Jorma Niven, I prepared a list of colleges to which we would apply for a position, making sure that we would each apply to different places. Should I state in my vita that I was Jewish? The three of us discussed this at some length and decided that there was no point, morally or strategically, in avoiding the issue. The fact is that none of us expected to get responses because of what happened on December 7, 1941, when the Japanese bombed Pearl Harbor. The draft had started before that, but with our entry into the war, the pace of the draft accelerated, and it appeared that a sizable fraction of the college population would be leaving the college campus. As it turned out, predictably, I was the only one of the three to receive no responses whatever to my inquiries. It was neither surprising nor disappointing to me.

When the state of Connecticut announced a civil service examination for psychologists, I took the exam. The announcement had been posted on the bulletin board at the hospital, several of the interns said they were going to apply, and I thought I would take my chances along with them. If you passed the first part of the examination, consisting of three essay questions, you would then be asked to an oral examination. I passed the written part and appeared for the orals in the seminar room of Yale's department of psychology in the Institute of Human Relations (a room in which I later taught for many years!). It was an intimidating experience, for two reasons. For one thing, whenever I went home from Worcester, the Greyhound bus would take a route through New Haven that passed the institute, never failing to arouse in me feelings of awe, inadequacy, and even puniness. The name Yale conjured up images of greatness, aristocracy, and power, a kind of Shangri-la that the likes of me could see but would never be part of. It was a White House in the land of psychology. The second reason was that the examining committee consisted of Robert Sears and Donald Marquis from Yale and Richard Wendt from Wesleyan. To a graduate student, they were a triumvirate of luminaries before whom I quaked. It is understandable if I have no memory of what they asked me or how I responded. What I do remember is that Marquis was incisive, Wendt was confronting, and Sears was friendly and supportive. It may be the case that my memory reflects my relationships with each of them in later years.

To my complete amazement, I came out first on the examination, which meant that I had a choice of three positions: Norwich State Hospital, Mansfield State Training School, and the Southbury Training School. The starting salary was $2,280! Jorma Niven borrowed his father's car, and in one day he drove me to each institution for interviews. Conceivably, I could have got to Norwich by bus or train, but that would have taken an entire day. Mansfield and Southbury, however, were in the middle of rural nowhere, my first lesson in how American society geographically segregated handicapped individuals.

My first interview was at Norwich State Hospital, where Dr. Florian Heiser was developing a vigorous department of psychology, one of whose staff members, Julian Rotter, had been an intern at Worcester State Hospital. It was a pleasant, stimulating, and brief visit, though it did not assuage my doubts about working in a psychiatric setting where psychologists were second-class citizens who administered tests and did test-based research. But I left there relieved that I could do far worse than Norwich.

Then we drove to Mansfield for my interview with the superintendent, Dr. Neil Dayton. The first question he asked was, "What is the origin of your name?" I resisted replying with Harry Older's favorite response: "You can go piss up a rope." Dr. Dayton then went on to tell me that he knew there was a 1937 revision of the Stanford-Binet, but that he still preferred the 1917 version because it was the only one used at Mansfield and he wanted no discontinuities. I left his office feeling that if I had to starve, I would not take a position there. Thank God I could go to Norwich, whatever my doubts! Both Norwich and Mansfield were architectural monstrosities, but Mansfield's internal morality was more of a match for its external appearance.

And then we went to Southbury, a new institution that had opened its doors a few months before. The next chapter is devoted to my Southbury years. Suffice it to say here that when we first glimpsed Southbury, we thought we had taken the wrong road and had come upon a magnificent college campus. It was the most atypical state institution that had ever been built, in terms of both architecture and rationale. And the superintendent, it turned out, was Mister, not Doctor, Ernest Roselle. I never had reason to change my opinion after that interview that Mr. Roselle could sell the Brooklyn Bridge several times a day if he set his mind to it. But Mr. Roselle was as morally straight as they come, committed to making Southbury as humane a setting as possible. Decades earlier, he had received a master's degree in education from a teachers' college, but that did not deter him from pursuing his real interest: architecture. There were several departments at Southbury, of which one was the medical, headed by Dr. Herman Yannet, a research pediatrician from Yale. It was made clear to me by all that I would be head of an independent department, responsible directly to Mr. Roselle. The beauty of Southbury—its architecture, sleepy hollow, and bucolic surround—together with the autonomy I would have obviated any serious decision making. On the ride home, we did a lot of singing, both of us amused that Brooklyn–Newark–New York me was taking a job in the middle of beautiful nowhere. I had determined that four times a day the Flying Eagle Busline picked up passengers on its way to its final stop in the Dixie Hotel on Forty-second Street in Manhattan. I would not be stranded. I began work at Southbury on July 1, 1942.

I have never met anyone who felt secure going to a professional (for example, a physician or attorney) who has just finished formal training. You seek an experienced person, by which you mean someone who has *independently* confronted a variety of situations in the real world, who has learned the difference between what the textbooks say and what unique individuals require, who has learned from mistakes, and who looks and acts as if your situation is old hat. There is a lot of wisdom in looking at the new professional in that way. Up until the time you receive your professional union card, you have been in a protected environment where what you did and how you did it were not your responsibility alone. You have been a student accumulating knowledge, skills, and attitudes, modeling yourself (whether you liked it or not) on your teachers and supervisors, always wrestling with the discrepancy between your sense of inadequacy or incompetence or ignorance and the need to appear "professional" to both your clients and supervisors. And then you are on your own, and the wrestling match takes on more fateful dimensions.

I was hoist by my own petard. If I had taken a position at Norwich, I would have been one of several staff members responsible to a senior staff psychologist. My duties would have been largely predetermined by the structure and traditions of an existing unit. If I had gone to Mansfield, I would have been the office boy for Dr. Dayton. At Southbury, there was an untrained young woman who had been hired on an interim basis to give Stanford-Binets when the school opened its doors several months earlier. I was to come to develop a department of psychology in a new institution with no traditions, and with a superintendent who had no clear idea of what such a department should be, except that it should be "good" and help establish Southbury as a national showplace. Mr. Roselle was not modest in his ambitions for Southbury. He wanted research less because he understood the role of research and more because published research would bring attention to the institution. I was no less ambitious than Mr. Roselle. But I was infinitely more insecure and struggled mightily to hide it. Where and how would I start? *I* was responsible for the interim psychologist, *I* had to tell *her* what to do. And to make matters worse, I had a secretary! What do you do with a secretary? From the role of student—in elementary and high schools, college, and graduate schools—I was catapulted to the position of boss!

A story is apposite here. My parents could not afford to come to my graduation at Clark. When I came home, I showed them my diploma and hood. My maternal grandmother was living with us at the time. She was an orthodox old woman who could speak little English. My mother explained to her in Yiddish that I had just got my Ph.D., that is, I was a kind of doctor. My grandmother was obviously puzzled and asked numerous questions, the answers to which obviously mystified her. She became silent, wrapped in thought, and then in broken English said, "So maybe now he should become a dentist?" The fact is that up until I took the position at Southbury, I was, like her, puzzled by what you did with a Ph.D. And when I arrived at Southbury, the answer was by no means clear. I was less puzzled, but still puzzled. I was on my own to an extent for which the Ph.D. did not prepare me.

What did "on my own" mean? If forced to, I could have answered the question in a variety of ways. But the answers would have been in the nature of labels lacking threads of coherence. You could say that I was a cast of characters in search of an author, that is, a cohering force. But that would be like during World War II calling sauerkraut "liberty cabbage." I was not my own author. I was a brash, ambitious, insecure, wide-eyed Jew, ex-Trotskyite, wet-behind-the-ears psychologist, closet playwright, whose fantasies clearly established that I wanted to be no less than a polymath. And, I now know, I was an American in that I believed that I had a right to reach for the stars, that I had a right to have opportunities (with the obligation to work hard to exploit them), that I had a right to question and seek to change the status quo: you could alter yourself and your society. This may strike some as the pieties of a patriot ignorant of American history and society, or as the insensitive, retrospective musings of someone who has "made it."

The fact is that it was not until the early sixties, when we began to take trips to foreign countries and interacted with foreign students in their late teens and early twenties, that I was quite taken aback by how un-American they were in outlook: how little they expected from their adult years, how they sadly expressed their overeducation for the positions they likely would get, how they envied the ambitiousness and optimism of Americans. Indeed, I found myself trying to disabuse them of their unrealistic, too rosy picture of America. But the fact is that being born and reared in American society makes it extraordinarily likely that one will grow up *expecting* far more from life than is the case in most other countries. If my expectations were (perhaps) above the average, it was an average far above that in most other societies. When I left Clark, I had high expectations, but I would not have explained them as in any way due to the fact that I was American.

It has long been the case in America that education—the more the better—is seen as the major vehicle for secular salvation. And in the past half century, given the dynamics of specialization and our obsession with credentials, graduate education has dramatically increased in duration, as has postgraduate training. I got my doctorate at Clark in three years. Today the average time for getting a doctorate in psychology is five or more years. (Our department has a number of students emeriti.) What that has meant, then as now, is that individuals are spending a third or more of their lives in parochial settings. My dictionary gives "narrow, provincial" as synonyms for *parochial*.

However broadening school may be for intellectual growth, it is experientially narrow and provincial, if only because you experience schooling from the vantage point of the protected, supervised, instructed student. John Dewey said that school is not a preparation for life, it is life. But he said that in the context of vehemently criticizing the customary vast disjunction between life in and out of schools.* He was discussing public schools, but his criticisms are only somewhat less true for environments in higher education. In any event, by the time you finish professional education, you have been institutionalized— personally, socially, intellectually—to an extent that makes entry to the "outside" world a very upsetting experience for many people. Suddenly, and it is rather sudden, you are on your own in a new role in a new environment, not geared to meeting your accustomed needs for support, collegiality, and (frequently) stimulation. You are no longer a student to whom hands are extended to help you traverse a predetermined course of growth. You are no longer a student to whom the environment will bend, in part at least, in response to your special needs. You are, so to speak, no longer a taker but a giver to others. Many students long for the day when they will leave this protected (to some it is overprotected) world, eager to apply their talents in the other world needful of them. For an undetermined number, and I do not think it is small, some degree of disillusionment or disappointment dilutes that eagerness. But of one thing I am certain: most students leaving their educational home feel alone in their new position, poignantly aware that the sense of belonging to a group has disappeared. I am not aware that this type of transition has received the study it deserves, except in relation to schoolteachers, for many of whom the transition can take on the proportions of catastrophe, requiring some to begin to consider other lines of work.

On the editorial page of the *New York Times* of December 2, 1986, Mortimer Adler said the following:

---

*It was not until 1983 that this theme was elaborated and conceptualized by me in *Schooling in America: Scapegoat and Salvation* (New York: Free Press). In that book I critique the axiom that education should and best takes places in encapsulated classrooms in encapsulated schools.

For more than 40 years, a controlling insight in my educational philosophy has been the recognition that no one has ever been—no one can ever be—educated in school or college.

That would be the case if our schools and colleges were at their very best, which they certainly are not, and even if the students were among the best and the brightest as well as conscientious in the application of their powers.

The reason is simply that youth itself—immaturity—is an insuperable obstacle to becoming educated. Schooling is for the young. Education comes later, usually much later. The very best thing for our schools to do is to prepare the young for continued learning in later life by giving them the skills of learning and the love of it. Our schools and colleges are not doing that now, but that is what they should be doing.

To speak of an educated young person or of a wise young person, rich in the understanding of basic ideas and issues, is as much a contradiction in terms as to speak of a round square. The young can be prepared for education in the years to come, but only mature men and women can become educated, beginning the process in their 40's and 50's and reaching some modicum of genuine insight, sound judgment and practical wisdom after they have turned 60.

I have to say that the "me" that went to Southbury lacked whatever Adler means by wisdom. Adler closes his article with these words: "An educated person is one who through the travail of his own life, has assimilated the ideas that make him representative of his culture, that make him a bearer of its traditions and enable him to contribute to its improvement." To me the two key words are *assimilation* and *culture*. If by these words Adler refers to an increasing, conscious, probing sensitivity to how one became what one is in a distinctive culture (whose past is not discontinuous with the present), the substance of which percolates throughout one's psychological bloodstream, I quite agree both with what he says and with his indictment of higher education. Wisdom resides in being able to adapt to the knowledge that soon after you emerge from one fog of ignorance you will find yourself in another, an ability that makes you gun-shy of proclaiming truths at the same time that you pursue them. Adler uses the word *travail* advisedly.

I was twenty-three when I left Clark and went to South-bury. Today, people on average are twenty-eight years of age or older before they go out on their own. The increasing pro-longation of formal schooling and training makes not for the seeking of wisdom but for a kind of travail that puts status, finan-cial rewards, and the accoutrements of "success" at the top of the personal agenda. We do live in America.

7

Professional Development in the Middle of Nowhere: The Southbury Training School

I have never known a psychologist, or any other social scientist, who came to graduate school with the intention to forge a career in the field of mental retardation. Psychotherapists frequently say that no less important than what a client talks about is what he or she does not talk about. Analogously, it is significant that American psychology has never paid much attention, in research or practice, to the field of mental retardation. The explanation is far from clear. Certainly, this lack of interest is not attributable to numbers, because however you define mental retardation, you are referring to several million people. And it takes no great imagination to conclude that when one adds the families of these handicapped individuals, you are talking about a very large number of people coping with diverse, difficult, and frequently destructive problems in living. It is also the case that the economic costs to families and government are considerable—staggering would be a more appropriate term. The only times, in American society at least, when we have become aware of the societal dimensions of the problem are when we have entered a war and learned how many people are intellectually unfit for service in the armed forces, which is what happened in World Wars I and II. Before these wars, mental

141

retardation was associated in the public mind with immigrants, delinquency, prostitution, race, and family tragedy.

To most people, mental retardation means two kinds of people: those with strange-looking faces and bodies who are recognizably human but unattractive if not repelling, and those who are biologically intact, very recognizably human and social, but lacking the "intellectual marbles" without which a productive life is barely possible. The former are the unfortunates, the latter the deserving or undeserving poor, depending on your outlook. Up until 1970 or so, if you were an undergraduate major in psychology, the assigned textbook in abnormal psychology would have a few pages on mental retardation accompanied by a photograph or two of a strange-looking human being; for example, an individual with Down's syndrome or another condition that is visually arresting. Who would want to work with *those* kinds of people? And there was and is little or nothing in graduate school to encourage you to believe that mental retardation can be a challenging area of practice or research. It was and is an area that seems to lack the stimulating appeal of the neuroses or psychoses. When I told my friends that I had taken a position in an institution for the mentally retarded, they asked me a question that I came to expect from others in subsequent years: "Isn't it depressing to work with *those* kinds of cases?"

I came to Southbury willingly, eagerly, enthusiastically, and with an ideological agenda. For one thing, as I discussed in Chapter Five, I had a passionate interest in the nature-nurture issue, especially in regard to the Kallikak type of mental retardation. In those days, retardation was labeled as *subcultural,* meaning that those individuals were the offspring of intellectually inadequate parents whose social functioning and context were quite appropriate to a Tobacco Road existence: poor, dependent, unhygienic, unstimulating, morally inferior, neglectful, lazy, shiftless. The more technical diagnostic label was *mental deficiency, familial type.* Their handicap inhered in their inadequate genes. I believed none of this. On the contrary, I felt that if I had been born into and reared in that kind of subculture (the prefix *sub* was the giveaway to the omnipresent value judgment), there but for the grace of God go I! And I knew that at least one-third of the Southbury population was of the subcultural type. My goal was to demonstrate how mistaken that conception of etiology was. Immodest I was not.

Being Jewish predisposes you to side with the underdog. If you have Marxist leanings, you are not prone to regard genetic explanations of social and intellectual development as hitting the mark. And if you have fantasies of greatness, challenging and disproving conventional wisdom and practice is one way to receive the attention and status you desire. Since I was Jewish, sympathetic to Marx, and possessed of fantasies of greatness, Southbury represented to me a golden opportunity. And, I must emphasize, at Southbury I had no institutional tradition to buck, no superior to whom I was professionally responsible. Unless I did something egregiously stupid, Mr. Roselle would stay out of my way.

I know of no psychological theory that includes luck as a variable in shaping lives. By luck, I mean that unpredictable confluence of events that makes for an exquisite match at a crucial time between internal needs and an external context, between ability, attitude, and predisposition, on the one hand, and an external setting or individual, on the other hand. I consider going to Southbury a matter of luck in several ways. If Southbury had been built and opened its doors other than when I was in the job market, I would have ended up elsewhere. If Southbury had been headed, as was the custom, by a *Dr.* Roselle, who would have been a psychiatrist, I might not have taken the position, and if I had, I could not have done what I did at Southbury (for example, psychotherapy with retarded individuals). Southbury not only was unique in terms of architecture, educational rationale, and "lay" leadership, but it had an amazingly high-quality board of trustees appointed by and directly responsible to Governor Wilbur Cross, former dean of the Yale Graduate School. Two of its members were academics: Dr. Stanley Davies, a sociologist of national status with a deep interest in mental retardation, and Dr. Grover Powers, head of Yale's department of pediatrics, which was nationally preeminent at that time.

If Southbury had opened a year earlier or a year later, my life would have been different. That would not be the last time that the quirks of timing would work in my favor. As I shall discuss in Chapter Nine, my coming to Yale was no less chancy and fateful. After all, if you are walking down a New Haven street, sad that no position can be worked out for you at Yale, framing in your mind a letter of acceptance of an offer from Michigan, you happen to meet John Dollard, and you tell him that you are regretful that he will not be your colleague, and then three hours later you have a firm offer from Yale— luck is a variable, however absent it is from explanations of the shaping of lives. Individuals do differ in the opportunities they create and take advantage of, but that is not the whole story.

Southbury was my first and mind-searing experience in group living in a complicated organization that was part of, and responsible to, a more complicated network of organizations we call the state. At the bottom of the organizational hill was South-bury, and at the top—like Kafka's castle—was the state, the major function of which seemed to be to make life difficult for those at the bottom. I quickly learned that if you were at South-bury, your world was divided (again) into the three people-places: inside (Southbury), "up there in Hartford," the state capital, and outside (the rest of the world). In terms of daily living, which meant day and night, the inside and the outside were phenomenologically salient. Most of the employees lived in the institution; the only thing you could rent or buy in that rural nowhere was empty land. Heads of departments had lovely houses. Although I was head of a department, it was essentially unpeopled. I was unmarried. I was given a small apartment in one of the two splendid-looking apartment buildings, splen-did on the outside but with a cold, long-halled interior spartanly furnished. I lived and worked with as motley a collection of peo-ple as you could imagine: teachers, maintenance people, nurses, secretaries, plumbers, electricians, carpenters, painters, and others whom I cannot recall. It is one thing to work with peo-ple varying widely in education, skills, age, and religion. It is quite another thing in addition to live with them, to see and be with them socially, to be "one of the gang," to avoid being seen as aloof, snobbish, or an isolate. To live in a semiclosed society in semitotal isolation during a world war when there were shortages of everything, travel was difficult, and I had no car—it was an experience.

It is valid, I think, to say that I am a friendly, outgoing person capable of being with and tolerating very diverse types of personalities. Some have said that I carry to an extreme the capacity to tolerate fools gladly. But it is less tolerance than a desire to like and be liked, to avoid areas of disagreement when I feel that they may ruffle sensitivities. I had no difficulty establishing pleasant, albeit superficial, relationships with most of the people at Southbury. The fact is that I had to establish relationships with almost everyone, because my major responsibilities included the placement of residents in appropriate cottages and the matching of working-age individuals with one or another work supervisor. Southbury, like every other state institution, would have come to a grinding halt if residents did not work. So each staff member (laundry, plumbing, ground maintenance, and so on) had a "detail" of residents to train. I had to be on good terms, therefore, with most everyone—and I was. More than any other department head, I knew what was going on in the daily lives of the residents and employees. I ate in the cottages as frequently as I did in the employee dining hall, if only because the cottage mother, father, and cook made an occasion of my joining them, and that meant far better fare than in the dining hall.

I gained friendships, weight, and information. The combination of the kind of person I was and my assumption that I could be of most help to residents and employees by knowing everything about everybody soon made me be seen as an important person. And by important, I mean that I was seen as someone who would use information to get things done, to right wrongs, to serve as mediator in the countless frictions that stamped life in the institution. And that was the dark side of life at Southbury: the seemingly endless number of interpersonal, interdepartmental, intradepartmental, sexual, and professional sources of friction. It was one big soap opera. I was not viewing it, I was part of it. Conceptually I was unprepared

for it. There was absolutely nothing in my graduate education
that exposed me to the nature of group living—anywhere. Psychology was about individuals, not about individuals in complicated social contexts. Psychology was based on a "cause-and-
effect" way of thinking, which, the longer I was at Southbury,
I came to see as grossly oversimplified, very misleading, and,
for the purposes of action, very self-defeating. The more I came
to know people there, the more I came to know myself, the more
disenchanted I became with an individual, cause-and-effect
psychology. Decades later I made a point that listeners and
readers have found humorous and true, although I intended no
humor: If instead of putting one rat in the maze, Thorndike
had put two, three, or more, we would have a more viable and
realistic social psychology than we do. The seeds of that comment were planted in my Southbury experience. At the same
time that I was learning, absorbing, and growing, I knew that
conceptually I did not know how to make overall sense of what
I was experiencing. When you are in the equivalent of Peyton
Place or General Hospital, it is hard, if not impossible, to take
conceptual distance, to come to grips with the overall picture.
It takes a Tolstoy, which obviously I am not, to make sense
of the myriad aspects (people and forces) of *War and Peace*. And
for me, Southbury was in microcosm *War and Peace*.

Far more than in the past, psychologists today who finish
their graduate education take positions in complicated organizations. They are prepared for those settings hardly better than
I was, and if my experience is any guide, too many of them
end up disillusioned, eagerness replaced by passivity, work
transformed into labor, cynicism a defense against smoldering
anger. I am not suggesting that there is a way of preparing these
kinds of psychologists so that working in these settings is more
satisfying and smooth. What I am suggesting is that ignorance
exponentially increases the travail. It is one thing to have some
idea of what you are getting into; it is quite another thing to
walk in chin up and hands down. Business schools do a far better job preparing their students for life in organizations than
psychology does. But the core problem is not a matter of knowledge, but how to grasp the significance of life in a cauldron of

people, purposes, structures, and traditions—a cauldron in which the temperature ranges from well above zero to the boiling and overflowing point. Can life be otherwise in a place like Southbury? Inchoately, that was the question that was struggling to get asked in my Southbury psyche. It did not get asked clearly until I left Southbury and found myself replaying that experience in the light of new experiences. If any statement I can make about my years at Southbury has validity, it is that my professional career in the subsequent four decades was a replaying, examination, and re-examination of my years there.

In my first year at Southbury, I administered more individual intelligence tests than I like to recall. For one thing, testing was my stock-in-trade. It was expected that each case folder would contain an assessment of level of intellectual functioning, a kind of proof that the individual's commitment to Southbury met legal requirements. In those days and for some years thereafter, commitment was via the probate courts, which meant that the state assumed the role of legal guardian. And legal guardianship meant that we at Southbury determined when and under what conditions a child could go home for visits, extended stays, or a work placement. In principle as well as in practice, it was similar to being sent to prison, that is, the state was in charge of your future. The words *parole* and *work placement* were somewhat euphemistic, because they referred to two (and only two) types of situations: if you were female, you were placed as a maid in a private home; if you were male, you were put on someone's farm. There were very few placements, and in every instance the individual placed was a "familial defective," that is, coming from a "Kallikak, subcultural" background. No one from a "nice" middle-class family was ever placed other than in their own home, which meant that they were rarely placed, because we and their families believed they were already in the best placement possible. And that brings me to one of the most important "lessons" I learned from my Southbury experience, a lesson that required me to unlearn and confront attitudes and beliefs grounded in ignorance and prejudice. It took me two years to learn the lesson, and the only thing that comforted me, once I learned it, was that, compared to almost everyone else at Southbury, I was a fast learner. It took almost three more decades, during which American society underwent some sea-swell social and legal transformations, before the lesson was more generally learned, albeit reluctantly and in a very superficial way.

We took great pride in Southbury's appearance, rationale, and mission. It was a unique place, and during my stay there I spent a fair amount of time shepherding visitors from around the country on a Southbury tour. The different types of small, homelike, residential cottages; a school building that would be the envy of any educator; a farm for which the adjective *model* would not be inappropriate; a magnificently equipped "industrial training" building; a hospital, spacious and no less magnificently equipped; an administration building that was an architectural gem; and well-kept treed and flowered grounds. It was, so to speak, Mr. Roselle's Last Hurrah, and he had made the most of it. So, if we took pride in Southbury, it was understandable. That pride was manifested in different kinds of ways, of which one was our feeling that the residents should be glad to be there. Compared to the homes and background from which many of them came, Southbury was a posh vacation resort. Why, then, did some of them run away? Why were we constantly being asked, "When will we be able to go home?" One of the first residents I came to know—because she ran away on my first weekend and I was part of the posse to find her—was Rosie. I had read her case folder, which was at least two inches thick, most of it consisting of accounts of previous runaways and descriptions of her home and family, a family that seemed a plagiarization of Goddard's description of the Kallikaks: "Rosie's father sold her mother to a friend for a clock" was one of the representative sentences in the case material. You had to be both retarded and crazy to want to leave paradise to go back to that environment!

What was the lesson I learned? It took months for it to dawn on me (the sun was still only on the horizon) that the desire to return home was *normal,* that however disordered and abusive the home setting was, it still was the only source of familiarity, security, and even intimacy the residents had ever experienced.

To us, the uniqueness of Southbury inhered in giving them a familylike existence dramatically different from and better than their own, and yet they wanted no part of it, they wanted to go home. Far from seeing this as a normal response to separation from the only social-family world they had ever known, we saw it as proof that they needed to be protected from themselves. Far from seeing it as normal, we saw it as a manifestation of their arrested development.

The lesson I was learning was that paternalism rendered you incapable of grasping and comprehending the world as it is experienced by those for whom you are or feel responsible. At Southbury, you saw the residents through the lens of a diagnostic label that explained everything and, therefore, nothing. You thought you were explaining human behavior, unaware that your explanation rested on an unexamined axiom: we and they had nothing in common. If *we* were in their place, we would get on our knees and thank God that we were placed at Southbury. Yes, the residents were human, but we could not accord them feelings and longings that follow separation from the only world they had ever known. How do you get inside of someone else's world? I was learning, and I am continuing to learn, that that may be the most important question in the training of any professional who, for clinical research purposes, has to understand others—not to "study" others but to understand others. In later chapters, I will elaborate on why I came to conclude that we do a poor job of training professionals in these matters.

Within Southbury, few things were as fateful in shaping a resident's life as his or her IQ. I would write detailed psychological reports based on a variety of verbal and performance tests, one section of which presented the quantitative scores. Rarely did anyone read the analyses of the test performance, but they did rivet on the different IQ scores. To most of my colleagues, if not all, the difference between an IQ of 65 and an IQ of 69 was a difference that made (or should make) a difference, the latter signifying a "smarter" person than the former. In those days, if an individual got an IQ score of 70 or above, the legal question would be asked: Have we grounds for keeping the person in the institution? No question would be raised if the IQ was 69, but if it was 71 or more, the question would be asked, because of legal considerations and *not* because of concern about what was best for the individual. In part, but only in part, this concern with IQ scores was spurred by the "dumping" phenomenon: as soon as Southbury opened its doors, communities sought to institutionalize as many of their special-class pupils as possible, shifting fiscal and educational responsibility to the state. And needless to say, the bulk of these white and black students came from "subcultural" backgrounds. Southbury sought to resist the dumping, and one of its weapons was the IQ score.* An IQ of 70 was the cutoff point. I was on the hot seat, caught in the middle between positions neither of which sincerely concerned itself with the welfare of the individual.

Whose agent was I? The answer was effectively decided by my temperament and ideology. I was for the underdog, with the result that I frequently locked horns with colleagues about who should or should not be admitted to or remain at Southbury. I won most of the battles, as much because of my passion as because my colleagues were, in those early months of Southbury's existence, still sensitive to moral-ethical issues; that is, Southbury still existed *for* its residents, and not vice versa.

If I came to Southbury with a lot of reservations about psychology's conceptions of and methods for "measuring" intelligence, those reservations quickly transformed into antipathy. For one thing, it was obvious that to theorize about intelligence as if it were a "thing" apart from personality and social context flew in the face of everyday experience. It flew in the face of what I knew about myself, my intelligence, my life. It also became obvious that psychologists who developed intelligence tests were amazingly ignorant of the fact that tests were used in political contexts and for political purposes, by which I mean that participants have unequal power—one uses information that will influence in some way the life of another person. And power

---

*It would be more correct to say that Esther resisted the dumping. Far more than I, Esther was sensitive and resistant to any situation in which the welfare of residents was being overlooked, neglected, or ignored. If I fought the good fight it was in part because Esther made sure I did.

as an omnipresent fact takes on added significance when tests are employed in complicated organizational contexts. *Whose agent am I?* That question, which should be consciously omnipresent, arises because of different power concerns of different parties. The power aspects of the context of testing were never discussed in the testing manuals I read, the classes I took, or the supervision I received. That is not ancient history. The situation is hardly different today. For the most part, psychologists still learn about tests as if they are employed only in a one-on-one context in a nonsocial, nonorganizational world. The realities are otherwise.

What have been psychology's contributions to knowledge and the public welfare? One of the many answers to that question has been the development of intelligence tests that validly predict level of subsequent performance in school, college, and work. There is a kernel of truth here, but there is the dark side that my experience at Southbury forced me to confront. I have never known a psychologist in the field of mental retardation who did not view intelligence testing as at best a mixed blessing and at worst a baleful influence. The same is true for that very large group of school psychologists who continue to struggle against the public perception that their sole function is to administer and score standardized, "objective" tests. And if that perception is part of the problem, psychology has to shoulder part of the responsibility for it. Just as economists educated the public to believe that they had developed quantitative means for understanding and measuring economic forces, thereby predicting and "fine tuning" the economy, psychologists oversold the significance of their understanding and measurement of intelligence. But why blame the victim?

What I failed to grasp at Southbury was that I was thinking about intelligence and testing in terms only of mental retardation. What I did not and could not see was that to be viewed as stupid or unintelligent in America was indeed fateful for one's existence. Put most generally: ours is a society in which, as individuals or collectivities, we are constantly judging people by their "smartness," regardless of whether our distinctions refer to the lower, middle, or upper levels. I read somewhere about an eminent person who had two sons, fraternal twins, one of whom ranked first and the other second in their high school graduating class. From that point on, they were referred to as the "smart one" and the "stupid one." If the labels were intended as humorous, they nevertheless reflected the pervasive tendency to make distinctions among people in terms of intelligence. And those distinctions, far more often than not, connote judgments about worthiness.

For seventeen years I served on the Yale psychology department's graduate admissions committee. Each candidate had taken the Graduate Record Examination, which gave two scores: the verbal and the quantitative. If the person got scores below 500, the application was routinely rejected. Above that cutoff point, your chances for admission were incomparably higher if your scores were in the 700s rather than below that, that is, the former were "smarter" than the latter. And we wanted the smartest ones, of course! But it was not only that we regarded them as smart but that we attributed other characteristics to them that suggested that they were more worthy: more ambitious, more creative, more motivated. Carl Hovland, who was then chair of the department, did an informal study of how well the scores correlated with faculty opinion about the quality of students' creativity and conceptual talents. He found essentially no correlation. That study, which was grist for my mill (I having recently come from Southbury), seemed to alter no one's judgment about scores and "smartness." But the clearest confirmation about the surplus values attributed to scores was the fact that if two candidates had similarly high scores, but one was male and the other was female, guess who was admitted?

A story is relevant here. It was in the mid fifties, and the department was aware that we had never admitted a black. We wanted to, but none had got scores above the cutoff point. Along comes an applicant from Brooklyn College whose personal statement and letters of recommendation *suggested* that he might be black. But his scores were in the 500s, which was not reassurance enough that he could get through the program. What should we do? Would we be doing him a favor by putting him with students with more astronomical scores? It was a long discussion, and the decision was made to admit him and to be prepared to give him as much help as he needed. The candidate, we learned on the first day of classes, was not black. He was Phillip Zimbardo, who needed academic and intellectual help the way a Rockefeller needs food stamps.

It comes as a surprise to people when they are told that there are societies whose language does not contain the word or concept *intelligence*. We are the most test-giving and test-taking society the world has ever known. We like to believe that our tests give us objective, dispassionate indices of ability that we use nonjudgmentally, that is, connoting nothing about worthiness. I am not disputing that these tests can validly, but imperfectly, predict performance. My point is that in our society, getting a higher rather than a lower score too frequently implies more worthiness, more value as a person. And if that implication is not made explicitly by the test giver, socialization into American society pretty much guarantees that the test taker will judge himself or herself on the continuum of worthiness. That was the case at Southbury and at Yale, and they are both representative of what is rife in the larger society. To discuss test development, test giving, and test taking independent of their significance for American society—what they tell us about our society—is egregiously misleading and an inexcusable form of cultural blindness.

At the same time that I was administering intelligence tests ad nauseam to the residents at Southbury, I began to administer Henry Murray's Thematic Apperception Test, a series of pictures to which the individual is asked to make up a story, a process in which the person interprets the picture according to motivations, relationships, and events peculiar to his or her experience. What is internal gets projected onto the external. Would mentally retarded individuals be able to make up, to *create*, coherent stories? Asking that question spoke volumes about how these individuals were (and too often still are) regarded: as devoid of an ''internal life,'' or possessing only a primitive personality organization. Would their stories make sense in that they would reveal what they are as persons: their hopes, fears, and so on? How different are ''they'' from ''us''? It is far clearer to me today than it was more than four decades ago that I was attempting to demonstrate—from a nontheoretical, personal-political, intuitive, perspective—that mentally retarded persons are like "us."

What those studies revealed is that they, like us, think about and yearn for loved ones; that they react with bewilderment, dejection, and despair to enforced separation; and that many of them are capable of responding sensitively and appreciatively to sustained interpersonal relationships. They dream and fantasize; they are no less and no more sexual than anyone else. In those studies, I accorded them the status of *persons* and *personhood,* emphasizing our similarities as thinking and feeling people and trying to counter the dominant view that they are incomplete, damaged, semiempty vessels who are obviously human but equally obviously devoid of the "inner life" we know so well. Those studies taught me a lot, but the major lesson was that they confirmed what was confirmable from my everyday social-personal relationships with the residents, if you viewed and experienced those relationships in the same way you would those with your friends, colleagues, and family. It was at Southbury that I learned how difficult it is to take the obvious seriously. "I am not my IQ, I am not the label you pin on me, I am not a baby"—in countless ways, none of them subtle, the residents sought to change our views of them. I call them residents, but in those days we referred to them as children, regardless of their age. I knew about the self-fulfilling prophecy long before it became a subject of psychological study.

Was it possible to develop a sustained psychotherapeutic relationship with some of the residents? And by that, we (Esther and I) meant a relationship explicitly geared to helping the "clients" understand better the sources of their covert and overt behavior, with the consequence that self-defeating behavior would be better controlled.* As I indicated earlier, one of our

*Esther and I met at Clark University in 1941. We were married on May 22, 1943. She joined me at Southbury shortly after that when she finished a second internship (the first was at New Hampshire State Hospital) at the Neurological Institute in New York.

major roles at Southbury was as troubleshooters: seeing and working with residents who were considered problems in school, work detail, or cottage. Troubleshooting is not psychotherapy, but the role positioned us to transform some of these instances into a therapeutic relationship if we so desired. We did so desire, but we had no formal preparation, no credentials. Where could we get supervision? Was there a psychiatrist who would be willing to supervise psychologists and who knew something about mentally retarded individuals and the institutions that housed them? And therein lies a story.

I have mentioned Dr. Grover Powers, who was head of pediatrics at Yale and the most influential member of Southbury's board of trustees. Dr. Powers trained more pediatricians who became heads of pediatric departments in medical schools than anyone in this country, before or after him. He was as distinctive a person as he was a pediatrician, administrator, and leader. He was stocky, somewhat fat, bald, slow moving, priestly looking, with a pipsqueak voice. On first meeting him, it was hard to square his appearance with his position and accomplishments. His grandfatherly manner, his soft warmth, his sensitivity were far more than skin-deep, but this was deceptive to anyone who concluded that Dr. Powers was passive or a pushover. He could be as firm as steel and direct as a bullet if the situation warranted it. And about nothing was he more concerned than providing a relaxed, supportive, accommodating atmosphere for children and their parents in the hospital. And when he spoke about these matters, it was not rhetoric.

Two things say a lot about him. The first is that he instituted the first mother–infant rooming-in unit in an American hospital. The second is that his department had its own mini-child guidance unit, staffed, with one exception, by part-time people: a schoolteacher, a social worker, a psychologist, and two psychiatrist-psychoanalysts, one full and the other part time. To my knowledge, it was the only department of pediatrics to have such a unit for training and service. The director of the unit was Edith Jackson, who was analyzed by Freud, a good friend of Anna, and an important figure in the early years of the development of child analysis. What was Edie Jackson (her

mother was Helen Hunt Jackson, who wrote *Ramona*) doing in
that department of pediatrics? How did she get there? Those were
the days when it was hard to find a department of psychiatry
that had a psychoanalyst on its full-time staff. The situation was
no different in pediatrics.

The answer to those questions was Dr. Grover Powers,
except that that answer obscures the fact that Edie was, to a
discernible degree, the female counterpart of Dr. Powers. From
Dr. Powers's perspective, Edie was the kind of person (*not* only
the kind of professional) who gave substance to the language
of caring and compassion. I spent one day a week with her in
the mini–child guidance unit, and when she and Dr. Powers
decided to develop the rooming-in unit, I became part of that
endeavor, an unimportant but welcome part. Edie and Dr.
Powers were immune to the virus of professional imperialism
and arrogance. I have had more than my share of good luck!

Esther and I became friends with Edie. So, when we
sought supervision for the psychotherapy we wanted to undertake at Southbury, we asked her whether she would be willing
to provide it. What the reader needs to know is that Edie had
a superego of galactic dimensions. For Edie to do anything
deemed irregular by custom or ruling aroused inner turmoil,
exquisitely illustrated by her response to us, a response that took
about ten minutes, most of which was anguished silence, to put
it mildly. Eliminating the silences, her response was "As a
member of the Boston Psychoanalytic Society, I am forbidden
to supervise nonmedical people in psychotherapy. I know that
you and Esther are responsible people and what you want to
do should be done, although I have no experience in psychotherapy with retarded people. I cannot supervise you. However,
if in your therapeutic work, which I hope you will do, questions arise about which you think I can be helpful, I will be
delighted to meet with you. But neither I nor you can call it
supervision." We were disappointed but did not feel rejected.
Edie probably had several sleepless nights. We never called upon
Edie, less because of not wanting to see her agonize and more
because, as we proceeded, it was obvious that anyone who did
not understand complex institutions could not be helpful to us.

In 1985 I was asked to bring together some of my writings in the field of mental retardation. In that book is reprinted a chapter from an out-of-print book in which I described our therapeutic work at Southbury. To give the reader some sense of what that work meant to us, then and in subsequent decades— I have always been in the field of mental retardation—I can do no better than to repeat my 1985 comments in *Psychology and Mental Retardation* (Austin, Tex.: Pro-Ed):

Only with the passage of decades was I able to see that our psychotherapeutic effort was powered by some conceptual illogicalities that demonstrated how much a prisoner of traditional thinking I was. Some readers will have discerned that the discussion of our results (and those of others) rested on this assumption: If an individual responds in the way that theory and practice say should characterize the psychotherapeutic relationship— however different on the surface that relationship may appear— then the individual is not mentally defective. Put in another way: The quality of response to the psychotherapeutic relationship is a test of the appropriateness of the diagnosis of mental deficiency (or mental retardation). There would be nothing inherently wrong about that assumption if three things were true: 1) the criteria for making the diagnosis of mental deficiency or mental retardation were unambiguous in language and implementation so that different diagnosticians arrive at the same conclusion; 2) the assumed relationships between the mental deficients implicit in the diagnosis and overt problem solving and interpersonal behavior were based on more than conjecture or a confusion between assumptions and fact; and 3) an earnest research effort had been made to test the appropriateness and helpfulness of psychotherapy. Instead of saying that the conceptual basis for the diagnosis of mental deficiency contained ambiguities and untested assumptions and, therefore, was a confusing and not a clarifying variable for social action and research, I was accepting the fiction that the diagnostic label validly described relationships (or a lack of them) among factors internal and external to the individual. More specifically, the diagnostic label stood for a condition "inside" the person that made a particular kind of relationship (i.e., the psychotherapeutic) impossible. So, when our efforts indicated that such a relationship was possible, the conclusion drawn was that the diagnosis was wrong. Instead of calling into question the nature of our conception of mental retardation, that conception went unchallenged and the argument focused on whether in this or that case the diagnosis was right or wrong. That mental retardation is not a "thing" in the way that a pencil or a stone is; that as a concept mental retardation is literally an invention of the human mind; that precisely because it is such an invention the chances are high that it contains unexamined biases and invalid assumptions—these considerations were far from clear to me. But there were more serious and harmful consequences of the traditional conception of mental retardation than whether the diagnosis was right or wrong in a particular case. The first of these consequences was that the diagnosis automatically precluded trying to establish anything resembling the features of a psychotherapeutic relationship, insuring that the dynamics of the self-fulfilling prophecy would be operative. (It was in all respects identical to the way in which psychotherapy used to be viewed as inapplicable to old people, even though here too, there were clear indications that such a sweeping generalization was unjustified. There was one big difference: Whereas one could question the validity of the diagnosis of mental retardation, one could not question whether or not an individual was "old"!) The second serious consequence of the traditional conception was the support it gave to society's view of where and how mentally retarded individuals should be placed and managed. Any view that contained the assumption that it was impossible to establish with certain "labeled" individuals a reciprocal, productive, sustained, change-producing relationship justified programs that essentially denied these individuals the status of personhood. This, of course, was not a deliberate denial but rather an instance of a typical and all too easy way in which a society justified how it manages its relationships with individuals it regards as different, be that difference one of appearance, behavior, or any other departure from what the society considers acceptable and normal.

As I look back on our psychotherapeutic work I am struck by a misplaced emphasis. Certainly we were justified in utilizing psychotherapy to learn about the technique as well as about certain individuals. And we were, of course, justified in suggesting that there was a fair number of individuals labeled as mentally retarded who were far more psychologically complicated than that diagnosis would lead one to believe. But in emphasizing the technique and our results, was I not posing the issues as professional ones? Was I not talking to specialists in the field of mental retardation? Imagine the situation in which professionals were convinced that what we had to say about mental retardation, psychotherapy, and therapeutic results was valid, and everyone was off and running to determine which, how many, and to what degree mentally retarded persons could benefit from the psychotherapeutic relationship. If at the time I wrote the chapter I had reason to believe that that is precisely what would happen, I would have been delighted, to put it mildly. Should not one take satisfaction from the knowledge that a field was undergoing a long overdue change and that people were now being helped in new ways? That satisfaction, however, should have been tempered by knowledge of three facts: The number for whom that approach was applicable was probably not overwhelming; the psychotherapeutic endeavor is one of repair and not of prevention; and as an endeavor of repair, its results are far from perfect. Put in another way, what I underemphasized was the need to examine professional and societal attitudes that made the clinical or repair endeavor necessary. To the extent that the emphasis was on repair, attention was being diverted from the features of our society that created the need for repair. And there could be no doubt that one of the major features was an attitude that essentially denied mentally retarded individuals the status of personhood, an attitude that powered the way society and its representatives responded to that heterogeneous group of people who had in common an assigned label. And in many instances society's response began to exert its influence on the day of the individual's birth.

Here, again, the notable exception was parents of mentally retarded children. Although there were differences among parents, as a group they related to their children not as empty objects but as persons sensitive to changes around them, in need of attention and love, and as deserving as any other of one's energies and respect. This is not to be maudlin or sentimental or to advocate parental love as a kind of psychologic universal solvent that either prevents or dissolves the frictions in living. The only intention is to convey that, as a group, parents felt for and with their children with a depth and consistency that was quite the opposite of what these children experienced from all other people who stood in some relationship to them. Granted that parental love can be a very mixed blessing and can be a pain in the neck to the professional who operates from an "I know best" stance, and granted that love is not enough—none of this lessens the significance and power of the central core of parental love: The child is a thinking and feeling organism, a person. It is what that core implies that the retarded child rarely experiences from others. As soon as you regard the child as capable of thinking and feeling and, therefore, of being influenceable and changeable—even if such attribution may be in part unrealistic—you have put a distinctive stamp of interpersonal sensitivity and reciprocity on your relationship with that child (pp. 78–82).

There are events in life that say to you, so to speak, "don't ever forget what you have just learned, because if you do forget, you will have blinded yourself to an eternal truth." One of those events took place in the context of my therapeutic work with Lottie. She was twenty-three, she had been institutionalized together with her mother and brother when she was six years of age, and she was a stormy petrel. How she had been able to maintain a sense of personal integrity and self-worth, I cannot explain. When she felt put upon or harassed by other residents or staff, she was capable of awesome anger and hostility, with the frequent result that she was subject to isolation and other forms of punishment. She looked younger than her age (why not?). I considered her attractive, and as I came to know her in the course of my daily meanderings around the institution, I concluded that Lottie was no more retarded than I was! Her tested IQ in 1928 was 59, in 1929 it was 74, in 1939 it was 45, and in 1944, when I tested her, it was 51. Why did I think she was basically of normal intelligence? For the sake of brevity, I sum up my answer in current popular jargon: she had "street smarts," in spades. The mental processes we imply by that phrase are in no way "measured" by our conventional tests. In any event, Lottie aroused in me a full-blown rescue fantasy: I was going to get her out of the institution. And necessary to the achievement of that would be a sustained therapeutic relationship that would prepare her for the day she would leave Southbury. I worked with her over many months, and the point was reached when she wanted and felt prepared to go on placement as a maid in a private home. The rescue fantasy was transformed into a reality! If my accomplishment was much less heroic than that of Itard with Victor (as described in H. Lane's *Wild Boy of Aveyron* (Cambridge, Mass.: Harvard University Press, 1976)) I felt that, at the least, I was carrying on a neglected tradition. I was not smug, just satisfied with myself.

Three weeks after Lottie left, she was returned to Southbury. She had been placed with a family who lived in a house where all rooms were on the first floor except for a large, bright, well-appointed room on the second floor, which was to be Lottie's room. The family made every effort to make Lottie feel wanted and told her that they knew that this was a new experience for her and that they would endeavor to make it a mutually rewarding one. The morning after her arrival, the family found Lottie downstairs sleeping on the living room couch. They explained to her that her room was upstairs and that she was expected to sleep there. They liked Lottie and concluded that her intellectual limitations were manifest in her lack of comprehension. It went on for three weeks; each morning Lottie would be found sleeping on the couch. Reluctantly, the family asked that she be returned to Southbury. I met with her and asked for an explanation. She would not respond; the silences were deafening, and I felt bewildered and impotent. Finally, sensing my turmoil and despair, she looked up at me and in a voice blended with exasperation and accusation she said, *"If you always slept each night in a room with thirty other girls, you would be afraid of sleeping alone in a room."*

That her assertion said much about her self-knowledge and Southbury was small balm for my feelings of stupidity and blindness. I learned more about mentally retarded people as persons and about the effects of prolonged institutionalization from my psychotherapeutic relationship with Lottie than from all the books I had read or the conventional wisdom I had heard. It confirmed my belief that no human being was understandable apart from the transactional relationships with complicated social-cultural contexts. That, of course, is a glimpse of the obvious, but Lottie taught me (and I mean that literally) how easy it is to avoid seeing the obvious. The lesson that Lottie taught me forever stayed with me. Was I as a person and psychologist understandable apart from living in the Southbury milieu? Was I understandable as a psychologist apart from having become one in a particular graduate school in America? Lottie had a more valid and sensitive conception of her transactional relationships with the Southbury culture than I had of mine with it. If anyone had asked me to be specific about how I affected Southbury and how it was shaping me, I would have had trouble answering the question. I had come to understand how Southbury (and her previous institutionalization) had shaped Lottie—*that* was an important set of issues for me, and I pursued them unaware that those issues *had* to be no less salient for understanding me than it was for understanding Lottie.

It was at Southbury that four themes or opinions got clarified, integrating intellectual and personal experiences reflecting my background, Jewishness, politics, education, and Southbury itself:

1.   If anything validly characterizes human history, it is the frequency and strength with which a society's dominant groups have underestimated the potentialities of those who are different from them.
2.   The most important problem we face is understanding, from the moment of birth, the individual-context transactions; that is, how the individual and context are both cause and effect, how the structure and dynamics of each, both part of an indissoluble whole, shape development that is judged positively or negatively by cultural criteria.
3.   We hardly understand those transactions, and there is a very strong tendency to resort to biology to explain what psychology describes and studies. If patriotism is the last (and frequently the first) resort of scoundrels, biological reductionism is the first resort of oversimplifiers who are allergic to messy complexity.
4.   Whatever conception you hold of what people are, it has to be challenged by efforts to show that they can be otherwise.

At Southbury, and in the decades since, those four opinions powered everything I ever did. Mental retardation, schools, resource networks, community psychology, projective techniques, test anxiety, the creation of settings, public policy, aging—behind each of these interests and work are the four opinions or beliefs. On the surface, I have worked in disparate areas. Phenomenologically, there has been but one common factor: the belief that I, and all people, can be more than what we are. Relevant here is another of my clinical mistakes. I do not, of course, seek to make mistakes, but when I do make a mistake it is a beauty, in two respects: its clarity and its power to instruct. It was not true before Southbury, but at and after Southbury I did not fear making mistakes. I could, I knew, capitalize on them, a stance reflective of a strange combination of arrogance, self-confidence, and humility.

Our offices were in Southbury's administration building, our windows facing front, allowing us to see who was going to enter the building. This was especially interesting on admission days, because we could see who was bringing whom for institutionalization. Together with the director of cottage life, we would meet and talk with the accompanying parents or guardians, observe and try to relate to the future resident, and make a decision about an appropriate cottage placement. It was our practice to see and test the resident a few days after admission to determine, among other things, if the cottage placement was appropriate. There were three types of cottages: for high-, middle-, and low-grade individuals, those labels referring to intellectual levels.

On one of these admission days, a car pulled up from which emerged a tall, stocky man who was holding, cradlelike in his hands, what appeared to be a large two- or three-year-old youngster. This was strange and upsetting, because Southbury did not admit anyone below the age of six—strange because someone had goofed, and upsetting because we would have to explain why we could not accept the child. As we soon learned, the young child was a thirty-year-old man, as physically and neurologically involved a case of cerebral palsy as we had ever seen, and we had seen many. His body was in constant motion (athetoid movements), every limb was involved, his face was distorted, there was constant drooling, and his facial expression was best called "wild." There was no doubt that he should be placed in a cottage that was "middle grade" but had its share of "low grades" who needed complete care. He was being admitted because his mother had just died, his father had died years ago, and there was no one to care for him. I also quickly concluded that there was no point trying to evaluate Mr. Humphrey in a matter of days. He had little intellectual potential, and aside from humane care, what we had to offer him he could not take advantage of. The question I asked myself was, why had the mother never considered institutionalization?

Three weeks later, I was passing his cottage and met Mr. Rooney, a delightful, sensitive, responsible man who was the cottage father. We chitchatted, and at one point I asked, "How is the Humphrey boy?" To which Mr. Rooney, face lighting up and gleaming, said, "He is a real smarty." I looked puzzled, and Mr. Rooney reacted by inviting me in to observe what Mr. Humphrey could do. He was lying, not sitting, in a wheelchair, looking exactly as he had when he was admitted. Mr. Rooney went to a cupboard and took out a checkerboard that had accompanied Mr. Humphrey to Southbury. In each square of the board was a letter of the alphabet, in sequence. Mr. Rooney said to me, "Now, you ask him a question that requires a one-word answer. Then, slowly, move your finger along the squares. Even though he is always in motion, he will let you know when your finger is on the right letter. He will really go into motion. In that way he will spell out the answer." I asked several questions (for example, day of week, name of institution), and he got each one right.

I felt appropriately humble and stupid, but also exhilarated, because here was grist for my mill: my/our capacity to be taken in by appearance and to underestimate what people are capable of. For days I was obsessed with several questions: What permitted the mother to believe that her infant had good intellectual potential? How did she engender, maintain, and sustain his attention and motivation? Does not this case raise questions about what we think we know about brain–behavior–social context relationships? What have intensive and comprehensive longitudinal studies of these kinds demonstrated? I could answer

the last question; such studies had never been done. As of today, they still have not been done. Of one thing I was and am
sure: to an undetermined extent, the self-fulfilling prophecy is
always operative, for good and for bad. In the case of mental
retardation, that is as true for the clinical and research professional as it is for parents, and too frequently its strength in
parents reflects what they have been told by professionals.

In my clinical and educational seminars, I devote one
meeting to a presentation of three of my diagnostic mistakes,
one of which is Mr. Humphrey. The other two cases are in some
ways more dramatic. The most obvious feature these cases share
is that a parent (in one instance a parent surrogate) believed
(too mild a word) that the young child had a capacity for development that was unpredicted by conventional diagnostic criteria,
psychological and neurological. There are, of course, parents
who hold such beliefs but whose efforts do not meet with the
success I describe in these cases. How to account for these differences? It is a question yet to be asked and studied in a seriously
systematic way. There have been "womb to tomb" longitudinal
studies of normal individuals. They are by no means numerous,
because to carry out such investigations is more a career than
a study, an obstacle-ridden, anxiety-producing, reputation-
delaying course that very few young psychologists (and even
fewer senior ones) are willing to traverse, even if appropriate
and secure funding is available, which rarely has been the case.
To do this kind of study with infants who at birth are indisput-
ably damaged, whose future is in all respects bleak? As a senior
developmental psychologist said to me, "You really have to be
mentally retarded to do that kind of study."

Experiences with the Lotties and Mr. Humphreys of Southbury forced me to relearn a lesson I had learned about myself
in other contexts. And when I say *forced*, I mean *forced:* it took
the equivalent of claps of psychological thunder to see what
should have been obvious. The lesson was that how I viewed
the world was determined by, among other things, the sense
of place. Put more correctly, my embeddedness in the culture
of place unwittingly but powerfully restricted and distorted what
I thought I knew and could explain. (There were, of course,

very positive aspects to this embeddedness, but you always pay a price.) So I had learned that Brooklyn–New York–Newark had colored and set limits to my understanding of the world. And that coloration and those limitations became understandable only when I left that "place" and went to Clark and Worcester. What I did not understand, again until I left them, was how Clark and Worcester colored and limited my view of the world at the same time that they expanded it. Worcester was not Boston, or New Haven, or Berkeley, or Chapel Hill. Clark was not Harvard, or Yale, or the University of California, or the University of North Carolina. Whatever their similarities, it is their differences that stamp you, that both expand and limit you.

Southbury was different, to a significant degree at least. For one thing, precisely because it was a place in the middle of nowhere, you could not escape awareness of the fact that it was a place remarkably different from the "outside world." The contrast was inescapable and stark. For another thing, unlike the other places I had lived in, at Southbury I was required professionally to deal with that other world. It is valid to say that I was less embedded in Southbury as a place than I had been in Clark-Worcester or Brooklyn–New York–Newark. But in one terribly important respect, Southbury colored and limited the substance and scope of my knowledge and understanding of the two worlds. If I became aware of the blind spot shortly before I left Southbury, it underlines the strength of place, that is, how living and working in a circumscribed place, assimilating and accommodating to people, roles, pressures, routines, and expectations give structure to your perceptions and conceptions and blind you to the existence of boundaries that structure inevitably erects.

What I was blind to was another glimpse of the obvious of which Mr. Humphrey was a good example. *All of the mentally retarded people I had come to know and I thought I understood were institutionalized people, who represented a very small percentage of the total population of retarded individuals; the great bulk of those individuals lived in the "other world."* In short, whatever I had experienced and learned was from and about an atypical population in an atypical setting. At most, only 5 percent of people with conditions covered by the umbrella term of *mental retardation* were in institutions. The rest were "out there" living in a variety of social-familial contexts in rural areas, villages, towns, and cities in distinctively different parts of this country. (How many Mr. Humphreys were out there?) To us at Southbury, it was inconceivable that America could get along without the Southburys of this world. We were institutionally egocentric: confusing what is with what should or had to be, overgeneralizing and overevaluating our roles, professional existence, and understandings. I knew that if I had taken the position at Mansfield instead of Southbury, I would have had distinctively different experiences, intellectually and personally. I would have thought about mental retardation differently. But whatever the differences, my conception and knowledge of mental retardation would have derived from a very atypical sample of people. If I was critical of psychologists who constructed theories based on studies of rats or college sophomores, I was incapable of seeing that the people I studied were an atypical sample.

What I have found fascinating in writing this autobiography is how strands of experience and thought stay in nonoverlapping psychological orbits waiting, so to speak, to be woven into a recognizable pattern. My guess is that more often than not these strands are never brought together. Why that is true for most people I do not know. I am the kind of person who has, at least in my adult years and especially in regard to psychology, always sought for connections among these strands of thought and experience. *Sought* is a somewhat misleading term, because it suggests a conscious or deliberate searching. That searching is present, but only from time to time. Behind the searching is a stance that if put into words would go like this: "However different my experiences have been or may appear, there *must* be connections among them that say something not only about an internal core but also about the nature of the external world. If I can discern the connections, they will allow me to say something important about how I and others see the world." To explain how the Southbury experience illustrates what I find difficult to put into words requires that I remind the reader that beginning in college there was one question that

gripped me: Why did the Russian Revolution fail? How does one
account for the transformation of a vision, albeit utopian, into
a nightmare that in the next two decades saw the deaths of millions and the imposition of a tyranny rivaling the worst in human
history? I had answers—more given than thought through by
me—but I knew they were at best incomplete. Those questions
remained with me after I had left the arena of radical politics.

That was one strand of thought and experience that accompanied me to Southbury. Over the several years at Southbury, another, seemingly unrelated strand emerged in the form
of this question: Why did Southbury, which began with such
a unique vision, such a validly self-conscious awareness of the
importance of its mission, slowly begin to manifest all of the
characteristics of insensitivity? Put in another way, for a year
after its opening, Southbury existed for its residents; after that,
the residents existed for the organization. There was nothing
witting about the transformation, you could not pinpoint the
time or event that signaled the change, the rhetoric of vision
or mission never changed, and to the "outside world" Southbury
remained a desired, revolutionary concept and place that deserved
emulation.

But change it did, and I knew it, but I had no conceptual
way of understanding why. You could blame the development
of a bureaucratic structure, inadequate leadership, departmental
rivalries, and the diminishing of a sense of willed selflessness—I
employed all of these and other explanations, unaware that I
was describing, not explaining, the transformation.

Just as when I left radical politics I continued to ruminate
about why the Russian Revolution failed, when I left Southbury
in 1945 I continued to try to understand why Southbury had
deteriorated (and has continued to do so until today, as newspaper accounts and court orders attest). It took almost two
decades for these two strands to come together and to lead me
to ask, could I create a new setting that would not fail of its
purposes? If I wanted (needed) to understand organizational
failure, should I not experience the creation of a new setting?
The origins of what I later called the problem of the "creation
of settings" and the Yale Psycho-Educational Clinic derived
from my radical politics and the Southbury experience.

I must here give voice to a conclusion to which I was forced by the writing of this autobiography. No one, least of all I, would dispute that one of the giants in psychology in this century was Piaget. He sought to and did illuminate some of the most important features in the development of the mental apparatus or schema that make logical, scientific thinking possible: that is, "formal operations" that are, so to speak, a protection against subjectivity and allow for the flowering of the possibilities inherent in logical-deductive thinking. I have never found Piaget convincing as explanation of how in my adult years I have arrived at the knowledge I have gained and the uses to which I have put that knowledge in my research, theorizing, and writings. Nothing that I have attained as knowledge in the sense that it was replicable by others, or was seen by others as "true," or became a stimulus to others in their thinking and actions derived from a deliberate employment of formal operations.

As I said above, whatever contributions I have made came about from an underlying, unverbalized stance that seems to propel me, not to see, but to be ready to see connections in strands of experience seemingly unrelated and that on the surface should be unrelated. No less characteristic of me—and something of which I am quite aware—is that the seeking of connections comes to the forefront after a "personal era" is over: after I have left Southbury, after I have left research on test anxiety, after I have left the Yale Psycho-Educational Clinic, after I have finished writing a book. I write books far less because I am clear about what I want to say than from a compulsion to make sense from what I have experienced. I enjoy writing, to the extent that the tortures of writing can be enjoyable, because I am exploring myself and becoming aware of connections. The "I" that begins to write is not the same "I" that finishes the book. I said earlier that I see my career as going from a fog into a clearing, into another fog, and then into another clearing, a very predictable psychological meteorology. Formal operations? They are a part of the story, but only a part.

Let me illustrate my conclusion by what happened after I finished ruminating about these matters and was ready to go on with and finish the Southbury story. I found myself asking: is there anything in my past experience that would throw light on my view that our private knowledge of how we think and work is dramatically different from the picture we project to others (for example, in our scientific and professional writings) or the picture that conventional wisdom or theory depicts, and to which we accommodate? More correctly, I did not ask the question, but rather I found myself feeling or assuming that there was something in the past that on the surface seemed unrelated but in fact could be connected to what was a private conclusion.

I must emphasize that I was completely secure in the feeling that what I would dredge up (or what would float up) would be under the heading "discrepancy between appearance and reality," "theories are a mixed blessing." What came up was an article by D. Taylor summarizing the conclusions of a meeting convened by the American Psychological Association on the scientific training of psychologists ("Education for Research in Psychology." *American Psychologist,* 1959, *14,* 167–179). It is an article I assign to every one of my students, and for two reasons. The first is that the participants, who met over several days, were as scientifically eminent as could be gathered. The second reason was in the major conclusion of the meeting: the picture you get of how scientists *think and work,* either from their publications or from the corpus of writings on scientific thinking and method, is dramatically discrepant from the "private picture" these individuals held. When you read the scientific literature, you cannot escape the impression of the researcher as one who seeks, gains, and transforms knowledge through vigorous, logical, objective thought processes, that is, complete formal operations. "That does not describe me or my thought processes"— that is what these scientists were saying.

As luck would have it, that article got dredged up the morning of the day I was to have my weekly lunch with Wendell Garner, a participant in that meeting and my closest friend at Yale. It wasn't all luck! I told him about what I had been thinking (Southbury, strands, Piaget, the meeting). He not only agreed with my conclusion (he is more than familiar with Piaget), but he went on to relate the following story. At one point in that 1959 meeting someone asked this question: "How would you describe your mental set when you read a research article or you are listening to someone reading a research paper?'' The question engendered embarrassment, because, it turned out, the consensus was that only in a very secondary way were they interested in understanding the writer or lecturer in his or her terms: what was done, why it was done, and how the results are explained. On the contrary, their set was: "Is there anything here that is connected to what I am thinking about and working on?" I am not interested here in labeling or describing the set further. Whatever you call it, it should not obscure what to me has long been a glimpse of the obvious: how we attain and seek knowledge, how that knowledge gets organized and how we organize it (two different processes), how we "play around" with that knowledge, and how we act in relation to that knowledge (be it as scientists or laypeople) is vastly more complex *and* interesting than Piaget's writings suggest. Piaget talked to and about young children and adolescents. If he had told us how he talks to himself, how he experienced the knowing process, he would have given us a more realistic picture in which the significance of formal operations and logical-deductive thinking would be less isolated in the mosaic of the knowing process.

I have always been interested in me, a fact that I know can be variously interpreted. What I mean by that fact is that I have always been fascinated and puzzled by what goes on in my head: thoughts, dreams, fantasies, questions—in their concreteness, substance, antecedents, and consequences, all leading to the conclusion that what went on in my head was unique in human history. That I was both unique and not unique was something that my exposure to psychology taught me, although my sense of uniqueness was always the center of my interest. There is no doubt that I was attracted to psychology because of what I wanted to learn about myself and the mysteries of my makeup. I had personal problems I wanted illuminated, but there was more to it than that. I was curious about myself. So, in every psychology course I ever took, I read and listened with the set, what was this telling me about myself? Was it true for me?

Which brings me to my entering psychoanalytical therapy. Being at Southbury presented some seemingly insuperable obstacles to an analysis. The war was on, I had no car, and the schedule of the Flying Eagle Busline was the opposite of convenient or dependable. Conceivably, by taking the early afternoon bus on Friday I could get into New York in time for an analytical hour and then another on Saturday. Was there an analyst who would be willing to see me on a one- or two-hour-a-week basis? Would the analytical fee rule out eating? On what basis could I justify asking Mr. Roselle to permit me to work a half day on Friday? The last question was the easiest to answer, because Esther and I wanted to take Bruno Klopfer's seminars on the Rorschach at Teachers College of Columbia University, and Mr. Roselle, to his everlasting credit, respected those who sought more training. If the timing was right, we could take the seminar and I would have the analytical hour.

I discussed these problems with David Shakow. He recommended that I talk with Dr. Bela Mittelmann, a well-known psychiatrist-analyst in Manhattan. David concluded the conversation by saying, "He will be easy on you." That was a puzzling statement that got clarified when I went to talk with Dr. Mittelmann. He was a short, mild-mannered man who smiled easily and warmly and whose facial expression always seemed ready to give expression to humor. He was a refugee, and before the meeting I had found out that he was married to a well-known clinical psychologist, Dr. Ruth Monroe. Somewhat later I learned (not from him, of course) that he was friends with Abraham Maslow at Brooklyn College. Several years later they coauthored a textbook in abnormal psychology.

I do not know whether David Shakow communicated with him before that interview. In any event, he could not have been more understanding of what I wanted and why. He agreed that I needed and could benefit from an analysis. But he could see me only on Saturday morning, and what he wanted to know was how many years I was ready to devote to being on the couch each Saturday morning. He was reassured by my reply, and I then asked whether what I would be experiencing on a once-a-week basis would be considered a kosher analysis. I forget the specifics of his answer, but he made it clear that he would regard it as kosher. The fee was $25 an hour, which in 1942 was about average. I was then earning $2,280 a year, from which $316 was deducted for room and board. I was not yet married, but, as I told Dr. Mittlemann, I was in love and intended to marry Esther within the next year.

What did I gain as person and psychologist from being on the couch? The distinction contained in the question makes no phenomenological sense. The experience was concrete and devoid of jargon and abstraction; it was about several interrelated "me's": lover, son, brother, psychologist, child, adult, Jew, friend, political radical, the whole shmear implied by that inadequate phrase "a person." But several things stand out as revelatory of me and relevant for the purposes of this autobiography. The first has to do with the set with which I approached the therapy, and it was in no way different from that with which I approached college, graduate school, or Southbury: I was going to have a mind-boggling experience that would broaden and deepen me, that would make me special in some way, that would answer my questions and make me wise. I looked forward to it with joy and eagerness. Of course, I wanted my personal problems to evaporate, but, truly, no less important was that I would understand "really" how the mind works, what Freud put into words but that to me was still largely words and abstractions. Spill my guts? That would be easy, and if it wasn't, think of what I would be learning!

Freud said that dreams were the royal road to the unconscious, but I expected that psychoanalytical therapy traversed many roads, all leading to the most stimulating vista of the human mind. Today, psychoanalytical language and theory have seeped into our language and world view in all fields in the humanities and the social sciences. But in 1942, psychoanalysis was outside of academia, its language or jargon unfamiliar but alluring, its difference from and challenge to academic psychology and psychiatry as obvious as they were unacceptable, and its status as a therapy a blend of shamanism, fascination, and indoctrination—another transplantation to American soil of an alien psychology that would remain alien. On the surface, the attitude of academia was one of dutiful tolerance and an abiding skepticism; something not to be accepted and yet something that could not be rejected out of hand. It is no wonder that the American Psychoanalytic Association set out to make psychoanalysis a respectable medical specialty to be studied and evaluated on a scientific basis; that is, to keep it out of the hands of those who would debase it. Institutionally speaking, that association did not regard psychoanalysis as an encompassing psychology that different people in different disciplines should and could make use of; it was a medical specialty. They were quite aware that there were people in different disciplines who showed interest in psychoanalytical theory and therapy, but that interest was no warrant for psychoanalytical training except for a miniscule (that is an exaggeration) number of people who promised *in writing* that they would not engage in psychoanalytical therapy. Neither then nor now do professionals, including psychologists, understand how psychoanalysis, as theory and therapy, was shaped by American medicine and the pathetic desire of American psychiatrists to be seen as "real doctors" in the halls of American medicine. To me, in 1942, psychoanalysis was a kind of "forbidden fruit" that I was going to steal and taste.

There is no doubt that the fundamental rule (for the patient) in analysis, free association—to let your mind wander and roam unconstricted by reason, logic, reflection, or conscious purpose—reinforced in me a habit of thinking to which I was, relatively speaking, accustomed. As I said earlier, I was always fascinated and puzzled by my associations, why certain contents appeared together in my head or how they might be related to each other. If anything had impressed me in my readings of Freud, it was that the stream of thought and its substance were not random phenomena but rather had interrelated personal significances, meanings, or motifs. I looked forward to getting on the analytical couch to ferret out these meanings, to make better sense of what I regarded as strange concatenations of thought and feeling tinged with pleasure, pain, fear, and anxiety. I did not seek analysis because of difficulties in working or social relationships or intimacies. Someone once said that analysis is most productive for those who need it the least. That was true for me, a statement that in no way glosses over the fact that I felt I needed the analysis to understand why I thought about what I did in the way I did. I was intellectually and personally curious about myself. Although the intellectual motivation was there, and strong, I knew that I was not walking into a seminar!

So, for example, in one of the early hours I was relating what memory said was one of my earliest experiences: I am standing on the roof of the building where we lived in Brooklyn and urinating over the edge. I am relating this almost casually, in part motivated by my conception of what one talks about on the analytical couch. As I was relating the memory, I became aware that it is a fiction, an obvious fiction. That my overprotective, Jewish mother would allow her three- or four-year-old child to be alone on the roof of the apartment building was ridiculous, let alone allowing him to stand by the edge to urinate! Besides, there was a parapet around the roof that was taller than I would have been. I was dumb struck. What I had always regarded as a "real" experience was sheer fantasy. But what was more fascinating to me than that fact were the strands of thought and experience, heretofore seemingly unrelated, that immediately, floodlike, cascaded before me in a most integrated and compelling way.

How do you adequately convey in language the disorganizing and organizing effects of such an experience (there were others) on your conception of self and the world? Of "truth"? Such experiences had two paradoxical consequences: at the same time that they made me more suspicious of how I explained me to myself, they reinforced in me the tendency to "let my mind go," that is, to seek connections among thoughts and experiences where none were evident. Put more generally, at the same time that the analysis "shrank" me, it emboldened me to regard myself as a representative sample of the human race: I was unique and representative at the same time. My goal was to capitalize on the uniqueness, feet of clay notwithstanding. It is my impression that it is only in the past two decades that psychotherapists have been called "shrinks." Intuitively, I feel that that label bespeaks a cultural change reflective of a strong need of young people for direction and external control. Choice of language is not a random affair. I never thought of my analysis as a shrinking process—humbling, yes, but primarily a process of enlargement.

It would be incomplete and misleading to convey the impression that the major benefit of my analysis resided in the illumination of my intrapsychic dynamics. The fact is that what was most impressive was how illumination depended on social context. No one would quarrel with the assertion that from day one of our lives we are social beings. To ferret out what that means and has meant in our lives—to know and experience it, to take it seriously—is quite another matter.

Let me illustrate this in the analytical social context: Dr. Mittelmann and me. On a number of occasions, I would get on the couch and begin talking. *Rambling* would be a more apt verb. I would not be aware that I was rambling but rather thought that I was talking about matters about which I felt either puzzled or ashamed or both. I would go on that way for as long as thirty or forty minutes, Dr. Mittelmann remaining silent. He would then ask me in his warm and quietly probing way, "What is your attitude toward me and the analysis?" And when I would begin to answer the question, what was puzzling and bothersome about what I had been recounting became comprehensible. What I had been recounting were *my* thoughts and feelings, but their substance and purpose were at every step a function of *our* relationship. What was true of the analytical relationship was no less true in any other relationship. That kind of understanding became second nature in me. In later years, when I supervised clinical students in psychotherapy, I was struck by how difficult it was for them to gain that understanding, if only because they had not had the kinds of experience that gave flesh to the dry bones of abstraction.

The analysis was of enormous help to me at Southbury. For one thing, I came to understand the residents in relation to me (and vice versa) in a more complex way, both in my therapeutic work and in diagnostic testing with standard and projective techniques. In addition, without ever saying so directly, Dr. Mittelmann accepted me, my work, and my ambitions. That was no small benefit. But there was one thing that he did on one occasion that forever stayed with me. It says a lot about him and how *an* experience can be influential. During an analytical hour, he said to me that he had made a mistake—"I was wrong" were his words—in an interpretation he had given me two weeks before. If *he* could make a mistake, how could *I* not emulate him? It is not fortuitous that in all of my teaching and in some of my writings my mistakes have played a prominent role. I like to characterize my development and career as going from and capitalizing on a major mistake in thinking and action, and then blithely proceeding to make new mistakes. I put it earlier as going from one fog into another. But each fog contained a major mistake.

Before beginning analysis, I was a partisan for psychoanalysis as theory, therapy, and a basis for research. The analysis strengthened that partisanship, but in one respect it planted the seeds for my later disenchantment with psychoanalysis as theory. I have emphasized that the analysis was totally devoid of jargon and theory. I cannot recall that words such as *ego, superego, id, resistance,* or *oedipus complex* were ever used, certainly not by Dr. Mittelmann. The analysis had a concreteness, a kind of palpability, an immediacy that psychoanalytical jargon and theory effectively obscure. One could argue that the purpose of theory is to explain, not describe, phenomena and, therefore, to seek to interrelate concepts that give added meanings to those phenomena. That is to say, theory is a necessary, organized fiction that derives from the concrete and the observable but is intended to come up with new or altered or more differentiated conclusions about the concrete and observable that subsequent experience will confirm. Before, during, and after the analysis, I steeped myself in the theoretical literature of psychoanalysis. I could not escape the feeling that its theory and its jargon illuminated little the phenomena from which the theory derived and for which it sought more powerfully encompassing explanations. But who was I to question the adequacy of theory, to say that the language of the theory seemed light years away from concrete experience, to criticize using concepts as if they were discrete pieces on a chessboard? I could and did parade my knowledge of psychoanalytical theory as if it stood in a clear relationship to my experience in analysis. I was a partisan, and if I had questions about the theory, that fact, I felt, said more about my conceptual inadequacies than it did about anything else. It was in every respect identical to my partisanship for Marxist theory. I stilled the doubting voice within me.

Analysis was a memorable personal experience. Southbury was a memorable professional experience. It was at Southbury that I met a man whose influence on my intellectual development was momentous. He deserves a separate chapter.

8

Discovering the Significance of Art for Psychology and Education

I called him Schaefer, he called me Seymour. When we met at Southbury in 1943, I was twenty-four; he was forty-five. I was American; he was a political refugee from Hitler Germany, having come here several years before. I was a psychologist; he had been a professor of art history and art education in Frankfurt. He lived in Manhattan. He had received a special fellowship from the Russell Sage Foundation to pursue his studies of artistic activity. He was visiting Southbury to determine whether it would be possible and feasible to conduct studies with mentally retarded individuals. That was what Mr. Roselle told me about Henry Schaefer-Simmern before I met him. Typically, Mr. Roselle was proud that Russell Sage had asked him to consider providing "the Professor" with a studio where he and his students could work. Mr. Roselle had already decided where the studio would be and what other material resources would be provided. My job would be to help select the kind of resident Schaefer considered appropriate to his goals and to be as helpful as I could be in making his stay at Southbury productive for him and us. He would be coming up for two or three days each week. A small apartment would be provided him.

Schaefer was a tall, large man with piercing eyes in a serious face. His English was comprehensible but with a decided German accent. Initially, he struck me as fitting my stereotype of a Prussian: deadly serious, rigid, authoritarian, forceful, opinionated. I had never met a political refugee from Hitler Germany. And here was one who struck me as "typically" German, the kind of person who made Hitler possible. It was not a difficult first meeting. We were both polite, obviously feeling each other out. How could I be helpful to him, I asked. He answered by attempting to explain his "theory" of artistic development and activity. It was hard for me to follow him, but two things were clear in what he said: artistic activity was a normal attribute of *all* people, and it was an attribute that the educational system and the culture of which it was a part effectively extinguished in its misguided belief that art was (had to be) the copying of reality. Schaefer's life goal had been and would continue to be to demonstrate the validity of his theory with individuals who were considered uncreative or considered themselves uncreative. He had worked with workers, institutionalized delinquents, among other groups. He had never worked with mentally retarded individuals, and that is why he was at Southbury. What he wanted from me was a list of residents with whom I thought he could work. We would then call each to my office and Schaefer would talk with them and ask them to draw anything they wanted, on the basis of which Schaefer would make his selection. I said I would prepare the list and he could begin to see each of these residents the following week, when he would begin his two- or three-day visits to Southbury. What he was after and how to prepare such a list mystified me. Were this man and his mission going to be an ongoing, unsought burden?

That first meeting had consequences for me. One was the memory it engendered of a traumatic event I had experienced in the third or fourth grade. It was during a class conducted by a "drawing" teacher. She came into the room with a coffee percolator, passed out paper, and told us to draw the percolator. I remember asking myself, why are we being asked to draw the percolator? I tried, oh did I try, to draw that damned percolator, but only by the wildest stretches of the imagination did it remotely look like the percolator. I looked around me and saw that the other children were drawing percolators that looked like Mrs. Pearson's percolator. Why couldn't I do it? Which is exactly the question Mrs. Pearson asked me. Psychologically I began to shrivel up, I was flooded with anxiety, and I wanted to cry. Was this what Schaefer was talking about when he said that requiring children to copy reality doomed them to failure and to regard themselves as devoid of artistic ability? Was this what he meant when he said that even if the artist wants to, he or she cannot duplicate reality because reality is too complex? Was I not one of those people socialized to believe that artistic ability was a special ability that the fates obviously had denied me? Schaefer became more interesting to me.

The second consequence was the realization that for all practical purposes I knew nothing about art. I knew the names of the great artists. I had gone to see the Van Gogh exhibit because it was an event, a happening, going to which testified to one's respect for "culture." In that first meeting, Schaefer had referred to several artists as if I knew who they were, and he had also emphasized that what he stood for was a direct continuation of the ideas of Gustave Britsch, Conrad Fiedler, and several others, all of whom were well-known figures in the field of theories of art and utterly unknown to me. Schaefer also had told me that he had the highest respect for John Dewey's understanding of the nature and significance of artistic activity. I did not know very much about Dewey except that he was identified with three fields: psychology long ago, philosophy, and education. Schaefer must have sensed my puzzlement about Dewey in relation to art, because he said that Dewey's book *Art as Experience* (New York: Minton, Balch, 1934) was a twentieth-century classic that I *must* read. (Schaefer was incapable of making a suggestion with neutral affect.)

The third was less a consequence in the narrow sense than a vague intuition that I was not in the same league with him, that he was a man of vast erudition capable of high-order conceptualizing and theorizing, that in any relationship with him I would be a student and probably not a good one. That in no way lessened my own sense of worth. I felt that I had met a man who lived and pushed the intellectual life to its limits, and I envied him.

Before going on with the development of our relationship—one that terminated with his death several years ago at age eighty-one—let me relate what happened at the second meeting, when I lined up a dozen or so residents for him to see. I have no clear memory of how I had selected them. All but three were female. Two of the males were known in the institution for their unusual interest in drawing and ability to draw. Their ages ranged from twenty to forty. Their IQs ranged from forty to eighty. Their formal diagnosis was familial retardation, variously called subcultural, garden variety, or Kallikak mental retardation. One of them, who plays an important role in this story, was also psychotic, but not obviously so. Why I included her I cannot remember. They had been at Southbury, or the older institution at Mansfield, from a minimum of three to a maximum of twenty years.

I brought each resident in and introduced him or her to Schaefer. They sat at my desk, and I sat a couple of feet away and could observe both of them. On the basis of my impression of Schaefer from the first meeting, I was fearful that his imposing bulk would intimidate the residents, that his German accent would not be intelligible to them, and that his serious, forbidding manner would be an obstacle to rapport. I watched him with that first resident, and I was flabbergasted. It was as if his entire musculature relaxed, his voice lowered and softened, and he looked at and spoke to the resident with *respect*. I do not know how else to put it. It was not only that he showed interest but that he regarded the resident with a mixture of curiosity, tenderness, and importance. He did not smile, he was always task oriented, and he was always accepting. Do you like to draw, paint, color? What do you like to draw? He gently asked these and related questions, and then he gave them a sheet of paper and requested that they draw whatever they wanted. When they were through, he looked with great interest at what they had drawn. Several questions might follow. Do you like what you have done? Would you like to try to do it again or draw something else? Is there anything about the drawing you do not like? That you would like to change? He spent at least fifteen minutes with each child.

During it all, I kept wondering on what basis he would select residents for his "studio." Would he choose Rudy, whose florid, semichaotic drawings had such graceful, flowing lines? Would he choose Selma, who drew stick figures, and very simple ones? Within one minute after the last resident left, Schaefer told me which six he had chosen. How did you choose, I asked him? He divided the drawings into two groups, spreading them out in a way as to make comparisons possible.

It did not require study to conclude that there was an obvious difference. The drawings of the residents who were not selected were, relatively speaking, complicated in a busy way, with overlapping lines, figures, and objects. The drawings of the selected residents could be called primitive, Selma's stick figures being an example. To me, the drawings of the unselected residents were more "artistic." I asked Schaefer why he made the choices he did. His answer remains vivid in my mind. It is not a verbatim quotation, I am sure, but the italicized words or sentences reflect his emphasis. In an intellectual discussion, Schaefer rarely uttered a sentence that did not contain at least one word to which he gave special emphasis. "These [referring to unselected residents] are drawings from *memory*. They tried to imitate *reality*. And the more they tried to do the *impossible—no* artist, *not even da Vinci,* can *copy* reality in all its details—the more the visual chaos. They did not draw according to an inner process of *visual conceiving* but according to their cognitions about reality, and, therefore, it is a memory game. Their artistic development has been *spoiled*. They tried to do something far beyond their level of visual conceiving. These [referring to the selected residents] are not yet *spoiled*. They drew what *they* can *see* in accordance with their level of visual conceiving. They did not *intend* to copy reality. To *you* it is primitive: there are no overlapping lines, each figure stands by itself, each figure is made up of circles and horizontal and vertical lines, *you cannot change the direction of any one line without changing the other lines.* Primitive, *yes,* but in accordance with *their* level of visual conceiving, their level of *gestalt formation.* They see on the paper what they *can* see, not what reality says they *should* see. They are not yet *spoiled.* They can develop. I shall work with them.''

I felt that what he said was terribly important, but I could hardly digest it. During the next few days, I found myself obsessively returning to what he had said. I replayed again and again my experience with having to draw the percolator. Could there be any doubt that what he had said explained in large part my inability to meet the requirements of copying reality, that trying to represent the curvatures of the percolator was way beyond whatever Schaefer meant by my level of visual conceiving? Was he not right in his view that artistic creativity is a universal human attribute that gets extinguished in most of us because we are unable to meet external criteria discrepant with our level of development, what he called our stage of development of visual conceiving? Was not his emphasis on the gestalt qualities of an artistic effort—that the integrity of the forms on the paper are reflective of an internal conceptual integrity—completely consistent with what I knew from the writings of the Gestalt psychologists such as Wertheimer, Koffka, Köhler?

About one thing I was crystal clear: Schaefer, like me, held the Rousseau-like view that our culture in general, and our educational institutions in particular, do an effective job in masking human potential. Unlike me, Schaefer held that view in relation to a specific type of human activity for which he was formulating a stage-developmental theory based on longitudinal studies of individuals. (There is more to it than individual studies, but that comes later.) Like me, Schaefer came to Southbury to demonstrate that "*even* mentally retarded people are capable of more than we think."

But there was another thing about those first two meetings that bothered and stirred me. Why was my education so utterly devoid of exposure to the world of art? And in education I include my graduate training in psychology. Not only had I never been exposed to psychology in relation to art, but I could not remember any seminar in which the nature of creativity had been discussed. I knew and used Goodenough's Draw-A-Man test, but that was an *intelligence* test. If Schaefer was right, as intuitively I felt he was, psychologists, like everyone else, believed that art required a special ability. You either had it or you didn't. And precisely because it was a special and infrequent ability, why should it be in the mainstream of the field? If someone had a special interest in a special ability, then he or she should pursue that interest, but that was no warrant for saying that it should be of general interest to psychology, or for it occupying time in the education of psychologists. And here was Schaefer insisting that artistic ability was universal and contained keys to understanding the nature and vicissitudes of human creativity!

Following the second meeting in my office—he was at Southbury for three days—I sought him out and plied him with questions. It was the beginning of a father-son, teacher-student, friend relationship. I did not know it then, but Schaefer was a lonely man. It was not only that his ideas ran counter to conventional wisdom. He was not an easy person to be with. That was the judgment of most people. Our forty-year relationship was a personal and intellectual delight. He was a man of single purpose: his work and his ideas were his life. He would talk about these matters with passion. Little else interested him. To say that he did not suffer fools gladly is truly an extreme form of understatement. He was not an ogre. He was not a hostile person. He was incapable of small talk. If you treated him with respect, he would be polite and gracious even if inside he had disdain for you. Schaefer was an elitist, and in a strange way. He felt comfortable with "ordinary" people who did not pretend to be intellectuals. In his words, they were not "spoiled." But God help you if you were an inhabitant of the intellectual world and, in Schaefer's view, a superficial thinker, a dilettante, a self-aggrandizing entrepreneur, a status-seeking climber— singly or in any combination. His disdain could be of majestic proportions, although he usually hid it and would avoid these people like the plague. His experience in and around academia produced few people he could respect. Few people met his standards either of intellectual seriousness or of personal conduct. If he cottoned to me, it was because it was obvious that I was interested in his ideas and work, respected him, was willing to be helpful, and put right out on the table that in matters of art I was an ignoramus who wanted to learn. I was and am no shrinking violet, and I could challenge and argue with him about anything without arousing the slightest sense of pique. We never articulated what was obvious. We loved each other.

As a result of my questions, Schaefer brought up the following week a series of "cases" each of which contained the artistic development of individuals none of whom ever considered themselves artists. Two were unforgettable. Indeed, my initial reaction was one of disbelief. When you looked at their first and their latest efforts, it was the difference between crawling and running, between knowing that one and one are two and being able to solve a quadratic equation. In all of the cases, the initial productions were simple and ordered, possessing gestalt qualities, but in no way impressive to a viewer. As you went from one drawing to another, you could see slight but increasing differentiation and complexity. By the time you reached their latest drawings or paintings or sculptures, you would have visions of delight at the prospect of having them on display in your home. But during and after viewing the several cases, I had a sinking sensation around the troubling thought that this single-minded, obsessed, intellectual missionary was totally unaware that he had instructed these individuals how to do or improve their drawings. My training as a psychologist may have been incomplete or deficient in a number of respects but not in regard to how easy it is for our passionately held ideas and values to influence and direct the behavior of others, especially in relationships of unequal power and status. If that was the case with Schaefer, it was also the case that I could not discuss it with him. I had better, I thought, tread very lightly. And, yet, there was a part of me that wanted (indeed, needed) to believe that he was right.

It is not a digression here to discuss Carl Rogers's *Counseling and Psychotherapy* (Boston: Houghton Mifflin, 1942), which was published the year before Schaefer came to Southbury. It is hard to exaggerate the impact of that book on me particularly and psychology generally. For one thing, here was a psychologist writing about psychotherapy; that is, presenting his therapeutic work and offering a very distinctive conceptualization that determined his technique. Nondirective psychotherapy did not *impose* restrictions on the therapist but rather enabled him or her to be exquisitely sensitive to what a client was saying in the here and now. Personal history, the results of diagnostic testing, unconscious meanings, and the like had relevance only insofar as they were contained in what the client *said* he or she was thinking and feeling *at the moment* in the relationship. The task of the therapist was to state or restate what the client said, as if one were holding up an auditory "mirror" for the client to see himself or herself, to examine and re-examine what they had said about themselves. And, Rogers argued and his cases indicated, that process of examination and re-examination enabled the client to clarify and reformulate perception of self and problem. The client possessed the seeds of change and growth; the nondirective technique enabled the client to see and nurture those seeds. The therapist did not direct or interpret but rather stated or restated the client's communication *as if* to say: "Is this what you are saying? Is this what you mean for me to understand?" So, to a client who says that he or she feels unloved, Rogers might say, "Are you saying that *no one* on this earth loves or has affection for you?" To which the client would likely say, "Oh, no, there are people who love me, like *A* or *B* or *C*. What I meant was. . . ."

That a psychologist was doing, theorizing about, and writing about psychotherapy in 1942 was startling in itself. But no less startling, truly revolutionary, was that he presented verbatim transcripts of the therapy. I said earlier that Rogers's book had impact on me and psychology. That is a misleading judgment, because his use and publication of verbatim transcripts threw down the gauntlet to the entire mental health community, especially psychiatry, to, so to speak, put up or shut up. It is as if Rogers was saying, "We have had a surfeit of theorizing, anecdotal evidence, case summarizing in regard to what we do and why in psychotherapy. What we have lacked are the raw data by which to judge the relationship among theory, technique, and outcome. In this book you have the raw data by which to judge my ideas, technique, and success." And the outcomes were impressive.

Just as I was not disposed to accept Schaefer's explanation of the work of his students—I could not dispute his "raw data,'' just as the reader could not dispute the validity of Rogers's transcripts—the mental health community was not disposed to accept Rogers's explanation of outcomes. The question that was raised most frequently and cogently was, how nondirective was Rogers? People pored over those transcripts searching for evidence that Rogers was not as nondirective as he said he was or his theory required. My own assessment at the time, not different from that of others, was that Rogers fell short of perfection but that he had a very high batting average. I reached that conclusion reluctantly, because nondirective therapy was so different from the psychoanalytical approaches to which I was very partisan.

All of this was buzzing around in my head during those early weeks with Schaefer. Was Schaefer as nondirective as he claimed? Was there not some kind of implicit affinity between Rogers's belief in a client's capacity to see and alter perceptions without substantive direction from the therapist, and Schaefer's insistence that the ''unfolding'' of artistic activity would be manifested if, and only if, you enabled the person to build on his or her level of visual conceiving uninfluenced by external criteria of how one should draw? And even if Schaefer and Rogers were correct in their explanations, how much of the outcomes they reported was due to the kinds of persons they were? There is theory and there is technique, but there is also a human being in whom they are supposed to be appropriately integrated. And if we know anything about that integration, it is how dramatically different it looks in different people. From my observations of Schaefer with residents in my office, I knew he was capable of being with them in a warm, sensitive, and dispassionate way—those observations were indeed compelling, contrasting as they did with his usual manner.

What came to mind was an experience I had at Clark observing Charlotte Bühler through a one-way screen with a young child. In 1939–40, Charlotte and Karl Bühler were at Clark for the year as visiting professors. Karl had been one of the greats in European psychology. He was known in America, but to a far lesser extent, because many of his works were untranslated. When he came to this country (he was not Jewish, Charlotte was), he was a defeated, depressed man but quintessentially the responsive gentleman. Charlotte, who had been one of his students, had a deserved international reputation in child development. And Charlotte not only considered herself a queen, but she acted and dressed accordingly. She was seen by students as fascinating, arrogant, cold, and impossible. On the first day of her seminar, she began by telling us of a meeting "at which I took place." She then asked us whether we had heard about or read anything of Freud. Midway in the seminar, she said that she wanted us to observe her with a child. *That* we had to see! It was inconceivable to us that she could do other to the girl than intimidate and scare her. We were flabbergasted by what we saw and heard. Neither before nor since have I seen anyone more comforting and sensitive with a preschooler, or elicit in a more nondirective way what interested the child; that is, follow where the child psychologically was and wanted to go. If she was directive, it escaped us. If we had a videotape of that session, I am sure one could find elements of directiveness, as in the case of Rogers. But those elements would not obscure her "ability" to build on what was in the mind of the child, to bring to configurated expression what was inside that young girl's head.

How did Schaefer get his students to develop artistically as his longitudinal case material demonstrated? How consistent was he with his view that every "unspoiled" person was capable of a stagelike development, each stage of which had its own visual-conceptual, gestalt properties that could not and should not be hurried or bypassed? Did he really enable or empower that process without "teaching" them, without telling them what and how to draw? I wanted very much to believe that Schaefer was correct, because it would confirm my conviction that we vastly underestimate human abilities, their nature, variety, and vicissitudes. But when I looked at those longitudinal case studies of "ordinary people," I had to be skeptical. And he was proposing to demonstrate his view by working with institutionalized, mentally retarded people! There was a part of me that said, a likely story!

I spent a lot of time in that studio at Southbury. Schaefer met with his students two or three consecutive mornings a week.

Over a two-year period, he started and ended with the same residents, probably six to eight in number. When you walked into the studio, you would be struck by the fact that each student was working in the most concentrated way on his or her drawing—not for five or ten minutes but over long periods of time. They might stop and *study* what they had done, add a line or figure, or take another piece of paper and start over. They might get up and converse with someone else about what they were doing, why, and the problem they were having. If you observed what each student was doing, you would have to note that no two students were drawing the same thing in terms of content, color, and complexity. You would label each of them as simple or primitive by the same criteria by which you would label a Grandma Moses painting; that is, there were no overlapping lines (early in their development), each figure or object was distinct, and the whole thing added up to a gestalt so that *if you changed the direction of one line, or changed a color, you would have to change almost everything else in the work.* You would also note that Schaefer sat at his desk working, usually writing. His interactions with the students were *always* dyadic. He never, but never, addressed them as a class. One of them might walk to his desk and show him what she had just completed. He would study it in the most interested, serious way. Early in the game, the student might ask him: "Do you like this?" And his set response was, "The important thing is whether *you* like it. Is there anything about it you would like to change or add? You are doing fine. If you started again, would you do it the same way? *Do you see what you want to see?*" That last question was, it turned out, crucial, because it required the student to reflect and study the work, and, far more often than not, it elicited some kind of dissatisfaction with this or that aspect, or a suggestion from the student as to what the next effort would be. Several times a student said, for example, that the tree he or she had drawn did not look like a "real" tree. To which Schaefer would respond with supportive emphasis: "No one can draw a real tree. There are too many branches, too many leaves. That is impossible. You have to draw it so that *you* see *what you* want to see." Schaefer was certainly directive when he would tell the students that trying to copy reality would get them into "visual" trouble—as he would say to me, "That leads to mental confusion and chaos, and the person gives up or draws an abstraction, not a visual conception." But that kind of direction was for the explicit purpose of reinforcing self-direction. Schaefer was able to get the students not to ignore reality but to transform it in ways satisfactory to the eye, what he called a visual conception, a configurated unity, however simple. He got them to study and reflect, happily to struggle and persevere, to a degree that was utterly unpredictable from their case histories and test results.

There were times when he would study a work and say, pointing to a particular part of it, "Were you having trouble here?" Or he might say about that part, "How do you feel about that?" And there were times when he would say to a student dissatisfied with what she had done, "Maybe if you took a larger piece of paper and worked with crayons, you might like it better."

The point of all this is that Schaefer intruded minimally into a student's development. And he was patient. Over a period of weeks, a student might have made a couple of dozen or more drawings with no two being the same. On quick glance, drawing *B* would look like drawing *A*, but, as Schaefer would show me, there was always something different. Drawing *C* would look like *B*, but again there was some kind of difference. It was only when you compared *A* with *Z* that you immediately saw development, a discernible change in visual clarity and gestalt qualities. He never hurried the students. He accepted and respected what they did. He treated them as if they were serious artists, and to Schaefer they were. "What their work has in common with that of da Vinci is the ordered, configurated, gestalt qualities of their artistic expression. They are, of course, at different stages, but that is no reason for overlooking that their work reflects an artistic process of visual conceiving and expression, a universal process and attribute."

There is a problem, this one between me and the reader. It is unsolvable if you mean by solvable that four divided by two is two. At best, language can give you a slight idea of a visual work of art. At worst, it conjures up imagery dramatically different from what the work looks like to the eye. Language may be the best means of communication we have, but as a way of describing art it is very imperfect. I have expressed my surprise and skepticism at what Schaefer had shown me about his previous students and what he proposed to demonstrate at Southbury. I assume that in reading this account the reader has felt frustrated at not being able to see what my words have tried to suggest. It would be strange if the reader felt otherwise. Shortly before Schaefer came to Southbury, he had begun writing a book. His felicity in writing English was barely fair. He was aware of this as he was of the inherent impossibility of using language to describe art. Schaefer accepted my offer to edit the chapters sentence by sentence. We would sit for hours, both of us struggling to make the text illuminate a drawing, to explain the drawing in terms of Schaefer's theory of stages of artistic development. Fortunately, his writing got clearer as he got into the book, reducing somewhat the frustration of finding the right words for what he wanted to say.

The book was finished after I left Southbury and Schaefer went to the University of California at Berkeley. It was published in 1948 by that university's press and has gone through numerous printings. The apt title was *The Unfolding of Artistic Activity*. I entreat the reader to look at and read that book. One of the last things John Dewey wrote was the preface to that book. Schaefer had made it his business to meet Dewey, because he considered Dewey's *Art as Experience* as one of this century's great books, a judgment with which I concurred after Schaefer insisted I read the book. Schaefer opened up for me the world of John Dewey, for which I am eternally grateful.

The employees at all levels of Southbury looked upon Schaefer as a "character," some suspicious because he was German and others, especially those in the education department, because they sensed that he took a very dim view of how the abilities of the residents were regarded and shaped. To most of them, what Schaefer was doing with his students was a frivolous luxury, a waste of good space, materials, and the residents' time and energies. After several months, given the finely honed efficiency of an institution gossip mill, word got around that the residents not only were making some very interesting drawings but were using these drawings to pattern and make rugs, place mats, and wall hangings. Without question, Selma was the resident that was most intriguing to the employees. She was very mentally retarded, introverted in the extreme, and probably schizophrenic to boot. She looked and acted like a cipher; she washed floors, worked in the hot laundry, and bothered no one. No one had visited her for years. Her case history contained a litany of every type of child abuse. Some of the employees had seen her work in the studio (which Schaefer made into a museum), and others began to visit the studio. Schaefer decided to publicly exhibit her work. Her cottage parents agreed to make the cottage into an art gallery for a two-day exhibit over a weekend. What happened over that weekend was what happens when a museum opens a Picasso retrospective, or when the president of the United States opens a world's fair. The crowds descended; there were waiting lines and much talk. What drew the most attention were Selma's rugs made from discarded clothing. More than a few observers would not believe that what they saw were Selma's *creations*. And in the middle of all this was Selma: now beaming, now tearful, now puzzled and overwhelmed by the attention she was receiving.

What Schaefer enabled these residents to accomplish has to be contrasted with another story. After the exhibit, several employees asked Schaefer to ''teach'' them. He was reluctant to do so, because he assumed that they were already unrescuably ''spoiled,'' that is, that they had overlearned the stance that the task of the artist was to copy reality. He liked the employees who made the request, he took satisfaction from the changed attitudes toward him the requests signified, and he agreed to meet with them two evenings a week. I observed carefully what went on during the initial weeks. I rarely have seen people struggling as hard or experience so much frustration. Not only was what they attempted to do in their initial efforts difficult in terms of composition—far beyond what Schaefer would say was their stage of visual conception—but they could not unimprison themselves from the tendency to judge their efforts by the criterion of external reality. They could not go back to the beginning, to those early stages where what the eye sees is simple and ordered and on the basis of which greater ordered complexity becomes possible. They wanted to run before they could crawl or walk. All but two gave up, but those two "got the message" and showed a startling development—startling to them, not to Schaefer. Those observations seared into my mind the conviction—to me it is an unfortunate, brute fact—that in their emphasis on memory and abstractions, their fantastic underestimation and ignoring of curiosity and creativity, the socialization and education processes obscure human capabilities. But, Schaefer would point out, that is not the case in all societies, present or past. Over the years, Schaefer had collected hundreds, if not thousands, of pictures of art (paintings, sculpture, and so on) from cultures in all parts of the world demonstrating stagelike progressions identical to what you will see in his book. What I learned from Schaefer about human abilities, cognitive development, and our educational theories, practices, and institutions influenced everything I have ever done. It is not happenstance that John Dewey saw fit to write the preface to Schaefer's book. Dewey, like Schaefer, saw that where you stand on the nature of artistic activity as an instance of creativity is where you stand on the processes and goals of education. There are very few others—frankly, no other names come to mind—who saw and wrote about that connection with the clarity and incisiveness (and implicit despair) of Dewey and Schaefer.

There was one disagreement between Schaefer and me, one of emphasis rather than principle. Schaefer presented his theory of the development of visual conceiving in a way that could give people the impression that the "unfolding" of artistic activity was, so to speak, programmed in the individual, that if you did not interfere in that unfolding, the development would run its "natural" course. I did not disagree with the thrust of his argument—you could not disagree with the longitudinal "data" he presented—but I felt that he was underplaying the roles of context and meaning. In short, he was underplaying the crucial role he played, past and present, in creating the social context and in acting in ways that enabled or empowered individuals to start and go forward. As with Carl Rogers and Charlotte Bühler, the outcomes of Schaefer's efforts were not independent of what he was as a mentor: the respect he showed his students, the encouragement he gave to them, the patience he had, and, crucially, his sensitivity to the problems a student would encounter within a particular stage and in moving to the next stage (for example, from exclusive use of horizontal and vertical lines to diagonal ones). I was already enough of a clinician to know that whatever the virtues of theory, its operational significance inhered in how it was manifest in practice. When David Shakow said to me that "Dr. Mittelmann would not be hard on you," he was essentially saying, "There are analysts and there are analysts, all subscribing to the same theory, but they don't all read and even understand what they subscribe to in the same way, *and those are differences that make a difference.*" However well I understood Schaefer's theory, never in a million years could I even approach doing what he did. What Schaefer had trouble confronting was his ability to create a context that had all of the characteristics that make for productive learning. When I would contrast the behavior of the Southbury residents in Schaefer's studio—truly a group within which each individual was distinctive and of which Schaefer was a member—with what you would see in classrooms in the school at Southbury, it was the difference between night and day. Schaefer, of course, knew this, but he could not bring himself to give it the significance it deserved. His main task in life, he said again and again, was to demonstrate that artistic activity and development were universal human attributes. *That* is what the world needed to know, and *that* was his mission. The emphasis I entreated him to consider would be the task of others, always a few, who would understand what he had done and written. He had to finish the book he was writing, because then he could start on his magnum opus: demonstrating his theory with art in scores of cultures, past and present. That book would take years, he knew. He was well into middle age, he had had a heart attack, time was not on his side. When he died several years ago at age eighty-one, the book was not finished. It took me years to understand that there was a part of him that felt that when he finished that book, his life would be over, his mission completed. It was as if he delayed and delayed its completion as a way of living with the mission, not completing it. Without the mission to keep him going, he would be more alone than he already was. Whenever we got together, in Berkeley or New Haven, I would implore, encourage, beg him to get it done. I had seen the "data" that would be in the book. I knew that he took yearly trips to Germany because there was a company there that could make the reproductions the way he wanted. To say that Schaefer was a perfectionist is a monumental understatement.

No one can understand me as person or professional without knowing my relationship with Schaefer. What I absorbed from him, as I shall shortly elaborate, took place in the best of all contexts in which the intellectual, interpersonal, and social features were indissolubly integrated. Schaefer would often say that I was one of a few people who understood his theory. I could never bring myself to say that that was a misleading judgment, that what I understood was the lack of boundaries among his theory, his practice, and *him*.

What did I get from Schaefer? Let me start with something that was both humbling and unsettling. Schaefer was the first person I knew who had a truly classical education. I once said to a friend, "Why should I buy the *Encyclopedia Britannica,* when I have Schaefer?" His knowledge of languages and world history was staggering. And when I say knowledge, I do not mean facts. It was knowledge organized for his purposes. It was as if all of human experience and knowledge existed for him to use depending on his immediate purpose. Rarely did we have a discussion without his connecting and illustrating it by reference to some past figure, event, or era, with line and verse. For example, I do not remember the specific focus of the conversation, but at one point he said something like this: "That is something Goethe understood and wrote about in his diary of his trip through Italy. He was in Perugia that summer, in July, and. . . ." On another occasion, when we were struggling for the words to describe the problem one of the residents was having in her drawing, Schaefer stopped for a moment as if lost in reflection and then said that what the resident was confronted with was beautifully illustrated in a series of murals painted by an unknown Egyptian artist several thousand years ago during the reign of a pharaoh whose name Schaefer gave, and then he went on to say in which museum it was housed. Philosophy, social history, intellectual history, religious history—it is as if he had it all in his head, productively organized and usable.

What was unsettling about this was not only the fact that I had not had a classical education but the dawning realization that education in America has severed its roots and connections with what was best in the traditions of classical education. The sense of history and rootedness—that was what had gone by the boards in education in America. Separated from the rest of the world by two vast oceans, we were also separated from our roots, from a sense of continuity. Schaefer understood this, but what he bemoaned most was our ignorance of the fact that the American world view was incomprehensible without the sense of history and continuity. But there was another source of my unsettlement. If I knew a fraction of what Schaefer knew, I would be a better psychologist. If American psychology grounded itself, as it did and does, in the narrow (relatively speaking) traditions of science, its view of humanity would have all of the deficits of rampant parochialism. A psychology that regarded creativity as a small and narrow tributary of the mainstream of psychology—worthy, of course, of study but not central to understanding human behavior—was an impoverished psychology. What Schaefer drummed into my head was that artistic activity was central for a number of reasons, not the least of which was the way it required us to look at the educational process in our schools. He would become literally livid when he described how our schools extinguished rather than nurtured the unfolding of human capacities. Working, as I was, in an educational institution (for the mentally retarded no less) meant that I was far from the mainstream of American psychology. That didn't bother me. What Schaefer did was to make me proud that I was in an arena of thought and work fateful for a society. Before I met Schaefer, I wanted to save the world. After I met him, I knew that I would do it in the field of education. I was no less grandiose than Schaefer. Our grandiosity was one of the ties that bound us together. If a part of each of us knew how unrealistic we were, we helped each other ignore it.

It was not simply that Schaefer had a classical education but that he milked it. From the time I met Schaefer, especially after I left Southbury and came to Yale in 1945, the substance and goals of education in America became a dominating interest in my life, but not without its problems. On the one hand, if I pursued that interest, I would have to not only re-educate myself but also forego a career in an academic psychology that regarded the field of education with at best disinterest and at worst derogation. On the other hand, I did have strong interests in problems that were more attuned to the zeitgeist in psychology that I wanted to pursue. The conflict would wax and wane. It would wax when I would meet or listen to senior members of the classics or history departments. It would wane when I was immersed in researching and writing about mental retardation, anxiety, and the clinical situation. And even when it waned, Schaefer was in my head reminding me of my ignorance of people, eras, problems, and traditions that as a student of human behavior I should and needed to know. I knew that our world was not born yesterday, but that is about all I knew. I read voluminously and indiscriminately, but it was untutored reading. Schaefer was out in California, and I was a beginning assistant professor at Yale. The only solace I had derived from the fact, which I successfully kept secret, was that I knew I was by classical standards the uneducated American. I judged myself, then as today, not by a relative but by an absolute standard.

A second benefit I derived from Schaefer was a heightened sensitivity to the obvious: You are what you are because, among other things, you are an American and not a German, or Englishman, or Frenchman. If you want to understand yourself or others, you cannot ignore the fact that you have been socialized into a particular society or one of its distinctive parts. The differences are reflected in language, behavior, and world view, differences that have to be understood before they are judged, although these differences predispose us to judge and to bypass understanding. To someone like Schaefer, these differences were not abstractions but stimuli to understanding. Interested (indeed,

obsessed) as he was in art in myriad societies and cultures—
how and why it differed in content, style, and level of artistic
achievement—his task was to understand these differences in
the terms of each distinctive society and culture. Schaefer was
more than an art historian, a type about whom he had very
mixed feelings. He was a historian of cultures. Schaefer was the
first person to force me to confront the implications of the fact
that I was American. He never did this directly, but it was impossible to be with him and not be aware that we were dramatically different kinds of people in part because he was German
and I was American. It was the differences that fascinated me.
One incident stands out, an incident that on the surface may
seem trivial and comic but to me made the cultural differences
between German him and American me real.

It was in 1943, several months after Schaefer had married an American woman, his second wife. We had a date to
go to the Metropolitan Museum in New York. I was to come
to his apartment, meet his new wife, and then go to the museum.
I had two immediate reactions when I entered the apartment.
The first was that Gudrun was as gracious and sensitive a woman
as I had ever met. In personality and appearance, she resembled
Eleanor Roosevelt. The second reaction was that the electricity
of conflict suffused the air. Obviously, there had been a quarrel. After about ten minutes, Schaefer realized my discomfort
(and his own), and he said, "Seymour, I want you to listen to
what happened yesterday and to give your honest opinion."
On the previous day, one of Gudrun's best friends from another
state had come to visit and to meet Schaefer. According to
Schaefer, she breezed into the apartment and when introduced
to him exclaimed, "Henry, it is a pleasure to meet you."
Finished with his account, he looked at me and asked, "What
do you think of *that?*" I looked at him blankly, expecting him
to continue the story, to clarify the question. He saw my puzzlement, a puzzled look appeared on his face, and finally he blurted,
"She called me *Henry*. *You* don't even call me Henry." Having
taken a year of German, I vaguely knew that the use of *du* and
sie depended on the depth of a relationship, and, therefore, for
a complete stranger to call Schaefer Henry was unforgivably

gross. I contained my inner laughter only because I realized, fortunately, that I was witness to a misunderstanding produced by two different ways of viewing social relationships, only one of the ways such views shaped relationships. The incident, of course, said a lot about Schaefer's personality, but to stop there would be to trivialize the implications of it. As a clinician, I had been taught that my task was to understand a patient in his or her terms. Nothing in my education and training had exposed me to applying the principle to individuals culturally different from me. Psychology was psychology, anthropology was anthropology, and putting them together was not an obligation of psychology! If my undergraduate education was far from classical, my professional education and training were even more parochial in terms of understanding diversity of human behavior in diverse cultures.

And that brings me to the Hampton Cafeteria on Madison Avenue in Manhattan. The cafeteria no longer exists, but when it did, it was the eating-meeting place of as heterogeneous a collection of Europeans as one could imagine, all part of the New York art dealers scene. Germans, Austrians, Italians, French— each talking in his or her language and each frequently replying in his or her native tongue without a break in the conversation. Because I was with Schaefer, they assumed that I understood what they were talking about. When they found out otherwise, and given my youth, they would frequently stop to explain to me why the conversation was as heated as it was. They were art dealers, but the range of their interests was to me phenomenal. If I had any tendency, which I did not, to overevaluate my education, the seminars in the Hampton cafeteria extinguished it. It was there that I began to learn that when an American is called a cosmopolitan, it does not mean the same as in Europe, where the world view of the intellectual cosmopolitan encompasses many nations, and the intellectual arena transcends national boundaries. At the same time that I was proud of the fact that America had given these Europeans a refuge, and I was convinced that we would be their beneficiaries, I was bothered by the thought that the traditions that had shaped them found inhospitable soil in this country. Their world view not only transcended national boundaries but was rooted in a present that had continuities spanning centuries and millennia. If in subsequent years I came to revere William James and John Dewey, it was because they were *in my field* the best examples of the intellectual cosmopolitan in the European tradition. No two people could be more American, but that was no bar to forging the broadest of world views.

The world of art: that is the world Schaefer opened for me. He took me to museums, stood me before paintings and sculpture, forced me to study what I saw and to articulate my judgments, which then became the focus of discussion. On one such occasion, alluded to briefly in Chapter Two, he stood me before a painting of a rural scene by Poussin. This was early in our trips, and my ignorance and biases were all too clear. I responded unreflectively by saying, "I don't like farm scenes." Schaefer looked down on me and said in a stern but fatherly way, "Your first job when you look at a work of art is to try to identify *the artistic problem* the artist was trying to overcome. The artistic process is a struggle involving color, form, composition, size, and content. Each painting has its own problems, some more difficult than others. We owe it to the artist, regardless of his level of development of visual conceiving, to judge his work in terms of what he wanted to accomplish." He then went on to say, "Study that painting with this question in mind: Can you change this or that color, this or that line, without changing anything else?" I studied the painting for some time, and it was as if a new world was opening before my eyes. If I changed this or that, I would have to change a lot else. I knew what a gestalt is in a way that I had never comprehended before! Schaefer went on to explain that when we look at a painting on a museum wall, we are looking at a final product that was preceded by a series of sketches, which could be voluminous, the purpose of which was to identify and attempt to resolve the inevitable problems and discrepancies that arise between internal vision or conception and the realities of color, line, size, and composition. This was (he would say in his own way) no stimulus and response, no cause and effect, but a constant back and forth, a totality of experience that included the artist and his materials,

both of which were always changing. For some time, I became
engrossed in viewing the sketches that led up to a painting before
me, endlessly fascinated, then as now, by the cognitive struggle,
the problem-solving aspects, the emergence of order, the creation of a configurated vision, that the artistic process required.
I had seen this take place in Schaefer's studio at Southbury:
the struggles of the residents, throwing away or tearing up one
paper and starting over with a new one, the look of satisfaction
when they liked what they had done, the frustration when they
did not like or saw a mess in what they had done—all part of
a total immersion, in Dewey's sense of the concept of *an* experience. Although Schaefer would tell me that what I was observing was in principle exactly the same as that experienced
by more highly developed artists, that the artistic process has
its own requirements wherever that process is found, I never
grasped the generality of what he said until we started to go
to museums.

Schaefer forever changed the way I look at, study, and
judge a work of art, regardless of the level of development of
the artist. But that is stating my debt in too narrow terms,
because in truth Schaefer provided me with a view of human
potential that I had long sought but never found. It was more
than a view or belief or act of faith. I had observed that potential where it was not supposed to exist. He had demonstrated
to my eyes enough "data" for me to accept as highly probable
that creative artistic activity was a universal human capacity.
And what I learned from him was grist from my own experiential mill: the nature of our social world either does not recognize
or it extinguishes that and other capacities. Schaefer knew that,
of course, just as he knew that what his students accomplished
was not independent of him and the contexts he created for them.
But that knowledge was to him of secondary importance to the
demonstration in case after case, in the present and the historical
past, of the unfolding of the stages of visual conceiving in the
creation of works of art. What was of secondary importance to
him was primary to me, but without his influence, the basis for
my convictions, the scope of my outlook, would be incomparably
more parochial than it is.

I have spent countless days in classrooms in and after Southbury. From the time of my relationship with Schaefer, there was hardly an instance when I would not find myself comparing the behavior of students in those classrooms with that of those in Schaefer's studio. In the one setting, I saw a pouring in of information, student passivity, rote memorizing, and an emphasis on outcome (the *right* answer) and token gestures to process. In the other, I saw struggle, eagerness, and perseverance in the effort to put "out there" a visual conception in tune with and satisfying to the eye of the creator: changing, distorting, simplifying external reality in a configurated way. In the one, individuality was hard to discern; in the other, it hit you in the face.

What Schaefer's studio represented to the residents, Southbury represented to me. No one was telling me what to do and how to do it. Although I was on my own in the middle of rural nowhere, I had Schaefer and Esther to stimulate and support me. I had the sense of growth and development, the sense that I was giving expression to my abilities and interests, sensitive to the "real world" around me but nevertheless intent on understanding and changing that world. I was not about to be judged by conventional external standards of what psychology and psychologists were supposed to be. Unlike the residents whom Schaefer chose as students, I was semispoiled. Indirectly but powerfully, all that Schaefer stood for and did served as warning to the dangers of being spoiled and as stimulus to going my own way. He was the greatest of my teachers.

The day before this chapter was finished, I was visited by two people, Bruce and Cathy Thomas, whom I had never met personally but with whom I had carried on a professional correspondence for several years. In the course of the conversation, they asked me about the role of Schaefer in my professional development. I had forgotten that in a letter I had suggested that they look at Schaefer's book in light of their interest in education and its inadequacies. When I asked whether they had seen the book, their faces lit up, and they tried to convey to me the impact the book had had on them. (The last time someone had taken the book out of the library had been ten years earlier, and apparently only one other person had read it from the time it was purchased.) Their reaction was identical to that of others to whom I had recommended the book. You really have to see before you begin to consider believing. Language is dull brass for describing works of art.

I reprint below a letter I received from a student of Schaefer's. Mr. Whitnaw did visit me in New Haven, and he projected onto a screen slides showing the development of several of his students. The development of the students was nothing less than staggering. Mr. Whitnaw obviously is a great teacher, but alone, like Schaefer was.

Dear Dr. Sarason:

I am delighted that you are going to do a chapter on Henry's work at Southbury. This would be most valuable for several reasons, chief of which is to give an intimate and well-documented look at Henry's actual pedagogical method and how that method found integration in the psychological sphere of mental retardation. Also valuable for the many who value *The Unfolding of Artistic Activity* would be your commentary as to the mise-en-scene, so to speak, which produced the book—the complex interactions of yourself, Henry, and the participating patients there. It would be interesting for people to know in more detail what psychological changes manifested (and how they manifested) in someone like Selma. Henry told me something about it years ago, but I have forgotten the details.

As I mentioned in my first letter, *The Unfolding* has been out for 36 years and it has not changed art education. Henry himself, in his lifetime, became deeply discouraged over the failure of the art education academy in this country to take serious note of his book. He told me in 1971: "I have often the temptation to throw up the whole thing (his art education work and the publishing of his great book on *The Essence of the Art Form*). I could go to Europe by the next plane. There I could look at exhibitions and enjoy art and live a completely different kind of life. But I have, I might say, a kind of guilty conscience in the face of such thought. I have a responsibility in full conscience to do this work." And I said: "And if you had not published the *Unfolding of Artistic Activity*"—he broke in: "Yes, but not more than ten people in the whole world understood that book"— And I interrupted: " . . . then my life would have been inexpressibly poorer, and I would have been diminished if you had kept the book a secret and written it, yet simply put it away.'' These are exact quotes from a conversation I had with him on the subject of exhibiting art. He had become so discouraged with the general art scene at this point that he did not even wish to have his own students exhibit work!

You see, Dr. Sarason, Henry suffered a great deal of ignominy, spite, misunderstanding, neglect and downright hostility from established academic art educators. He was extremely sensitive to this, especially so, since he himself was a professional in education, fully qualified, and a great teacher whose students produced work of outstanding quality. He was good, and he knew it. He had something of utmost importance to offer to educators, psychologists, artists, architects and laymen, to mention only a few categories.

But, with the advent of Abstract Expressionism in the 1950's and the steady rise of a kind of graphic and pictorial work which was profoundly anti-Gestalt, the temper of the times was against his implementation of the hard-won conclusions which make up his book, his work and his life. He had told me: ''When I left Europe I looked at the continent receding over the horizon and I took a solemn oath that I would take this Idea to the United States and make it a living Reality.'' He fulfilled this oath by publishing *The Unfolding* and by the productive years which followed in the forties and the fifties. But, as he got better, the general art scene got worse! He would go to Europe in the summer and there be told by young art students that the old Gothic painters like Grunewald and Durer (if there *are* any like them!) were nothing but ''old nonsense.''

When Henry died I asked the responsible parties at St. Mary's College to put on an event which would review and sum up his achievement as a writer, thinker, and active art educator. Somehow, this never got done, I don't know why, and it always bothered me that such a man should thus slip, unnoticed and unacclaimed, out of this world. Perhaps one of the reasons for the hostility and neglect which he suffered was the fact that excellence in a field is not always admired, but often envied. Also the fact that he was never noted for his tact and had little of the small talk and social personality so useful in the educational field. He was passionately devoted to The Artistic Form and he was delighted when he found another who shared that passion. And he had little time for anything else.

The temper of the times has changed. People are beginning

to understand that anti-gestalt pictorial products have nothing
to do with art in its most fundamental, ancient and highest sense.
Many professionals are beginning to see that *quality* is the hallmark of artistic excellence and indeed excellence in any field,
whether it be psychology, artisanship or architecture. Recently,
my wife and I had the good luck to meet a fine architect, world-
renowned, currently engaged in building a university in Japan.
He is also a professor at the University of California, but not
too busy to take an interest in the project of building a house
and studios for us here in Northern California. He lives in Berkeley, and when I met him I mentioned that Schaefer-Simmern
used to live a few blocks away, and that his books had reminded
me of the ideas in *The Unfolding*. Well, Dr. Sarason, this man
caught on fire! He said when he was studying architecture at
Harvard that he had read *The Unfolding* every day and had kept
it by him as a source book. But he had no idea that Schaefer-
Simmern had lived in Berkeley, or that his work had continued
at all after the publication of the book. He has very kindly offered to sponsor a lecture for me at the University of California.

Now, then, the reason I suggested the lecture to you: I
did so because I was reasonably certain that there are also many
people at Yale, faculty and students in art, in education, in
psychology and philosophy who would be deeply interested in
the visual results of Henry's long career as well as the pedagogical
means by which these came into being. When I lecture and show
the slides, people are amazed. They can't believe that work of
such outstanding quality, and such a radically simple approach
to art can be such a well kept secret. They are also astonished
to learn of the existence of *The Unfolding* and that it is still in print.

There is also the paradoxical factor of diminishing returns
as time races onward. When Henry told me in 1971 that only
ten people in the world understood this book, he was speaking
correctly. Now, 12 years later, I am sorry to reckon that those
numbers have shrunk. As far as I know there are no young
people who have taken up this Idea with the vigor and conviction which will make it operable to future generations. There
is, thus, a certain urgency, depending on our viewpoint. Quite
possibly, the availability of *The Unfolding* may be lost for many
generations and only rediscovered years hence by some group
or individual. In this case they would have to reconstruct it from
the external evidence inward—no easy task! But I think such
a creative hiatus would be a pity since it is the living instruction that gets the message across, and there are still a few left

who worked directly with Henry, having grasped the pedagogical method in their bones, so to speak, and thus can transmit it without distortion.

But my reason for writing you was simpler still: You were with Henry in the old days and you helped him get his book written, both by your active cooperation and your true understanding of what he was doing. Above all, he needed that understanding and in you he had it. You are one of the ten people who understand the book. He told me that. So, you see, when I heard that you were doing some writing about Henry I thought the least I could do would be to offer you a lecture. And though the materials I show are not specifically about mental retardation, they apply (as you well know) with equal force on the scale of measurable "intelligence" up or down. Selma was no genius, but look what she produced! I show slides of her work to my eight-year-olds and tell them about Selma and the discipline she brought to her art. My children can relate directly to her work and feel strong encouragement through her example.

Anyway, I wanted *you* to see the kind of achievements which have flowered since *The Unfolding of Artistic Activity* was published, both for specific application in your field of expertise and for the larger frame of reference where psychology relates directly to the human potential.

Again, thanks for your letter.

Sincere regards,
Kevin Whitnaw

9

1941–1945:
When the World Changed

An autobiography, even one limited to a professional development, founders to an undetermined extent on the problem of keeping an appropriate balance in explaining the interweaving between inside and outside factors. You "know your mind," you know that you exist in a larger society, and you know that both are not discrete but part of some kind of whole. Far more often than not, we explain ourselves to ourselves in a narrow inside-outside context: family, place, community, school, religion, ethnicity. I say *narrow* because we are not set or schooled to see ourselves as partial products of a larger society, aspects of which are in us in ways that quotidian life does not require us to fathom. So, as I have emphasized, I have sought to pay more than lip service to the fact that I was born and reared in America. If I adhered to a chronological account of my career, this chapter would begin the story of my more than four decades at Yale. I would begin by describing why and how I came to Yale, but however factual the account, it would not add up to the truth, even if inevitably a partial truth. To understand why and how I came to Yale requires an explanation that goes beyond the psychological, personal, or phenomenological. If I spent most of the war years at Southbury—as far from the turmoil of war as one could imagine—things were happening that were setting the stage for the greatest and speediest transformations in psychology and the larger society. A stage was being constructed, a drama was being written and produced, that would make my coming to Yale a possibility. If anyone had told me when I came to Southbury in 1942 that I would be at Yale in 1945, my diagnosis and prognosis of their mental condition would have been gloomy indeed.

The world was changing in ways unknown to me but ways that would transform me. What some of those transformations are will occupy this chapter. What I shall relate may be regarded by the younger reader as history, but that would be making two grievous mistakes. The first is that you cannot understand psychology and the larger society today without comprehending how much of that history is in the living present. The second is that the younger reader is unaware that, like my life in the war years, his or her life is being determined in part by transformations today in the larger society. The script seems different, the actors are different, but the stage is no less large, and we see only a part of it. But if we see only a part of it, that is no excuse for not trying to see and know more. We do not have to have a Greek chorus to tell us what the present portends for us the actors. Unlike the Greek tragedies, the present is pregnant with many futures, even though we live our days as if that were not the case.

The bombing of Pearl Harbor on December 7, 1941, produced a shock of recognition in everyone. Suddenly, the rhetoric of the American concept and traditions of freedom took on an immediacy, a practical reality, it did not have before. America was vulnerable and under challenge. If we had taken our freedoms for granted, we no longer could do so. It was remarkable how many people, theretofore critical and disparaging of American society, came overnight to see that the future of freedom in this world depended on this country. If we had been blind to the strength and ambitions of the faces of tyranny, we were now paying the price. As some would put it, materialistic and capitalistic America had forgotten what it was about; Pearl Harbor was the signal of its comeuppance. What requires emphasis is that for two years after Pearl Harbor, it was by no means clear that the Allies could survive, let alone be victorious.

War (especially a world war) may be the only time in the history of a country when it willingly and quickly gives up doing business as usual. Entering the war meant that almost every adult would experience some kind of alteration in role, place, context, and outlook. Whereas in peacetime who does what is relatively clear—we have long been a credentialing society—the pressures of war do not obliterate the usual criteria for roles but bring to the fore the question: who can learn to do what? That question had salience hard to exaggerate, because it was obvious (and I do mean obvious) that this country simply did not and could not have the trained human resources to fill the roles that the armed services and the industrial sector required; indeed, demanded. Women, in and out of the armed services, became important human resources. Old people were encouraged to seek employment. If you were a highly trained cardiologist-internist, as my brother-in-law was, you could end up in chemical warfare. If you were an ophthalmologist, you could find yourself doing psychiatry. If you were an experimental psychologist, you could find yourself doing screening of pilots. And not infrequently, if you had only an undergraduate major in psychology, you became a psychologist in a unit dealing with battle casualties. "Don't tell us what you are. We'll tell you what we need and what you will become"—that was what infused the thinking of the policy makers in the armed services and beyond. Professionalism was important, but it was a luxury. A war was on, and credentials were a problem, not a solution. For the moment, no one was arguing otherwise.

For months after Pearl Harbor, it was by no means clear whether many of our colleges could survive in light of their being denuded of students and faculty. What prevented such a disaster was the recognition that the war would be long and that despite the improvisation in roles, the armed services would need an irreducible minimum of physicians, engineers, language specialists, and the like. Colleges and universities, with government support, became training and educational centers for the different armed services. Young people found themselves in colleges and universities to which they had never dreamed they could be admitted. The educational process was speeded up; preparation for the military was part of the experience.

Esther and I were married on May 22, 1943. We honeymooned in the Sherman Square Hotel at Broadway and Seventy-second Street. We were awakened each morning at 6:00 A.M. by students from some New York college doing their marching drills. In Chapter Six, I said that I was the only one of three graduating students at Clark University in 1941–42 who never received a reply from colleges to which I had applied for a position. I attributed that to the fact that I did not conceal that I was Jewish. That was a factor, but so was the fact that in that year colleges were uncertain about how they could survive.

Like all other professionals (and their professional organizations), psychologists sought to contribute to the war effort. Some were inducted as officers, others served in the capacity of consultants. A comprehensive history of that involvement has yet to be written, an unfortunate omission, because I have never talked to any participant who did not assert that both he and psychology were transformed in those years. Those transformations came about in several ways. First, and most obvious, some psychologists were asked to deal with psychological problems they had never even dreamed about. For example, how do you select, train, and evaluate individuals who will be engaged in spying? How could all that was known about Hitler—his biography, autobiography, past and current speeches—be used to predict his future military moves? Why were so many pilots crashing in the process of landing? Can you predict who will be a good pilot? In light of the large number of illiterates who had been inducted, was it possible to get them to read at a third- or fourth-grade level in no more than three or four months? Was it possible to quickly rehabilitate soldiers who had broken down under the stress of battle, and to do so near the scene of battle? In light of food shortages, how could we affect the eating habits of people? These were, understandably, not questions that the small, laboratory-based, basic science–oriented field of psychology had given thought to. But they were questions that when willingly confronted dramatically broadened psychologists' horizons about diversity and complexity of behavior in diverse contexts. What on the surface appeared to be "applied" problems were challenges to whatever were considered basic psychological princples.

If confronting new problems widened horizons, it was also the case that the dominant theories and research literature were frequently inadequate or wrong when applied to new and complicated contexts. In 1899, in his presidential address to the American Psychological Association in New Haven, John Dewey (as had William James before him) warned about the dangers of extrapolating from theories and data derived from laboratory studies of human behavior. The wisdom of that warning was confirmed in World War I, and again confirmed in World War II. A clear example was the way that James Gibson was forced to change his theory of space-depth perception in order to explain the frequency of pilots' crashing in the process of landing. World War II required psychologists to deal with an order of complexity to which they were unaccustomed, and their theories were not very helpful. It says something praiseworthy about psychologists that they unlearned inadequate theories and developed more adequate ones so quickly. If knowledge of one's pending execution focuses one's attention, so did the pressures of World War II. It is deserving of emphasis that it was by no means clear that the Allies would survive. Japan went from one victory to another in the Pacific, China, and Southeast Asia; Hitler was in the process of taking over Europe, North Africa, and a lot of Russia. Pride in one's previous scientific work had no role in persisting with ideas and methods that were inadequate.

Regardless of specialty, psychologists could not ignore one brute fact: the number of recruits who could not adjust to military life, or who broke down under battle stress, was staggering. Psychologists' eyes and their sympathy became attuned to abnormal behavior to a degree for which previous experience, in and out of the university, had not prepared them. Awareness of that brute fact brought in its wake the feeling not only that psychology had a role to play, a role to develop, but that the arena of clinical problems had general significance for the field. This change in attitude was one that predisposed many nonclinical psychologists from the university to look more positively and respectfully at clinical psychology. Before World War II, American psychology oscillated between being an aclinical and an anticlinical discipline. The war years produced a degree of attitude change that would, after the war, serve to make clinical psychology a part of graduate education.

But the brute fact affected more than the fully trained psychologists connected with the war effort. These psychologists were, relatively speaking, miniscule in numbers. There were many more people without the doctorate who found themselves in psychological roles that opened their eyes to the frequency and challenge of human breakdown. And their numbers were nothing compared to those of the college-educated recruits who were not in psychological roles but who were inevitably witnesses to the nature and consequences of breakdown in their peers and in those for whom their officer status made them responsible. The novels, plays, and films that the war years stimulated validly reflected what millions in the armed services had seen and experienced. It is not happenstance, of course, that the film *The Best Years of Our Lives* received an Oscar. Years later, I came to label the postwar years as the Age of Psychology, or the Age of Mental Health. The societal transformation that label was intended to suggest was a direct manifestation of what millions of people, in and out of the armed services, had seen and had had to confront during the war years. Lives had been transformed, the structure and dynamics of conventional family life had been altered, the racial issue came to the fore as never before, the role and status of women changed, there were vast shifts in the population from one part of the country to another. In combination, these and other factors converged to make salient the question: what is the meaning of it all? How do you pick up the pieces? How do you put them together? World War II— the first truly *world* war—was a convulsive struggle in more than a military way. For literally millions of people, it was experienced as a personal disruption of future orientation and world view. The traditional sources of faith, hope, and meaning had been undermined. More people felt more alone and bereft of personal security and identity than ever before. The stage was being set

214 The Making of an American Psychologist

for the Age of Psychology, in which people were predisposed
to seek personal help to obtain a new compass to guide living.
It is not surprising that, with the end of the war, the philosophy
of existentialism and the "God is dead" pronouncements became
popular fare.

If psychology and psychologists were being transformed,
a similar transformation was occurring in psychiatry. How does
one explain the fact that American psychiatry before World War
II was a biological psychiatry and within a few years after the
war it was largely a pyschoanalytical psychiatry? That question
has hardly been studied or discussed, and yet that transformation was startling. It is beyond my purposes to attempt anything
like a comprehensive answer, but certain aspects of it should
be stated. As in the case of psychology, psychiatrists had to confront the fact that their theories and practices were either inadequate or ineffective in meeting the problems they confronted.
It is one thing to explain and treat personal misery in a state
hospital or in the confines of a private office. It is quite another
thing to confront it in unfamiliar contexts, under unfamiliar
pressures, and in relation to populations varying widely in education, race, ethnicity, intellectual level, and cultural background.
That was an eye-opener for all psychiatrists, whether they came
from the academy or from private practice. But among those
who came from private practice were psychoanalytical psychiatrists who viewed academic psychiatry with disdain. They were
more ready to apply their theory and experience in new ways
that gave promise of being more adequate to the needs of the
military. Despite their small numbers, they occupied important
roles. Dr. William Menninger, from the nationally known center
of psychoanalytical thought and practice, became chief psychiatrist of the army. Why he was chosen and how he used his office
to position his psychoanalytical colleagues in important positions,
I do not know. But the rising influence of psychoanalysis in psychiatric circles during the war was not only a matter of informal,
political factors. They saw themselves and came to be regarded—
especially by younger psychiatrists not completely socialized in
academic psychiatry—as a breath of fresh air, as a movement
whose time had come.

Before World War II, academic psychiatry had little to say about the social-psychological significances of the rise of fascism in Germany. If only because so many of the leading analysts were refugees from Germany and Austria, they brought attention to psychoanalysis by their writings in which they attempted to explain the psychological substrata undergirding the rise of Hitler. If before World War II psychoanalysis was outside of American academic psychiatry, its influence was nevertheless spreading. The war years accelerated that spreading. There was one other important factor: most analysts (and a significant portion of the psychiatrists who received training during the war years) were Jewish. For them, Hitler and fascism were not abstractions but threats to existence. And for them, Freud represented a Moses-like figure whose contributions had opened up new vistas about the nature of humans, vistas that Hitler sought to obscure or obliterate. To Jews, Freud—like Einstein—was a revered figure, even if they could not comprehend the nature of the contributions of either.

At Southbury, I comprehended nothing of what I have described above. I was not only not in the armed services, I was not in the university. I was in bucolic Southbury. But I did go into New Haven one day a week to work with Edith Jackson in pediatrics. It was suggested to me (by whom I cannot remember) that I should endeavor to get further training in diagnostic testing with Dr. Catherine Cox Miles, who was the clinical psychologist in psychiatry and a professor in the department of psychology. She had gained national visibility by her work with Lewis Terman on gifted children. I met with her, and she arranged for me to see some patients in psychiatry with supervision. She was a somewhat formidable, constricted person whose approach to testing was conventional in the extreme. The point of the story is not Dr. Miles but what I learned about the department of psychiatry. The head of the department was a German, Dr. Eugen Kahn, whose major claim to fame was his concept of organic drivenness, and there were few psychiatric conditions to which he found that concept inapplicable. I was already a partisan of psychoanalysis, and I had also become aware that the Institute of Human Relations (which housed the departments of psychology and psychiatry and the Gesell Institute of Child Development) was a buzzing center of psychoanalytical thinking. What I did not know until I met Dr. Miles was that doors between the two adjacent departments were closed, physically and psychologically. The interest in psychoanalysis was in and around the department of psychology. Psychiatry was in another world, ruled by Herr Professor. I saw only a handful of cases in psychiatry, but they gave me a glimpse of that department that I found disheartening and mystifying. Dr. Kahn would have nothing to do with psychoanalysis as theory and practice. And, knowing as I do now the psychologists who were seeking to integrate psychoanalysis into a general psychology, it is very likely that their disdain for Dr. Kahn was not a secret. The doors between the two departments were closed, but they didn't have to be: no one on either side of those doors seemed to want to pass through. That was in 1943. Approximately five years later—as a result of a palace revolt led by young psychiatrists who had returned from the service—the department of psychiatry became, overnight it seemed, a psychoanalytical enclave; Dr. Kahn was relieved of all duties, and a new era began.

Why did psychoanalysis become the regnant orientation in American psychiatry after World War II? There is no simple answer. It was not planned that way. Too much was happening to too many people during the war to allow for a simple, coherent answer. It is perhaps best to say that a zeitgeist was being forged during the war years that would become manifest on an institutional level once the war was over. War has intended and unintended consequences, and it is the unintended consequences that make history so interesting and important.

But there was one source of planning during the war that served to give direction to what would happen to psychology and psychiatry after the war, a source that would begin to give some degree of coherence and substance to the emerging professional zeitgeist. It is ironic that the beginning of a war forces government to think about and plan for the postwar period. It is forced to do so for two reasons: moral and economic. In the case of World War II, the moral reason was put this way: We have to be ready to give the best care possible to a staggering number of people who will require health services on a short-term, long-term, or lifetime basis. And among those who will require services, those with war-incurred psychological disabilities will be a significant fraction. The economic reason was a direct consequence of the moral: What will it cost to give these scarred veterans the kinds of care they deserve and a grateful society wishes to give?

You didn't need special knowledge or wisdom to conclude that since this was going to be a long war, and millions of people would be in the armed services, several million would incur one or another type of disability, that the Veterans Administration would be faced with a seemingly impossible task when the war was over. Not long after the war began, the Veterans Administration started planning for the postwar care of veterans. Time was not on its side. The war was on, the casualty list was high and growing. The future was all too clear. If improvisation is the name of the game during war, the name of the game after the war would and should be different. To my knowledge, no one has studied and described in depth how that planning proceeded, who took part formally and informally, and the degree to which they tried to anticipate the consequences of their policy recommendations. The ahistorical stance has long been weak or absent in American psychology and psychiatry. As best as I have determined over the years, the psychologists and psychiatrists who represented their professions in the planning tended to be young, favorable to (at least not critical of) psychoanalysis, and eager to bridge the gap between their professions and the larger society. The morality powering the planning was never lost sight of: the veterans deserved the best from society, and psychology and psychiatry had to organize themselves to provide the best.

The import of the decisions can be put in the following statements.

1. Whereas following World War I, health facilities for veterans were built away from population and medical centers, with untoward consequences, the new facilities should be

placed in or very near medical centers (medical schools and hospitals) having a major voice in the organization and administration of the new facilities. The new facilities would be part of a teaching and research program.

2. In order for veterans to receive the care they deserved, clinical psychologists and psychiatrists would be needed in numbers far exceeding those that would be available at the end of the war. To lessen the shortage, departments of psychology would be encouraged and fiscally supported to enlarge their training programs. Entrants to these programs would receive financial support at a level that would attract a large pool of applicants and allow departments to be selective.

3. Although graduate programs in clinical psychology did not exist, the need for clinical psychologists sophisticated in diagnostic testing and research had to be met. A special effort would have to be made to get departments to institute such programs consistent with their scientific-research traditions.

4. For the veterans to receive the best care possible from the mental health fields, it was essential that that care be based on research on (and evaluation of) whatever therapies and therapeutic contexts gave promise of improving patient status. Without a program of clinical and experimental research, the quality of care would inevitably decline.

5. Our society had to be ready to underwrite building, training, research, and service programs at a heretofore undreamed of level.

It would be both misleading and unfair to say that the speed with which graduate departments developed clinical programs after the war was because of the financial plums the Veterans Administration was dangling before them. The financial incentives were important, but, independent of them, those academics who were returning from the war effort to the university were, generally speaking, predisposed to look favorably on the creation of a new graduate area in psychology. The transformation of psychology and psychologists during the war would continue and be manifested institutionally after the war.

Most of what I have described about the war years I learned after I came to Yale in 1945. Southbury was working out fine for me (I thought), and I looked forward to spending more years there until I would get a more lucrative position in another state institution. My one day a week in pediatrics with Edie Jackson was stimulating, I had Schaefer and Esther, and we could pursue our interests pretty much as we wished, within broad limits. In 1944, Don Marquis, chair of the Yale psychology department, asked to see me. He told me that he was leaving Yale to go to the University of Michigan to chair and develop their graduate programs. His wife, Dr. Dorothy Marquis, was a part-time clinical psychologist in pediatrics. One of her responsibilities was to supervise the occasional Yale graduate student in a practicum. Would I be willing the next year to give part of the day I spent in pediatrics to the supervision of two female graduate students who wanted a practicum? If I was willing (which of course I was), I would be given the courtesy title of assistant clinical professor, a title that at Yale meant that I was a practitioner and not a researcher. I had met Don and Dorothy a number of times and was both taken with her friendliness and intimidated by Don's Socratic incisiveness. Besides, he had written with E. R. Hilgard *Conditioning and Learning* (East Norwalk, Conn.: Appleton-Century-Crofts, 1940), a kind of bible to graduate students. Don must have been aware that I, alone and with Esther, had published several papers that I know Dorothy had commented on favorably. It did not occur to me that Don might have been impressed by the fact that here was a young psychologist working in a state institution and publishing papers, two of which had been in the *Journal of Abnormal and Social Psychology*. Nor was I in any way aware of what Don knew: psychology would be different after the war, clinical psychology was going to enter the scene, governmental funding would be available, and Ann Arbor would provide a far larger and more complex stage than Yale to give expression to Don's prodigious intellectual, leadership, and administrative talents.

A year after he left Yale, Don called to offer me an assistant professorship. I was puzzled and flabbergasted. I never imagined I would be in a university, and I truly did not know what I would be letting myself in for. He asked Esther and me to visit, which we did. What I saw there was the initial stage in the development of what soon would be the largest and certainly one of the best departments in the country. I saw myself as a little boy among men—big men.

I was prepared to accept the Michigan offer. I was given two weeks to arrive at a decision. To explain why I was prepared to go there requires that I relate what happened in the previous weeks in regard to coming to Yale. That year, Carl Hovland had returned to Yale as chair of the department, succeeding Marquis. We got to know and like each other. He wanted to have a clinical program at Yale, and a few weeks before the call from Marquis, he asked whether it were possible for me to spend more than one day a week at Yale. That, I knew, would be impossible for me to arrange, but even if it could be arranged, it did not seem to me to be in my best interests. He came up with other possibilities, such as spending half time in the student mental health unit and the other half in the department. That seemed to make more sense, but it turned out to be impossible. It was not clear to me why a full-time position in the department could not be arranged. There were, I later concluded, two reasons. The first had to do with Carl Hovland, the person. Carl was one of those rare people—as brilliant as he was decent, as cautious as he was foresightful, as sensitive as he was supportive. He was the rarest of human beings. But Carl was not of the cast of mind that permitted him to take action, to make commitments, unless he had thought through the ins and outs of action. He wanted a clinical program, but it had to be one that would fit in with the traditions and values of the department. The fact that I was on the scene and available was not in itself justification for appointing me before there was clarity about what a clinical program should be.

The other reason, interacting with the first, was that this was his first year back, and in Hovlandian fashion he was casing the joint, so to speak, feeling his way. Starting a clinical program was only one of his problems. I have no doubt whatsoever that Carl saw irony in the fact that in bringing clinical into psychology, the field was faced with a dilemma. In order to develop a program, you needed the kind of faculty who did not exist in the university. You would have to get people who after their doctorate had not been able to get an academic position (like me), and who had taken clinical jobs in state hospitals and clinics. Obviously, that pool differed in three respects from that of those who had been "chosen" for positions in the university. First, many of them were Jewish. Second, by conventional criteria—performance in graduate school, letters of recommendation, ability to do research—some had not passed muster. Third, they had grown up, so to speak, outside the university. With the end of the war, the "Jewish question" was no longer a factor, although Dr. Frederick Thorne, who after the war started the *Journal of Clinical Psychology*, stated in an early editorial that the influx of Jews into the field would put a distinctive and not necessarily positive stamp on it. In any event, one could not gloss over the fact that staffing clinical programs would bring into the university what for it would be a new breed. To someone like Carl Hovland, criteria of intellectual ability and quality of research performance were crucial.

There had been a competitive relationship at Yale between Hovland and Marquis. They had respect for each other, but their relationship was a cool one. So, when I told Carl about the Michigan offer, he sought to get a comparable offer from the Yale department. Crucial in this respect were Walter and Catherine Miles, who were in England at the time. Carl wired them to get their approval for an offer to me. They did not approve. Carl asked me to delay acceptance of the Michigan offer until the last minute, giving him time to dream up a viable alternative. I saw him the day before I had to call Don. He felt bad that his hands were tied, and he wished me well. I left his office, walked out of the Institute of Human Relations, and started to turn right to go to my car. But I wanted a cup of coffee, and I turned left to go to a corner eatery. There I met John Dollard, whom I had come to know through Edie Jackson. John had visited me at Southbury, had discussed with me some research we had done on diagnostic test patterns, and was very interested in our psychotherapeutic efforts. He liked me, and it must have been obvious that I had unbounded respect for him. When I told John that I would be going to Michigan, that I would prefer coming to Yale, but that Carl could not come up with a comparable offer, he wondered whether Carl had thought of an institute research appointment that would not require departmental approval. Would it be okay if he talked to Carl? I told him about the time constraints.

By midafternoon, I was offered a full-time appointment in the institute. But I had nothing in writing, and insecure me was not about to decline the Michigan offer for one I really did not comprehend organizationally. Besides, Carl had casually said that the appointment would ultimately be sent to the provost for what would be a routine approval. And what if the provost, like the Mileses, said no? Carl sensed my insecurity and tried to reassure me that the provost, who was vacationing in the southwest, would present no problem. Would Carl, I asked, be willing to call the provost? He did, the approval was given, and I declined the Michigan offer. The experience mightily reinforced my coffee drinking.

These anecdotes only in part explain how I came to Yale, or why I got the Michigan offer. More important (certainly not less important) is an explanation of what had happened in the cauldron of the war years: myriad factors that were part of social, professional, and individual upheavals that led to the emergence of clinical psychology as a distinctive area in graduate education. At that time, I had no way of seeing or comprehending the transformations that were taking place. Phenomenologically, *I* was a decision maker, *I* was determining my future, *I* was the captain of my fate, the master of my soul. If that was phenomenologically valid, it had all of the features of tunnel vision. It took several years before I began to see how unreflectively but powerfully imprisoned American psychology is in an individual psychology that ignores the larger social-cultural stage. The individual is figure, and that larger, complex stage is an ignored background.

Relevant here is the reaction of Esther and myself when we visited Carl in his home to work out the details of the appointment. When Esther and I left the chairman's home in a New Haven suburb, having come to final agreement about the offer and my acceptance, evening had come, together with a spring mist that made the blooming dogwoods (in which the area abounds) look unusually heavy. We had about three blocks to walk to the bus. We never took the bus. When we left the chairman's house, we said not a word to each other for about a minute; we just walked hand in hand. Then, as if by some prearranged signal, we turned to each other and shouted: "We are free!" That utterance was the first time I had allowed myself to say something out loud that reflected vague fears about spending our social lives in an institutional setting, and being intellectually confined by having to focus on a particular patient population. There was a part of me that knew that by my going to Southbury the confines of my career had already been determined: my positions might change, my status and income increase; I would write and do research, and I would try to branch out, but all of this would be as a clinical psychologist in a state institutional setting. When I daydreamed about all the great and wonderful things I would do in my lifetime, the physical setting in which these would be done was a Southbury or one of its different kin. For the first two years at Southbury, I enjoyed these daydreams. I was lucky, I had it made! I had a career line, thank God. I knew what my life would be like, and I liked the prospect. If anyone had told me that I was uncritically buying the one life–one career imperative, I would have signed his commitment papers. It was after a couple of years, and it was only in part a function of my marriage, that I would have fleeting and disquieting thoughts about what the long-term future looked like. But I never really allowed myself to pursue these thoughts. Where would it get me? Besides, wasn't I learning and doing a lot, and wasn't there a lot more to do? What more did I want? Sure, institutional life and work leave something to be desired, but you have to put these negatives into perspective.

I never could bring myself to discuss this openly with anyone, particularly with Esther, who never hesitated to tell me how she regarded institutional living. I resented her putting into words what I feared to let myself think about. Why get upset about what you cannot alter? I saw the future and accommodated to it. So when we walked into freedom upon leaving the chairman's home, masculine me could for the first time acknowledge

what I had previously allowed (= required) myself to believe
was weakness and irrationality. I had been in prison and thought
it was freedom. Relative to any other institution I knew or heard
about, I did have freedom at Southbury; relative to Yale, it was
a concentration camp.

It took more than a year to get used to my new freedom.
I felt like a college freshman who, after years of having the school
day structured for him, finds himself with a lot of "free time."
I began to realize how well planted the work ethic was in me:
you go "to work" in the morning, and you do "work" until
five o'clock, and if in that interval you didn't "do" work—the
kind of activity that could be filmed and proved you were "working," and that proved to yourself that you hadn't goofed off—
you felt and were guilty. You could enjoy this work, there was
no law against it, but one of its essential ingredients was that
you were satisfying an external criterion of worth. So, when I
spent evenings and weekends writing, that was "writing," not
"working"! I coped well with my guilt, and it helped me understand how much a product of my culture I was. I came to understand that the prime function of a university was to create the
conditions for its faculty to learn, change, and grow. Yale existed for *me* and the rest of the faculty. No one bothered me or
even suggested that I do this or that. It took me six months to
learn that I had call on various departmental resources and that
the more you claimed "call on," the more it was interpreted
that you had an active research program. It could also be interpreted as being pushy and imperialistic, but at least it was in
a worthy cause!

My experience at Yale was the reverse of that of many
of my undergraduate students who leave Yale for "the real
world." As one student put it, "I bitched and yelled when I
was here. It all seemed so irrelevant and theoretical. I couldn't
wait to get out. But I do miss this place! I was more myself here."
If Yale's primary function is the welfare of its faculty, it is a
function only somewhat more exalted than its concern for its
undergraduates, most of whom understand this only after they
have left. I understood freedom not when I lost it, but when
I got it. I could write a large volume on universities in general

and Yale in particular, and its contents would be far from a paeon of praise, but I would go to lengths to ensure that the reader understood that the university is the most refreshing oasis of freedom in our society. It is by no means surprising that as masses of young people streamed into our colleges and universities after World War II, they absorbed, directly and indirectly, values and outlooks that were much more those of the university than of the larger society.

The switch to Yale taught me much about myself. First, I had and needed to have a diversity of interests. Diversity of interest and stimulation was essential to my well-being, to the extent that if I felt a lack or waning of either, I would become uneasy. Not only did I have to feel that in the present I had diverse interests and goals, but it was also important that I knew in outline the different things I wanted to be involved in and writing about in the future; for example, five or ten years from now. After decades at Yale, it is hard for me to recall a day when on the way to the office I did not have the thought, "And what interesting things are going to happen today?" My days were unpredictable and interesting to an extent I did not dream possible at Southbury. What I am trying to say about my days is not unlike what I experience in writing. When I begin to write, I have a pretty good idea of what I want to say, the ideas I want to put into words, and the organization of and interconnections among ideas. But shortly after I begin writing, the ideas and their interconnections begin to change, and I end up with something discernibly different from what I initially planned. Writing is a form of exploration full of surprises (and tortures). In fact, I have gained the least in an intellectual sense (and found the task relatively uninteresting) when I was writing up journal articles based on empirical research; by the nature of the task and materials, I had to be impersonal and do justice to data "out there." In more discursive writing, I was playing with my ideas, and I never quite knew where they would take me, where I would take myself.

Another thing I learned about myself—related to the first point as well as to the Southbury experience—was that I did not wish to remain with a particular issue, in research or otherwise, for an indefinite period of time. That is, when I began something new, I already knew that there would come a time when I would want to move on to something else. Before moving on, however, I would have to make written sense of what I had experienced. I became dimly aware of this when after two years at Yale I felt an internal compulsion to write a book reflecting what I had done in and learned about the field of mental deficiency. Put in another way, I needed to feel that I would be changing career every few years or so. The beauty of the university is that it permits and encourages such changes; the obstacles are usually internal and not external.

The two major things I learned about myself—the need for diversity of interest and stimulation and the opportunity to change career directions—are obviously not peculiar to me. On the contrary, as I pointed out in earlier chapters, they were and have increasingly become characteristics of people in our society, particularly those who are highly educated. In myriad ways we have been taught to hunger for new experience, whether it be for a new car, coffee maker, home, exotic trip, clothes, drugs, deodorant, the latest form of self-exploration, movie, or picture book on the new geography of sexual positions.

We can scapegoat Madison Avenue for some of this, but it is my belief that Madison Avenue and American industry have followed wants as often as they have created them. The hunger for the new, exciting, and rejuvenating experience goes much deeper than Madison Avenue and requires a far more complicated explanation. The hunger goes beyond material things and can be found in our theories about how to raise children and to live our lives, about how we must encounter and confront ourselves so that we experience our protean nature and free ourselves from our procrustean bed. When, after World War II, Dr. Benjamin Spock's 1946 *Common Sense Book of Baby and Child Care* became the child-rearing bible, it was not because parents were truly ignorant of how to keep a child alive and healthy or because pediatricians did not exist or because help and advice from friends and parents were not available, but rather because they thought it contained the psychological formulas ensuring two related things: the discovery, nurture, and expression of children's diverse capacities and the foundation on which they could scan and experience a very diverse world. Implicit in all this was that you had to avoid unduly imposing your tradition and cultural heritage on the child before he or she could comprehend what it was all about. My parents never read Spock, but, like many immigrants, they did not come to this country to recreate for their children the conditions of their own upbringing. If they did not find the streets paved with gold, they did see them as paved with opportunity for their children, and being Jewish made it very likely that the major thoroughfares would be called Learning, Education, and Professions.

None of this, of course, explains my great needs for diversity of stimulation and change. It explains in part my ambition, and I do not want to underestimate what it meant in my early schooling to be regarded as bright and encouraged by teachers to set my sights high. The Great Depression altered my sights, and when early in those years I came down with polio, it must have been traumatic in the extreme for my parents. It was traumatic for me, but, dialectically, it also created the condition in which fantasy could run riot, and in the two years when the upper part of my body was encased in a brace or cast, I lived through at least a dozen different careers.

I find it very difficult to think about what might have happened to me, my career, and even my marriage if I had stayed at Southbury. Indeed, when I do think about it, I experience a mini-panic. The thought that I would have stayed on, blotting out the many ways in which I was being shaped to adjust to institutional living, constantly managing the war between my values and institutional practice, fooling myself that I was not becoming an "organization man," unaware (making myself unaware) of the larger arena of ideas and writings, a confined person in a confining setting—even today I cannot allow myself to pursue that train of thought for more than a few minutes.

But there is one insight that I gained from that train of thought, one that attended clarity and that I wrote about thirty years after I left Southbury and that had its origins in my Southbury experience.* The insight is in the form of a question:

*Sarason, S. B. *Work, Aging, and Social Change: Professionals and the One-Life, One-Career Imperative.* New York: Free Press, 1977.

What is it like to have a career in which it becomes clear that the chances are high that what you will be doing ten or twenty years from now will be much the same as what you are doing today, that your need for change and growth will not be satisfied? Personal experience and observation forced me to conclude that too many people avoid confronting that question, with consequences adversely fateful for their individual lives and, therefore, for the larger society. American psychology has shown little interest in this issue, even though it is, I believe, a crucial one in American society in that the dynamics the issue suggests have changed and will continue to change that society. I shall be eternally in debt to my Southbury years, but only because events beyond my ken and control permitted me to escape the trap that Southbury would have been. Of course, Seymour Sarason played a role in that escape. But it was a role in a larger drama that at the time I did not understand, let alone write. It was a drama of change in American society that would alter my life even though I was a truly insignificant actor.

10

Socialization at Yale

For the past several years, in the initial meeting of one of my graduate seminars I have said, "Take a piece of paper and in about fifteen minutes, answer two questions: (1) List the schools of which Yale is comprised. (2) Outline the steps by which Yale selects and appoints someone to its faculty." All of the students have been at Yale for a year or more. Almost all had been in comparable universities as undergraduates. No student has ever listed all of the schools that make up Yale, although a few have come close. In regard to faculty selection and appointment, no student has come close to a realistic picture of those steps, their chronology or rationale.

The ostensible reason for the assignment is to provide a basis for discussing the question: How is it possible to spend six, seven, or more years in a particular type of setting and know so little about how it works? The other reason is more personal in that it serves the purpose of confirming the conclusion that when I came to Yale I was, for all practical purposes, totally ignorant of how a university is organized and how it works in the ways it does. I was far more ignorant than the average student in my seminar. Dana College was no preparation for understanding Yale. And neither was Clark University, from the standpoint of size and complexity.

Phenomenologically speaking, I did not come to Yale but to the department of psychology, housed in a building away from the "campus." I put quotation marks around "campus" because Yale is in the Broadway and Forty-second Street area of downtown New Haven. The department of psychology was then five or so blocks away in the medical center, but psychologically it would have made no difference if it had been a mile away. The department was housed in the Institute of Human Relations, containing the department of psychiatry, Gesell's Institute of Child Development, the department of psychology, part of anthropology, a labor-management institute, and, when I got there, a counseling service for returning veterans. They were unconnected units, and I had no understanding of the parts, let alone of a whole. I knew that Mark May, a psychologist, was the director of the institute and that he had funds to disburse for conducting research and making research appointments. Nobody explained anything to me. I did not have the security to seek explanations. I was like the child full of sexual curiosity and questions but surrounded by folks who did not seem disposed to satisfy them. It was not really, as I now know, that no one seemed disposed to provide me with explanations, to help me in the socialization process, but that my questions would have been regarded as unimportant in terms of why I was at Yale. And why was I at Yale? The answer would have been "to do *your* own thing," and everything else was of secondary or tertiary importance. And "your own thing" meant initiating and sustaining a research program. In subtle and not so subtle ways, the unverbalized message was, "You were not brought here because you are a nice guy or a good teacher. You were brought here because we think you can do worthwhile research, and don't ever forget that."

In itself, the message was not intimidating, but the consequences and context were. One of the consequences of such a message is that it reinforces individualism. If each member of the faculty has his or her own distinctive research program, if each has organized his or her life and priorities around a certain problem, relationships are not likely to be close. The university, we are used to hearing, is a community of scholars. That is playing loose with the word *community*.

The Yales of this world are a collection of ambitious, assertive individuals. I do not say this critically but rather for the purpose of stating that at the same time that the university does an extraordinarily good job of supporting individual effort, it does not foster those ties that bind one member with another. As a beginning assistant professor, ignorant of the ways of the university and the department, being completely on my own to organize my thinking and days, it was less intimidating than it was puzzling. Everyone was friendly, but everyone seemed preoccupied with their research interests. Complicating my adjustment was the fact that Esther and I could not find an apartment (the housing shortage because of the war was acute), and she returned to Clark University for the year to finish her residence requirements for her doctorate. I was both alone and lonely, except for weekends when I would go to Worcester. I had a lot to do: read, decide about research focus, and prepare and teach seminars. But I was poignantly aware that I was in a setting in which rugged individualism was a prevailing value. I missed the sense of community, and my reaction to it became a theme in my writings in later years. It was also one of the spurs to the creation in 1961–62 of the Yale Psycho-Educational Clinic, a deliberate effort to organize my own academic family. Almost everything I have ever done or written has been autobiographical.

What was truly intimidating was finding myself in a place loaded with luminaries whose work I had been required to read in graduate school: Carl Hovland, Clark Hull, Walter Miles, Robert Yerkes, John Dollard, Neal Miller, Leonard Doob, Frank Beach—what was the likes of me doing in the same place as the likes of them? I recounted in Chapter Six how puny I felt sitting in the seminar room at Clark where there hung photographs of those who had got their doctorates or had taught at Clark. It was one thing to look at photographs of outstanding people; it is quite another to have to interact with them, to appear as if you deserve to be with them. It was not only that they were "names" in psychology but that each of them appeared intellectually secure and capable of a level of critical and systematic thinking that far surpassed my own.

The icing on this cake of intimidation was that their substantive interests were not mine. I was the sole full-time clinical psychologist in the department. There was practically no overlap between their interests and mine. I was not interested in learning, human or animal. And the emphasis on research designs, statistical rationales, and the superiority of experimental manipulations over correlational methods was both boring and beyond my level of sophistication. I envied them for their knowledge and methodological skills. I would have liked to know everything they knew and do everything they could do. At the same time, I was never in doubt that my substantive interests were not theirs. My respect for them was unbounded. They had first-rate minds. But it never occurred to me to alter in any way my substantive interests. The one thing I did gain from those senior colleagues was that the rules of evidence held regardless of what you studied. If they conveyed the attitude that the study of clinical problems was characterized by sloppy, slipshod methods and thinking, I refrained from articulating my perception that sloppy thinking and trivial pursuits were rather general in psychology. Indirectly but powerfully, those colleagues forced me to examine my ideas more critically. I took from them what I needed for my purposes, which did not include what they considered to be important problems.

There is another way of describing this state of affairs. It is hard to exaggerate how after the war the ethos of science suffused the intellectual climate, especially in psychology, which had long sought to establish itself as a science. Science had been a decisive factor in winning the war, and science would be the vehicle for building a new and better world. There was acceptance of the belief (in the society generally) that the application of science to human and social problems would, for the first time in history, illuminate and dissolve millennia-old problems in individual and social existence. B. F. Skinner's *Walden Two* (New York: Macmillan, 1962) is a clear example of how a scientific and technologically sophisticated psychology could bring us close to utopian living. Undergirding that belief was another one: it was American science that would lead the way. If the potentials of science were to be realized, it was only in America that these developments could take place.

As I look back at those early years at Yale, I am struck by the insularity of view. It was as if the rest of the world did not exist and we did not have to take account of non-American formulations of the nature of the human animal and social existence. American psychology had emerged from and then cut its roots in philosophy in its efforts to become a science. One of the consequences of World War II was a further rejection of philosophical traditions in Europe and elsewhere. Science was concerned with clear formulations, data, proof, system building, prediction, and control. I was totally unaware of this insularity from philosophical traditions, although my relationship with Schaefer had dented somewhat my insularity. And I was also caught up in the belief that science could solve human problems.

The bedeviling conflict within me was the recognition that I was far more interested in ideas than I was in research. I was more a critic than I was an investigator. I was more a philosopher than I was a psychologist. So, for example, I was more interested in why American psychology took such a narrow view of intelligence than I was in demonstrating through research that intelligence was not a "thing." If the early papers I wrote at Yale were about projective techniques, it was because those techniques, which derived from European sources, rested on rationales that provided observations of problem solving that the traditional conceptions of intelligence ignored. That these techniques did not have demonstrable reliability and validity, that conclusions drawn from the data they provided depended on who was drawing conclusions, that the clinician is an imperfect observer and interpreter, bothered me, but not to the point where I would commit the mistake of ignoring the problem those techniques were devised to address: how different human problem solving looks as a function of variation of task. That was the problem that my Southbury years made central to my interests.

When you join a department in the university, both sides have embarked on a socialization process. That is not so obvious in the case of a new member who comes in at a senior level, that is, who has an established reputation and track record, and the question of whether the individual meets and will strengthen department standards has been answered. A full professor is not asked to join a department if there is any doubt about that person's scholarly and research standards and accomplishments.

It is quite different in the case of a wet-behind-the-ears, beginning assistant professor intent on "making it." From the moment of arrival, that person on the make seeks to determine how his or her senior colleagues make judgments of the quality and quantity of one's work. It is a seeking that can powerfully influence what one thinks, the direction of research, and the forging of a sense of professional identity.

Matters are not helped any by the fact that no one tells you how to think, what to study, and in what ways. You are on your own, but it is an "own" that inevitably seeks to incorporate the standards of judgment of senior colleagues. How much one incorporates varies considerably from individual to individual, and the intellectual and personal consequences are no less varied. If only from novels, plays, and movies, we are all familiar with the fact that trying to "make it" in large private and public organizations is a soul-searching, soul-searing, soul-changing affair. It is no less so in our major universities. The stakes are high, the rites of passage are suffused with anxieties, and for most the door of the room at the top remains closed. I do not say this critically but as a statement of fact about membership in a major university. The phrase "a major university" really says it all, because when you come to such a place you *know* that you are going to try to make it in the "big leagues," not in the minors. No one wants to fail and end up in the minors. How do you go about "making it"? The young assistant professor wants to be socialized, but not at the expense of becoming other than what he or she is. But what if what you are is judged not good enough? Anyone who views the university as an oasis of personal tranquillity and easy ascent to the presumed joys of a full professorship has no understanding of the culture of the university.

On the day (April 24, 1987) I began writing this paragraph, the first page of the *New York Times* had an article about a Harvard professor (who is also president of the American Political Science Association) who had just been denied membership in the National Academy of Science. Within the academy, a campaign led by a Yale professor of mathematics had been mounted to deny membership because that professor's work was "pseudoscience." I cannot judge the merits of the case. But I can say that the case is quite typical of the seriousness with which one's work in the university is scrutinized and the depths of the conflicts that can be engendered. A year earlier, a member of the Harvard department of sociology was denied tenure shortly after one of his books had received a Pulitzer Prize. That case was also given a good deal of play in the national media. These cases are atypical only in terms of receiving public attention. They are not atypical of how membership in the university gets determined in a drama of individual ambition and institutional rules and traditions. It was not until I became a full professor that I understood the agony that I and most of my colleagues experienced in deciding the fate of others. As one colleague said after a meeting of several hours about whether to give tenure to someone, "How did *I* ever make it here?" Few who have made it do not carry scars from the process.

In light of the above, it will come as a surprise when I say that I was minimally caught up with whether I would make it at Yale or not. That I wanted to make it goes without saying. But I viewed that prospect no differently from the fantasy of receiving a gift of a million dollars. Brooklyn–New York–Newark me could not see myself as possessing the social and academic credentials to remain at Yale. My social insecurity derived from one fact and one perception. The fact was that I was the first acknowledged Jew in the department. The perception was that Esther and I came from a social-cultural-economic background dramatically different from that of other members of the department. They were middle- and upper-class Protestants, we were economically poor Jews who felt socially marginal. We were able to afford a large, heatless apartment at the edge of the ghetto, making do with two kerosene heaters. Everyone else had their own houses or far better apartments. We did not see ourselves (and assumed—wrongly—that others did not see us) as fitting the mold of Yale people. The point is that I did not expect to remain at Yale, and it did not bother me.

I have tried strenuously to re-experience those early years at Yale to test the conclusion that I was not caught up in a struggle to stay at Yale. What becomes clear in that replaying is that

I regarded everyone else at my rank (let alone those above) as possessing more academic "ability." They were far better researchers and scientists than I was. I did not feel in competition with them. I envied and respected them for their talents, and I knew that by conventional academic criteria there was no point in being competitive. And yet, strange to say, it minimally (if at all) altered the judgment that what I thought and had to say was important, that I had to be (to employ a cliché) true to myself. I was a clinical psychologist. I viewed it, as did others, as a new and "soft" field, the scientific underpinnings of which left much to be desired. However interested I was, however necessary it was to establish such underpinnings, my interests were broader than that.

How do you select and train clinical psychologists? How and why do clinicians vary in what they observe and interpret? How does one milk the potentials of the single case? What represents a contribution to knowledge? Why is clinical psychology tying itself to a repair-oriented medical psychiatry instead of relating itself to a more prevention-oriented role in schools? Why is no one, but no one, interested in the cultural significances of the field of mental retardation for understanding American society? Was clinical psychology being put into a mold that would inordinately restrict its development? These were not questions or issues about which I had clarity. I was too uninformed and unformed for clarity. But these questions and issues fascinated me. I was aware of my ignorance but not daunted by it. If I was not a scientist, which is not to say that I was in any way antiscience, so be it. I felt fortunate to be in a place that, despite its intimidating aspects, allowed me to go my own way. I would leave Yale not with resentment but with gratitude for having been exposed to first-rate minds from whom I would have learned a good deal about the rules of evidence. In those early years, I had no idea where I would end up. I was too caught up in my academic beginnings to worry about transitions and endings.

And then there were the graduate students, who were sources of joy, help, and intimidation. For one thing, they were extraordinarily bright, curious, and fast learners. By the end of their first or second year at Yale, during which they took the basic "scientific" courses, they were far more sophisticated than I in matters of statistics, methodology, and research design. Indeed, in the one systematic, conventional research project I initiated a few years after I came to Yale, I could count on their sophistication to make up for my weaknesses. But what characterized the graduate students who came to Yale within the first five years after the war was an openness to knowledge and viewpoints, a soaking up of knowledge, that became increasingly rare as the years went on. Herbert Kelman, Paul Mussen, Seymour Feshbach, Patricia Pittluck Minuchin, Florence Schumer, George Mahl, George Mandler, Jerome Kagan, William Kessen, John Conger—these are some of the names that come to mind. Some were as old as I; the others were no more than three or four years younger. With students like that, you did not have to worry about intellectual stimulation. They, like the faculty, were imbued with the feeling that psychology was at the beginning of a new era of growth in size, knowledge, and status. Psychology would (would have to) make a difference in the new post–World War II era. We were in on the ground floor. It would not be a small building.

Many of the students were Jewish, in marked contrast to the prewar situation. For the most part, they were from the New York City colleges, coming from backgrounds similar to that of Esther and myself. They were "hungry" Jews: ambitious, hardworking, and reverential of learning. Esther and I now felt socially less alone. If we felt socially marginal among the faculty, that was certainly not the case in our relationship with graduate students. Shortly after I came to Yale, the religious composition of the faculty (in psychology and elsewhere in the university) changed dramatically. Up until the end of the war, Clark Hull had been the most commanding presence and influence in the department. He was, the rumor mill had it, anti-Semitic. He was also anti-Catholic, anti-Oriental, and anti- a lot of other religious and ethnic groups. In fact, everyone was surprised when Hull took Harry Yamaguchi as a research assistant, and when, before that, Eliot Rodnick worked with him. When I joined the department, Hull was still active but ailing. The

academic baton had been passed on to others, many of whom
had been his students or had been influenced by him but who
were devoid of the virus of discrimination. This change was occurring not only in colleges and universities but in the society
at large, but it took place most quickly in academia.

To my knowledge, no one foresaw that the virtual abolish-
ment of anti-Semitism in the university (reflective as it was of
a more general acceptance of equality of opportunity) was only
the beginning of a dynamic that within fifteen years would require the university to open its faculty doors to other groups,
women and blacks in particular. Why in the case of Jews did
the change take place so quickly and without federal legislation,
whereas in the case of blacks and women, external prods were
necessary? In the case of blacks, the problem between 1945 and
1960 was not hiring blacks to the faculty but finding blacks with
the credentials for being admitted as graduate students. Long
before there was federal legislation, the Yale department was
eager to admit black students, but few applied and none met
criteria for admission.

With women it was another story: the obligations of marriage and family were seen as incompatible with the demands
of the scholarly and research life. That women could earn a doctorate no one would deny. Many would deny that they had the
"cast of mind" to be outstanding contributors to the field.
Underneath it all was the perception or intuition that the presence of women among the faculty would be socially difficult,
uncomfortable, and problematic—the same argument that had
been used against hiring Jews in universities before World War
II. But whereas Jews had been seen as intellectually able but
socially and personally overly pushy, ambitious, and competitive, women and blacks were seen as intellectually passive and
interpersonally dependent, that is, the opposite of the individual-
istic, autonomous, striving white male faculty members in all-
white, all-male departments. The fact is that the intuition was
a valid one but very one-sided. It was valid in the sense that
the presence of women and blacks would present social and interpersonal problems, just as were presented for decades in those
departments that had a Jewish member. The occasional "out-

sider" who was brought in from the cold was, and remained, an outsider to the insiders. That requires no special explanation. But where the intuition was incomplete and insensitive was in not comprehending the psychology of the outsider: how being seen as different, or thinking you are being seen and treated as different and feeling different, can produce the consequences of the self-fulfilling prophecy.

If as a Jew I understood this well (but not completely), I confess that the personal lesson did not sufficiently sensitize me to what other types of outsiders would experience. But that is part of a later and more complicated story. My coming to Yale was an example of how universities were changing. *That* I and others were aware of. What this professional self-absorption prevented us from seeing was that America was changing, that an accustomed world view was being transformed, if not shattered, and that this would show up in diverse but unsettling ways that would alter the relationship between the university and its societal surround. More than any of the other social sciences, psychology—by tradition and substance—was unprepared for comprehending the larger picture. American psychology was quintessentially a psychology of the individual. All else was an undifferentiated, unexplored background. If only because of my abiding interests in political theories and movements and the need for everything I did to have relevance for social problems, I was critical of my field. But it was the criticism of an amateur. I still lived in two rather separate worlds: the world of affairs and the world of the university. I knew something was wrong, and that included not knowing how to think about it. I would reread J. F. Brown's attempt to integrate Marx, Freud, and Lewin, awed by his conceptual courage but unsatisfied with the result. I retreated, in part at least, to the confines of clinical psychology and its enamorment with the intrapsychic. It was not an unproductive retreat, but it was a retreat nevertheless. It would take me fifteen years before I acted on the maxim that if you want to understand your social world, try to change it.

If I had to choose one social phenomenon from the immediate postwar years that contained and heralded societal transformation, it was the GI Bill of Rights. To paint a picture of the American university in those years and leave out the significance of that legislation for the university and the society, then and now, is to plumb the depths of obtuseness. Here was a piece of legislation that had massive impact and has as yet to be studied. I find that amazing and depressing, as blatant an example of the blind spots in American social science as one will find. That legislation was quintessentially American in several respects. First, it reflected the American view that education (the more the better) was for the individual the secular equivalent of religious salvation. Second, it was a manifestation of American optimism that a new world was aborning and America had the crucial part to play. Third, the university was no longer a luxury for society but, as its role during the war had demonstrated, was essential for capitalizing on the potentials of science and technology. Fourth, the least a grateful society could do for its veterans was to give substance to the rhetoric of equal opportunity. Powering the GI Bill was a memory and a fear. The memory had to do with the Great Depression still vivid in the minds of citizens. The fear had to do with the possibility that going from a war to a peacetime economy could be socially destabilizing.

If I had to sum up in a phrase the message the GI Bill communicated to millions of veterans and the larger society, it would be "great expectations." It was a message that many veterans who never expected to go to college, finish college, go on to graduate and professional school, or have the opportunity for refresher courses and experiences in their profession (especially in medicine) heard and acted on. As individuals they were given a new lease on life in a new world, a world yet to be fashioned. If they flocked into the university with great expectations, they found themselves in departments suffused with great expectations about the future of their fields.

And did they ever flock! In terms of physical plant and living accommodations, the university was unprepared for such quick growth. Villages of army Quonset huts sprang up overnight. Babies and small children were familiar campus sights. The population explosion had begun, although few understood what its consequences would be. That in psychology there would be an explosion in knowledge no one doubted. That clinical psychology would contribute to that explosion I had no doubt, at the same time that I was aware that in the field at large there were psychologists who had questions about how this new field might adversely affect the establishment of psychology as a science. I am sure that there were members of the Yale department who harbored such questions, but they adopted a supportive, wait-and-see stance. The department and the Institute of Human Relations had been and continued to be places in which psychoanalysis as theory, practice, and research was the focus of interest. John Dollard and Neal Miller were writing their books the goal of which was to integrate psychoanalysis into a more general psychology.

With such a tradition and in such an ambience, the question was not whether to have a clinical program but rather how to develop a quality program. There were universities that decided against having a program. A noted psychologist, Samuel Fennberger, voiced the view that clinical psychology could have the effect of killing the goose that laid the golden eggs, the scientific eggs. At a meeting of the American Psychological Association at the University of Pennsylvania (for a few years after the war, you could have such a meeting on a university campus), I found myself in conversation with, among others, Walter Hunter, an eminent experimental psychologist who had left Clark to head up the department at Brown. The conversation concerned the core courses that would make up a clinical program. I voiced the opinion that a course in projective techniques was essential. Walter Hunter replied, "If you can show me that those techniques have scientific validity, I would agree to such a course. But you cannot." As a lowly assistant professor in the presence of one of the greats of the time, I refrained from saying that it was precisely because clinical psychology had been kept out of the university that it lacked a firm foundation in research, and not until it became a part of the field could such a foundation be laid.

It was apparent that the assimilation of the new field by psychology would not be a smooth one. To expect otherwise demonstrated ignorance of the processes of institutional change, of the force of tradition, and of long-standing practice. It would not be a matter of personalities, although those are always complicating factors. It would be a matter of societal, institutional, and generational change. The Age of Psychology or Mental Health was upon us, and the university in general and psychology in particular would never be the same. The walls between the university and the larger society were beginning to erode. Would clinical psychology be the Trojan horse that would overwhelm and conquer psychology from within? Some feared that possibility, others enjoyed the fantasy. None predicted that within three decades the American Psychological Association would be composed of dozens of divisions, virtually making it impossible to answer the question, what is the core of psychology? And no one predicted that in the foreseeable future only a few cities would be able to accommodate the annual meeting of the American Psychological Association. Clinical psychology played an important role in this transformation, but it was only one of a number of factors.

For several years after I came to Yale, *I* was the clinical program. I taught the courses in diagnostic testing and projective techniques. I spent countless hours each week observing students in their testing and going over their written reports. I was also major adviser on dissertation research. I developed and oversaw a clinical proseminar that met twice a week, two hours each time, that was as comprehensive as it was time-consuming. I developed a course in psychoanalytical theory, perhaps the first such graduate course in the country. All of this I did willingly and enthusiastically. That I was teaching more than a normal load goes without saying. In fact, at that time I did not know what a normal load was, and I was not interested enough to find out. I knew what clinical students needed, and my job was to give it to them. By present-day standards, it was a very demanding program. Aside from clinical courses, the students took seminars in statistics and research design and a departmental proseminar. In addition, I urged students (really twisted their arms) to take Neal Miller's course in learning, not because I was interested in the literature on learning (most of which was about rat learning) but because I felt that they should not pass up the opportunity to see how a first-rate mind operates. Many of the students did take that course, and a majority agreed that it was instructive to observe a creative, rigorous, penetrating mind at work.

The fact is that I very quickly became allergic to the emphasis placed on learning in the department and the field generally. The talmudic controversies that occupied that area I found boring and much ado about nothing. That learning was an important and ubiquitous process was obvious. Nobody needed convincing on that score. Humans were animals, and the nature of animal learning should, therefore, be a major focus in psychology. But in America, animal learning was rat learning, for the most part. I tried to get interested in Hull, Guthrie, Tolman, Skinner, and others, but I had to conclude that they were trivializing an important problem. And for me, the problem was the developmental and social arenas in which learning of diverse sorts took place.

It says a good deal about Neal Miller, as it does about John Dollard, that they collaborated on efforts to conceptualize learning in the contexts of social imitation and psychotherapy. Their book on personality and psychotherapy was very influential on the new field of clinical psychology (*Personality and Psychotherapy*. New York: McGraw-Hill, 1950). For one thing, it sharpened the debate about whether psychoanalysis could be formulated in a way that suggested directions for research. It brought (albeit indirectly) to the fore two questions: How could psychologists, influenced by the writings of Miller and Dollard, do research on psychotherapy if they had no training in psychotherapy? Should (and how should) training in psychotherapy be part of a clinical program? Their book received a mixed critical reception, as might have been expected. Although I was critical of it, I recognized that it was a valiant and needed effort with which the field would have to deal. The conflict between psychology and psychiatry about who could or should do psychotherapy (let alone psychoanalysis) was heating up. To the extent (and it was not small) that their book fueled the interest of clinical psychologists in the processes of and research on psychotherapy, it focused attention on the consequences of the tie between clinical psychology and the psychiatric setting. The cold war between the two professions had started; it was to become a hot one in a few short years.

It is not happenstance that the person with whom I felt an intellectual affinity and with whom I became a friend was Frank Beach, who left the Museum of Natural History to come to Yale shortly after I did. He was already an eminent comparative psychologist, and it was considered a major feat when he accepted the offer to come as Sterling Professor, the most prestigious chair at Yale. Frank's virtues were many, not the least of which was a combination of humility and forthrightness. In an early conversation, he told me that when he accepted the offer, he had made it clear that he really was not a psychologist. At the same time that he was interested in many animal species, his focus was on sexual behavior. Frank was as much a biologist, ethnologist, and endocrinologist as he was a psychologist. He saw psychology as unduly narrow and erecting theories derived almost exclusively from studies of the Norway rat as a disaster. He predicted correctly that in psychology the field of animal learning would become moribund.

To a youngster like me, hearing these views from an eminent psychologist was a salutary warning that I had to avoid accommodating my interests and opinions to what was mainstream psychology. Frank was a born and bred Kansan. In his own field, he was the opposite of parochial; he was an internationalist in his grasp of the literature on sexual behavior in humans and other animal species. And he had an abiding interest in cultural variations in sexual behavior. The event that emboldened me to seek a relationship with Frank Beach was his presentation to the departmental colloquium, an honor reserved only for full professors who had come from elsewhere to join the department. Frank had put on the blackboard several graphs and tables. At the beginning of the question period, one of the graduate students started it off by asking, "Professor Beach, have you considered doing a Fourier analysis of your data?" With no reaction time, Frank replied, "If I knew what it was, I might consider doing it." Such candor was and is unusual. I had to get to know him.

In my first year at Yale, I gave little thought to what would be the focus of my research effort. I was quite aware that I was expected to do research, not an article about this and an article about that but a sustained programmatic effort about an important problem. There were seeds of important problems I could identify, but none gripped me, either because they were important but uninteresting to me or because they would require an immersion in methodological issues that were to neither my taste nor my sophistication. It did not take long for me to confront the fact that what I was most interested in was me: what I had experienced at Southbury and certain personal problems that had been obstacles in my development. In short, I decided that what interested me the most, and what I could do best, was making sense of my past. I had the security or arrogance to assume that whatever sense I made of my past would have general significance.

The first decision I made was less a decision than an indulgence of the ambition to transform the field of mental retardation. From the day I left Southbury, I felt that I could and should not leave the Southbury experience in the unused past. Indeed, in 1947 or 1948, when the National Institute of Mental Health (NIMH) was in its infancy, I submitted a research proposal to study the child-rearing practices of families who contributed disproprtionately to the Southbury population: the so-called subcultural, garden-variety, Kallikak type of mental retardation. I knew both the families and areas (urban and rural) I wanted to begin with. The focus would be to observe and describe the familial-cultural context into which these individuals were born and reared.

There was no doubt in my mind that I would be able to demonstrate that these contexts did not foster the kind of intellectual stimulation that was necessary if individuals were to be able to meet standards of intellectual-educational performance that the larger society valued. As I was wont to say, familiarity with these contexts would convince you that children who manage to survive in them, far from being biologically inferior, should be viewed as biologically hearty, if not superior. That proposal was submitted years before labels such as "deprived," "underprivileged," and the "culture of poverty" became a part of everyday language. It was also submitted at a time when interest in mental retardation was virtually nil in psychology. The proposal was rejected, largely on the grounds that the observations I would make would have uncertain reliability and validity. That, or course, was true, but, I reassured myself, are there not times when uncertainty about adequacy of methods should not stand in the way of trying to describe and understand an important, unstudied problem? Why couldn't they see that the problem cried out for attention, that its significance went far beyond the confines of mental retardation to the nature of American society and the diverse cultures it contains?

A decade later, when I was a member of an NIMH panel to evaluate research proposals, I found it ironic that support was being approved for "womb to tomb" studies of white, middle-class individuals and their families in an effort to describe the origins and vicissitudes of personality and intellectual style. Every one of these approved studies was methodologically weak, but they were supported for two reasons. First, they were trying to illuminate, theoretically and practically, important developmental issues. Second, with few exceptions, they were studies derived from psychoanalytical theory and were carried out by psychoanalysts. For two decades after the war, psychoanalysis as theory, research, and practice was a major focus in American psychology, especially in the fields of clinical and personality psychology. It was seen as the wave of the future. Compared to psychoanalysis, mental retardation was a nothing field. I believed that psychoanalysis was the royal road to understanding human behavior. I was probably the only person who believed that psychoanalysis and American society would be illuminated through studies of mentally retarded individuals.

I think it is fair to say that those "womb to tomb" studies were research disasters that contributed little or nothing to anything. They were overdesigned, submerged by data, and fruitless. In their pathetic efforts to ape science, to appear methodologically sound, they managed to lose sight of the individual and the context. As these studies came up for renewed support, they were one by one disapproved. I do not have a copy of my research proposal. If I did, I am sure I would find it wanting in a number of ways. But presumption would not be one of its defects. Like the anthropologist going to a so-called primitive culture, I wanted to become part of, to observe, to understand particular individuals in a particular cultural-familial context. To this day, you cannot find in the professional-scientific literature a developmental-longitudinal study of mentally retarded individuals. Unlike Topsy, they apparently do not grow! We are relatively insensitive to how fields are prejudiced in regard to certain conditions and substantive problems. Particularly in America, mental retardation was and still is an ''oppressed'' field of study.

The rejection of my proposal emboldened me to write my first book, *Psychological Problems in Mental Deficiency* (New York: Harper & Row, 1949). That book had several purposes or themes. The first was that the customary definition or criteria for mental retardation, and the psychometric ways those criteria were judged or met, were narrow, misleading, and harmful—that is, they confused labeling an individual with understanding him or her. So, for example, if your neighbor's child who has an IQ of 180 takes your cat and chokes it to death, you will not say he did it *because* he has a high IQ. But if the child has an IQ of 50, the chances are enormously high that you will say he did it *because* he has a low IQ. The Aristotelian mode of thinking is rampant when it comes to reacting to a mentally retarded individual. The second purpose of the book was to challenge the tendency to explain atypical behavior and development in purely biological terms, that is, to oversimplify phenomena by indulgence of biological reductionism. The third purpose was to illustrate how projective techniques demonstrated that mentally retarded people were *persons* possessed of feelings, fears, hopes, and strivings like the rest of us. A related purpose was to bolster that argument by a detailed presentation of Esther's and my psychotherapeutic efforts. The fourth purpose was to indicate how institutionalization—its purpose, length, and ambience—guaranteed that return to family and community would be difficult and frequently impossible. The final purpose or theme, the thread on which all other purposes hung, was to emphasize the significance of cultural context: family, community, geographical region, institution.

That book was as much polemic as it was critique, as

much social commentary as it was a marshaling of evidence, an ideological statement as much as it was an effort at scholarship. Although I did not write that book in the first person, it was a very personal statement. It was making sense about what I and Esther had experienced and done. (Esther was a spur to my interest in projective techniques and psychotherapy.)

I wrote the book in the academic year 1947–48. I knew nothing about how you get a book published. I called Harper, was referred to the senior editor (Edward Tyler), told him I had a manuscript about mental retardation, and asked if he would be interested in seeing it. He was interested (I did not know that editors are always interested, on the phone at least), and I sent it off to him. We arranged to meet in New York three weeks later. When we met, he told me that he liked the manuscript, but there was a problem: who was interested in mental retardation? Being not far from Madison Avenue, I made my pitch that mental retardation was a coming area and that Harper and I would be getting in on the ground floor. I believed it; Mr. Tyler was unconvinced. He thought awhile, and then said something like the following: "The first printing of a book like yours would be twenty-five hundred copies. But it will not sell that many. If you will take reduced royalties on the first printing, we will publish it even though we expect to lose money on the book. Frankly, we are looking for good books on which to lose money because we are making so much money on textbooks since the GI Bill pays for the books that veterans need. We cannot keep up with the demand for Gardner Murphy's book *Personality*. So we are willing to publish your book even though we will lose money even if you do take reduced royalties." I assumed that his judgment reflected what outside readers of the manuscript had told him. Since Gardner Murphy was one of their consultants, it is likely that his was the decisive judgment. I, of course, was prepared to sign on the dotted line even if they had asked me to eschew royalties on the first printing.

The book received the kind of reviews that authors hope for but rarely get. Over the years, scores of individuals have told me how eye-opening the book was for them. It is not undue modesty on my part to say that if the book was regarded as the best statement yet on the psychology of mental retardation, it said as much about the pedestrian quality of previous books as it did about the virtues of mine. The impact of the book had two sources: I did make mental retardation interesting, and it did talk to what many practitioners had experienced and thought. It was the right book at the right time. The book was minimally influential in psychology. One might have expected that it would be influential among clinical psychologists, but that was unrealistic, because they were riveted on the neuroses and psychoses, which had for them far more—incomparably more—sex appeal than mental retardation. It was in schools of education that the book was influential. They were responsible for preparing special-class teachers and school psychologists, and although the book was not written as a text, it was used as such in those programs. I became far more well known in education than in psychology. I enjoyed that modest celebrity, although it in no way altered my opinion that in the land of the blind, the one-eyed, astigmatic man is king. I had already learned (how I do not know) that the more you know, the more you need to know. I have always been both impressed and unimpressed by my accomplishments.

The book was decisive in determining the systematic research program I would undertake. In a section of the book devoted to the interpersonal dynamics of the testing situation, I described a bright college student who was asked by his psychology instructor to take a test in front of the class. The test was the Kohs Block Designs, composed of wooden cubes each side of which is differently colored. Some sides are half this color and half that. The subject is shown a card containing a design and asked to assemble the cubes to mirror that design. The designs range in difficulty from the simple to the complex. The student I described was pathetically inadequate to the task, embarrassing to him and to the instructor as well as to the class, in which he was a star student. The student was obviously anxious, feeling at the beginning of the testing that he would fail and be ridiculed, disappointing his mentor. The point of the anecdote in that section of the book was that test performance, be it of a bright or of a mentally retarded person, had always to be understood (among other things) in terms of the attitudes and feelings the testing situation arouses. In real life, there are no boundaries between intelligence and personality.

If anything was obvious in my diagnostic work at Southbury, it was how anxious individuals could become when they were tested. The customary explanation was that their intellectual inadequacies were not caused by anxiety and other reactions but were the cause of those reactions. I argued that such an explanation was too one-sided, an instance of the IQ becoming the etiological explanation for almost everything. Coming to Yale and participating in the selection of graduate students gave further strength to my belief that the worth and fate of people were too frequently and simplemindedly determined by test scores.

I decided to start a research program on the measurement, antecendents, and consequences of test anxiety. Testing, for myriad purposes in myriad settings, was a feature of American life. If it was such a feature of the society, why had virtually nothing been done to understand how people felt about tests and what tests did to them? Were tests, unlike X-rays and drugs, exempt from the phenomena of side effects? I wanted to demonstrate that test performance varied as a function of test-taking attitudes. Like the book, the research I would carry out would be relevant to the problem of most interest to me: relationships between performance and context. We were (still are) used to hearing that intelligence is what intelligence tests measure. That definition always bothered me. I finally figured out that the statement was a misuse of language in that the verb *is* conveys the message that intelligence is a thing in the sense that a stone *is*, that intelligence exists the way a stone exists. That, of course, is nonsense. The concept of intelligence was a cultural invention for the purpose of making distinctions among people. The concept is relatively new in human history. It is precisely because it is a cultural invention that one must fathom its cultural origins and uses, and one must be very wary of regarding "it" as a thing. We measure things because we know how to measure them. But that we think we know how to measure them, as in the case of intelligence, in no way means that we have solved the cultural-conceptual-definitional problem. It is like the way some people "measure" progress, another bedeviling cultural invention.

The truth is that I was that college student. I knew, from on and off the analytical couch, what test anxiety was. If I was right in my understanding, and if I was approximately right that I was a representative American sample of one, the research would confirm what I already knew. David Bakan, a well-known but still vastly underrated figure in American psychology, once pointed out that by traditional outlook the best experiment is one from which you learn nothing new—that is, everything comes out the way you expected. That is true for the fifteen years I directed the research program.

Another factor that made for the decision to initiate the research program was that I would keep it simple—no fancy designs, complicated procedures, or esoteric statistical analyses. The first thing I did was to get up a self-report questionnaire on test-taking attitudes that could be used with college students. The second step was to administer the questionnaire to several hundred students (Yale was all male then). I would say to the students, "In the course of your life you have taken hundreds of tests. Yet there has been very little study of how people feel about tests and how those feelings affect, positively or negatively, how you do on tests. This questionnaire is an opportunity to report about how you feel in testing situations. When you are through, we have a request that you should feel free to ignore. The request is that on the back of the questionnaire you write as much as you want on your opinion on the role of tests in American society." To our surprise, approximately a fourth of the students wrote essays, many of which were very perceptive and almost all of which served the purpose of venting their anger in regard to having one's fate determined by test scores.

George Mandler was my first research assistant, and he did the initial study comparing high- and low-anxious students— all obviously bright by conventional criteria—on a learning task. As expected, the high-anxious students did significantly poorer than the low-anxious students. We did many such studies, using different tasks and varying instructions, with similar results. Indeed, there was only one study where the expected results were not obtained, and that was an attempt to replicate the initial study. In the replication study, conducted by Alan Towbin, the direction of the findings was as expected but not statistically significant. How come? The instructions were the same: "You are going to be given a task highly correlated with intelligence." The only difference was in experimenters. Fortunately, in the replication the session ended by asking the students several questions about their perception of Towbin—his status, manner, and so on. Those questions were asked because in our conversations Alan had expressed reservations about using those intimidating and deceptive instructions. Alan and George were two very different people. George was and looked older, was far more secure and assertive, and being in the role of the dispassionate researcher facilitated role playing and dissimulation. It was crystal clear from the postsession interview that the students had viewed Alan as another student, a nice guy who in no way aroused in them self-doubt or fear. Alan became a superb clinician. George left the clinical area and became a respected researcher in cognitive psychology. Alan and I submitted the study for publication, but it was rejected on the grounds that it was a glimpse of the obvious. Of course it was, but it was no less a glimpse of the obvious that researchers wrote up and published their findings as if the characteristics of the experimenters were unimportant. What was true then is no less true today.

Just as the rejection of my proposal to the National Institute of Mental Health emboldened me to write the book on mental deficiency, the rejection of the Towbin study led to my writing another book, *The Clinical Interaction* (New York: Harper & Row, 1954). The goal of that book was to marshal evidence that identified those variables that influenced any dyadic clinical interaction and that, when ignored or glossed over, led either to misinterpretation of an individual's behavior and performance or to confusing controversies in the literature, or to both. The issues go far beyond the clinical interaction to the myriad interactions that characterize research on human behavior. The history of American psychology is replete with "findings" that later had to be discarded, or dramatically reinterpreted, as it became clear that the conditions of the testing or research, the nature of the instructions, the age, sex, and background of subject and researcher, and the characteristics of the stimulus materials had been ignored or grievously underinterpreted. The clinical interaction is terribly complicated not only because it has fateful consequences but because it is an event in which two people are in very different roles conditioned by the culture. My experiences at Southbury and with the test-anxiety research (and my work with an anthropologist, to which I will come shortly) left no doubt in my mind that the clinical interaction contained some of the major practical, methodological, and theoretical issues in psychology. To understand another human being requires acute sensitivity to contexts near and far, past and present, idiosyncratic and normative. The "understanders" are part of the contexts, and if we know anything, it is that they, like those they seek to understand, vary enormously.

The anxiety research and that book were, to me, glimpses of the obvious. But who pays attention to the obvious? And then there are those who deny the obvious. It was in the early fifties that I read a news bulletin from the Educational Testing Service in which it was said that they had no evidence that anxiety played a role in SAT scores. I could not believe my eyes. That the evidence for making such a statement was not given goes without saying. I assume they were aware of our studies. But even if they were unaware, and even if they had no evidence, how could they say that taking the SATs was an affectively neutral affair? What conception of American society could they have in order to say that tests used for admission to college, graduate schools, and professional schools would be approached as if one were going to a movie? Ignorance is one thing; irresponsibility or social stupidity is another.

I find it noteworthy that in the postwar years researchers have developed scales to get at how truthful an individual is in responding to personality inventories or how his or her responses are reflective of a tendency to give socially acceptable answers. These scales are tribute to a more sophisticated understanding of what the testing situation engenders in people. Why is it, then, that in the case of ability testing, where on average the personal stakes or consequences are higher, test anxiety is not routinely determined? For my purposes here, I am not referring to the one-on-one clinical interaction where the clinician can make a judgment, although the reliability of such judgments is far from high—more correctly, undetermined. I am referring to group testing, to which we all are exposed in our lives in schools, and which are the basis for sorting individuals into variously labeled groups.

There are, I found out, two parts to an answer to the question. The first is that these tests are not given for the purpose of understanding individuals. The individual is his or her score, and that is the basis of an administrative decision. If the first part of the answer is baldly aclinical or anticlinical in purpose—that is, it is not for the purpose of being helpful to individuals—the second part of the answer is no less obtuse: testing is not for the purpose of the prevention of problems. The rhetoric justifying the testing program may be otherwise, but in practice, it is not for the purpose of understanding and prevention but for sorting. I am not opposed to sorting in principle, but I am opposed to sorting when it does not take into account factors that adversely affect performance. I undertook the test-anxiety research to demonstrate that test anxiety was one such factor.

In order to broaden the research and to further demonstrate the role of test anxiety, we undertook a longitudinal study in which we followed a large number of first- and second-grade children through their elementary school years. It was quite an undertaking and could not have been done without the efforts of Kennedy Hill and Philip Zimbardo. That research left little doubt that test anxiety was an important factor in the test performance and scholastic achievement of many children. There is also no doubt that the stated purpose of schooling is to help individuals "realize their full potential." In responding to that phrase, I am torn between laughing and crying. I want to laugh because that statement is so wildly discrepant with the fact that the individual child is not regarded or understood as an individual until after he or she manifests a problem, and it has to be a problem that interferes with institutional routine. I want to cry because those who make the statement are well intentioned, often in important public policy roles, and blind to the obvious.

We live in the era of mass society, which is not one in which individuality is treasured. Psychology, especially American psychology, is not without blame in this matter, and for two reasons. For one thing, it fostered in the minds of people an overevaluation of tests and scores as a basis for decision making, vastly if not irresponsibly ignoring and glossing over the dynamics of the contexts in which tests are used. And, for another thing, American psychology has always distanced itself from the educational arena, viewing it as an arena of "applications" and not one from which basic laws and principles can be obtained. Before World War II, those in the clinical and educational endeavor were second- and third-class citizens in American psychology. If after the war, clinical psychology got a status it never before had had, the educational setting has remained outside the mainstream.

In 1973 Theta Wolf published a biography of Alfred Binet (*Alfred Binet*. Chicago: University of Chicago Press). I wish that it had been published earlier, because Wolf makes it clear that Binet—one of a handful of psychologists whom Piaget respected—was essentially a clinician who devised his intelligence scales not primarily for the purposes of screening and placement but as an aid for understanding and helping individuals in classrooms. His concept of "mental orthopedics" required that conclusions derived from test performance be translated and implemented in ways appropriate to what should happen in a classroom. For Binet, test scores were not ends in themselves but only one source of information in a helping process. Wolf leaves no doubt that the Americanization of Binet's scales by Goddard and Terman was an unfortunately clear example of running with Binet's scales on the highway of methodology, standardization, and quantification and ignoring his conceptual framework, in which the individual was central. I suppose I have to say that neither in principle nor in practice am I opposed to methodology, standardization, and quantification. What I am saying and have long believed is that when the process and context of measurement have the effect of pushing individuality into the background— the individual *is* his or her test score—let us face the reality that that is what we are doing, and not pretend that we are illuminating or accommodating to individuality.

My attitude toward certain types and uses of psychological tests derives from personal experience and political outlook. And by political outlook, I mean the perception that increasingly each of us is being slotted or grouped by means and criteria that make for impersonality and attribute to us characteristics that may or may not be valid for either our needs or the stated purposes of others. The dynamics of growth and bureaucratization have led to a superficial acceptance of the need for efficiency at the expense of respect for individuality. I am reminded here of a friend who after several days in the hospital exploded to her physician by saying, "I am more than my blood tests, X-rays, temperature, Blue Cross status, and appendix!"

Rare is the individual who does not bear resentment at being identified with some kind of test score, who does not experience an infuriating impotence in the face of faceless impersonality. As a Jew, I did not want my behavior to be interpreted in terms only of Jewishness. As a psychologist at Southbury, I resented the unfairness of reacting to its residents in terms of labels and test scores. And my resentment was as nothing compared to that of the residents. As a faculty member at Yale, I was bothered by the degree to which admission of graduate students depended on grades and test scores. I understand well the dilemma that arises when you have to make decisions about large numbers of people, often having to do so quickly and with the awareness that our tests are far from perfect. It is one thing to accommodate to necessity; it is quite another thing to invoke necessity as an excuse for not seeking to improve your procedures—and that is frequently the case. It is unacceptable to use your procedures to accomplish your purposes and to gloss over the mistakes and injustices you make in regard to the purposes and needs of the test takers. When I used the adjective *political*, I was referring to the obvious fact that the testing situation was one of unequal power, and when we forget that, we have undercut our obligations to individuality. Testing is quintessentially a political and moral endeavor. It may be more correct to say the "interpretation of tests," as blacks, women, and other groups constantly remind us. It took a long time, and the upheavals consequent to World War II, for American psychology to recognize that the development and use of tests were more than scientific and technological problems.

I was drawn to clinical psychology because, among other reasons (there are always other reasons), I was interested in understanding myself and others. In its emphasis on understanding and helping individuals, clinical psychology represented to me an antidote to the number-crunching or score-worshipping use of tests. For me, the fascination of testing inhered in the opportunity it provided to observe the quality and style of individual problem solving, be they in response to an intelligence test, or an inkblot, or a picture to which the individual was asked to organize a story. To administer tests according to a manual of instructions does not require special gifts or extensive training. And the same is true in regard to scoring the tests in accordance with given norms. What makes testing clinical rather than psychometric is the degree to which performance is seen as embedded in the dyadic relationship between tester and testee, that is, the attitudes, feelings, and social behavior the testing situation engenders in the participants.

If I learned anything in being psychoanalyzed, it was that what a person said and did was minimally comprehensible apart from the social context of two people in two different roles. That is a glimpse of the obvious—easy to state but very difficult to take seriously, especially for the beginning clinician, who is so preoccupied with self (and with fear that he or she will not administer the test correctly) that he or she is rendered blind to the interpersonal significance of the context. What I would do frequently in my case seminars was to analyze blindly a Rorschach protocol a student had obtained. I did not do this to flaunt or parade my intuitive talents. And I did not do it to suggest that life-history data are unnecessary or an obstacle to understanding. I am respectful of data as long as they do not lead to premature and arbitrary conclusions, as the "demand characteristics" of the life-history data frequently do. I analyzed these protocols blindly in order to illustrate how from the very first utterances (formal or informal) of the test taker, I was asking myself, how would I have to think or feel to say *that*, in *that* way, in *this* kind of an interpersonal situation? I was not advocating "hell diving" into the unconscious: dredging up exotic material and formulating hypotheses of dubious validity or practical significance.

Those were the days when psychoanalysis was so attractive to many psychologists (especially graduate students) that the "deeper" the interpretation, the more sophisticated you felt or were regarded. I was a partisan for psychoanalysis, but not to the extent that I looked kindly at interpretive pyrotechnics that made the conscious here and now seem irrelevent or even boring. As I pointed out in Chapter Seven, never—but never—did my analyst resort to hell diving or to the use of the jargon of theory. He stayed with me in the concrete present, his interpretations rarely going much beyond what I thought and felt, clearly or inchoately. Understanding others requires, at a minimum, an interpersonal sensitivity that derives not from the dictates of theory but from a willingness and ability to put yourself in somebody else's role. But why seek such understanding? The answer is that such understanding is the basis for actions geared to being helpful. And as I shall discuss later in this chapter, it was the reactions to the professional constraints on action that in a few years altered the field of clinical psychology.

In planned and unplanned ways, my interest in and clinical facility with projective techniques gave direction to my personal and professional lives. For this to be intelligible to the reader, especially the younger one, I have to discuss briefly several features of those years. The first is that America had emerged from World War II as the most powerful economic and military nation. That meant that America became involved in and was frequently responsible for cultures and societies wildly different from our own. That was most clear in regard to the diverse cultures in the vast Pacific Ocean. To administer these territories required an understanding of their cultures that for practical purposes hardly existed.

It is not happenstance, therefore, that anthropology took on an importance to the governing authorities it had never had before, and that new role was manifested in government-sponsored research programs in major universities. It seemed as if anthropologists were spending as much time on exotic Pacific islands as on their campuses. Numerically, anthropology was (and still may be) the smallest of the social sciences, but it too witnessed a dramatic growth after World War II. But its influence on the social sciences was dramatically disproportionate to its numbers. That was true before World War II. The most general reason was that anthropological data presented a clear challenge to any effort to illuminate the "nature of human nature." Put in another way, anthropologists spent a lot of time exposing the blindness of social scientists (especially psychologists) to the fact and significances of cultural diversity. It had long been the case that anthropologists were far more knowledgeable about psychological theory and research than psychologists were about anthropological literature. In psychology and psychiatry, there were, so to speak, a handful of people who strove to forge connections between psychological theory and anthropological data.

Without question, however, the individual who played the most decisive intellectual and interpersonal role in making these connections was one of the giants of American anthropology: Edward Sapir. For two decades before he came to Yale in the thirties from the University of Chicago, Sapir (who among other things was a superb linguist) wrote incisively, sympathetically, but critically about the significance of Freud for a conceptual integration of anthropology, psychiatry, and psychology. (When Sapir came to Yale, he brought Dollard with him as an assistant.) Long before Freud became a significant figure in American psychology, he was someone whom anthropology was seriously confronting.

The significance of Freud for anthropology was obvious: he had presented a general theory of individual development (and of the origins of culture) that he said was valid regardless of cultural variations. That this would not sit well with anthropologists was predictable. But they did not ignore Freud. Scores of "cultural and personality" studies were done to test Freud's position. Was the oedipus complex a universal phenomenon? Was castration complex inevitable in male development? Was penis envy unavoidable in women? Was Freud's view of historical patriarchy tenable? Were child-rearing practices an explanation of adult personality? If anthropology was critical of Freud, it respected him to the point that it sought to evaluate his ideas.

In the decade after World War II, cultural anthropology attained a degree of salience for psychology and psychiatry that it had not had before. It also saw the rise of a psychoanalytically oriented clinical psychology, most clearly seen in the theory and use of (and research on) projective techniques. And it also saw the field of psychiatry become a kind of enclave in the psychoanalytical movement. Culture and personality became a "hot" area, a nexus for interconnecting diverse fields. And few places rivaled Yale (the departments of psychology and anthropology, the Institute of Human Relations) as an interdisciplinary center. For example, across from my office were those of Ralph Linton, George Murdock, Clellan Ford, and John Dollard. And elsewhere in the building were John Whiting, Irvin Child, and Frank Beach. It was in that decade that Ford and Beach spearheaded the development of the Human Relations Area Files, a multiuniversity setting to organize and make available in practical form data from diverse cultures around the world. The world was indeed their oyster. For me and the graduate students, it was an atmosphere that challenged, stretched, and deepened our imagination and knowledge. That was the case in other major universities, and if you peruse the literature of these fields in that decade and compare it to that of today, you will understand why the adjective *parochial* is appropriate for the current scene. It was a decade during which it seemed as if an integration among the social sciences was occurring. What seemed to be happening did not last long, but that is a story for later chapters.

Enter Thomas Gladwin. Tom was a graduate student in anthropology. He had graduated from Harvard, had done some graduate work at Columbia, and during the war had been employed at Lockheed in designing aircraft. (Tom was, among other things, a competent engineer.) He was married and had several children, who lived with his wife in California while he finished his residency requirement at Yale. In 1947 or 1948, he took my seminar on projective techniques because the next year he (and his family) would be on the islands of Truk in the

South Pacific, where he would conduct an ethnographic culture and personality study. One of the things he wished to do was to use the Rorschach and the Thematic Apperception Test (TAT) with the Trukese people, perhaps the most frequently used tests by anthropologists at that time (certainly the case with the Rorschach).

Before taking off from Yale to California to Truk, Tom asked me whether I would be willing (when he got back) to interpret the test protocols. Of course, I said yes, and for several reasons. First, it would be a new and challenging experience. Second, I could not help learning a good deal about culture and personality, even if my interpretations were wide of the mark. Third, I had the confidence or arrogance to believe that despite the fact that the protocols would be those of individuals obviously different from myself, I would be able to put myself in their test-taking shoes: *they* would be in what for them was a new problem-solving situation, and how they responded to the challenge would say *something* about them and their culture. For me, the beauty of the projective techniques was less in what they would reveal about the content of past experience, unconscious memories, or fantasies and more in the responsibility it gave the individual to determine how he or she will respond to a task in a dyadic relationship of unequal power. There was, as I emphasized to students, nothing mysterious about what I was about. Once you are secure in your understanding of an individual's test-taking attitudes—which can vary during the course of the testing—there is much you can deduce about that individual. If I believed that, it was because I knew it was true for me in my encounter with tests. I was a respresentative sample of one.

Tom did not return after a year on Truk. He stayed on as a native affairs officer in the territory for several years. I would hear from him once a year or so. I forgot about him until five years later, when he showed up at the beginning of a new academic year, ready for both of us to go to work: for me to interpret the tests and for him to start writing the ethnography. I did not greet him warmly. As I said to Esther, I needed to interpret the tests the way I needed a hole in my head. It would take months of hard thinking and writing to do what he wanted. I really had no choice. His dissertation depended on my interpreting the tests. Besides, from our discussions several years earlier, I had concluded that Tom had a first-rate mind and an intriguing background and personality. He was the first person I had come to know who was independently wealthy, a fact that Tom did not like to discuss and about which he had agonizing ambivalence. To Brooklyn–New York–Newark, Depression-scarred me, Tom Gladwin came from and lived in a different world, and that was intriguing. But he, like me, sensed an intellectual kinship and shared values about what was important in living.

He agreed to several conditions I suggested. I would spend a few weeks going over the Rorschach protocols. When I felt ready to interpret them, he would listen and write down my interpretations of a protocol as I went from the first to the tenth Rorschach card of an individual, culminating in a brief summary of what I considered to be highlights. He was not in any way to participate in the interpretation, an unnecessary caveat, because Tom was skeptical about the validity of what I would come up with. Having seen a couple of protocols he had sent me from Truk, I knew that some of the responses referred to flora and fauna that were mysterious to me. Therefore, the only questions I would put to him would be for the purpose of his telling me what these flora and fauna were like. When we were done with the Rorschach protocols, I would write a general statement about what I thought these protocols said about Trukese culture and personality. Finally, I would not interpret the Thematic Apperception Test protocols. To do the Rorschachs would take several months. I simply did not have the time to spend more months on those protocols. It was less a matter of time than the energy-draining consequences of going step by step through a protocol. I did not ''score'' the Rorschachs. I ''listened'' to the test taker as he or she engaged the task.

The protocols, my interpretations, and my conclusions are contained in a monograph by Tom and myself, entitled *Truk: Man in Paradise* (New York: Viking Fund Publications in Anthropology, 1953). The title reflects the irony that in an idyllic setting that in all respects caters to the needs and wants of its people—nutritionally, physically, esthetically—the culture is riddled with conflicts.

One of my conclusions deserves mention here. It was the dominant one, and when we were through with the protocols, Tom told me that it was the one perplexing and troublesome to him. I had concluded that Trukese women, in contrast to men, had far less conflict in regard to assertive and aggressive behavior. It was, I must emphasize, a conclusion that derived less from the content of their responses (although that played a role) than from the style with which they responded to the test situation. As Tom told me later, that was a conclusion that he had not noted: initially he thought I was wide of the mark, if not dead wrong, and yet it rang a bell. And the bell it rang led him to go over his notes and count the frequency of two types of events. The first had to do with the custom of arranged marriages; more specifically, those times when the male or female was against the arranged marriage. In each of these instances, it was the woman who successfully resisted the proposed marriage. The second event was suicide, which is disproportionately high on Truk. Every suicide was by a male. It is interesting that in 1985 (I think) I was reading the *New York Times* and I came across a news article (not a little squib) in which the high rate of male suicide in Truk is discussed. I cut it out and sent it to Tom in California. It was news to neither of us.

When we finished the Rorschachs, Tom asked me to reconsider the agreement not to do the TATs. He knew the time and torture the Rorschachs took, but he also believed that if I did the TATs, it would significantly contribute to the thesis and its subsequent publication. Would I be willing to do it if I would become a coauthor in the publication, as he thought would be justifiable and fair? I said no. It was *his* thesis. He had conceived the study and carried it out. Yes, I contributed to the work, I was glad I had participated, but essentially it was his creation. Also, I did not want to risk appearing to be using my faculty role to get a publication. I was uncomfortable. The answer had to be no. On his own, Tom took the matter up with his department, who said that it would be ethically correct for me to be a coauthor on the publication of the thesis. I did the TATs.

Tom became for me another Schaefer-Simmern. He opened my eyes to the fact and significance of cultural diversity. Like Schaefer, he taught me how American I was in my world view, how much I did not know about culture and world views, how my grasp of reality—of what was right and wrong, of what was natural and proper, of what was "progress"—derived from being born and reared in a particular society. Tom, I hasten to add, was never pedantic or didactic. But in his quiet, firm way, he would raise the incisive question and force me to take distance from what I said and thought. Tom was one of the powerful stimulants causing me to re-evaluate my relatively uncritical acceptance of psychoanalytical theory as a general theory of human behavior. I shall never forget one evening, during the time he was preparing the thesis for publication, when he talked for an hour or so, semihumorously building up an argument that a significant feature of Trukese personality was not penis envy but vagina envy. He delighted in making shreds of Freud's *Totem and Taboo*. But he respected Freud. He took him seriously.

In later years, Tom was wont to say that as a result of our friendship and collaborations, I went from psychology to anthropology and he went in the reverse direction. There is a kernel of truth in that judgment. We were good for each other. We could yell, shout, criticize, and insult each other because we had that kind of relationship familiar to anthropologists: the "joking" relationship. We took each other far more seriously than each took himself. I shudder to think how grievously impoverished my personal and intellectual life would have been without Tom. Today, I feel sorry for graduate students in psychology, because they are living at a time of stultifying specialization that renders them ignorant of the cultures of the world. Between 1945 and 1955, it was hard for psychologists and other social scientists not to be respectful of a cross-cultural perspective. America had become a global power, *the* global power, and that got reflected in the conceptual concerns of social scientists. The arbitrary boundaries among the social sciences became more permeable. Cultural egocentricity became hard to maintain. The plasticity of the human organism was difficult to ignore. America was not the world. Although it never received the attention it deserved, in that decade it seemed as if Dollard's critique of American psychology in his 1935 *Criteria for the Life History* would lose its bite. I am not describing that decade as a kind of intellectual Camelot. It was not. But compared to today, it *was* Camelot.

Three years after the Truk monograph was published, I was asked by the American Association for Retarded Children (now Retarded Citizens) to take a year's leave to assess what was going on (and where) in regard to research on and programs for mentally retarded individuals. I agreed to do it provided that funds would be available to allow Tom to collaborate with me. He was then at the National Institute of Mental Health, and the additional funds I requested would permit him to hire a research assistant to help him do a literature search. The fruit of that collaboration was published in two places, first as a Genetic Psychology Monograph entitled *Psychological and Cultural Factors in Mental Subnormality* and then in a book by Masland, Sarason, and Gladwin entitled *Mental Subnormality*. Masland was a neurologist who was titular head of the project responsible for covering the medical literature.

Tom was initially reluctant to collaborate because he knew so little about mental retardation. Indeed, he was not interested in mental retardation. That, I shouted at him, was the damned problem: mental retardation was a pariah field in the social sciences, and gifted minds like Tom's were morally and intellectually irresponsible in their ignorance and derogation of that field. He would, I told him, make a far more lasting contribution to the world by concentrating on mental retardation than by worrying about the neuroses and the psychoses. I was playing to what I knew was distinctive in Tom: a galactic-sized superego, personal and social.

Those publications received a good deal of attention. I am proud of the parts I wrote, but my greatest satisfaction was and is in the fact that I enticed a first-rate anthropologist to write a fascinating think piece on cultural retardation. I continue to meet people who tell me about the impact of those publications on their thinking. When they elaborate on that impact, more often than not they single out chapters written by Tom. To those readers who have no interest in mental retardation (they would be in the majority by far), I would suggest that they read Tom's 1970 book *East Is a Big Bird* (Cambridge, Mass.: Harvard University Press), a description and explanation of how the natives in the South Pacific go in their small boats hundreds of miles over the trackless ocean and unerringly get to their destination. The last chapter is about poverty in America! When you have read the book, it is likely that your appetite will have been whetted to read Gladwin on culture and mental retardation. Hope springs eternal.

11

The Origins of Modern Clinical Psychology

I have discussed the emergence of modern clinical psychology as a consequence of World War II. But there was one societal change antedating the war that made that emergence seem right, natural, and proper—so much so that it went unnoticed. Up until the Great Depression of the thirties, it was more than rhetoric when people would say that that government is best which governs the least. This stance was not intended to suggest that the federal government should be indifferent to all the disasters—personal, economic, health—that can befall its people but rather that the citizens of the states and their communities should take responsibility for deciding which services should be provided for which individuals or groups. Education, for example, is never mentioned in the Constitution, not because it was considered unimportant—quite the contrary—but because it was considered to be a local affair and not one into which a national government should intrude. The constraints put on the national government did not stem from esthetics but from a reading of the history of the uses and abuse of power by central government. As I described in Chapter Three, when I got polio I was aided by the March of Dimes and the New Jersey State Rehabilitation Commission. Helping me was not a federal obligation. If I had lived in some other state, I would never have been able to go to college.

To those born after World War II, this stance toward the federal role may seem incomprehensible or callous, or both. Such a reaction, however, too easily glosses over the tension between two moral principles: the obligation to provide help to dependent people and the obligation to do so in ways that are respectful of individual needs and dignity. There had been a long-standing fear in America that if such help became an obligation of federal government, the quality of such help not only would be poor but would be subject to the abuses of power. This is not to say that the help provided by states and communities would be adequate or helpful or nonintrusive but rather that the dangers of a federal role had to be avoided because they were potentially more insidious.

The Great Depression changed all that. In his campaign for the presidency, Franklin Roosevelt called for reduced spending, a balanced budget, and reform of the banking system. He did not advocate federal programs to reinvigorate the economy. The problem was, as he said, in part psychological: "We have nothing to fear but fear itself." Within days of becoming president, he confronted the dimensions of the reality of the economic disaster and its socially destabilizing implications. Federal programs were almost invented overnight, and the Congress passed a cascade of legislation intended to help diverse groups. All of this was viewed as a *temporary* move until the damage was repaired, allowing the government to resume its nonintrusive role. That, of course, did not happen. Not only did the federal government continue to have an active role, but a majority of the people accepted and pressured for a continuation of the exercise of federal power. With the approach of World War II, the federal role increased. If what happened was both understandable and necessary, the fact remains that the perception of the role of government in the lives of people had undergone a radical change.

As a political radical of the Trotskyite persuasion, I viewed Roosevelt's New Deal as utterly inadequate to the disaster at hand. I was totally unaware of the possibility that as central government—regardless of whether it was socialistic, communistic, or capitalistic—became increasingly a factor in the lives of its citizens, there could be, would be, adverse consequences. That should have been, but was not, obvious to me given what happened in Russia and Germany. In principle, it was argued, what happened in those countries could have been avoided if only the right people with the right ideas and values had attained power. That there are predictable problems and consequences to powerful, centralized, bureaucratic government was an issue that I did not confront. Nor did I know that not only was the issue political-governmental but it was an issue that surfaced in any large organization—industrial or otherwise. I had not read Max Weber, and I had never heard of his "iron cage" forged by institutional growth and bureaucracy. Weber's underlying pessimism (like that of Freud) did not take hold when his work became influential in optimistic America. Far more often than not, psychology is viewed as a social science. My formal education in psychology hardly exposed me to seminal thinkers in sociology and political science.

These are not the words of a political conservative or of an ex-radical who has undergone conversion and who now proclaims a new truth or ideology. They are the words of someone who, like many others of differing backgrounds and political affiliation, has had to face the fact that the more responsibility and power that are given to central government, the more the consequences have the features of a very mixed blessing. And those consequences have led most people to view political authority with cynicism, resentment, and, too frequently, destructive impotence. It is not happenstance that Kafka's novel *The Castle* has become a metaphor to describe the puniness and powerlessness of the individual struggling to comprehend the layers of authority that determine his or her existence. Nor is it happenstance that in the post–World War II era, words such as *alienation, isolation, anomie, loneliness,* and *"opting out"* have become part of common parlance.

Let us for a moment take a recent event that may to some seem trivial and unimportant. Early in 1987, the Internal Revenue Service issued a new form for estimating income and taxes. The uproar in this country—even in Congress—was wondrous to behold. The form was incomprehensible to educated people, including many tax advisers. To less educated people, it was a complete mystery. Now, those who developed the form were not motivated to produce a financial inkblot. As a colleague of mine said, "There are only two explanations. It was either done by choosing words according to a table of random numbers, or it was done by people totally ignorant of and unresponsive to those they are paid to serve." It was not a world-shaking event, but it was an instance that mightily reinforced in people the feeling that they exist to conform to impersonal bureaucracy, that the distance between the individual and the decision makers in the castle on top of the mountain is unbridgeable. What happened as a result of the uproar? The people in the castle uttered their mea culpas and came up with a new form that was less bewildering but by no means clear. Fortunately, we live in a society in which resentment to abuse is not extinguished and in which courageous "whistle blowers" can muster support to counter the stupidity, insensitivity, or sleaziness that can characterize large, centralized, central government.

But abuse of power is only one of the dangers inherent in an increasing federal role. No less important is the tendency of central government to initiate programs that, however well intentioned, too frequently seem oblivious to consequences that later come to be seen as adverse. It is not that the federal policy makers seek to foist these programs on an unwilling or unresponsive public. Quite the contrary, these programs often have widespread public support. But there are several aspects to the forging of a policy and the passing of legislation that need to be recognized. The first is that the initiative or responsibility for developing policy starts somewhere in central government and is defined in ways that justify the initiative; that is, it requires federal initiative. The second aspect is that the need for a program or policy on the part of government receives support or pressure from interest groups who, no less than those in government, have a vested interest in shaping the federal initiative. I am in no way impugning the motives of these groups, or those of the federal bureaus, but rather emphasizing the obvious point that the participants in the process define the problem in terms of their perceived interests. And all of them assume and proclaim that their interests best represent the public interest: in the short and long term, the untoward consequences will be overshadowed by the positive ones. The third aspect is that more often than not, the influence of the federal participants is decisive in shaping the policy and legislation. It is a process marked by conflicting views, compromises, and the resort to the use of formal and informal influence and power.

Hundreds (if not thousands) of books have been written about the federal policy process in the post–World War II era. And that is the point: with the end of World War II, the federal government was given—and assumed—the role of initiator, and there is hardly a sphere of social function that does not bear the imprint of a federal social policy. If those books attest to a truly radical change in the role of central government—a largely silent transformation-revolution in how people view government—they also bear witness to the view that in terms of consequences and of the public interest, the role and effectiveness of central government have been, at best, a mixed blessing.

These prefatory comments are prologue to my view of what happened and why to clinical psychology in the post–World War II era. The fact is, as I have already pointed out, that the shape and direction of modern clinical psychology were a direct consequence of federal initiative. The war was over, the world was forever changed, there was no turning the clock back, there were mammoth problems confronting our society, and Washington became the center of action and attention. It was all understandable in the context of the times. What the participants (including me) did not comprehend were the predictable realities and booby traps inherent in the unprecedented role that central government was being given. It was not all that unprecedented if one took seriously the efforts of the government to cope with the Great Depression. But the history of those efforts, the lessons they contained, remained as past history rather than as experiences to be mined. It is not hyperbole to say that we saw ourselves either in a new world or faced with the golden opportunity to create a new world. It is impossible to exaggerate how World War II altered world views. This was particularly true in the United States, which, alone among the nations of the world, appeared to have the resources and resolve not only to better its society but to prevent the dissolution of the traditions of Western society. The optimism that had always characterized America was reinforced rather than diluted by the war.

Let me restate briefly some background factors that led to the emergence of modern clinical psychology:

1. The federal government (the Veterans Administration) had long had the responsibility to care for veterans with service-incurred disabilities. Even before World War II, there had been serious questions about the quality of the services provided. The inadequacy of those services was never directly confronted until we entered World War II.
2. With our entrance into the war, it became obvious to the VA that we lacked then, and would lack in the future, the health facilities and professionals to provide quality service.
3. The VA began to plan for a new system of health facilities that would be intimately related to, and in part administered by, medical schools and centers. The closer the ties (geographically and otherwise), the better.
4. To obtain the quantity and quality of health professionals necessary to staff the new system, the VA would under-write the training of these people.
5. The planning did not take place in "splendid isolation" in VA offices. Representatives from diverse medical schools and medical specialties participated in the planning. It was obvious to all that the new system would require participation, assent, and cooperation of the medical establishment.
6. Psychologists participated in the planning process. For one thing, the mental health services that would be required were staggering. For another thing, departments of psychology had not been in the business of training clinical psychologists. Clinical psychologists would be needed in the roles of diagnostic testers and researchers. As in the case of psychiatrists and psychiatric social workers, the VA would have to secure the cooperation of graduate departments of psychology to develop formal training programs. VA facili-

ties would be the training sites of graduate students in clinical psychology, their training extending over a period of two years.

Now for some glimpses of the obvious. The first is that the federal government had needs regarding (or a vested interest in) the direction that clinical psychology should take. Put in another way, the government—understandably, responsibly, and forcefully—wanted a clinical psychology that would meet its conception of what veterans would require. The second is that it advocated a clinical psychology that would in essence be agreeing to the underlying, indeed explicit, government rationale for what clinical psychology should become. In fact, almost all new university programs willingly affiliated with the VA. From the standpoint of university departments of psychology (and also psychiatry), affiliation had a number of benefits: generous stipends for graduate students, consultation funds for faculty members, and the expectation that VA facilities would present many opportunities for research and research training. In other words, departments of psychology had needs and vested interests, and again, I do not use the adjective *vested* pejoratively. They were in favor of starting clinical programs, the government presented a rationale and funding that would be helpful, and the autonomy of departments would in no way be restricted. There was a meeting of minds about what clinical psychology should be. There was no coercion or arm twisting, although I can personally attest to hearing some "hard sells." In some instances, the decision to start programs was unrelated to knowledge or expectation of government support. In other instances, the justification of programs was based on the fact that such support would be forthcoming. The decision to start a program at Yale was unrelated to what the VA sought to do.

Why was I opposed to affiliating the Yale program with the VA? The general answer was that the rationale for clinical training advocated by the VA, and the fact that a significant number of students would be trained in the VA, were inimical to the development of potentials of this new field for the society generally; that is, in some ultimate sense, the public welfare.

That the government had legitimate needs I, of course, did not question. But if the training rationale of the VA became dominant in the new field, it would be putting it in a conceptual, service, and professional straitjacket, constricting its potentials at its birth.

The specific answer to the question was in several parts. First, I considered it unduly restrictive that a VA trainee had to have his clinical experience in a VA facility. Second, that experience would give the trainee almost no exposure to women. Third, it would give him no exposure at all to children. Fourth, it would restrict the trainee to two functions: diagnostic tester and researcher. Fifth, precisely because the VA facility would be under the control and direction of the medical-psychiatric community, the clinical psychologist would be a second-class citizen, a member of an underdeveloped colony, so to speak, of a remarkably imperialistic medical profession. The contrasting experiences I had at Worcester State Hospital and the Southbury Training School were not lost on me.

There was another part of the answer, which over the years became clearer to me and required that I put my money where my mouth was. If departments of psychology adopted the VA rationale, it meant that they were treating clinical students differently from those in other areas of specialization. For example, graduate students in social or developmental psychology are directly educated, trained, and supervised by faculty in their specialization. They are not farmed out to sites and psychologists outside the university, except in very limited ways, to obtain experience crucial to their specialization. That is precisely what the VA rationale entailed: the forging of the identity of mental health professionals outside the university; that is, the role models for the clinical trainee would not be the clinical faculty of the department. Those faculty would serve as consultants to the outside facility, which would mean that from time to time they would visit and discuss with trainees and staff how things were going and what problems were being encountered, the frequency of visits depending on variables of distance and amount of consultant funds.

The university consultant was not, obviously, a clinical role model for the trainee. The process of consulting can be helpful and fruitful to both trainee and site, but that should not be confused with the functions of being an observable role model for clinical behavior. What did it mean to say that a department had a clinical faculty that had relatively little to do with the clinical student during the crucially formative internship experience? What did it mean to say that a clinical student would get a Yale degree while his identity as a clinician had not been forged at Yale? My questions had nothing to do with the quality of VA staff. Generally speaking, in those early years the VA psychologists were serious, mature people of quality. And, I must emphasize, my concerns in no way questioned the need of the VA for clinical psychologists. What I opposed was cooperating with a program that required that the student do his (mostly his) internship in a VA facility. And included in my criticism were departments of psychology that clearly had not thought through the educational and professional implications of what they were willingly agreeing to. Why agree to something in regard to clinical students that not in a million years would they apply to any other type of graduate student?

From my perspective, what was at stake was no less than the future of clinical psychology. If the VA rationale was accepted, clinical psychology would be put into a mold that would be in neither its or the public interest. What were the alternatives? As a result of many discussions with individuals in and around the process from which the VA rationale emerged, I had to conclude that what I later called "the universe of alternatives" had hardly been considered. The government had pressing needs, so did departments of psychology, and those needs seemed to coincide. And, fatefully, there was an existing rationale for what training in clinical psychology should be, and no one was more influential—by virtue of experience, status, and brilliance—in advocating the principles of that rationale than David Shakow, who in the pre–World War II years had administered at Worcester State Hospital the best clinical training program in the nation. He spoke and wrote forcefully and persuasively about the internship: its centrality, its personal and professional goals, its *site,* and its relationship to the university. In spirit and substance, the VA rationale bears the imprint of David Shakow and Worcester State Hospital. There really was no serious consideration of alternatives. There was no doubt not only that the rationale was in the best interests of the VA and psychology but that those interests were identical with the public interest. And it is that presumption that too often is blithely accepted in the policy process involving government and professions. What is good for "us" is good for the country.

Let us imagine the following situation: It is during World War II, and a group of psychologists decide to meet for several days to discuss how and why clinical psychology could become a distinct graduate area in ways that not only would exploit its potentials (and psychology generally) but would be responsive to the public welfare generally. They would, of course, be aware of the needs of the VA, but that would be only one consideration and not the major one. How could psychology generally, and clinical psychology in particular, become socially responsive in the short and long run to the public welfare?

It is safe to say that several questions would soon occupy the group. What are the drawbacks of steering the new field to an almost exclusive emphasis on the repair or remediation of personal misery? Granted that any kind of clinical practice deals with problems that have already developed, does that mean that the training of the clinical psychologist should be relatively devoid of an emphasis on prevention and, therefore, on developing roles appropriate to a preventive orientation? Should we go the traditional route of separating repair and prevention, a route that the history of clinical professions (particularly the medical ones) suggests is ultimately defeating of the public welfare? Does psychology have anything to offer in regard to prevention that should influence the education and training of clinical psychologists? Would the potentials of psychology generally, and clinical psychology in particular, be unduly constrained by tying the new field to the psychiatric community? Should the new field be stimulated and encouraged to ally itself with nonmedical sites and professions where the integration of the repair and preventive orientations appears possible and viable? Can we justify a modern clinical psychology that does not have meaningful and productive relations with our public schools? Is it possible to build into the new field a stance, a conceptual framework, a practical vehicle that would lessen the chances that this new field would be put into a professional straitjacket? How should we keep our options open so that we can evaluate the different ways the public welfare could benefit from psychology as science and profession?

As we shall see shortly, the situation may be imaginary, but the questions are not. They did get raised, but I do not want to get ahead of the story. The point I want to emphasize here is the obvious one that there were alternative ways one could think about the shape, substance, and direction of the new field. To the VA and their advisers, the rationale they formulated met their needs and explicitly assumed that that rationale best met the future needs of psychology and the public welfare. I do not, of course, question the sincerity or seriousness of the VA and its advisers. The fact remains that they came to the problem with certain handicaps. Their clinical experience had been in a medical setting, their conception and knowledge of societal needs were superficial, they were under the pressure of time, and their major concern was to steer clinical psychology in a direction that would meet VA *medical-psychiatric* needs. In short, they were not disposed seriously to discuss alternatives—that is, different—perspectives and criteria. They were, as most of us were, babes in the woods in matters of professional interests and concerns, especially confronted as they were by visions of generous funding and new facilities.

Now to an instructive anecdote that illustrates how we can be unfortunate prisoners of time and place unless our education builds into us schemata that aid us in taking distance from our time and place. One has not only always to say, as John Dollard emphasized, "in our culture" but to add "at this time and place." This anecdote related to a future condition that already existed in the present but to which no one was paying heed. If the cast of characters had had the conceptual tools to help them divorce themselves from the compelling quality of their concrete present, clinical psychology might not have made the kinds of commitments it did.

The anecdote is about a meeting that took place either shortly before or shortly after the Boulder Conference on Clinical

Psychology discussed later in this chapter. I do not remember the point of the occasion or the names of most of the dozen or so people who were there. I do know that there were representatives of university clinical training programs and staff from the regional and central VA offices. At one point, a VA staff person said, "Do you realize that the young veterans we are talking about will someday be old veterans, and we have a lot of those now from World War I, and we will not have the appropriate knowledge or facilities?" Nobody, including myself, responded to his comments, and the meeting went on, probably to rehash the problems of training clinical psychologists. But it is as if his words were seared on my brain. I knew that what he said was important, but it took years for me to appreciate its wisdom. I would like to believe that he understood, like no one else at the meeting, the difference between preventive and clinical thinking. His totally uninfluential comments were, of course, confirmed in subsequent years. The VA is now responsible for more geriatric cases than any other societal agency—responsible but unprepared.

Why did that individual's comment stick with me? Why did it continue to haunt me? The answer is that the comment implicitly indicted the process from which emerged a rationale that guaranteed that clinical psychology—indeed, all of the mental health professions—would be insensitive to and neglectful of predictable social problems. Just as that rationale ensured that a field such as mental retardation would be far from the focus of these professions, it also ensured that the aging process would have the same fate. The point of the anecdote, thus, is that after World War II a health policy was being forged that was narrow in scope, not grounded in an attempt to conceptualize the nature of society and its social order, amazingly ahistorical, and resting on the belief that the future would be a carbon copy of the present. It was a policy forged by professionals who had no way of asking, how are the ways we are defining problems and modes of attack a function of where *we* are in the social order? How should awareness of our place in the social order serve as a warning that we are subject to certain biases and distortions in regard to our society and its needs? How does our place in its social order—the result of a host of selective factors that interact with a distinctive, prolonged education that emphasizes how different we are from the rest of society—prevent us from recognizing that, like it or not, we are part of the problem because we are in the stream of social history? One cannot ask these kinds of questions without being realistically humble. *Humbleness* is not a word that easily comes to mind when one reviews the mental health movement after World War II. Personal, intellectual, and professional arrogance comes more quickly to mind. The roots that clinical psychology had in American psychology were shallow, but they at least contained the fertilizing ingredient of skepticism. But that ingredient came only from an individual psychology, and it was (and still is) inadequately sustaining when psychology in general and clinical psychology in particular entered the arenas of social reality and public policy. In those arenas, an individual psychology is a mammoth distraction.

I, or course, was not alone in my fears about unduly tying clinical psychology to the VA. Indeed, the creation shortly after World War II of the National Institute of Mental Health was intended to gain recognition of the fact that there were many groups and sites in our society that had unmet mental health needs. One of its first programs was to provide training funds to departments of psychology that were intended to broaden training and education in clinical psychology. The new institute was in principle not in competition with the VA. It was testimony to the fact that veterans were but one group that needed and deserved more and better mental health professionals. The important early history of NIMH has yet to be written, an omission not surprising in the ahistorical mental health fields. My experience in those early years with NIMH staff was that they were a most unusual visionary group who were trying to introduce breath into the mental health fields. The conceptual leadership at NIMH came primarily from psychologists on the staff. Interacting with them was dramatically more stimulating and refreshing than interacting with VA staff, where the exclusive concern was the welfare of veterans. It was the difference between a staff constricted in outlook by its medical-psychiatric culture and traditions and a staff trying to be true to the traditions of social science. Nevertheless, it was also apparent to me that the decisive policy-making power at NIMH was in the hands of psychiatrists and not psychologists. Unfortunately, many of the NIMH psychologists who played major roles in those early years are dead. It is my opinion, based on many interactions with them, that when (if ever) a comprehensive history of those early NIMH years is written, it will support my conclusion that from the beginning there was a real tension between them and their medical-psychiatric administrative peers and superiors. If that tension was muted in those early years, it became more obvious and fateful as the years went on.

Agencies, especially governmental ones, are accountable for the funds they disburse. It is, therefore, not surprising that the VA and NIMH had to raise and answer the question, by what criteria should we decide whether to give training funds to departments of psychology for their clinical training programs? The question, of course, was a legitimate one. But the danger was, as even a superficial knowledge of governmental policy making would suggest, that the need to be accountable can result in rigid criteria that produce uniformity and not diversity. *That* was the real danger, and the degree to which that danger was confronted would be decisive for the future of clinical psychology.

That brings me to the 1949 Boulder conference (proceedings discussed in V. Raimy, *Training in Clinical Psychology*. Englewood Cliffs, N.J.: Prentice-Hall, 1950), which was so fateful for determining the directions clinical psychology would take. That conference was underwritten by the VA and NIMH. The goal of that three-week conference in Colorado was to forge a consensus of what graduate training in clinical psychology should be; that is, to articulate clearly the criteria, narrow and broad, that the two agencies could use in making funding decisions. The participants were representatives of university departments that had or were planning to have graduate clinical programs. Representatives from psychiatry, psychiatric social work, school pscyhology, psychiatric nursing, medical education, and master's-level programs participated. In all, there were seventy-three participants. Several things were obvious. First, most of the "outside" representatives were from the medical community. Second, most of the representatives from departments of psychology had gained their clinical experience in medical-psychiatric settings. Third, the most prestigious (deservedly so) clinical psychologists (for example, David Shakow, Starke Hathaway, William A. Hunt, Charles Strother) were or had been intimately involved in medical-psychiatric settings. Fourth, it was not that anyone stacked the cards in the direction of tying clinical psychology to the psychiatric setting, but rather that, by the time of the conference in 1949, that direction had already been taken. Boulder was fateful not because it moved clinical psychology in new directions but because it legitimized an orientation that already had been established during and immediately after World War II.

The Boulder conference began with a brief introductory statement by Dr. Robert Felix, director of NIMH, an energetic, idealistic psychiatrist who was "liberal" in that he vigorously advocated an important role for the clinical psychologist. He was more "liberal" in private conversation than in his public statements. Robert Felix was an astute politician-statesman, and he well knew how zealously the American Psychiatric Association guarded its leadership in the mental health arena. So let us listen to an excerpt from his opening remarks:

If my experience as a medically trained person is worth anything, I would say that, although the best possible didactic and laboratory training is very necessary, the technique and attitudes learned in clinical clerkships, wardwalks, internships, and residencies leave a lasting impression and are the shapers of attitudes and concepts which, for better or for worse, last a lifetime.

Although I recognize the dangers involved in discussing problems outside one's field of competence, nevertheless, because of my firm conviction regarding the critical role to be played by the clinical psychologist, I hazard to enumerate here a more detailed listing of the functions of the clinical psychologist as I see them. It seems to me that the diagnostic function includes much more than the determination of intellectual status. I, for one, in my clinical practice of psychiatry have never been too concerned about the numerical figure supplied me by a psychometrist to indicate the intellect of a patient. Were this all I wanted in a diagnostic way, I would not use a psychologist at all. I can tell to my own satisfaction within reasonably broad limits, whether an individual is very dull, dull, of average intelligence, or above average.

If I wish a somewhat finer determination, I can either do my own intelligence testing or have it done for me by a psychological technician. There are other diagnostic data that I need and that the properly trained clinical psychologist is peculiarly prepared to: (a) supply me, (b) interpret for me, and (c) confer with me in planning the treatment of the case in the light of his findings. I refer to procedures for the evaluation of personality structure and dynamics and for the exploration and appraisal of vocational interests and potentialities. Much of this information does not come as much from test material as from the clinical experience and judgment of a psychological diagnostician—the properly trained clinical psychologist. As we move into the broad field of mental public health, however, there is another diagnostic role that the clinical psychologist must be adequately prepared to fill. It is essential that we know the size of our mental illness problem in order to lay strategy to attack it, and this means the proper identification of mental disorders that exist in a community undetected until a special effort is made to identify them.

The identification of mental illness or emotional problems in a community, while of scientific interest, is in many ways a disservice to a community if reasonable facilities are not available to deal with the problems discovered. This means the utilization of all therapeutic skills available and the development of potential skills to the point at which they can be useful and relied upon. The fulfilling of this function, it seems to me, involves the treatment of psychological disorders and the promotion of the mental health of the individual or the group by the utilization of appropriate and established psychological techniques and principles of therapy under psychiatric direction. As more and more clinical psychologists enter active working relationships, in hospitals, clinics, and elsewhere, the psychiatrists and other mental health personnel there have naturally developed some conflicts and problems centering about the specific functions of each. As this relationship continues, and each learns to know the other better and to understand his sphere of competence, and as all grow to understand the tremendous scope of mental health work, these conflicts will inevitably decrease (pp. xvi-xvii).

My heart sank when I heard these remarks. Although he did not intend it (I think), he described the clinical psychologist as tester in the service of the psychiatrist. He also left no doubt that the clinical psychologist should receive his training in a psychiatric setting, that training being modeled on what he regarded as the virtues of medical-clinical training. Although he had the courage to say that there were and would be professional conflicts in regard to functions and roles, he had no doubt that the curative aspects of the passage of time, together with goodwill, would "inevitably decrease" these conflicts. That, I knew, was an indulgence of wishful thinking exacerbated by ignorance of the history, traditions, and realities of American medicine. I geared up for battle. That was not easy, because I was at the conference as a young upstart, a nontenured associate professor who was inevitably in awe of the well-known, influential participants who were there. I took a stand on several issues. Why was the proposed curriculum weighted in favor of such elective courses as neurophysiology, pharmacology, and neuroanatomy? Why should clinical psychology be tied to a setting that would not expose its members to such areas as mental retardation, criminality, physical handicap, and vocational planning and adjustment? What about prevention? Did not Dr. Felix rightly emphasize the importance of the community, early detection, secondary prevention?

These issues were raised and joined, and the outcome was predictable. Only a handful of people at Boulder took the position I did. I do not think I ever expressed it at Boulder, but I know the following thought crossed my mind: If the funding for the development of clinical psychology were coming from other sources with no strings attached, would clinical psychology move in the direction it was going? In some vague way, I knew that the conference was not confronting the age-old maxim that the hand that feeds you is the hand that can starve you, that money as an incentive is almost always powerful and frequently unwittingly corrupting. And by corrupting, I mean that dependence, in whole or in part, on a funding source facilitates rationalizations that constrict one's thinking about alternatives more congruent with one's initial values, expectations, and capabilities.

The problem is made more difficult when one is part of a professional field the internal policies of which reinforce the tie with the exernal funding source. By virtue of the nature and details of the origins of modern clinical psychology, it is not surprising that one of the characteristics of its development has been concern with achieving independence from and a kind of parity with psychiatry. This concern catapulted the field into the arenas of politics, legislation, lobbying, and public policy. It was a move to gain and preserve independence, not to change the conceptual substance of mental health policy. It was a move to be considered as good as and as financially deserving as "them." It was not a move that challenged the underlying conceptions of public policy; for example, its focus on the individual organism deriving from an asocial psychology. Nor was it a move that stemmed from an attempt to identify past conceptual mistakes but, rather, one that recognized past organizational mistakes. Self-scrutiny has never been a notable characteristic of professional organizations. I should amend this statement, however, by saying that professional organizations do scrutinize their political-organizational mistakes, but only when their status is threatened. The recognition that a field may have based itself on faulty conceptions of the nature of its subject matter always reflects sea-swell changes in the society, affecting the field along a time dimension quite different from our usual experience of time.

What happened in the subsequent decades was predictable. Far from the battle between clinical psychology and psychiatry lessening, the conflict increased. It also widened in the sense that it went far beyond the confines of clinical settings and the two national associations to the courts and the halls of legislatures. And central to the conflict was who, professionally and legally, was entitled to practice psychotherapy? That became the all-engrossing issue. The conflict around that issue became exacerbated by the economic dynamics of the growth of health insurance: no less than the psychiatrists, the clinical psychologists expected and sought to be reimbursed for their therapeutic efforts as individual practitioners. No one has yet seen fit to describe, dissect, and explain how the battle was fought. It was really a war, with many battles in many places, costing large sums of money, involving thousands of people, many casualties, and an endless stream of articles, pronouncements, position papers, and vituperative rhetoric. Although no armistice has ever been declared, and certainly no peace treaty has ever been written, for all practical purposes the clinical psychologists have emerged as victors. They have established themselves as independent clinical practitioners.

Wars always have intended and unintended consequences. And it is always the case, especially in prolonged wars, that memory of their origins becomes faint or markedly transformed. So, for example, if you read the proceedings of the Boulder conference, it is apparent that the consensus was that the arena of psychotherapy should not be off limits to psychologists; that is, the issue was joined, albeit subtly and politely. But it is no less apparent that most, if not all, of the participants did not look with favor at the possibility that any significant number of clinical psychologists would become independent practitioners, and for two reasons. First, the major obligation of the clinical psychologist was to his or her discipline: to contribute to its substantive and methodological base. There were many ways one could do that, but common to all was the obligation to contribute to strengthening and improving the discipline. This obligation could not be discharged by the private practitioner unconnected with or isolated from research or training centers. Second, in the future as in the past, psychology as a basic or applied activity should be practiced in societal institutions devoted to the public welfare. Psychologists were not and should not be economic entrepreneurs. Indeed, the willingness with which psychology brought clinical psychology into its mainstream was in part because it was envisioned that these psychologists would work in public institutions: VA facilities, state hospitals, and community clinics. It is fair to say that the bulk of the participants at Boulder looked with disfavor and unease at the possibility that clinical psychologists, like the physician in medicine, would become private practitioners. You did not go into psychology to make money! If that sounds strangely idealistic, you must remember that most of the psychologists at Boulder were academics who had grown up in the field, a small field, when it was primarily ensconced in the university. The point of all this is that the professional war between psychology and psychiatry did not begin and heat up around the issue of private practice or even salary differentials (which were large) but rather around the question, who owned psychotherapy?

I never envisioned a time when clinical psychologists would be in private practice to any significant extent. It was not that I was in principle opposed to private practice but that I felt that psychology's obligation was to society and its major institutions, to the reform and improvement of those settings in which the less fortunate of our society were to be found. It is probably the case that my attitude on this score derived from my political history. As I have said earlier, I was critical of psychology because its substantive concerns seemed so far removed from societal concerns. And I enthusiastically greeted the possibility that by becoming part of American psychology, clinical psychology could force the field to a more realistic understanding of our society. To me, clinical psychology, like any other organized field, had an explicit or implicit political agenda. It was inevitably embedded in and reflected a political context. It could not avoid using and being used by the political system. To me, clinical psychology was more than an endeavor to repair individual misery. It was also an endeavor to identify and influence institutional contexts that engendered and reinforced that misery. Clinical psychology had to be, broadly speaking, a social psychology. To the extent that clinical psychology tied itself to medicine and psychiatry, its ties to the social sciences becoming weak or nonexistent, it would become another in the category of lost opportunities.

Within a few years after Boulder, during which time psychologists began to flee from the VA and the state hospitals, it became apparent that psychiatry was beginning to lose its claim to ownership of psychotherapy. And in challenging that claim, the new issue in the professional war became the right of clinical psychologists to engage in private practice. This change in issues was facilitated by two interrelated facts. The Age of Mental Health manifested itself in many ways in many parts of the society, as any analysis of the mass media would confirm. Lying on the analyst's couch became a status symbol. And flocking in droves into graduate programs in clinical psychology were students who had assimilated the ideology of the Age of Mental Health. Psychotherapy was the strongest magnet attracting these students, and the personal satisfactions and financial rewards of private practice were slightly less strong magnets. Before World War II, clinical psychology did not exist as a field in American psychology. Within two decades after World War II, clinical psychology became the largest field. Before World War II, only a handful, so to speak, of psychologists were outside of and unconnected with the university. Within three decades after the war, a majority of psychologists were outside of and unconnected with the university.

At some point, one leaves explanation and goes to judgment. There are those who view the fantastic growth of clinical psychology as an unalloyed good. They view the dominance of the field in the American Psychological Association as just and healthy. They take satisfaction from the fact that many thousands of people are being treated each day by thousands of clinical psychologists. And they interpret the brief history of modern clinical psychology as one in which stultifying tradition (within psychology and between psychology and psychiatry) had to be overcome, altering in a productive manner the relationship between psychology as science and as profession. They see psychology generally and clinical psychology in particular as vital endeavors serving the public interest, and, therefore, they must zealously and vigilantly discharge the obligation to ensure that standards for practice are high and vigorously monitored.

If you are not a clinical psychologist (for example, if you are a cognitive, social, or biological psychologist), you likely see the past and present rather differently. You will see psychology as having grievously de-emphasized research and research training. You will see the influence of clinical psychology in graduate departments and the American Psychological Association as baleful because of the disproportionate time, energy, and resources given to psychology as application. You will look nostalgically back at the time when scientific training in general psychology was the primary goal in the admission process and the curriculum. Credentialing departments and practitioners, lobbying in Washington and state capitals for the professional interests of clinical practitioners, protecting and ensuring the interests of clinical psychologists in regard to third-party payments, taking positions on and advocating public policies that are controversial and divisive—these are activities that have attained an importance that makes you feel a stranger in your discipline. Whereas the annual meeting of the American Psychological Association used to be a scientific meeting—and the newly elected president was an eminent researcher or theoretician from the university—you see it now a professional circus run by and for practitioners who have elected as president a "political," not a scientific, individual. And it is very likely that you are no longer a member of the association, having chosen to join the Psychonomic Society, which is primarily for the scientists in psychology.

The schism that these extreme views depict has a long history in American psychology, although up until World War II it was more potential than an actuality. Today, that schism is all too real. There are two radically different cultures in psychology, and the most startling consequence has been the development of professional schools unaffiliated with a university. In fact, these professional schools—some giving the Ph.D., others the Psy.D. degree—now train more clinical psychologists than do all university programs combined. This development simply could not have been imagined by anyone at the Boulder conference. If someone had broached the idea there (less than forty years ago), a fund would have been started to defray the costs of that person's long-term stay in a mental hospital. The merits of this development aside, one cannot avoid asking this question: Why was the report of the Boulder conference, and a similar report on psychiatric training by the American Psychiatric Association, so utterly unpredictive of what would happen in both fields? Someone has said that it is hard to be completely wrong. But when I look at these reports today, I am tempted to regard them as exceptions to that generalization.

I was and am no seer. At the time of Boulder, I could

not and did not predict in any specific way how the field would be transformed. But at the core of my being, I knew several things: our society was undergoing accelerated social change to which the new field was insensitive; embedding that field in the medical-psychiatric culture would have untoward consequences; and the view that governmental support would be enduring, consistent, and unfettered was proof positive of ignorance of the nature of our capitalist, market-oriented society. I wanted to believe, and there were periods when I did, that the direction in which clinical psychology was being steered was good for psychology and the public welfare; that is, the positives outweighed the negatives. Was it not a good that important research areas began to be developed that were like a breath of fresh air in American psychology? Was it not a good that rat-based theories of human behavior were being challenged, supplanted, or influenced by psychoanalytical observations and theory? Was it not a good that in challenging the professional imperialism of psychiatry, more clinicians would be available to help more people? Was it not a good that clinical psychology was attracting so many extraordinarily able, idealistic students? Of course these were goods. But after Boulder, as each year passed, my nagging doubts became stronger. Let me explain.

I trust that I have made it clear that I believe any field of human endeavor, especially if it is in the human services, should be judged by the degree to which it understands and is responsive to the social forces and structures that produce or help maintain human misery. Baldly put, it is not enough for individual practitioners in a field to understand and be responsive to an individual in need. It goes without saying that helping an individual is itself an endeavor that requires neither explanation nor defense. But I expect that the collectivity of which the individual practitioner is a part is no less interested in doing something about the social conditions that produce misery. I am talking not about rhetoric but about action of some kind, action in regard to institutional and social change. What became increasingly clear as the years rolled on was that clinical psychology was becoming a passive profession: clinicians responding in their offices on their turf to individuals who had *actively* sought *them* out. They dealt with what came to them, and those who did not come were not in their ken. What was no less vexing was that the people they saw were quite unrepresentative of American society; more correctly, dramatically unrepresentative of all those experiencing human misery. What was more vexing was that clinical psychologists seemed unaware of how skewed a sample of people they saw. And nothing was more reinforcing of this parochialism than the embeddedness of the field either in the medical-psychiatric setting or in a theoretical-psychiatric way of thinking or theorizing or in both. In brief, clinical psychology was fast becoming a field unbased in and unrelated to the social sciences. It was to me a monumental irony that in its challenge to long-standing traditions of American psychology, clinical psychology had unknowingly bought the most durable aspect of those traditions: a riveting on the individual organism.

From my perspective and values, it was essential that clinical psychologists should be no less exposed to children than to adults. Indeed, I argued forcefully that from the standpoint of prevention and the public welfare, the majority of clinicians should be encouraged to work with children in the diverse settings that were shaping them. My fantasies to the contrary notwithstanding, I did not expect that clinical psychology would or could take on all of the problems of all of the people experiencing personal difficulties. But I did expect that as a new field it should seriously deliberate about how its limited resources could best benefit the society. At the very least, I argued, such deliberation could not justify a state of affairs in which only a very small number of clinical psychologists had anything to do with children.

The fact was (and is) that the preponderance by far of clinical psychologists were and are trained to work with the individual adult. This socially unfortunate situation has a complicated explanation in which several factors are significant. The first is that many of the training sites (for example, the VA) did not have children. The second is that working with children is "messy," requiring as it does working with families, schools, and other agencies that tax one's patience and in regard to which

one has little influence or control. (It is not happenstance that
in medicine the fields of pediatrics and child psychiatry are very
small fields.) And the third reason is that those who presided
over the creation of modern clinical psychology never asked the
question, where in terms of the public welfare could this new
field make its most effective impact? But at the time, there was
another factor, which was the most influential of all because
it reflected a mammoth change in American society and the
American psyche. I have alluded to this factor before, but it
now requires being made more explicit. It is a factor the explanation of which requires a separate book, because it is a factor
that cannot be understood apart from the history and nature
of American culture. But this is a professional autobiography
and not a scholarly endeavor, and I restrict myself here and in
the next chapter to how my views of that factor emerged and
changed. Let me just note that it is a factor that emerged full-
blown in post–World War II Western society, but not to the
degree and manner in which it was institutionalized and pro-
fesssionalized in America. Only in America!

World War II produced cataclysmic changes in American
society. If the war was not an etiological force for those changes,
it accelerated those changes at a dizzying pace. I have labeled
the postwar era as the Age of Psychology or the Age of Mental
Health. It would be no less appropriate to call it the Age of
Psychotherapy. By historical standards of time, it was as if, overnight, psychotherapy appeared on the social scene as a socially
sanctioned way of getting personal help. Shortly after the war,
Leonard Bernstein composed the concerto ''The Age of Anxiety''; in novels, films, and plays, the psychotherapist became
a familiar face; and in the mass media (radio, later TV, the
Sunday supplements of newspapers), the world and workings
of psychotherapy were frequent topics. Whereas before World
War II going to a psychotherapist was something you kept secret
because others (=society) would regard you as ''crazy,'' after
the war the message broadcast to the society was: ''You should
regard your need for personal help no differently from your need
to correct a phsyical illness. It is nothing to be ashamed of. It
does not mean that you are abnormal. It means you need a certain

kind of help, and that help is available, and if you get it, you will get better. You are not alone." That message and its variants became omnipresent. And, of course, no groups proclaimed this message with more vigor than those constituting the mental health fields. That the demand for psychotherapy vastly exceeded the supply was noted but glossed over. These advocates were unschooled in economics and the dynamics of a market economy and, therefore, were in a few years unprepared for what began to happen: the limited supply of psychotherapists would be discernibly increased by the phenomenon of "everybody getting into the act," with or without degrees or the traditional academic and experiential credentials.

When I say that psychotherapy became both faddish and fashionable—some clinical training programs required their students to obtain psychotherapy for themselves—I refer especially to the reading public; for example, college students and faculty, the multitudes who were members of book clubs, and those who read among that cadre of self-styled avant-garde intellectual monthlies the influence of which is disproportionate to their numbers. Sigmund Freud, Erich Fromm, Karen Horney, the analytical couch, the phenomena of dreams and the benefits of catharsis, the wondrously mysterious relationship between psyche and soma—these and much more were in the social and intellectual air. Textbooks in psychiatry and abnormal psychology changed dramatically. All of this had two major effects, one obvious and the other subtle. The obvious one was that psychotherapy—and in the decade after the war, that meant prolonged psychoanalysis or its briefer versions for those less affluent (not poor, just less affluent) or Rogers's nondirective approach—became, as literally never before, a way of getting help with personal problems. The subtle effect was that the role of the psychotherapist came to be seen as fascinating, socially significant, boundlessly and personally rewarding, and a sign that one possessed special gifts. That kind of role had already been achieved by American physicians, again to a degree unexcelled in Western society. But very few of the many who wished to become medical healers could afford the education or, if they could, were admitted. And, let us not forget, if you were an "ethnic," especially if you were Jewish, the odds against your getting into a medical school were immorally high.

With the emergence of modern clinical psychology in the Age of Mental Health, a way was opened to become a healer without going through years of medical education and training. Of the many who entered the new field, a significant percentage did not want to be physicians. They wanted to be healers of the psyche, to apply the new knowledge about the mind to those in personal difficulties. From what they had read in texts and novels, what they had seen in films, what some had experienced as patients, what they had read or had been told about Freud's fears that analysis would *in America* be made a medical specialty—these new entrants into this field were not about to let their dreams about becoming a healer stay in the realm of dreams.

I assume, and my experience in this matter is not miniscule, that most people have had fantasies about being a healer of the psyche. It is an alluring prospect that satisfies many needs, good and bad. I am reminded here of something that Wolfgang Köhler said in one of his publications. He was describing a social occasion at which there are a chemist, a mathematician, a physicist, and a psychologist. It is, he said, very unlikely that when the chemist, the mathematician, or the physicist says something about his field, the others will see fit to challenge it. But as soon as the psychologist opens up his mouth, everybody becomes a psychologist! What Köhler described decades ago remains true today—but with one significant difference: if on these social occasions you label yourself as a psychotherapist, you are viewed as someone with special knowledge and techniques not possessed by the others and, therefore, not likely to be challenged. The air of mystery has always surrounded healers. And like other healers today, the psychotherapist revels in this reaction and tends to do nothing to dispel it. It is to Freud's everlasting credit, one of his enduring contributions, that he described how personally corrupting the role of psychotherapist can be. When he recommended that analysts ought to be reanalyzed every five years, it was not to ensure that the analytical fraternity would be economically secure. Freud's comments derived

solely from his observations of himself and others in their therapeutic role in their offices. He could not anticipate the situation where on a societal level the psychological healer would be
accorded a social status, a social power, a social image that that
healer has today in American society.

If I am emphasizing the negatives, it is for the purpose
of underlining what I regard as one of the most unfortunate
developments in modern clinical psychology: it has for all practical purposes become a one-topic field. Several years ago, at
the annual meeting of the American Psychological Association,
I came across a fat paperback entitled *Two Hundred and Fifty
Psychotherapies*. Some of these therapies were accorded a couple
of paragraphs, others several pages. If you are the optimist who
regards the half-empty bottle as half-full, you will regard this
book as a sign of vitality, as a sign of dissatisfaction with tradition and of a healthy quest to explore new avenues of help. If
you are the pessimist, you will tend to see it as a Tower of Babel,
as an indication that the field has run amok. If you have the
arrogance, as I do, to regard yourself as a realist, you have to
conclude that something is wrong somewhere. But my opinion
is not based only on that one book. Indeed, that book served
merely to crystallize disquiet from several sources. For example, in the past decade I have asked this question of colleagues
(clinical and otherwise) around the country, all from my or the
next generation: Have you noticed any change in the characteristics of graduate students over the years? The initial response
is one of thoughtful silence, as if a troublesome note has been
sounded. No one ever goes on to say that he or she has not noticed
a change. Almost all go on to say something like the following:
"They are as bright as ever, and there are a few who are really
dedicated to getting a rounded education. But most of them come
with a very narrow, trade school attitude: they want to become
psychotherapists, and the more experience we can give them
along those lines, the better. Most take positions where they
can engage in full- or part-time practice. In fact, a surprising
number explicitly decide that they do not want to be in the
university, which is quite a change from our days."

I began to ask that question because of what I had begun
to see happen at Yale, where our department has long prided

itself on being one that would admit only those graduate students intent on a research career in their specialty. And what I observed was that an ever increasing number of students were interested primarily in becoming psychotherapists and taking positions where they could practice. Indeed, one of the troublesome problems in the department was in regard to nonclinical students who after they came to Yale sought to switch over into the clinical program because of their interest in psychotherapy. In some cases, the desire to switch had to do with fewer job opportunities in their nonclinical field, but that says as much about the clinical endeavor as magnet as it does about the job market.

For two consecutive months in 1986, I counted the number of times I received in the mail advertising announcements for a workshop on one or another type of psychotherapy. None was of the soft-sell variety. None was cheap. Apparently, a fair number of well-known figures spend a fair amount of their time on a national circuit of workshops. I received forty-two such announcements. In no way do I derogate these workshops or the need for continuing education. I have attended several of them with profit. I mention them to emphasize the degree to which psychotherapy has become the major preoccupation of clinical psychologists, social workers, educational counselors, clinical sociologists, and those referred to by that ambiguous but status-according label of "allied health professionals." Phillip Rieff was more than prophetic when he titled his 1966 book *The Triumph of the Therapeutic* (New York: Harper & Row). As best as I can determine, few who attend these workshops have ever heard about or read that provocative book.

I am not indicting students and workshops. I am criticizing the development of clinical psychology into an individual-oriented, market-economy profession unaware of its embeddedness in the history and nature of American society. Clinical psychology has become almost exclusively a profession of repair, a large enclave conceptually isolated from or insensitive to those conditions and societal dynamics that when glossed over ensure the manufacture of problems and the need to have more and more repairers. In earlier decades of this century, American psychology was justly criticized for basing so much of its theorizing on the Norway rat and the college sophomore. American social psychology was quintessentially a psychology of the isolated organism. It was not social in the wider political-sociological-economic-anthropological sense. The concept of culture has never been central to American psychology. This, I am tempted to suggest, largely explains why it was relatively easy for clinical psychology to become riveted in a narrow theoretical and technical way on the individual, with society in the background as an inkblot. There was no awareness at the Boulder conference that it was steering modern clinical psychology down the same road American psychology had long traveled. The individual patient is not the Norway rat or the college sophomore, but he or she is nonetheless the sole window through which clinicians see and explain the world.

History, Voltaire said, is written by the victors. And, as Rieff so well noted, the therapeutic has been victorious in American society and psychology. As a result, the history of (at least) clinical psychology is usually described as a progressive step in that its emergence in the post–World War II era is seen as a calculated effort to be responsive to the public welfare. More than that, given the context of those days, the emergence of modern clinical psychology is described as inevitable. And in typical American style, the fact that clinical psychology has become such a large field whose services are in great demand is blithely assumed to be evidence that the way things are is the way things should be. In typical American style, clinical psychology is not disposed to ask whether it has not fallen prey to what is quintessentially American: we are on an onward and upward course, more is better, nothing succeeds like success, the future will be a carbon copy of the present, we have overcome an obstacle-ridden past, and we must zealously guard what we have achieved.

The emergence of modern clinical psychology was a progressive step. Like all such steps, it was a step away from a past into a future. But that past was unrealistically understood and confronted, and that future—already in that present—was almost totally ignored. It was a step accompanied by a missionary zeal that effectively submerged a dispassionate, historically based, socially analytical consideration of the universe of alternatives.

Today, we are used to hearing about cost-benefit analysis, which is another way of saying, given the different directions we can go, how do we decide what will be most beneficial for our purposes? Whose purposes? That question never really got discussed at Boulder, or by any group meeting before Boulder. It was as if the question had one answer. It seemed obvious where (conceptually and regarding site) clinical psychology should go and how it should get there. And it also seemed obvious that what was good for psychology would be an unalloyed good for the public welfare. There were a few, such as myself, who were not persuaded. (And I do not include among these unpersuaded those academic, nonclinical psychologists who believed that leaving the laboratory and the university was trafficking with evil.)

Earlier I characterized clinical psychology as a passive profession. Let me elaborate on that by noting how reactive rather than proactive the field has been. Modern clinical psychology began by reacting to federal initiatives. Within a short time, it began to react to the stultifying imperialism of the medical-psychiatric community. Then came the sizzling sixties, which forced the field to react to issues of race, gender, poverty, and sexual style. Then it began to react to the consequences for practice of private and governmental health insurance policies. As a result of escalating health costs and the efforts of public and private agencies to contain those costs, the field again found itself reacting to new policies and a new array of health provider instrumentalities. The point is that in the post–World War II era, clinical psychology has been a reactor to and not an anticipator of social change. From my perspective, any field (such as psychology) that has a human service component should be judged by the degree to which it understands, anticipates, and takes action in regard to changes in society. That, of course, means that I expect the field to have a relatively explicit conception of the nature of the society in which it is embedded, a conception that sensitizes it to what is and will be changing on the social scene and how as a field it can lead and not only react when forced to. That may be asking too much. Not to ask it is irresponsible and self-defeating to the field in some ultimate sense. I am quite aware that the history of the clinical professions is characterized by a divorce between the repairers and the preventers. It is not happenstance that schools and departments of public health, where prevention is taken seriously, are second-class citizens in medical schools. That is a history that did not intrude into the deliberations at Boulder. Clinical psychology has been poorer because of that. Divorce may solve one set of problems. It creates others.

What I have said in this chapter will not sit well with many people in the field. I have described what my thinking was in regard to clinical psychology and how my ambivalence seesawed between advocacy and criticism. By the usual standards of historiography, I am sure that some of the things I have reported do not reflect the whole story or are not free from bias or distortion. Autobiography should not be confused with history, although history has to take autobiography into account. Whatever exists about the history of clinical psychology I would not dignify by calling it history. Clinical psychology—indeed, the mental health professions generally—has yet to be described comprehensively as a social-historical phenomenon in its peculiarly American aspects. The American story is rather different from that of other Western countries. If we were more sensitive to that fact, we would take more seriously another obvious fact: precisely because our clinical psychology is an American clinical psychology, it must reflect what is good and bad in American society. Clinical psychology did not arise in a social vacuum. It was not predestined to go in one and only one direction. The assortment of forces at play in its birth and development was no less heterogeneous than its social-intellectual genes. There was a universe of alternatives, but its dimensions were poorly discerned. That is a fact of history but not a lesson of history. To me, the lesson is that it is in the nature of culture that it constricts our awareness of the many possibilities in that universe of alternatives. We are literally schooled to constrict what possibilities we will allow ourselves to consider. This, I hasten to add, does not mean that history is a playing out of the inevitable, Karl Marx and other philosophers of world history to the contrary notwithstanding. I am reminded here of what William James said about free will: the scientific validity of the concept of free will aside, believing in free will is a difference that makes a difference in living. To use his very American phrase, it is a belief that has "cash value." To believe—in one's personal and professional lives—that there is a universe of alternatives, and that if we cannot fathom the whole of it, that is no excuse for not seriously trying, is a difference that makes a difference in the world of social action.

12

America:
Freud's Greatest Defeat

I am less than an amateur historian, and a frustrated one at that. But my feelings of vocational frustration are dramatically diluted in strength when on occasion I realize what an awesome and difficult task the historian faces when he or she is trying to explain social phenomena—an event, a movement, an era. Setting the stage—indeed, determining what the stage consists of; identifying the cast of characters; distinguishing between the major and minor actors; locating and evaluating archival data; controlling for the tendency to read the present into the past; differentiating between facts and the truth; fathoming world views different from your own—these are only a few of the aspects that make understanding and writing about the past as problematic and difficult as it is fascinating and important. And the wider the historian's scope, the more the problems multiply. Adhering to the highest standards of historiography is as difficult an intellectual endeavor as an individual can confront.

These musings intruded and bothered me throughout the writing of this book. Although this is an autobiography and, therefore, an account of a self, I justified writing it as a way of conveying how my professional career took place in a certain society that had distinctive features, not the least of which was its changing character. If I felt compelled to be more personal than I had anticipated, it was because I decided that the features of this society would be better understood by the reader if I did so. America is as much a focus of this book as I am. But I am hoist by my own petard, because that larger and more important focus raises questions about the ways I understand the relationships between American psychology and American society. And by *understand,* I mean my delineation of the facts and the truth. So, for example, I have discussed the role of the VA and NIMH in shaping modern clinical psychology. From the standpoint of the historian, my account will not pass muster, because I have not gone into the archives, or interviewed systematically the actors who are still alive, or identified in detail the considerations, pressures, and influences that entered into their deliberations. That the VA and NIMH played decisive roles is an indisputable fact. But the truth has to do with the interrelationships among facts, what was, so to speak, between and not on the lines, what was axiomatic and therefore unverbalized, who was decisive and why, and the interplay between formal and informal sources of power as well as between the legislative and executive branches of the federal government— and all of this suffused in a zeitgeist as crucial as it is bewildering to relate to these developments. Someone once said that just as patriotism can be the refuge of scoundrels, the concept of zeitgeist is employed by those too lazy to concretize it in regard to a particular social phenomenon; that is, it explains everything and, therefore, nothing. I have tried to avoid that laziness, but the fact remains that requirements of autobiography set limits to concretizing in detail how I and my field reflected zeitgeist and its changes. Autobiography and scholarliness are not exactly the best of bedpersons.

These musings are particularly appropriate to the present chapter, which deals, among other related things, with several questions: Why in this century did psychoanalysis steadily become a distinctive feature in the American cultural scene? Why did that influence take on explosive proportions after World War II? Why did it come to dominate modern clinical psychology? Why has that domination markedly decreased in the past two decades? Why in these two decades has American psychiatry changed so dramatically from a psychoanalytical to a biological emphasis? These questions are obviously not answerable only in terms of this or that individual, or this or that professional group, or by the substance of psychoanalytical theory, or by any evidence that as a therapy psychoanalysis was a demonstrably superior one. Psychoanalysis was not only a theory, a therapy, and a research area. It was also a movement in that many of its advocates, lay and professional, saw and proclaimed it as a vehicle through which individuals and the culture could and should be transformed. If taken seriously, as I and many others took it, psychoanalysis would inform and transform schools, marriage, child rearing, the law, and any field concerned with "human nature." However you distinguish between a field or discipline, on the one hand, and a social movement, on the other hand, psychoanalysis has historically had features of both. And that was much more the case in America than in any other Western country.

The slow but steady spread of Freud's influence is no great mystery. Put briefly but, I think, fairly, Freud addressed and described feelings, attitudes, events, habits, processes, and tendencies that Western people had difficulty denying: by virtue of being social and biological organisms, we cannot escape sexuality and its vicissitudes, shame and guilt, defensive and self-protective maneuvers, propelling anxiety, dreaming, the pursuit of pleasure, and conflicts attendant to interpersonal relationships. People could and did deny Freud's explanations, but they had less success in denying the relevance of his descriptions for their lives. So, when Freud described a case of a phobia in a five-year-old boy, he clearly distinguished for the reader what little Hans said and did from his theoretical explanation. Some people said that little Hans was a pervert and hardly a basis for testing a theory. But for many others, what Freud described rang familiar bells. At the time of and before Freud's early writings, there existed a relatively large literature in Europe on human sexuality. Freud's writings did not go unread, and he did not go unrecognized. "Old" Europe was not young, Puritan America. But that statement requires qualification, because in the latter half of the nineteenth century and the early decades of this century, many American psychologists and physicians either received their training abroad or felt obliged to spend some time in a European (mostly German or Austrian) center of learning. They could talk and read French and German, just as Freud could talk and read English and French. And these Americans read! That Freud was not an unknown in American psychology at a time when that field was truly miniscule in its numbers is best indicated by the invitation accorded him, Jung, and Adler to attend the twentieth anniversary of the founding of Clark University in 1909. That invitation was extended by the first president of Clark: G. Stanley Hall, the father of child psychology in this country. It was, for the time, a much publicized occasion that contributed to Freud's reputation in academic and lay circles in America. This did not mean that Freud and psychoanalysis became topics of household conversation but rather that among what is called the intellectual community (for example, academics, writers, artists, social essayists), psychoanalysis became food for thought. Psychoanalysis was not an overnight sensation. American culture was not disposed to receive cordially what psychoanalysis seemed to be saying about the human organism. Indeed, most people viewed psychoanalysis as a sign of European moral decadence, from which America needed to be isolated no less than from European political decadence. But if American culture was inhospitable soil for psychoanalysis, it was not lethal soil. The seeds were planted, and in two of those ecologies, the growth took very different forms relevant to my professional life.

Although American psychology did not embrace Freud and his theories, it did not ignore them. In those early days, American psychology can be characterized as a field intent on demonstrating its credentials as a science. And that meant an emphasis on methodology, experimentation, and replication. Theory was important, but its value inhered in the direction it gave to studies, preferably in the laboratory, that allowed for the manipulation of variables and statistical analysis. Psychology was reacting to its former embeddedness in philosophy, a reaction that made it gun-shy in regard to grand theorizing. Freud presented a challenge to American psychology. For one thing, he made it crystal clear that he regarded psychoanalysis as psychology, not a medical-psychiatric discipline. For another thing, he described human behavior, he was an acute observer, and nothing in whatever he wrote suggested an antiscientific bias. Criticism of Freud was threefold. The first had to do with his emphasis on the role of sexuality. The second was the elaborateness and language of his theoretical explanations. And the third was the matter of provability: how could what Freud himself called the mythology of psychoanalytical theory be demonstrated by the usual canons of scientific procedure and evidence? And matters were not helped any by Freud's position that the nature of theory would engender obstacles to its acceptance in people predictable by the theory. Freud never left his readers in doubt that his was a general psychology, not one peculiar to neurotic or psychotic individuals.

If Freud was by no means embraced by American psychology—if he was viewed by most psychologists critically and even hostilely—he was not ignored. He became part of the psychological stream, albeit a minor one. In an earlier chapter, I indicated that by the twenties and thirties, psychoanalysis had become a focus of interest at Yale and Harvard. They were notable exceptions in American psychology, and even in those two places the political power in and the theoretical orientation of the departments were not exactly favorable to psychoanalysis. As a graduate student in 1939–1942 at Clark University, where Freud had given his introductory lectures on psychoanalysis, one might expect that I would have been exposed to psychoanalytical theory or, at the least, had been told about that 1909 occasion at which were some of the finest minds of the time (for example, William James, Franz Boas). Were it not for the fact that Saul Rosenzweig (a Henry Murray product from Harvard and the Psychological Clinic) at Worcester State Hospital taught the abnormal psychology course, I would not have received even this brief formal exposure to psychoanalysis.

The point I wish to emphasize is that the response of American psychology to Freud was primarily on conceptual, intellectual, and scientific grounds. It was not to psychoanalysis as a therapy or a practicing profession. It was to psychoanalysis as an ambitious, encompassing, general psychology. It is as if American psychology said, ''Freud deserves a hearing. There is less here than meets the eye. Don't ignore him. But be wary. Interesting ideas do not a science make. American and Viennese psychology are very different breeds. Ours is the scientific wave of the future.'' Those were the messages I got as a student in undergraduate and graduate schools. To many graduate students, that message was a description akin to forbidden fruit and, therefore, something we wanted to know more about. And when on our own we began to read Freud, we (at least I) found ourselves reading about ourselves. By the time World War II began, Freud was more in the stream of American psychology than its literature would have suggested. And the best indication of that was when the *Journal of Abnormal and Social Psychology* devoted a special issue to reports by eminent academic psychologists of their experience in psychoanalytical therapy (Volume 35, 1940). The rivulet was spilling over its banks.

The story of Freud and American psychiatry in the pre–World War II era is a radically different one—the same seed but with a very different growth pattern. At least two facts were decisive. The first is that of the small number of psychiatrists who were initially attracted to psychoanalysis, almost all lived and practiced in New York City (Boston came later). A few had been analyzed in Vienna by Freud, and they in turn ''trained'' their local colleagues. The second fact is that they were individual psychiatrists outside of academia; that is, they were practitioners who essentially constituted themselves as a passionate advocacy group. They were disciples, possessing all of the defects and few of the virtues of disciples. Their feelings of marginality and isolation stemmed not only from the response they received to their doctrines but also from the fact that most were Jewish.

For a long time, New York was the Mecca for psychoanalytical training. To trace the spread of psychoanalysis to other urban centers in America, you have to start with that small group that organized the New York Psychoanalytic Institute. From the outset, that group was intent on ''purity,'' a slavish devotion to Freud's writings. By concentrating on what Freud and his inner group wrote, they "managed" to ignore a distinctive feature of the Vienna circle: it was deliberately, explicitly comprised of people from very diverse professional disciplines. Possessing a medical degree was not a "must." To someone like Freud, whose goal was to develop a general psychology, restricting psychoanalytical training to physicians was anathema, which he indeed proclaimed. The fact is that the New York group ignored Freud in this regard and essentially transformed psychoanalysis from a general psychology to a medical-psychiatric ideology. This transformation was peculiarly American. It was a transformation that I regard as Freud's greatest defeat, a kind of example of snatching defeat from the jaws of victory. Freud did open up new vistas, and he did want to see psychoanalysis, as theory and research, percolate into all of those disciplines concerned with human history and conduct. And if Freud had rigid criteria about what was and was not psychoanalysis, and if he did not look kindly on dissenters and defectors, he knew that the promise of psychoanalysis would be disastrously diluted if it remained a medical specialty. At least as I read Freud, now and when I was in college, the development of psychoanalytical therapy was regarded by him as the least significant of his contributions or goals. In America, therapy became for all practical purposes the main focus. The rhetoric was, of course, otherwise. Just as no one is publicly against motherhood, no one is opposed to research. In the New York institute, and the other institutes around the country it helped spawn, what passed and passes for intellectual discourse, let alone research training, is at best farcical and at worst tragic. This development, of course, made it virtually impossible for psychologists to enter the psychoanalytical arena. I knew this when I was in graduate school, but no one explained to me how this had come about, how different the American scene was in this respect from the European scene. A couple of years after I came to Yale—when psychoanalysis seemed to erupt into the university and the culture generally—I sought to become a candidate at the New York Psychoanalytic Institute and was not accepted. I was crestfallen. I even considered going to medical school if that would increase my chances. That says as much about the zeitgeist as it does about me. Long before I was rejected by that institute, I had developed a deep antipathy to what in later years I called professional preciousness: an obsession with and dependence on formal criteria for entrance that deny opportunity to many who, despite the lack of formal credentials, could meet standards of professional performance. It was that preciousness against which clinical psychology fought in its fraternal war with psychiatry. Today, clinical psychology strikes me as having no less a sense of preciousness toward those who lack doctorates or come from other fields. Freud's concept of identification with the aggressor may be relevant here!

The second decisive factor shaping the pattern of growth of psychoanalysis in America has to do with psychiatry's response to it. I said earlier that American psychology did not warmly embrace Freud. Compared to psychiatry's response, that of American psychology was love at first sight. At the turn of the century, American psychiatry was still largely a mental hospital profession with strong roots in neurology and neuroanatomy. It was barely represented in what was then an already changing medical school scene. Even in those few medical schools that were then of good quality, psychiatry was a second- or third-class citizen, when it was a citizen at all. American psychiatry was biological in the extreme. Freud received a hearing in American psychology. By contrast, he was virtually ignored by American psychiatry.

One of the distinctive features of the history of American psychiatry (up until today) is its efforts to become a recognized, respected part of American medicine; that is, to be seen as a profession with "real" doctors who are vital to an understanding of psyche and soma. That upwardly mobile quest had several consequences. First, it steered psychiatry away from any meaningful relationship with the social sciences. Second, it similarly stifled any tendency to base the field on a comprehensive general psychology. And third, it disposed the field to view the substance of psychoanalysis as a danger to its goal of becoming a scientific, institutionally respected endeavor. I think it fair to say, although it would not have been put this way, that academic psychiatry saw Freud as a psychologist, and a poor one at that.

After all, Freud did cover the intellectual-psychological water-front while psychiatry was trying to carve out a small niche for itself in American medicine.

Psychiatry's response to Freud has predictable effects on the psychoanalytical psychiatrists, who, it must be kept in mind, were on the outside looking longingly into the house of academic psychiatry. It mightily reinforced their position that psychoanalytical training had to be restricted to physicians, with occasional acceptance of a nonphysician who promised in writing that he or she would not practice psychoanalysis but would do research relevant to psychoanalytical theory. And it no less reinforced the desire of the psychoanalytical community to become part of academic psychiatry. Purity of doctrine, exclusiveness in selection, a formal curriculum for training—these become the major concerns of the training institutes. Their goal was to preserve and protect psychoanalysis from heretics from within and without. They possessed the truth, but far from the truth setting them free, it walled them off from the world of ideas and fertilizing controversy. As Freud recognized, with friends like that, he had no need of enemies. Freud did not look kindly at American society, and he long feared the negative transformations that would take place in psychoanalysis in this country.

Hitler complicated matters for the American analytical institutes, because his rise to power caused many analysts to come to America. Among them were some of the leading intellectual figures of psychoanalysis, and a fair number of them were not physicians. Should these nonphysicians, all of whom had Freud's blessings, be admitted as full members of the institutes? The answer, constitutionally determined, was no. They could have a special, second-class-citizen status. A few declined such status; the others agreed to this demeaning restriction. I heard a little about these goings on while I was a graduate student at Clark reading and rereading Freud's *The Question of Lay Analysis*. To me at the time, it was an instance of the good guys versus the bad guys, the cowboys versus the Indians. I simply did not have the background to place the issues in the context of European traditions, American culture, and the rise of "scientific" American medicine. My education in American psychology was about individuals, not about individuals in culture and history.

I find it hard here to stay on a chronological track. In 1986 I wrote a book, *Caring and Compassion in Clinical Practice* (San Francisco: Jossey-Bass). In that book, I devote a chapter to a man and a report that were of enormous significance for American medicine. The man was Abraham Flexner, and the report was *The Flexner Report on Medical Education in the United States and Canada* (Washington, D.C.: Science and Health Publications), published in 1910. That report crystallized several features of medicine at that time. First was Flexner's description of the truly deplorable state of medical education, and the adjective *scandalous* might be more appropriate. The second feature was the necessity to further the tendency for medical schools to become part of the university. And the third feature was the importance of developing a medical curriculum that was based on the traditions and findings of science. Flexner (an educator, not a physician) was the right man at the right time with the right foundation and financial backing to bring to public awareness the need for a new medical education. I say "right" because that is the way he and his report are universally described. There is justice in that characterization, but in my book I state my reservations, which I will take up in a later chapter. What is important at this point is that Flexner presided, so to speak, over the wedding of American medicine and science. His report was published one year after Freud's visit to America. I note this in order to emphasize the fact that American medicine was intent on basing itself not only on science but, more specifically, on certain laboratory sciences, such as physiology, chemistry, and physics.

When the Boulder Conference on Clinical Psychology insisted on the scientist-practitioner model, it was an insistence that lineally descended from Flexner's scientist-practitioner model. It is hard to exaggerate how eagerly and quickly American medicine embraced the traditions and findings of science within a few years after Flexner's report. Science became part of the zeitgeist as never before. Now, when you read Flexner—and I consider it a must for anybody with an interest in American intellectual, social, and institutional history—you will find very little about psychiatry or psychology. Psychiatry, mental hygiene, nervous and mental diseases, public health: they cannot be found in his index. It is not that Flexner was unaware of these areas but rather that the wave of the future for these problems was in neurology, neuroanatomy, and histology. Those would have to be the scientific underpinnings. It is not happenstance that American phychiatry and medicine virtually ignored Freud. And I assume that the small group of New York psychiatrists who were attracted to Freud—and Flexner's report got good play in the New York papers—were impressed not only with the importance of presenting oneself and one's field as scientific but also with Flexner's insistence on upgrading the educational requirements for admission to medical schools. It was by no means unusual in the nineteenth and early part of the twentieth century for someone to enter what passed for a medical school after two years of high school or a year or so of college. I offer the hypothesis that the escalating concern with improving medical education and drastically upgrading the credentials for admission to medical school was a factor in the guildlike attitude the psychoanalysts took toward nonphysicians. No less than the leading physicians of the day, they sought improvement and quality through purity.

While I was in graduate school and reading much that I was not required to, I was dimly aware that there were dissensions around doctrine in the analytical community. Karen Horney, Erich Fromm, and Clara Thompson were some of the analysts whose writings departed from orthodox doctrine. It was more than a departure from doctrine but as much a broadening of the societal context in which analytical theory began to be seen. I had no way of knowing the depth, divisiveness, and guild ramifications of these controversies. What these "diluters of the faith" were saying struck responsive chords in someone like me who lived in two worlds: academic psychology and the arena of social change and affairs. What I did not know—and did not really know until 1987—was that in its earliest decades in Europe, especially in Vienna, there was a serious interest in the relationship, theoretical and practical, between psychoanalytical and political theory, between theory and the world of affairs. And the person who organized and led this circle of analysts was the one who wrote a book that immediately after World War II became the bible of orthodox psychoanalysis, which most clinical psychologists had to read. The man was Otto Fenichel, and the book was *The Psychoanalytic Theory of Neurosis* (New York: Norton, 1945). How does one account for this massive, orthodox tome and Fenichel's passionate concern for social analysis and change? Why has that seeming paradox gone unnoticed and undiscussed in America? Why did Fenichel, after he emigrated to America, essentially hide his political and social concerns at the same time that he devoted his energies to keeping his circle intellectually alive? The answers to these and other, related questions are contained in Russell Jacoby's 1983 book, *The Repression of Psychoanalysis: Otto Fenichel and the Political Freudians* (Chicago: University of Chicago Press). It is the story of personal tragedy, intellectual courage and heroism, and stultifying guildism, and confirmation of Freud's worst fears about the medicalization of psychoanalysis in America. Fenichel was orthodox, but, like Freud, he believed that the future of psychoanalysis was not in its therapy but in its interrelationships with other bodies of knowledge relevant to understanding society and spearheading social change. I cannot refrain from quoting Jacoby:

Fascism compelled the political Freudians to retreat. As Fenichel put it in his parting lecture from Prague, the political Freudians must withdraw and preserve classical psychoanalysis; this was the best the times allowed. The situation in the United States reinforced this deployment of energies; conditions did not prompt political Freudians to advance a more social or militant psychoanalysis. The weakness of a credible Marxism; the relative newness of psychoanalysis; the geographic dispersion of the analysts; and the tenuous legal status of the immigrants all worked effectively against a political psychoanalysis. In addition, the medicalization proceeded most rapidly in the United States, undermining the cultural and political implications of psychoanalysis.

Fenichel's public writings reflected these realities; they barely breathed of his private and political sentiments. But a reader who read to the final pages of his straitlaced *Psychoanalytic Theory of Neurosis,* attuned to the cautious idiom, could pick up a number of clues. Fenichel espouses here a rigorous historical perspective. He writes:

"Neuroses do not occur out of biological necessity, like aging. . . . Neuroses are social diseases . . . the outcome of unfavorable and socially determined educational measures, corresponding to a given and historically developed social milieu. . . . They cannot be changed without corresponding change in the milieu."

In the final pages of this text Fenichel reiterates several of his principles. Sharp limits beset the therapeutic possibilities of psychoanalysis. "Faced with the enormous neurotic (and non-neurotic) misery of today, we are sometimes near to despair, realizing that we can only help five to ten persons a year." There is "consolation," however, in the "general application" of psychoanalysis.

"Not because primitive instincts are still effective within us do we have wars, misery and neuroses; rather, because we have not yet learned to avoid wars and misery by a more reasonable and less contradictory regulation of social relations, our instincts are still kept in an unfavorable form."

After almost six hundred dense pages of categories and descriptions, these inelegant formulations effectively smothered the message of socialism, "a more reasonable and less contradictory regulation of social relations" (pp. 120–121).

It should be noted that Fenichel unsuccessfully fought in America against the position of the analytical institutes on lay analysis.

In Chapter Nine, I briefly discussed why and how World War II facilitated the legitimation of psychoanalysis in the society generally and the university in particular. For at least two decades after the war, clinical psychology was heavily influenced by psychoanalysis. I was a prime example of that. The speed of that legitimation is nothing short of amazing. It was as if overnight a new "new testament" had been unearthed (a kind of Dead Sea Scrolls), which had to be confronted and assimilated. To be on the analytical couch was a badge of distinction (as I can personally attest), to be admitted to an analytical institute was to become part of a small priesthood, and to become a training analyst was the equivalent of becoming a member of the College of Cardinals, the number of colleges increasing as a reaction to the rigidity of the orthodox institutes in matters of doctrine and selection. In saying this, I intend criticism of myself as well as of the churchlike analytical institutes.

At the beginning of this book, I said that I see my intellectual-professional development as one in which I was in a particular fog, then the sun came out and my mind cleared, only later to find myself in another fog, then another parting of the clouds, and so on. I was in a fog until I read Freud. But the fog returned, I now know, a few short years after I began teaching an intensive and comprehensive seminar on psychoanalysis. It may well be that that was the first required seminar on psychoanalysis in a graduate clinical training program. I say that not to establish any claim to priority but to indicate the speed and force of the legitimation of psychoanalysis after World War II. However you define the zeitgeist of the time, psychoanalysis was an important feature of it. It was the wave of the future, but I lacked the sophistication—I was possessed too much of the ahistorical stance—to know that waves inevitably dissipate their energies as new ones roll in. That is why I have such respect for historians for whom it is axiomatic that "this too shall pass."

Anyone who seriously begins to read Freud quickly confronts a new and strange lexicon. At the time I am talking about, words such as *ego, superego,* and *id* were not part of everyday parlance. In the Freudian scheme, *ego* is not simply I, *superego* is not simply what we ordinarily mean by *conscience,* and *id* is the most ambiguous of the three. And what about *catharsis, libido, penis envy, thanatos, introjection, structural formulations, topographical formulations,* the *death instinct,* the *partial instincts, sublimation?* And if you read later theorists, such as Hartman, Lowenstein, and Kris, there were phrases such as the *autonomous ego,* the *conflict sphere part of the ego,* and *regression in the service of the ego.* Those were models of linguistic clarity compared to some of the concepts found in Melanie Klein's writings on child analysis. Until I began to teach the seminar, what fascinated me was not the language of the theory but the concrete, detailed case descriptions or case fragments, especially those by Freud, who was not given the Goethe prize for literature for nothing. I tried valiantly to comprehend his theorizing, but as I look back, I must conclude that I was confusing comprehension of theory with the ability to memorize and repeat it. There was a part of me that knew that I was not comprehending—that I did not have that gut feeling that I understood the nature and interrelationships of the components of the theory—but that, I assumed, was a deficiency on my part. I knew, I had already decided, that I was not a theorist, that I had a rather concrete style of thinking that was uncomfortable when I had to weave explanations of complex phenomena. Who was I to entertain for more than a moment the thought that maybe the emperor had no clothes? (That is precisely the way I reacted during my Trotskyite days when I tried to understand the writings of Marx, Engels, Hegel, and Kant. I found them sleep producing and very confirmatory of my intellectual deficits.) But one thing I knew then as now: Freud's theories were efforts to deal with real and important concrete problems (no less than in the case of Marx). If I was incapable of being critical of the theory, if I was fearful of saying that the logic of it was not all that apparent and the gulf between it and concrete phenomena by no means narrow, it said as much about me as it did about intimidation by authority. I was a privately questioning but publicly devoted disciple. Some day, I hoped, the clouds would part and there would be light.

    It is one thing on your own to struggle with psychoanalytical theory. It was quite another thing to teach it to bright, serious, question-asking graduate students who were immersed in a milieu where you were supposed to take nothing for granted, let alone on faith. And during the years I taught that seminar, those graduate students were intellectually assertive to an unsurpassed extent. Somewhere in his writings, Jerome Kagan thanks me for introducing him to psychoanalytical theory. What I could not tell Jerry then was how much anxiety he engendered in me by his questions, which assumed a knowledge and ability on my part that I did not possess. If ten minutes or so went by without Jerry asking a question, it was because he was mulling over something I had said earlier, and I could count on his interrupting the discussion to bring us back to something I had said. His style of participation was unique, but many other graduate students were no less disturbing to my equilibrium. I did not have to worry about being kept on my intellectual toes. The problem was how to keep from sinking.

I knew that I could not come to class and regurgitate what was contained in the assigned readings. (Unlike the situation in later decades, I could count on students having seriously read assignments.) My task was to elicit questions and to help the students understand the substance and scope of the theory, how the theory had been changed by Freud and others, and the relationship between theory and the contents and vicissitudes of psychoanalytical therapy. I spent a summer preparing for that first seminar, and it was then that I began to realize how slippery, ambiguous, and indefinable many of the concepts were. I well remember rereading Freud's *Beyond the Pleasure Principle.* It raised troublesome questions. What could I anticipate when we took up Freud's fanciful meanderings in *Totem and Taboo?*

What that summer of preparation forced me to begin to confront were all of my reservations about Freud's hydraulic conception of the mind: comprising energies that got attached here and there, got transformed in mysterious ways, even got "neutralized," and seemed to power everything in diverse ways depending on where in the mental "apparatus" these energies found themselves. The mind was a self-igniting "place" in which war rather than peace was the constant condition. It was a place comprising zones and structures containing gremlinlike energies.

How should I teach the course so that the students could comprehend what Freud had been about, and do this fairly, sympathetically, and critically? How do I get them to distinguish between the clinical and observational material that gave and gives rise to the theory, on the one hand, and the theoretical superstructure, on the other hand? Those questions are misleading, because they suggest a pedagogical clarity on my part that I did not possess. All that I really knew was that there would be problems and that I had to avoid the stance of indoctrination and authority as a way of masking my insecurities. The worst thing that could happen was for the students to conclude that Freud had not identified some of the most significant problems and processes of human behavior.

What I found myself doing early in that first seminar was using my own experience in analysis, my own personal life, for illustrative examples of psychoanalytical theory and therapy. Far from finding it difficult or embarrassing, I found it no end relieving. I was the world's expert on myself. I had no difficulty using my life to give flesh to the bones of theory. As a pedagogical device, it worked well and allowed me to feel free to be critical of the language and mythology of the theory. There were limits, of course, to what I would reveal about myself, and in admitting that to the class I would repeat ad nauseum, "What Freud *described* is no less true of us than it is of the classes of people labeled neurotic and psychotic. And by us I include Freud, as he himself never denied. We can criticize his theorizing, but we cannot avoid coming to personal grips with his descriptions."

I began teaching the seminar at about the same time that our neighbor in the building, the department of psychiatry, experienced a palace revolution. What had been a bastion of biological, antianalytical psychiatry was transformed into a psychoanalytical enclave. Fritz Redlich, a young analyst, became chair of the department. Fritz was Viennese in the best intellectual and cosmopolitan sense of that label. He was the opposite of parochial. Before becoming chair, he had developed an intellectual relationship with Neal Miller and John Dollard. He was interested in and knowledgeable about the social sciences. One of the first things Fritz did when he became chair was to invite members of our department to participate in meetings in his department, and to develop seminars for residents. But he did one other thing relevant to this chapter: he gave adjunct appointments to the most emiment psychoanalysts on the eastern coast. He started Saturday-morning meetings to which these analysts came. I attended many of these meetings. I, of course, said nothing. I was there to soak up wisdom, to learn more about the relationship between theory and clinical material. Two of the analysts were mightily impressive: Lawrence Kubie and Robert Knight. What impressed me in their discussion of clinical material was what I can only call their earthiness: sticking with what was observable and using amazingly little of a theoretical superstructure. They had penetrating and organizing minds. They brought seemingly disparate phenomena together, they gave them a meaning that made practical sense. And they did this in a way that left no doubt that they thought in a psychoanalytical framework. But the impressive fact was how little of the theoretical superstructure was reflected in their comments and interpretations. In one informal interchange with Knight, I falteringly indicated that although I could follow his line of reasoning, I could not see the relevance of the superstructure; that is, I could not see what it would have contributed to the issues that had been discussed. I am sorry that I cannot repeat his reply verbatim, but he left no doubt that my reservations were not without merit.

What those meetings recalled for me was a colloquium that Kurt Lewin gave at Clark when I was a second-year graduate student. I had made it my business to read a fair amount of his writings, to which I responded most enthusiastically because of his implied critique of American psychology, especially those writings that so clearly distinguished between the Galilean and Aristotelian modes of thinking. I had also struggled with his papers in which he used concepts of topology, a branch of mathematics, in his theorizing. To Lewin, it was obvious, topology had relevance for what he was trying to explain and conceptualize. To me, it was Greek and no more, and here again I castigated myself for my ignorance and intellectual deficits. So, when I and others heard that Lewin was coming, we welcomed the possibility that the significance of topology would be made more clear to us by this most creative, intellectually provocative, ingenious thinker and experimenter. His presentation was a model of clarity, one of the most thoughtful I have heard, then and since. But there was not a hint of topology. I questioned him about this, but he politely indicated that he would prefer not to get into the matter. To my knowledge, Lewin's excursion into topology was brief, never to rear its head again in his writings.

If all actors want to play Hamlet at least once in their lives, I think that all serious researchers want to develop a theory.

It was Kurt Lewin who said—and few statements have been more repeated in the psychological literature—that there is nothing as practical as a good theory. But what are the criteria of a good theory? There are good researchers and lousy researchers; there are good theories and lousy theories. This is not the place to answer that question except to say that in those early years I was vaguely coming to the conclusion that a good theory not only explains what you already know, but directs you to relationships of which you have not been aware. Put in another way, it is not enough to translate, so to speak, what you know and observe into another language. The trick is not in the translation but in the illumination of new possibilities. From that standpoint, I found Lewin and Freud wanting. As the years went by, it did not surprise me to see critiques of orthodox analytical theories escalate in frequency by those within and without the analytical community.

One other experience has to be mentioned here. It concerns Dr. Richard Karpe, an émigré psychiatrist-analyst from Prague who practiced in Hartford and had a clinical appointment at Yale. Sometime in the late forties or early fifties, he began supervising the analysis of a young woman by Dr. George Mahl, a former student in our department to whom Fritz Redlich had given a full-time research appointment. In the course of the analysis, Richard and George had concluded that it was important for the success of that analysis that the husband should go into analysis. Would I be willing to conduct the analysis under Richard's supervision? I had come to know Richard socially, and I liked and respected him a good deal. I jumped at the opportunity.

I am not about to present a case history or details of the course of the analysis, which was terminated after several months. Suffice it to say that the husband was a frightened, anxious individual whose volcanic anger and hostility to almost everyone in his social world were not far from the surface. To me he was always pathetically acquiescent and even subservient. He was handicapped by a problem with one of his legs from a birth defect. Two features of the man were fascinating to me. The first, and the one that made analysis impossible, was that he was the most unpsychologically-minded person I had ever encountered, and that was also the reaction of Richard Karpe. It was a grievous mistake to have made analysis the treatment of choice. The second feature, no less fascinating to me than the first, was how thoroughly Italian he was. Physically, socially, and culturally, he lived in a walled Italian world. He was a foreigner in his native America. Almost from the start, it was obvious to me that you could not understand this man only in narrow psychological terms or within the confines of psychoanalytical theory. But my task was understanding in the service of being helpful to someone with severe interpersonal difficulties. Psychological and cultural understanding could not be separated. The problem was how to take them into account in regard to therapeutic tactics and strategy. Though Richard was nonplussed, he was flexible enough to suggest that we alter our approach, but to no avail.

The point of the story, however, is not that psychoanalytical theory and the therapy derived from it were inadequate guides in this case. Nor is it the point that an error in selection was made. What became apparent to me after many long discussions with Richard, and after the case was terminated, was how little of analytical theory ever got mentioned or used. What was the relevance of this or that aspect of doctrine? Psychoanalytical theory is not a random collection of concepts. And it certainly is not a simple affair or an arid exercise of the imagination. It is a serious affair intended to illuminate human behavior. Why did so little of it get reflected in our discussions? I took this up with Richard. His reply was in four parts. First, much of the theory was simply not relevant to the conduct of therapy. Second, when it came to explaining any particular sample of behavior in or out of therapy, the theory simply did not provide the guidelines whereby you could go from theory to behavior. Far from providing guidelines, it gave you an almost limitless array of possibilities for interpretation. Third, despite their public posture, most practicing analysts view the complexities and elaborateness of analytical theory as a mythology that, like most mythology, contains kernels of truth. Fourth, as long as theorizing remained in the bailiwick of the analytical community, the dynamics of orthodoxy would continue to be counterproductive. Richard, like many émigré analysts I have known, looked appalledly at the narrowness and rigidities of the American psychoanalytical institutes. I once said in humor to Richard that although I rejected Freud's concept of a death instinct, it did "explain" the behavior of the analytical institutes in regard to the life of psychoanalysis. He got and agreed with the point.

Finally, my reservations about psychoanalytical theory and therapy, my anger about the crippling orthodoxy within the analytical community, were fed by a publication that became a "nonbook." Its authors were internationally eminent analysts. I refer to F. Alexander and T. M. French's 1946 book *Psychoanalytic Therapy* (New York: Ronald Press). Here in the most clear and compelling fashion, Alexander and French (and their colleagues) state that the traditional relationship between analytical theory and therapy was faulty; that is, it was erroneous to assume that psychoanalytical theory ruled out the possibility that untoward human behavior—the kind of problem behavior that analysts sought to change—could be desirably altered and sustained in relatively few sessions, *even one session*. They were questioning not only analytical therapy *qua* therapy but the substance of certain aspects of the theory itself. After all, if it could be demonstrated that the kind of problems ordinarily confronting analysts could be in a clinical sense "cured" or dramatically ameliorated in a few sessions, then analytical theory could not remain intact. In that book are contained case after case (it is not a small book) demonstrating the cogency of their position. They do not argue that there is no place for traditional analytical therapy. If they do not employ the elaborate theoretical superstructure of analytical theory—it hardly appears in their discussions—it is clear that they distinguish between what is useful and nonuseful in the theory. And they do not argue that their brief, obviously psychoanalytically influenced approach is a new panacea. What they assert is that under certain conditions, certain people with certain problems can relatively quickly experience marked changes that endure and that are not predictable from theory.

That book was as disconcerting to the analytical community, practitioners and theorists, as if the pope had announced his conversion to Islam or his assent to abortion. It quickly became a nonbook in that community. But not only in that community. That book came out when modern clinical psychology started and adapted to a large extent a psychoanalytical orientation. For all practical purposes, the book was ignored. At Esther's insistence, I had read the book, and it helped me not only to crystallize my developing doubts about the status of analytical theory and practice but also to begin to comprehend how Freud's ability and courage to change his position about both therapy and theory—to turn theory upside down as he did in regard to the origin and role of anxiety—were not examples that would inform psychoanalytical training in America.

In 1986, again at the prodding of Esther, we attended a workshop in Boston by Peter Sifneos, a psychiatrist-analyst very well known today for his work on brief psychoanalytical therapy. He told the following story, which starts with a horrendous catastrophe in Boston: the fire in the 1942 Coconut Grove nightclub in which many hundreds of people were killed. Dr. Edward Lindemann, a noted figure in preventive mental and public health, immediately set up "stations" around the city to deal with individuals and families directly or indirectly affected by the catastrophe. Dr. Sifneos, who was either a medical student or psychiatric resident at the time, participated in the effort and was very much influenced by how helpful one can be in brief contact with trauma-affected people—so much so, that when he later began his analytical training (I am understandably not sure of the chronology), he also began to experiment with brief therapy. His analytical supervisor told him that such experimentation would not sit well with the establishment figures of the Boston Institute, a bastion of orthodoxy if ever there was one. But then as now, Dr. Sifneos was his own person, and despite warnings about his future in the institute, he began a program of research. He wrote a paper, which was accepted for the convention program of the American Psychiatric Association. His anxiety level escalated when he found out that Franz Alexander would be a discussant of his paper. Alexander was one of the foremost figures in psychoanalysis, and to a beginner like Sifneos, Alexander represented mainstream thinking. Sifneos expected a very rough time. Why did Sifneos relate this story at the workshop? *During his analytical training, he had never heard of Alexander and French's work and book. He had to go to the convention to learn about their work.* In the cathedrals of psychoanalysis, there is no place for heresies. Nonbooks and nonpersons receive their status from closed minds, a lesson I had learned in my Trotskyite days when Trotsky's name and role were erased from Russian history except for mention of his status as a traitor. In the past decade, French and Alexander have been "rediscovered" by researchers, mostly clinical psychologists, who have sought to evaluate the efficacy of brief therapies, analytical or otherwise.

To explain why and how psychoanalysis took hold when it did in America is in principle identical with the task of explaining how from the moment of birth the transactions between "inside and outside" gave shape and substance to psychological life. And I use the word *transactions* advisedly, in order to emphasize the reciprocal relationship between inside and outside; that is, you cannot define one without the other, each is "in" the other, they are together and always changing in relationship to each other. I have not offered a comprehensive explanation of why psychoanalysis took hold when it did, why in a few short years after World War II it percolated into the intellectual bloodstream of every discipline that in some way deals with human behavior and history. What I have done, using my own personal and professional development, is to indicate why psychoanalysis was so magnetically attractive; why certain disciplines were for so long inhospitable soil for psychoanalysis; the role of the isolationist and the within-the-walls features of the analytical community; and the ways in which World War II transformed professional lives, disciplines, public policy, and power relationships within disciplines. I must emphasize that we as yet do not have the story of how *during the war* there took place in the corridors of power in Washington (in government and national professional organizations) a transformation in thinking and sources of influences that, among other things, began the process of the institutional legitimation of psychoanalysis. But when and if that story gets told (in my lifetime, I hope, but I doubt it), we will still have to explain why with the ending of the war that slippery thing we call zeitgeist became so hospitable, relatively speaking, to psychoanalysis. And when I say hospitable, I am not ignorant of the fact that there were pockets of resistance, some very important ones, that were not about to go along with the tide. I am aware that the Boston–New York–Washington corridor should not be confused with the rest of America, although that corridor was most influential, and that influence spread. It would be more correct to say that the influence spread inland from the corridor in the East, from enclaves in Los Angeles and San Francisco, with notable assists from Chicago and Topeka.

Personal experience and a national event or "happening" are very suggestive of why psychoanalysis took hold when it did. The personal experience occurred in the forties when Frank Beach told me that his friend Alfred Kinsey would give a departmental colloquium. I had not heard of Kinsey, and Frank proceeded to educate me about the purposes and scope of Kinsey's work. And, he stressed, it was very important to Kinsey that he obtain 100 percent samples to minimize criticism of biased sampling. Kinsey, his presentation made obvious, was as single-minded a person as I have ever seen. He was an evangelist for the scientific study of sexual behavior of all people in all types of social and vocational groups and of all ages. Kinsey was no psychologist or social scientist. He was an entomologist of world renown. And he knew his Freud, and their disagreements were many. He was not out to disprove Freud's explanations of sexual behavior but rather to secure that kind of information on the basis of which one could begin to disentangle biological and social factors in sexual development. Although he was convinced that Freud's biology was either wrong or outdated, or both, and that Freud had no normative basis for his explanations, Kinsey's interview schedule and technique sought to stay on a descriptive level, that is, type and frequency of sexual practices. Kinsey was no theorist, if only because he regarded theory in the absence of compelling and voluminous descriptive data as mischievous and obfuscating in its consequences.

I signed up to be interviewed by Kinsey's senior colleague, Pomeroy. The interview lasted over two hours, but it seemed like ten minutes. The questions were short, clear, and to the point. The interview flowed even though I was spilling my guts as if I were on my analyst's couch, with the difference that in the interview I experienced no resistance. The style of interviewing could only be described as warmly businesslike, as if I were being quizzed by a most skilled market researcher about my purchasing habits. The only disconcerting note in the interview derived from the conflict between answering the questions quickly and candidly, on the one hand, and my reactions of amazement and respect for Pomeroy's obvious interviewing skills, on the other hand. At the end of the interview, as I was leaving, Pomeroy handed me a stamped post card and requested that I send it back to him with the desired information. And the desired information was the length of my penis on erection. With unaccustomed aplomb, I said, "Of course!" I went home, showed Esther the card, we laughed, and the next morning the card was in the mail.

I relate this experience for several reasons. Kinsey had begun his research years before I was interviewed, and he had encountered all kinds of obstacles, legal and otherwise, to what he was doing. If Kinsey disagreed with Freud, he felt an affinity with him in terms of a hostile reception to the study of sexual behavior and practice. In the years immediately after World War II, that kind of reception was noticeably reduced. The zeitgeist was changing. There is no doubt that Freud's theorizing about sexuality was one stimulus to Kinsey's thinking and research. What has not been noted is Kinsey's role in bringing more attention to psychoanalytical theorizing about sexuality. I do not want to exaggerate this reciprocal influence, because the more important factor was that the intellectual community and the public generally had begun to reflect a sea-swell change in matters of self-expression. And by "matters of self-expression," I mean a greater need and willingness of people to make more permeable the boundaries between their private and public selves. (Nowhere was this more clear than in the world of art.) If a decade earlier I had been asked to be interviewed by Kinsey, I am not sure that I would have agreed. If when I agreed to be interviewed I did so enthusiastically, it was not only because I felt an obligation to show my support for a scientific study but also because I was reflecting a changing attitude toward the untoward consequences of traditional conceptions of personal privacy, of a walled-in, isolated, private world. Freud and Kinsey each in his own way painted a picture of the negative consequences of the clash between biology and culture. In the aftermath of World War II, increasing numbers of people began looking at that picture with different eyes. And that brings me to the "happening," one of the most revealing cultural events of this century.

Kinsey's first volume of findings was published in 1948 (Kinsey, A., Pomeroy, W. D., and Martin, C. E. *Sexual Behavior in the Human Male.* Philadelphia: Saunders). Imagine a situation wherein for each of the 365 days before a publication you were able to plot the frequency with which Kinsey's study was mentioned in the mass media—not only frequency but also the amount of space and, in regard to radio, the amount of time. If anybody did that study, he or she would find that with each passing week, Kinsey's forthcoming study got more and more space and time and that for several weeks before publication, frequency and time took on cascading proportions. If someone had found that a giant meteor would be hitting the earth within the month, it would not have received more attention. And the situation was no different for several weeks after publication.

Yale was by no means atypical in the number of meetings and symposia that were held in psychology, psychiatry, and other parts of the medical school. In the department of psychiatry, the reaction of the analysts ranged from derision to reasonable disagreement. But one thing was clear: Kinsey's work markedly furthered the recognition of psychoanalyis, albeit by Kinsey's conclusions, which were at variance with those of the orthodox analytical community.

The events surrounding the publication of the book spoke volumes about the changing zeitgeist. Is frequency of a sexual practice an index of its biological normativeness? If it is, what bearing does it have on our attitudes and legal codes in regard to these practices? Unless one believes that the thousands of people interviewed by the Kinsey group managed a mammoth

326 The Making of an American Psychologist

deception or spoof—or were wildly unrepresentative of the American population—how do we think about and deal with their findings? What does all of this say about American society? Would the same results obtain in other societies? These were not questions that occupied only the scientific community. They literally became public questions. Sexuality did not come out of the closet, it exploded out of it. However differently people answered these questions, the furor surrounding the publication of the book altered perceptions of the American past and present. And it instilled the thought that the script for the future would probably have to be rewritten.

Although they were not alone in this respect, the analytical community did not know how to deal with the report. On the one hand, some of the findings clearly supported Freud's conceptions of the significance and protean nature of sexuality. On the other hand, the findings challenged or contradicted key analytical explanations of the origins of sexual behavior, especially in regard to homosexuality. It came as no surprise to me that the analytical critics tended to respond in narrow psychological terms, in the process of overlooking the obvious fact that in the development of his theorizing, Freud seesawed in his evaluation of the roles of biological constitution, psychological factors, and culture-civilization. To me, the challenge that Kinsey represented to analytical theory was how to explain two interrelated things. The first was the sizable frequencies of many sexual practices and attitudes. The second was how to explain why the Kinsey report had become a social, cultural, national event. What did these two things say about American culture? Although Kinsey almost compulsively avoided in his reports going beyond his data, he was never in doubt that the significance of his work inhered in its implications for culture and cultural change. Kinsey was far more than a data-bound scientist. I well remember walking with him and Frank Beach down Broadway after he had addressed a packed ballroom at some national convention. It was a notable walk: Kinsey did all the talking, and he made it clear that the ultimate significance of his work was less for psychological theory, by which he usually meant psychoanalytical theory, and more for understanding and changing culture.

In their response to Kinsey, the analytical critics exposed all of the adverse consequences of the medicalization of psychoanalysis in America. Enclosed within an elaborate theory of the individual organism, they were unable to look at Kinsey's data and the "happening" in terms of what they implied for American culture. It was, of course, true that Kinsey's data had implications for psychoanalytical theory and therapy. It was also true that in responding to Kinsey, the analytical critics revealed what had long been obvious: the pervasiveness of value and moral judgments in psychoanalytical theory. And it was no less true that Kinsey had not given the world the last word on sexual development, behavior, and practices. I am not suggesting that these critics should have lain down and played dead before the onslaught. What was pathetic about all of this to me was their predictable inadequacy in placing the controversy in a more comprehensive context. It reminded me of the recurring nature-nurture controversies, in which passionate advocates, each drawing different conclusions from a body of data, seek and sustain polarizations that grossly oversimplify a fantastically complex problem. That is what I saw happening between Kinsey the entomologist and the analysts as narrow psychologists. I did not expect more from Kinsey. I did expect more from the analytical spokespeople. Then as now, I believed that Freud had given us a set of heuristic ideas that were of enormous significance for what I regard as the most important process and problem: how from the moment of birth do we begin to absorb our local and wider culture? To me, Kinsey's data were fascinating and important and gave urgency to what I considered the most important problem. If in regard to that problem Kinsey's data "proved" nothing, they had to be taken into account by anyone concerned with that larger problem. But the polarizations that those data produced made dispassionate discussion of the problem virtually impossible.

Decades later, I read an article by John Dewey that brought me back to the Kinsey controversy. It was written in 1896, and it was titled "The Reflex Arc Concept in Psychology" (In J. R. Ratner (ed.), *John Dewey: Philosophy, Psychology, and Social Practice*. New York: Capricorn Books, 1965). It is no less relevant

today than it was in 1896. The event with which Dewey chose
to illustrate his argument is "the familiar child-candle instance.
The ordinary interpretation would say the sensation of light is
a stimulus to the grasping as a response, the burn resulting is
a stimulus to withdrawing the hand and so on." Dewey then
goes on to demonstrate in a clear and compelling way why the
explanation in terms of stimulus and response is both incomplete
and misleading. Dewey the logician and astute psychological
observer makes a shambles of the reflex arc concept, an achievement that had absolutely no influence on the direction that
American psychology took and still takes. At the end of the
article, Dewey points out that the way the reflex arc concept
is employed is an instance of the "psychological or historical
fallacy": "A set of considerations which hold good only because
of a completed process, is read into the content of the process
which conditions this completed result. *A state of things characterizing an outcome is regarded as a true description of the events which led
up to this outcome;* when, as a matter of fact, if this outcome had
already been in existence, there would have been no necessity
for the process" (italics mine).

   What that statement triggered in me was the "biological
fallacy." Kinsey's data can be regarded as "outcomes," and
it is unjustified to regard those outcomes as a true description
of the events that led up to the "outcomes." That does not mean,
of course, that Kinsey's hypothesis of biological normativeness
is wrong, just as Dewey points out that there *is* a distinction
between stimulus and response. But the hypothesis begs the question, what were the events, processes, and conditions that brought
about the outcomes? The beauty of Dewey's paper is in his
demonstration that something that seems so simple to explain
as the child-candle instance is far from simple. Complex explanations are not inherently virtuous, as I learned in regard
to psychoanalytical theory. But in the realm of human behavior,
nothing has created more mischief than the tendency to rush
to judgment about the relationship of outcome to etiology.

   When I look back over the changes in thinking I experienced in regard to Marxism, the nature-nurture controversy,
the Kinsey controversy, the relationship between childhood

events and adult behavior, I see myself (then and now) on a road that began with the marker "gross oversimplification," which was soon followed by the marker "bewildering complexity." Life was easier at the beginning of the road. I have learned to live with bewilderment even though I have been rendered incapable of rushing to judgment.

I shall return to some of these issues in Chapter Fifteen when I take up the sizzling sixties and the Black and Jewish experience in America. By the time that decade rolled around, I had developed a serious allergy to easy explanations, the joyful passions of polarized controversy, and an asocial American psychology. Intellectually speaking, I no longer felt marginal. I felt like an outsider who no longer wanted to come in.

What might have happened if psychoanalysis had not undergone medicalization in America? It is inconceivable to me that the story would be as sorry as it has been. This is not to say that Freud's legacy has been squandered. There have been notable changes and additions to that legacy that I believe will stand the test of time. Nor do I assume that if medicalization had been avoided, the potentials of Freud's core contributions would have taken an unbroken onward and upward course. But I believe, as I believe in few other things, that the outcome would have been desirably better if psychoanalysis had become more a part of an unfettered marketplace of ideas. It is to be regretted that when psychoanalysis crossed the ocean there was no intellectual analogue to a Sherman Anti-Trust Law. There is much that I can criticize about the American university, as Veblen did early in this century and Robert Nisbet has done more recently. But those criticisms aside, the fact remains that in the university there is no place for the copyright of ideas. When that begins to happen, we had better close shop, go home, and pray. And for those of us who cannot pray, we can weep. Freud deserved better.

I have three heroes in psychology. They were contemporaries. They were very different kinds of persons, coming from radically different family and social backgrounds. What they had in common was an education, a fund of knowledge, a restless cast of mind, a generalizing cast of mind, and a kind of courage that enabled each in his lifetime to undergo dramatic transformations in thinking and outlook. The extent of their knowledge of human history was awesome, to someone like me utterly humbling and a source of envy. From their truly Olympian heights, they could see a past and envision a very different future. And they wrote—did they ever write!—in the endeavor to make their ideas public and influential. They were always questing. In the case of each, the world had difficulty pigeonholing him. Was William James a physician, a psychologist, a philosopher, an educator, a logician, or a social commentator? And the same for John Dewey. Was Sigmund Freud a physician, a psychiatrist, a psychologist, a philosopher, or an imaginative storyteller? Could they be called scientists? Small minds need small categories.

As I reflect over what I have written in this chapter, it becomes obvious, to me at least, how opposed I am to the institutionalization and canonization of great people and their ideas, accompanied as those processes usually are with self-serving possessiveness and credentialing. I intended this chapter as a critique of the medicalization of psychoanalysis from the perspective, of course, of my own experience. But the critique is unfair to the extent that I may have misled the reader to conclude that I blame individuals, as if the history of the medicalization is understandable primarily in terms of individuals and their motivations. That history, yet to be written up in historical detail, began at a particular time in American society, and it was shaped and given direction by features distinctive in the culture. And it is a history involving a feature that up until today has been at the center of this country's history and changing world view: the clash between American and Western European thought and outlook. (This is particularly clear in James, Dewey, and Freud.) How then, I can hear readers ask of me, can you justify a critique of history? My answer is in two parts. The first is that it reminds us that we are cultural products of time and place. And the second is that it should stimulate us (however puny the results) to transcend our times as James, Dewey, and Freud did.

I stopped teaching the seminar in psychoanalysis when I became aware that I was teaching Sarason and not Freud. That, I felt, was unfair to the students. I had ample opportunity to present my position in other courses and in the myriad contacts I had with the graduate students. Besides, there was another member of the faculty (George Mahl), for whom I had the highest respect, who could do justice to the goals of the seminar. In addition, since some of our students did their practicum and internship next door in psychiatry, they would be exposed to Ray Schaefer, whose analytical orientation (then!) was quite orthodox. He left Yale about that time, and his place was taken by Sidney Blatt, who possessed to a high degree exceptional clinical skills, research sophistication, and the analytical orientation.

There was no need to worry about indoctrination. Next door to me was David Hunt, who had joined the department after getting his degree from Ohio State, where he had been a student of George Kelly and Julian Rotter. David's presence was a constant reminder to me and the students that there was more than one perspective from which one could profitably view and study human behavior. It was not but should have been apparent to me that David had that kind of questing mind that could not be contained within the confines of a narrow clinical psychology.

On the surface at least, by the mid fifties I had "arrived." In 1953, the department voted to make me a full professor, a decision I gladly accepted, although I still did not see myself as an intellectual peer of my colleagues. Then as now, I saw myself as a Brooklyn-Manhattan-Newark Jewish kid (I was thirty-four) who had just been bar mitzvahed. There was an element in me that agreed with Groucho Marx's quip that he would not join any country club that would have *him*. By 1956, I had finished a book, *The Clinical Interaction* (New York: Harper & Row), which was a kind of summing up of my clinical experience. It also represented, I knew, the end of one phase of my development and another fog rolling in. It was also at this time that I was collaborating with Tom Gladwin on the monograph on psychological and cultural factors in mental retardation, an experience that confirmed in me that American psychology was self-defeatingly acultural in outlook. And the test-anxiety project was by all conventional standards a resounding success, although I was unable to steer the project from the arena of research findings to that of action based in those findings. How could we utilize our findings to get teachers to recognize and to help highly test-anxious children? I applied for grant support to the National Institute of Mental Health. As in the instance a decade earlier when I applied to the institute for support to study the cultural contexts of "familial, garden-variety" retarded individuals, I made it clear that I was not certain what would be the best way of beginning such an effort and that I would have to play it by ear. The grant request was denied, but they continued to support us in the more conventional mode of doing one study after another. If it indicated anything to me, it was how little comprehension psychologists had about the American classroom in particular and schools in general. That I already knew, but what the denial of our grant request made clear to me was that I was more the activist than the researcher. And it was at this time that Burton Blatt entered my life. Henry Schaefer-Simmern enriched and altered my life. So did Tom Gladwin. And so did Burton Blatt. None of them was a psychologist by training. Each in his own way sought to change the world. But Burt, more than the other two, spent his life trying to change the world. And he did.

So let me tell you about a person who, more than anyone else I have known, helped bring about a social change of which all readers will be aware, even though the name Burton Blatt will be unfamiliar to most readers of this book.

13

Psychology
and American Education

Every ten years or so, America takes dead aim at public education, indicting it for this or that depending on which societal issues have forced themselves onto the public agenda. And you can count on our universities to provide articulate critics who will lead the assault. I have lived through several of these cyclical bouts of scapegoating. When I came to Yale from the Southbury Training School—which was a public educational institution, albeit a special one—I was unprepared for the low regard in which the field of education was held. And, I quickly learned, that was not peculiar to Yale, although the virus of disdain was virulent there. It was not that anyone believed that the *field* of education was unimportant, but that they believed that the *people* in it were of inferior quality. At that time, Yale had a graduate department of education, awarding the doctorate to those who, it was hoped, would be the intellectual and research leaders of the field. If only because of where our department was housed, I met but hardly knew members of the department of education. What I did know was that the new president of Yale, A. Whitney Griswold, who was a historian, was a very articulate critic of our schools and "educationists," by which he meant the members of the department of education. Within

several years of becoming president, he eliminated that department. Griswold was one in a long line of university critics who
believed that the ills of our schools would be remedied if teachers
had a more comprehensive liberal arts background, if they were
more steeped in the subject matter they taught. My experience
at Southbury and my experience in schools in connection with
the test-anxiety research forced me to conclude that Griswold's
diagnosis and prescription were wildly oversimplified. I already
knew, albeit in an unformed way, that there was a "culture of
the schools" that if not studied and understood would defeat
any effort at reform. I could run off at the mouth with criticisms
of schools, teachers, and administrators, but I knew that the
answers did not lie in simple prescriptions. It is hard to exaggerate what a wound it was to the American ego when in 1957
Russia orbited the first *Sputnik*. Criticism of our schools from
university scholars had begun to escalate before 1957, but immediately after that the cascade of criticism and recommendations was dramatic. President Griswold became a national figure
in the "grand debate" on educational reform.

I saw that debate from the vantage point of my interest
in mental retardation and special education. And what I saw
was that, as in the past, when people talked about education
they were not talking about that very sizable group of children
whose needs were either ignored or unmet in schools. These
people were oblivious to the plain fact that our school systems,
especially our urban ones, were composed of two systems: one
for "regular" children and one for the "irregular" ones. And
the size of the irregular ones was mounting as the nature and
composition of our cities were changing. The debate was another
clear but unfortunate example of an educational debate that
managed to ignore the obvious.

There was no one at Yale with whom I could talk about
these matters. By virtue of my book on mental deficiency, I had
achieved instant recognition in that part of the field of education concerned with atypical development. I was invited to talk
in these departments around the country, and I received several
interesting job offers. I learned from my travels the derogatory
status of special education in schools of education. Given my

predisposition to side with the underdog, these experiences strengthened my identification with the field of education. Professionally, I lived in two separate worlds: psychology and education. In psychology, I was a relative unknown; in a part of education, it was a case of in the land of the blind the one-eyed astigmatic man is king. Relevant here is a story of the first examination given by the American Psychological Association for those clinical psychologists seeking the elevated status of "diplomate in clinical psychology." I was too young to come under the grandfather clause and, therefore, took the exam with about twenty other people in a small room in the City College of New York. We were in total agreement that it was as mystifying, demeaning, and stupid an exam as we had ever seen and taken. The clearest part of the exam was a section composed of two columns: one listing fields or special areas in psychology and the other names of people. We had to draw lines connecting name with area. By the time we came to that section of the exam, the level of anger in the group was high. At one point, I heard people sitting near me in that crowded room mutter, "Who the hell is Sarason?" There was no proctor in the room at the time, so I told them—we had not been introduced—to draw the line between Sarason and mental deficiency. That my name was in that section surprised me. That no one in that room could connect my name with my area did not. Even today, I meet psychologists who are surprised to learn that I have written, and continue to write, about education and mental retardation.

Burton Blatt knew of me when he came as chair of the small department of special education to New Haven State College in 1955. That college (now Southern Connecticut State University) had a few years before been the New Haven State Teachers College. Although Yale and Southern Connecticut were in the same city, they could just as well have been on different planets. Had it not been for Burt, I would probably have lived my life in New Haven without ever having set foot in that college. It continues to amaze me that two colleges can be in the same community without any meaningful intercourse between them. Yale, obviously, feels no need for such intercourse. It is a great university with many resources, financial and intellectual, and a perceived mission that makes it unnecessary, indeed impossible, to view Southern Connecticut as a potential asset to it. Yale is self-sufficient in a way that Southern can never be. Yale is a have, Southern is a have-not. That I have always understood. But if I understood it, I could not excuse the snobbishness that accompanied it. To preserve greatness is one thing; to cloak it in the garments of snobbishness is quite another. To be rich is no crime, but to be unwilling to share your riches with the poor is certainly no virtue. Today, as a nation, we take it for granted that aid to underdeveloped countries is both politically necessary and morally sound. That is not the way the Yales of this world look upon the Southern Connecticuts of this world. And that is what has always bothered me: the lack of a sense of obligation to share riches. If that sounds impractical, or inappropriate, or bleeding-heart utopianism, I will be satisfied if the reader agrees with me that snobbishness and derogation are inexcusable.

Burt made it his business to meet with me. And by "made it his business," I refer to the serious exuberance with which he made it clear that I was someone who was very important to him. That was disconcerting on several grounds. First, I was not used to meeting people who say right out loud how much my writings have influenced them and, therefore, that they want to get to know and work with me. In the Yales of this world, I have never been greeted with such exuberance and deferential respect as Burt displayed. Second, I was leery of his motivation to work with me, fearing that in some ways I would be exploited. Third, although I was far from having a low opinion of myself, I thought that anyone who regarded me as highly as he did— on first meeting, no less—should have his head examined. That first meeting was at a cocktail party at his house, and I had the feeling that I was center stage, except that I did not know what the script was. Esther, whose initial sizing up of people far exceeds mine in validity, said on the way home, "Watch out. He can't be real. He will use you."

Anyone who has known Burt—he died in his fifties several years ago—will understand our initial reactions. He was an exuberant man. He was in all respects as giving a person as you will ever meet. He was without guile. He was religious and took his Judaism seriously. He was incapable of exploiting anyone for his own purposes. He was amazingly well read and self-tutored in philosophy and history. He was incapable of tolerating injustice. He was at Southern Connecticut State College, he had a D.Ed., not a Ph.D., degree, but he had the imaginativeness, productivity, and quality standards not always in evidence in our elite institutions. He was ambitious for himself and others. As few people I have known, he lived comfortably in the world of ideas and social action. He was a builder and mover. He was a rough-cut diamond of a person.

Burt was a godsend to me. For one thing, he gave me a friendship all too rare in this competitive world. He gave me intellectual stimulation and companionship I sorely needed. He helped me put in perspective and conceptualize my experience at Southbury and in the public schools. And he served as a model to me of integrity and courage in action. Far more than most in academia, he had an impact on this society.

During his years in New Haven, I spent as much time at Southern as I did at Yale. The reason for this was that we came to agree that the best contribution we could make, given our resources and where they were, was in thinking through where we stood on the preparation of teachers. Burt had been a teacher for several years in the New York City schools. At Southbury and in the schools where we were conducting our test-anxiety research, I had come to observe and know well scores of teachers. I had concluded, among other things, that the training of teachers ill prepared them for what they encountered in a classroom. Although we did not initially agree on all points, we did agree on one obvious fact: teachers were psychological diagnosticians and prescribers. Whatever else their roles required of them, phenomenologically they were always making decisions and acting upon observation and interpretations of behavior. And, we agreed, generally speaking they were not good psychologists. This had nothing to do with their intellect, motivations, and fund of abstract knowledge. It was not a matter of taking this or that course in which one read and discussed principles of behavior. What was lacking in the preparation of teachers was the opportunity to scrutinize and experience the process of going from diagnostic observation to prescriptive action. It is a process we engage in all the time, usually unreflectively. And that was our point: teachers seemed to engage in the process unreflectively in a situation where the stakes are high. And if that was the case, it was also the case that there was nothing in their training to make them more reflective about the process. Neither in their practice teaching nor in their courses were they forced to focus on their role as psychological observer and prescriber.

How could we test our ideas? What we would need were a classroom, a good one-way-vision facility, a teacher, and ten or so children. In typical fashion, Burt got them all in a period of a few months. The course we offered was called "The Observation Seminar." The students were undergraduates in their third or fourth year who had elected to go into teaching. Here is what we said to them at the first meeting: "There is a classroom next door with one-way-vision facilities. Each time we meet, we are going to observe the teacher and children for about a half hour or so. It is impossible, truly impossible, to observe and not to find yourself asking questions about this or that child, or why the teacher did this and not that, why she responded the way she did, and many other types of questions. After we observe, we will come back here and discuss your questions. It may be that we will return to observe because of something that comes up in our discussion. Let's go in and start our observations." It was as simple and open-ended as that.

The first problem we ran into at the first meeting was as productive as it was unforeseen: the students had extreme reluctance to articulate their questions. The most obvious reason was the fear that their questions would be regarded as wrong or silly by Burt or me. But that, we quickly learned, was the tip of the iceberg. Of course, our presence would initially not be facilitative, but that did not fully account for their thundering silence. What finally emerged, with great difficulty, was that this was the first time they had been told that their questions, opinions, reactions would be respected and taken seriously, and they did not believe we meant what we said. They literally had been trained to give a *right* answer and not to give voice to disagreements, unclear feelings, or doubts. As one student put it, 'Who am I to pass judgment on what I observed?'' It was staggering to us how hard it was for these students to take seriously that question asking is one of the royal roads to usable knowledge and wisdom in action. It has been noted over the decades that teachers teach the way they were taught, and that is generally true in the university and our public schools. The observation seminar demonstrated that to us in spades. We gave that seminar each of the years Burt was at Southern. When he went to Boston University and then to Syracuse University, we continued to offer it to groups of undergraduate and graduate students in education. Groups varied, of course, especially as we moved into the sixties, but we could count on two "findings": reluctance to articulate questions and doubts, and the emerging awareness that the teacher was a psychologist, not a technician.

In 1962, Burt, Ken Davidson from the test-anxiety project, and I wrote *The Preparation of Teachers: An Unstudied Problem in Education* (New York: Wiley). In it we described our experiences with the observation seminar. But the larger theme of that book was that the preparation of teachers was minimally relevant to what teachers confronted when they began to teach. We were not the first to say that, but like those before us, no one was disposed to listen, let alone act. Although the book was favorably reviewed, it went out of print extraordinarily quickly, even though it was published at a time when a great debate was raging about what we should do to improve our schools. Our teachers should be better steeped in subject matter; they are required to take too many technique, Mickey Mouse courses; the criteria for selection into teaching are too low or nonexistent; education tends to attract unimaginative people who score low on tests of intellectual ability; the basic research upon which a viable pedagogy should rest does not exist; schools of education are factories and dens of intellectual iniquity that do not belong in the university—these are only some of the scathing criticisms around which the debate raged. In our book we did not directly confront these criticisms, each of which is a legitimate issue for debate on the assumption that strongly held convictions

about something as important as public education should be
aired and debated. We took several positions in the book. First,
these criticisms had been voiced in earlier debates, and reforms
had been instituted. Why were these reforms so ineffective?
Could it be that these criticisms were misdirected? The fact is,
we argued, that the criticisms now being made were amazingly
ahistorical and asociological. They were ahistorical in that they
ignored the fact that our universities never wanted education
to be part of them, which is why for over a century there were
teachers' colleges—for a long time two-year affairs—that had
to go it alone. And why was it that when universities began
to develop departments and schools of education, it was, so to
speak, over the dead bodies of the arts and sciences faculties?
And if schools of education are inadequate, ineffective, and of
poor quality, is it possible that part of the explanation inheres
in the dynamics of the self-fulfilling prophecy? How does one
explain the long-standing derogatory attitude, in the university
and the society generally, toward teachers in particular and
education in general? Could it be that the current debate should
be described as another instance of blaming the victim? As in
previous debates, issues of cultural history were distinguished
by their absence. The debate at its core was one grand ad ho-
minem: whatever was wrong with our schools could be remedied
by supplanting present personnel with brighter, better-educated
people. As any college debater learns, you pile on the facts and
you ignore the complex truths. I found myself in the familiar
position toward the opposing sides in the debate: a plague on
both your houses. It was comforting to have someone like Burt
on my side.

But what really got to me was the sheer ignorance the
critics displayed of what I later termed the culture of schools.
From listening to and reading the critics, it was obvious that
they had no understanding of how classrooms and schools were
organized and worked; that is, how teachers, administrators,
students, and parents were socialized in the complexity we call
a school, how the force of societal tradition pervades and determines what schools are as cultural entities. And the critics of
the late fifties and early sixties were irresponsibly ignorant of

how the composition of our schools, especially our urban ones, was changing ethnically, racially, and socioeconomically. The position of the critics was ass-backwards. Instead of starting with what a classroom was like, what problems a teacher confronted, how he or she handled these problems and why, why classrooms tend to be uninteresting places, what sends teachers up walls, why intellectual collegiality hardly exists in schools, what it means in practice to recognize and deal with intellectual and personality differences among students, what is meant when we say that a teacher teaches children, not subject matter—instead of starting with the culture of the classroom and the phenomenology of the teacher and how the preparation of the teacher prepared for them both, they started with course requirements, the revision of curricula, criteria for selection, and criticisms of the devil: John Dewey.

I said earlier that concern and controversy about public education, as in the case of the business cycle, are a cyclical affair in America. The actors change, the language changes, and the emphases vary, but the issues have been remarkably similar. And that is no less true of the results, which is why in the middle of the debate it was easy to predict that in ten years or so another debate would take place. (The next one started in 1981 with President Reagan's presidency.) But in the debate of the late fifties and much of the sixties, there was a new feature. Historically, it derived from the fact that the Constitution of the United States says absolutely nothing about education. That was not happenstance, of course, because education was considered a parental and local responsibility and one into which the federal government should never intrude. When in President Eisenhower's first term the decision was made to support public education, those who participated in that decision were acutely aware that they were departing from a long-standing political-moral decision. What informed that decision was the postwar population explosion, the changing composition and character of our cities, and the financial inability of our cities to cope with these changes. The debate, therefore, was not only about educational theory, practice, and reform, but also about the role of federal policy.

In regard to a federal role, Burt and I were between a rock and a hard place. On the one hand, we could not deny that our urban school systems lacked resources of all kinds. On the other hand, it was obvious to us that federal policies and support would have minimally desirable results. When compared to Burt, I would have to be viewed as an extreme pessimist. Early on I had concluded that the federal role was an understandable but misdirected and wasteful effort. This was also at a time when I was beginning to unlearn the deeply ingrained American attitude that in the face of a recognized societal problem, you garner resources, of which we have always had much, and you "solve" it. Whether it is education, cancer, or mental illness, if there is a national awareness and resolve, the material resources to solve the problem will be forthcoming. It is an attitude that is as oversimple as it is commendable. And it is commendable. But by the middle of the debate, Burt and I had to conclude that the federal role was having the unintended consequence of obscuring the extent of our ignorance about "the culture of schools and the problem of change," a book that began to germinate in my head and that I wrote several years later (*The Culture of the School and the Problem of Change.* (2nd ed.) Newton, Mass.: Allyn & Bacon, 1982).

What Burt did for me was not only to keep me in the field of education but to dramatically enlarge my understanding of it. If I had inclination to be an armchair philosopher or critic of matters educational, it was suppressed by virtue of our relationship. Burt was an activist. Once he decided that a situation was unjust, morally wrong, and inhumane, Burt Blatt could not close his eyes or walk away. And it truly made no difference if he had to tangle with his administrative superiors or important public figures. Precisely because in these forays it was obvious to others that Burt did not have a purely personal agenda, his desire for personal gain being virtually nonexistent, and because of his sense of humor and respect for the feelings of others, Burt's actions produced upset but not hostility.

Burt and I disagreed on one issue. Both of us agreed that the residential training schools for the mentally retarded were pathetic, inhuman places that rendered their residents incapable of returning to the community. At their best, they were like peaceful cattle farms. At their worst, they were only a notch above concentration camps. (That, I knew, was no less true of our mental hospitals, but they minimally entered our discussions, bonded as we were by our experience with training schools.) Soon after Burt came to Connecticut, he began to serve on advisory boards that had responsibility for these institutions. Burt believed that these institutions could be reformed. I did not. My reasons were several:

1. These institutions were in the middle of nowhere, separating child from family and community. They were "total communities" separated from anything resembling normal living. And that was true for residents and staff alike.
2. It is in the nature of these institutions, regardless of original intent, that the residents come to exist to meet the needs of the institution and not vice versa. The needs of residents become secondary or tertiary to those of maintaining organizational structure, program, and conformity.
3. Embedded as these institutions are in a state bureaucracy in which fiscal and policy decisions are made by people unfamiliar with the institutions, and subject as these people are to myriad pressures from and embeddedness in their own bureaucratic locales, institutions are rendered virtually incapable of flexible, innovative, or meaningful change. No less than the residents, the institution is "locked in." To survive, not to change, is the name of the game.
4. The staff that had the most to do with the residents' experience were the least paid, educated, and respected employees. They were hired hands, treated as if they had no heads. But if they were seen as having heads, no one seriously bothered to shape the thinking inside of them.
5. The thinking that undergirded institutional programs guaranteed a prolonged residency having two consequences: a sizable and growing waiting list and, in the dynamics of the self-fulfilling prophecy, making the patients look more incapable of returning to family and community.
6. Ours is a society that has long responded to "different" or "deviant" people by segregating them. The costs—fiscal, psychological, social, moral—have been enormous and self-

defeating. We have gone on the assumption that if these institutions exist, they must, they should exist. With less money and more humaneness, the bulk of the residents could be accommodated in our communities. There are alternatives, but we will never explore them as long as we allow ourselves to hope that they are salvageable. They are not salvageable.

Burt and I fought long and hard about these issues. It was not that we disagreed at all about what these institutions were like. Indeed, Burt, being Burt, was more upset than I was. He simply believed that they could be desirably altered, and I believed that they were hopeless. Burt began to see it my way when I hammered home the significance of his doctoral thesis, which was a comparison of two groups of handicapped children: those who had been placed in special classes and those who had remained in the regular classroom of the public school. His research and review of the literature indicated that those in the regular classroom did as well as, and frequently better than, those in the special class. That conclusion came as no surprise to Burt, who in his years as a public school teacher knew well that children put in special classes were usually there for reasons unrelated to alleged mental retardation. And the special classes in those and previous decades were called "opportunity" rooms, usually near the boiler room. They were "separate but unequal" rooms.

Early in the sixties, Burt was called to head up the department of special education at Boston University. I visited there weekly, and our argument continued. In 1965, unbeknownst to me, Burt arranged to take photographs inside training schools in Massachusetts, Connecticut, and New York. In each institution, a top official gave Burt permission to be accompanied by a photographer who had a small camera attached unobtrusively to the belt of his trousers. Burt promised that whatever use he made of the photographs, he would never disclose the name or site of the institution. It speaks volumes about Burt that he was trusted to keep his word. The photographs were taken during the Christmas season of 1965 and in 1967 were published as a photographic essay, *Christmas in Purgatory* (Newton, Mass.: Allyn & Bacon). Before its publication, an abridged version was published in *Look* magazine (Oct. 31, 1967, pp. 96–103), and that issue brought more letters to the magazine than any other piece it had ever published. It was a photographic essay in human degradation. As Burt noted in *Exodus from Pandemonium* (Newton, Mass.: Allyn & Bacon, 1970, p. 13), "This story—my purgatory in black and white—which, ironically, was conceived of and written on the 700th anniversary of Dante, represents my composite impressions of what I consider to be the prevailing conditions of certain sectors of most institutions for the mentally retarded in this country. It is the hope of calling attention to the desperate needs of these institutions for the mentally retarded in all dimensions of their responsibilities that this study was undertaken and this story written." Burt was subjected to enormous pressure to reveal the names of the institutions, but he refused to do so. I shall never forget how shaken Burt was after he returned from a meeting with Senators Robert and Ted Kennedy. Burt wanted the Kennedy Foundation to publish the essay. In the fall of 1965, Senator Robert Kennedy, in the midst of his senatorial campaign, had visited some of these institutions in New York, and his reports of what he saw were greeted with disbelief and incredulity. He was, his critics said, playing politics, using the unfortunates of this world for his own narrow purposes. Burt knew, of course, that what Senator Kennedy had reported was not only valid but not peculiar to the institutions of New York. It turned out, however, that the Kennedys would publish the essay only if they could name names. And they tried to persuade Burt that more was at stake than keeping one's word with those who had given Burt access to their institutions. As Burt wrote, "I did not believe it was necessary to disclose the names of the institutions we visited. First, to reveal those names was, assuredly, an invitation to the dismissal of those who arranged for us to photograph their deepest and most embarrassing 'secrets.' However, involved was not only a matter of promises made to altruistic people but also an avoidance of the impression that the problems exposed were and are local rather than national ones" (*Exodus from Pandemonium,*

p. 12). Burt was quite perturbed by his encounter with the Kennedys. He arranged for publication elsewhere. He, of course, refused any arrangement that would bring him any financial gain.

To me, Burt's *Christmas in Purgatory* said that the situation was worse than I had thought. And more hopeless. But Burt was not ready to give up. He was more sympathetic to my position. But he was overtaken by events. He was invited by the governor of Massachusetts to address the assembled legislature, and when he did, he essentially conveyed the same message that Dorothea Dix had given in 1843 to the same legislature, except that Burt had pictures. The governor persuaded Burt to take a leave from Boston University and become deputy commissioner for mental retardation, a position the aim of which was to clean up the Augean stables. To do so, however, required a special act of the legislature changing the requirement that the deputy be a physician! As a result of that stint, Burt was convinced that reforming these institutions was an exercise in futility. He wrote a book about that experience titled *Exodus from Pandemonium,* probably the best of the several books he subsequently wrote.

Few people contributed more than Burt to bringing the scandalous conditions to national awareness and giving impetus to deinstitutionalization. Burt was like the biblical prophets: it was not enough to proclaim a truth once or twice; he made it his business to proclaim it again and again, especially when he became aware of how the assumption that these institutions were necessary was bedrock to the outlook of officialdom.

Aside from what I got from Burt as a friend, I shall always be in his debt for how through him I was never far from the arena of social action, public policy, and issues of justice. His experience and outlook contributed mightily to counteracting whatever parochial tendencies I may have had. Burt was far more than an educator or social activist. He had a passionate interest in American and biblical history. He was the most omnivorous reader I have ever known. But above all, he was a moralist, possessing the most sensitive of personal radars to injustice and inequity. Burt was always evolving. The more you got to know him, the more your conscience took shape and direction. Unlike most activists and moralists, Burt had a firm grasp of the traditions of science and a respect for data. And he understood the American university as few of us who spend our lives in it do. Burt was born and reared in Brooklyn, but the world was his oyster. He loved and respected his roots. When I think of Burt, which is very often, I think of someone who was at war with injustice but at peace with himself. When Burt died, I understood as I rarely had before what it means for a part of yourself to die.

I wrote the foreword to *Exodus from Pandemonium*. The following is from that foreword:

A couple of years ago it became necessary for me to become acquainted with nursing homes for the aged. As the reader probably knows, there has been a fantastic number of these facilities built in recent years primarily because of the Medicare program. They are very modern, well-equipped settings and many more of them are being and will be erected. Psychologically speaking, however, they are hell-holes in which patients languish until death. From the standpoint of the patient, life is silent and usually in bed. The patient is completely and cringingly dependent on others for all or most of his needs, and any display of anger or complaint is viewed either as a personality defect or the consequence of senility. The actual amount of patient-staff contact, visual or physical, during the day is amazingly slight. These conditions are not due to deliberate human abuse. When one talks to the staff one gets two responses which are identical to what Dr. Blatt describes in the case of those who care for the mentally retarded in our institutions. First, the shortage of personnel is acknowledged (since these facilities are *businesses,* there is no likelihood that more personnel will be hired because that would obviously cut profits). Second, and somewhat in contradiction to the first, it is stated that there is not much one can do for these old people. The self-fulfilling prophecy is always at work!

I was describing these conditions to an undergraduate class, which is not a group one should expect to get personally upset by what happens to old people. They had some kind of intellectual appreciation but it was and could be no more than that. As I said to them: ''You get all upset about what you think is wrong with your education—and you should. You have a burning sense of injustice about racial discrimination—and you should. You and others spend a lot of your time tutoring ghetto children—and you should. You demonstrate about the senseless loss of life in wars—and you should. But the aged in our euphemistically labeled nursing homes or convalescent hospitals is not a group you know about or can feel for or have an interest in or towards whom you have the kind of obligation you feel with other groups.'' This was not said critically but as a statement of fact relevant to something of deep concern to them: man's inhumanity to man. Following this particular class, one of the students asked if he could do his research paper on convalescent hospitals. As luck would have it, he had complete access to a new convalescent hospital and he proposed to spend three weeks there, dividing his time among the three shifts. He was also a photography bug. He did a study which, unfortunately, cannot be published. He presented his data and pictures to the class. What is noteworthy is that although the students were shook up, the student who did the study was far more upset than anyone else. Like Dr. Blatt he experienced the hell-hole and was aware that his words (and even his pictures) could not communicate the depth of his feelings.

I take satisfaction in being one of the first people to argue for deinstitutionalization. When I read the 1954 Supreme Court decision on segregation, it provided me with a legal-moral rationale for opposing institutional segregation. I knew that that decision had implications far beyond our public schools. But I made one grievous mistake that I could have avoided if I had taken seriously what Burt described about his experience as deputy commissioner. It was an obvious point that Burt had made, but neither he nor I saw its significance until it was too late; that is, its significance for the tactics and strategy of deinstitutionalization. The obvious point was that those who would be responsible for carrying out deinstitutionalization had three strikes against them before they got to bat. First, they were carrying out a policy with which few of them agreed. Second, their professional lives had been spent in or around institutions. Third, they had absolutely—and I think "absolutely" is not an exaggeration—no understanding of communities: how they are organized and work, how they would respond to those who would return to their communities, and the crucial importance of developing formal and informal constituencies and support services. In their hands, deinstitutionalization became a technical-fiscal problem, whereas at its roots it was the old American problem of the community's response to "immigrants," to those who are different, to those who force us to change (or move). Burt and I realized that there was no way that the goals of deinstitutionalization could be achieved without some strong, articulate, and politically related community resistance. But what neither of us appreciated was that those who would carry out the policy of deinstitutionalization would do it as mindlessly as they did. It was like asking the fox to guard the chicken coop. Of course, these policy implementers were not malicious foxes. But their ignorance had comparable consequences. That was as true in the case of the deinstitutionalization of the mentally ill as it was for the mentally retarded.

I think it was de Tocqueville early in the nineteenth century who said that Americans are prepotently disposed to transform moral into legal issues. It is also the case that we tend to transform social problems into technical ones; that is, to define the problem in a way that suggests a technical solution. That has been the case with deinstitutionalization. To the policy implementers, their task was primarily logistical: how to take people from one site and deposit them in another, making sure that all papers were in order, new fiscal arrangements worked out, and appropriate medication accompanying the residents who were leaving. Deinstitutionalization was carried out in a manner comparable to that marking the building after World War II of our national highway system: you know what you want built; you know "how" to build it; you start leveling this or that, here and there; and, presto, you can get on an interstate in New York and never see a red light until you leave the interstate someplace on the West Coast. We have been the Romans of the modern era. What this system did to the people living in the parts of our cities that were demolished, what it contributed to noise and gas pollution, the mammoth population shifts it encouraged, how our cities qua cities were affected—these were not possibilities in the heads of the technocrats who designed the system. They knew how to design and plan a high-way system, just as others like them knew how to build residential institutions and just as others knew how to take institutionalized residents and dump them in our communities.

I blame myself severely for not realizing early on why deinstitutionalization would be, relatively speaking, a human disaster that would so arouse communities as to justify their prejudice that the handicapped individual should not be in the community; that is, in any "nice" part of it. This is not to say that if I had been more observant, I could have made a difference in what happened. I feel bad simply because I did not take the obvious seriously. But my mistake was not without its instructive consequences, because I learned that an unwittingly favored way of obscuring a problem is to label it as "applied" and, therefore, one whose solution requires that you use "basic" knowledge to figure out the appropriate techniques to use. Deinstitutionalization was never an applied or technical problem unless you have that cast of mind that permits you to accept the illusion that America has been truly a melting pot; that is, that time has melted away the ingredients of prejudice, hostility, and rampant individualism, and our communities are blissfully homogeneous. Deinstitutionalization, like immigration, cuts to the heart of the American world view, in which we see ourselves as treasuring individualism at the same time that we proclaim and yearn for the sense of community. And by cutting to the heart of our world view, it forces us to recognize that the strength with which we hold its values of individualism is greater than that with which we hold to the values of community. We should be grateful that there is a tension, that one has not completely swamped the other. It is a tension that is a fact of American life. Understanding that tension in America, past and present, is by no means easy, even though that tension has marked our society almost from its inception. And when one had to deal with that tension, as was required by deinstitutionalization, there was precious little "basic knowledge" upon which to build a "technical" approach. But that conclusion sounds, to a part of me, mischievous, because it glosses over the plain fact that those responsible for carrying out the policy simply did not know with which problem they were dealing.

Burt would have loved this. On the evening of the day I finished this chapter (October 12, 1987), I tuned in on the TV news program at 6:30 on ABC (Channel 7 in New York). Each night the program devotes a few minutes to something of "human interest." And what was this particular segment on? It was on the pathetic and scandalous conditions at the Bridgewater State Hospital in Massachusetts. In Burt's *Exodus from Pandemonium*, there is a chapter by George Albee, a former president of the American Psychological Association and, like Burt, a passionate crusader against man's inhumanity to man. The chapter is entitled "Tear Down the Walls of Hell!" Burt had invited Professor Albee to discuss at a colloquium at Boston University a film about that state hospital. The following is from the chapter he wrote after he previewed the film:

Titicut was what the Indians used to call the area around Bridgewater, Massachusetts, where there is now a state hospital for the criminally insane. (There are lots *worse* places than Bridgewater, but all of them are also state hospitals!)

The *Titicut Follies* is a movie produced and directed by Frederick Wiseman. Mr. Wiseman is a lawyer who keeps asking embarrassing questions about the way society treats its victims—its criminals, its insane—and also its other victims who live in ghettos almost as confining as the walls of the hospital you have just seen. His earlier movie, called *The Cool World*, a film of the book by Warner Miller, was a great critical success but a financial failure. The present movie is also in trouble!

The state of Massachusetts is violently angry with Mr. Wiseman. Especially angry are the politicians of the state, who claim that by making this film he invaded the privacy of the inmates without first obtaining their permission. The politicians say that the inmates will be embarrassed if they ever recover and learn that they have been thus exposed to the public. Mr. Wiseman, on the other hand, says that the public's right to know is most important. He claims that photos in a mental hospital are no more of an invasion of privacy than photos of an auto accident. Maybe they are no worse than photos of a bombed and burned group of children in a Vietnamese village. The courts will decide.

Some cynics say that the politicians in Massachusetts are more worried about their own embarrassment at letting the world see the kind of horror that some Massachusetts citizens are experiencing. The film has won prizes in New York and in Europe, but if Massachusetts has its way it will be banned from further showings anywhere. There is a kind of magical thinking here. Maybe if no one knows about them these places will not quite exist.

You have just *seen* Hell. You may feel a sense of shock. But you haven't *smelled* Hell yet. Every citizen, especially every Legislator, and particularly every Governor, should be forced to spend time each year on a back yard. The sights are bad enough. But the smells are worse.

They say that Governor Rhodes vomited during his first visit to a state institution. But his reaction has not resulted in any improvement in our state system. Next time he should spend a week and vomit every day (p. 57).

I have seen the film—Burt had arranged a private showing. (Wiseman has been prohibited from distributing it.) Albee's controlled rage is more than justified. It is obvious from the TV segment I saw in 1987 that Bridgewater has been "cleaned up," which is to say that the hospital looks less run down and filthy and the employees more aware that Bridgewater is a hellhole for them and the patients. And that is the point: Bridgewater is still a kind of a cattle farm the products of which no one wants or knows what to do with. This reminds me of Burt's presidential address to the American Association on Mental Deficiency. Burt had revisited and took photographs of the institutions that were in his *Christmas in Purgatory*. They too had been cleaned up. There was no overcrowding, there was more equipment, and there were no obvious signs of inhumane treatment. The fact is that nothing was going on: the residents sat or stood alone, oblivious to the equipment and to anything or anyone else in this world. They were pictures of eerie silence, the kind of silence I have seen countless times in nursing homes.

The TV news program was not a sterling example of investigative journalism. They did not mention Wiseman's *Titicut Follies* or, of course, Burton Blatt. That would not have surprised Burt, who knew too well how short societal memory is for the cyclical uproars, let alone what Dorothea Dix said a century and a half ago about the inhumaneness of our "humane institutions."

I said earlier that Burt would have loved this story. That was, of course, an inappropriate attribution. He would likely have turned over in his grave. Burt had a marvelous sense of irony in regard to how the road to hell is paved and repaved with good intentions. I can see that ironic smile on his face.

I owe Burt a belated apology. With few exceptions, his books are variations on a single theme: the self-defeating dynamics of our residential institutions. I refrained from saying to him, "Burt, you have described the way things are. You have said it all. Why not now turn that creative mind of yours to something else? You know the fate of prophets." I am glad I never said this to him as clearly, directly, and strongly as I felt it. Burt understood prophets far better than I did. Prophets in the biblical tradition, unlike the rest of us, don't walk away from injustice. They know that their audience is incapable of one-trial learning. Their message, requiring as it does a radical change in our thinking and action, is too demanding even though a part of us agrees with the message.

In the next two chapters, I describe a decade in my life that I can only describe as my Camelot years. The years of creating and directing the Yale Psycho-Educational Clinic were years of unsurpassed stimulation, excitement, and new learning. Those years allowed me to integrate the worlds of action and academia. What heretofore were worlds kept apart now came together. As I shall describe, there were many factors and events that propelled me to start the clinic. But one of them was Burt Blatt as a model of someone who put his money where his mouth was. Burt was a risk taker, a characteristic that affected anyone who had contact with him.

14

The Camelot Years:
The Yale
Psycho-Educational Clinic

The Yale Psycho-Educational Clinic was started in 1962. Its prehistory is composed of experiences and events to which I find it hard to assign weights. Starting the clinic represented a dramatic change in direction and living style. Saying it that way probably conveys the incorrect impression that I was clear about the new direction and what it entailed. That was not the case. What I was clear about was that I *had* to move in new directions, that I would have to make it appear as if I knew what that direction would be even though "inside" the future was an inkblot. I was willingly moving into a new fog with the most inadequate of radars. I was not really troubled by this. I had, of course, doubts and anxieties, but I had the self-confidence to believe that somehow clarity would be achieved as I felt my way, step by step, into the process of creating a new setting. My basic stance was that my acute awareness of what I did *not* want the clinic to become would help me avoid succumbing to the pressures of convention. If I was unclear about where I was going, I was crystal clear about where I had been and what I was against. I had the security of being a tenured professor. I had proved, to myself at least, that I was capable of making a respectable contribution to more than one field in psychology.

The bald fact was that I did not fear failing in the new endeavor. I did not want to fail, but if I did, I would somehow capitalize on the experience. What worried me mammothly were the consequences of failure for those who would join me in the new effort. Those consequences literally never left my mind. I could afford to fail; they could not.

Let me now turn to the factors that constitute the prehistory of the clinic. The picture that will emerge will be more orderly, integrated, and rational than in fact it was. Reconstruction of the past implies a constructed past: a kind of personal edifice that, like all edifices, has a definite form. In my case, at least, both in the past and present I find myself trying to figure out what form my personal edifice has. That may be why I find theories of personality and development inevitably misleading. They assume a degree of integration—an orderliness in day-to-day psychological living—that I think is overrated.

Each of the books I have written has had two personal significances: each has been about my recent past, and each consciously is a separation or break from that past and a search for a new direction. That was certainly the case when I finished *The Clinical Interaction* in 1956. I was no longer interested in thinking about and dealing with clinical problems. I no longer wanted to be director of the clinical training program. I was fed up with the battles with psychiatry. And I concluded that clinical psychology had hopelessly mired itself in settings that were self-defeating of their purposes, that dealt with an unrepresentative sample of our society, that utilized approaches that created long waiting lists, and that were ahistorical, acultural, and unable to think within a preventive orientation. Clinical psychology had no sound social psychological base. It had no way of understanding the society of which it was a reflection. My earlier past reasserted itself. I wanted to be part of something that would deal with society, something that would allow me better to understand the social world in which I lived, something that would allow me a more socially active role. If I was ready to break with my past, I was at sea about what I might do. I became restless.

It was in the late fifties. It was the weekly meeting of our test-anxiety group at which we kept track of each person's research activities (among other things). One of the people reported on findings from his most recent study. And he reported that the predicted differences between high- and low-test-anxious kids were clearly obtained. That was not surprising, because almost every study we had conducted had come out as predicted. We were monotonously successful. At some point in the meeting, I heard myself saying, only in half jest, "I am willing to bet that if we filmed high- and low-test-anxious kids drinking from Coca-Cola bottles, we would find statistically significant stylistic differences." When I heard what I had said, I realized instantly that I was no longer thinking, that I was running a kind of research factory, and that I had to phase out the project. If I didn't do that, I would continue to be a victim of success. All of the external "reinforcers" were incentives to continue. But the voice within was stronger than the external reinforcers. It took three years to phase out the project, during which time I was trying to figure out what I might do next.

We are used to hearing that the sizzling sixties were preceded by the silent fifties. That is sheer nonsense. Any decade that covers the Korean War, the McCarthy hearings, the 1954 desegregation decision, the emerging militant civil rights movement, the orbiting of the Russian *Sputnik,* and the use of the National Guard in Little Rock was not silent. If the social cauldron was not at the boiling point, it was certainly escalating in temperature. Of one thing I was sure: our northern urban centers and our schools were as prepared for desegregation as I was to go to the moon. We were living in a fool's paradise in which one of the reigning myths was that desegregation was primarily a southern problem. By that time I had come to know schools quite intimately, and more than ever I became convinced that our urban schools were places that manufactured human problems, especially in those central-city schools that were increasingly black in composition. The legal pressures to desegregate were, I felt, adding insult to injury. Issues about busing were stormily debated. The morality and legality of busing were not issues for me. What seemed obvious to me was that busing would make for white flight and would make the goal of desegregation impossible to achieve. But these considerations aside, what was egregiously clear was that the well-meaning proponents of busing were truly ignorant of what I came to term "the culture of schools." More than a few of our friends and colleagues viewed Esther and me as prejudiced, if not reactionary. When the Supreme Court issued the desegregation decision in 1954, we were alone in believing that achieving the goals of that decision in the North would meet countless obstacles—in our schools and communities—that would expose the unrealistic optimism implied in the Court's phrase "with all deliberate speed."

The conscious decision to create a new clinic was made immediately after a special meeting in the Yale Child Study Center. At the end of the fifties, I had to assume full supervisory responsibilities for two clinical students doing their internship next door in the Child Study Center, a child psychiatry setting. John Doris, a former student who later became a treasured coauthor with me on two books, had been chief psychologist there but had left to go to Cornell. One of the interns of the previous year came to me to complain about the inadequate therapeutic experience she had in that center. (Clinical psychology interns were "allowed" to see two children in therapy under the supervision of a child psychiatrist.) In one case, the family terminated the therapy, and in the other case, there was reason to believe, as the supervisor did, that the child was not amenable to therapy. As a result, the intern felt that she had had an incomplete and inadequate experience, and she requested that I seek to arrange for her to see two other children. I asked for a meeting with the senior staff of the center, all psychiatrists and all psychoanalytically trained. From the moment the meeting began, I felt myself to be in the "hat in hand" stance, asking for a handout. It was difficult for them, too. We knew each other, liked and respected each other. But it was immediately clear that they would not agree to my request. It was a calm meeting, we were all restrained and constricted, and the outcome was clear: the student could not be given additional cases. I left the meeting, walked down the hall to the office of our chair (Claude Buxton), described to him what had happened, blew off volumes of steam, anger, and frustration, and ended by saying, "Claude, we have to have our own clinic." And his reply was, "Let's see how to do it." For the rest of that day, I was asking myself questions. Why did I say that to Claude? What was I committing myself to? What did I mean by a *clinic?* Why was I so impulsive? Should I go back and tell Claude to forget what I had said? What resources would I need, how much of them would be forthcoming from the department, would the tenured faculty approve such a new venture? What in hell would we be doing in our own clinic? Was this the new direction I wanted to go? I was bewitched, bothered, and bewildered. I had conned myself. Or had I?

That night, Esther said in her accustomed way that I had to be stark, raving mad not to go ahead. I could count on her. That, of course, I knew. The next few weeks were spent in thinking, self-analysis, tentative planning, and trying to outline and articulate what I wanted the new setting to be. Those weeks were fascinating, because I was forcing myself—more correctly, I felt I was being forced—to get clarity about where I had been and why I wanted to go elsewhere. What did I want to get out of the new venture? What did I want to prove to myself? What did I want to demonstrate to the world? Specifically, how would this new setting be different from every other clinic I knew? What emerged—not always as clearly as I put them now—were the following:

1. It would not be a clinic to which clients came for "treatment." It would be a place from which staff would go to community settings to be helpful in regard to problems in the setting, not problems "in" individuals. These would be human services settings of one kind or another.
2. One of our overarching goals would be to comprehend these settings within the context of the history and cultural characteristics of the community: political, economic, religious, racial.
3. Another overarching goal was to gain knowledge of and experience with attempts to change settings. Why were settings resistant to change? What were the differences in process and outcome between efforts at change from within and those stirred by pressures from without the setting?

4. We were creating a new setting. Why was a literature on the creation of new settings nonexistent? Why is it that whatever we think we know about creating new settings comes from retrospection years after the beginning? Why did so many new settings fail of their purposes or take on features the polar opposite of their original intent? What was the role of leadership? As leader, I would have the opportunity to experience the creation of a new setting, and it was an opportunity about which I would someday write. And I defined a new setting as one in which two or more people got together in new and sustained relationships to achieve stated goals. Marriage was the smallest example; revolution was the largest. Creating the new setting was an instance in which I could explore two questions that dominated my past: why did the Russian Revolution fail? Why did the Southbury Training School lose its innovative force and go downhill?

5. The clinic would have a variety of people, some with and some without academic credentials. They would be chosen according to their interests and skills. Up to an undetermined point, *everyone* would be doing what everyone else did, the opposite of what is termed "differentiated staffing." There were several people without academic credentials I knew could be valuable assets in whatever we did, and I would seek to get them.

6. Although we would be prepared to explore any community setting in which we could be helpful and learn something, working in schools would be a first priority. How could we be helpful within the confines of a classroom and school? And we would attempt, in line with a preventive orientation, to concentrate on elementary schools, preferably in the inner city. No less important than trying to be helpful was the goal of understanding the culture of schools. We could not allow ourselves to forget that our task was to contribute to knowledge by organizing and writing up what we learned.

7. Our resources were and would always be very limited. Somehow we would have to slow down the treadmill on which it was too easy to act and not think; that is, to sur-

vive at the expense of being true to one's mission. If we
could not create the conditions wherein we could learn,
change, and grow, how would we help others to do it?

8. Given my experience in the Great Depression, my in-
    securities around money, my expectation that another
    collapse was inevitable, would we be able—we would
    have to be able—to go on "forward financing": to stash
    money away so that if the world was coming to an end,
    we would be able to live graciously for at least a year?
    We could expect some support from the department—
    one, maybe two new positions, space, a secretary—but
    not nearly enough tangible support to do what we would
    want to do.

9. In phasing out the test-anxiety project, I was losing a "fam-
    ily," a group of friends and colleagues that mightily lessened
    the feelings of aloneness that are a consequence of the rugged
    individualism that the university fosters. The new setting
    had to be as satisfying and stimulating an interpersonal and
    intellectual give-and-take as the test-anxiety project had
    been. I wanted to be neither lonely nor alone. Life is with
    people (the title of one of my favorite books, which is about
    the Jewish shtetl in Eastern Europe, gone forever thanks
    to Hitler).

There was one other thing about which I was clear, and
which I state here reluctantly, because it makes me seem more
saintly or wise than indeed I feel. Of course the new setting would
bear my imprint, but I could not allow it to become *my* setting.
I would have to do for others who joined me what I wanted to
do for myself. I had to capitalize on their interests, skills, and
assets, but not at the expense of their creativity and independence. They would not exist for me. Each person would have
to give something of his or her time and energy to maintain
the setting—each person, including myself, would have to do
something that he or she would not love to do—but the setting
had to have the same obligation to him or her. That is what
we owed each other. And that had to be clear from day one.
To exploit our new opportunity meant that we would explicitly

and willingly exploit each other. It would be exploitation in the service of independence and diversity. These were, I knew, statements of pious virtue. Could I act appropriately? The fact is that I had no doubt that I could. I had, if the opinions of others had any validity, done this with the test-anxiety project. The new setting would be a very different cup of tea. The stakes were higher. The directions were far less clear. Our boundaries within and without the department and university would be far more porous and problematic. There would be problems in "foreign relations." Unlike mistakes you make in planning and carrying out discrete research studies, we would now make mistakes that could and would have percolating consequences for us and the department, involved as we hoped to be with a variety of community settings. Like it or not, we would be enmeshed with and dependent upon individuals and agencies with their own peculiarities, agendas, pressures, and what I came to call organizational craziness. Mistakes would be inevitable, if only because we were giving up the clinical stance and its emphasis on the individual client in need of repair *in our offices,* and trying to become part of the turf of others for the sake of learning and helping. We would consciously be forging a new professional identity, a process as conducive of mistakes as it was of new knowledge. We wanted to become a new kind of psychologist, except that we did not know in any concrete sense what that kind was. Psychology did not provide us guidelines. I called the new setting the Yale Psycho-Educational Clinic to pay homage to Lightner Witmer, who started the first psychological clinic at the University of Pennsylvania in 1896, his emphasis having been on educational problems. Psychology has all but forgotten Witmer. I stumbled on his writings in connection with my work in mental retardation, and I was amazed at how well his clinical findings stood the test of time, albeit unrecognized. I wanted the new nonclinical setting to be as innovative as the one he created. And, I vowed, what we did, learned, and wrote would not go unrecognized. We would make a difference in this world by trying to understand and change it, which is what experimental research is all about: understanding by changing phenomena. My fantasies or ambitions have never been modest in scale. Fortunately, my reality testing keeps the fantasies where they belong.

If during those weeks I was achieving some clarity, I was at the same time made aware of a very troublesome dilemma. We were starting from a stance of relative ignorance, our mutual task was to learn, but we were unclear about what it was we wanted to learn. That was exciting, not troublesome. The dilemma was wrapped up in the question, what did we have to offer community settings, why should they mess with us, what credentials did we have or could we establish? We would not be a clinic in any traditional sense; that is, you could not walk in seeking diagnostic and therapeutic service. Matters were not helped any by the rumor mill. New Haven is a small city, and it quickly got around that a new "clinic" was being planned. The expectation was that we would be in competition with other university and community clinics. One might think that the announcement of a new clinic would have received a positive response, because existing clinics were unable to handle the number of cases that came their way. But that expectation founders on the fact of the "universal complaint" of human services agencies: they are not given the resources to deal well with the number of problems referred to them. Therefore, they are constantly searching and pleading for more resources; that is, money. If another clinic appears on the scene, it is one more potential source of competition for scarce resources. This was no surprise to me. But their response had the benefit of requiring me to articulate that we would not be in competition with them and that our immediate and most important focus was developing ways of being helpful to teachers *within the confines of the classroom and school.* That my statements were received with skepticism again did not surprise me. They were worried about what we would do. I was worried about whether we could get into schools and, once in them, what we could do to justify remaining there.

Here I must discuss a factor that was crucial in the creation of the clinic but that never was noted in the scores of books and articles that derived from that setting. In overlooking that factor, I was unwittingly confirming something I had already begun to criticize about American psychology: to the extent that

an explanation of events is based on a psychology of the individual organism, the explanation will be egregiously incomplete and misleading. More concretely, the clinic is not explainable primarily in terms of the kind of person I was and the ideas
I had. Obviously, those were important factors, but they have
to be seen in the context of time and place, of history and geography, of a changing society, of the role of chance factors. For
example, when the clinic started, I had lived in Connecticut for
twenty years, several years at Southbury and the subsequent
years in New Haven. Now, Connecticut is a very small state.
As the saying goes, if you sneeze in one part of the state, you
hear it in all other parts. At Southbury I had got to know the
state from a particular political, social, and economic perspective. And the picture became more rounded from the perspective of living in New Haven. As a state, Connecticut was knowable to me in a way that would not have been possible if I had
lived in New York, Texas, or Indiana. And by *knowable*, I refer
to people, places, agencies, and institutions. My social, intellectual, professional, institutional network of relationships was not
small. I knew, and was known to, many people. When we started
the clinic, there was a variety of resources potentially available
and useful to me, to an extent not possible for someone relatively
new to both the area and the state. The point is that I never
plainly said to people who wanted to create a similar setting that
"replication" required at least one person firmly embedded in
the area and state. Anyone who reads the research literature
in psychology knows well how difficult it is to comprehend the
"methods" section of a research study. It is a puzzle, to say
the least, which is one of the reasons replications founder. And
in many instances, you find yourself asking, how did these
researchers get to the point where they could do their study in
the setting they did in the way they did it? The reader comes
into the picture after the "prehistory," and that prehistory is
crucial for those who seek to understand and replicate the study.

Another example: Long before the federal "War on
Poverty" of the sixties, the Ford Foundation had given grant
support to several cities to mount innovative programs in the
"gray areas" of these cities, the initial emphasis being on juve-

nile delinquency, racism, transforming the schools, and empowerment. It was a program intended to alter agency-political-
educational interrelationships. It was a program on which the
later federal programs were based. New Haven was one of the
cities chosen, largely because of two people: Mayor Richard Lee
and Mitchell Sviridoff, a labor leader, chair of the board of
education, and probably the mayor's closest associate. They saw
early on that New Haven was a dying city with a downtown
that was already on its deathbed. And they predicted that if
nothing was done about the several black ghettos, the schools
black children attended, and their lack of employment opportunities, the downhill slide would be marked by speed and conflict. They considered the existing human services network of
agencies to be part of the problem, not of the solution. Briefly,
they came up with a plan that would essentially create new forms
of human services agencies. Thus was created the community
action program called Community Progress, Inc. (CPI). Although it bypassed existing agencies, CPI used some of its funds
as a carrot to stimulate change in the existing agencies. Lee and
Sviridoff were two unusually bright, hard-driving, politically
astute thinkers and social activists. They took a dim view of
academics and Yale, but they made sure that CPI had Yale's
blessings, albeit none of its material resources. In those days,
Yale was in but not of New Haven. The picture is somewhat
different today.

By the time the clinic was ready to open, CPI was picking up a head of steam. With the election of President Kennedy (and the discovery of "poverty in America"), CPI was
in on the ground floor in getting federal funds. Sviridoff, who
headed CPI, began to spend a fair amount of time in Washington
as a consultant and seeker of funds. He was a super salesper-
son for New Haven. (I well remember standing in Times Square
in 1964 or 1965 and reading the news bulletins flashing on the
Times building. To my surprise, the following appeared: "On
a per capita basis New Haven receives more federal grant funds
than any other city in the United States.")

Although I did not know Lee or Sviridoff, I had read their
prospectus for starting CPI, and it was obvious that as a clinical

psychologist I was reacting against many of the things that they as social-political activists were reacting against. I was trying to move in new directions, and so were they. Earlier than I, and with greater urgency, they concluded that they had either to alter, or subvert, or bypass conventional thinking and practice in human services agencies and schools. Their sense of urgency was greater than mine. They *had* to act. There was too much at stake. Although I thought that they promised too much, and vastly underestimated the obstacles to change, and I predicted ultimate disillusionment, there was an affinity I could not deny. I needed them, and I began figuring out why they might need me and the clinic. I did not want to approach them until I had a clear basis for doing so. Getting to them would be easy; forging a reciprocal relationship was far more problematic. I knew that they would respond favorably to our proposed way of being helpful within the confines of classrooms and schools. But did I want to get enmeshed in the New Haven public schools, which were scandalously inadequate? And I had reason to believe that the chief school psychologist in New Haven viewed anyone from Yale, especially if he was a psychologist, as several notches below the deepest level of evil. She looked like a witch, and my contacts with her forced me to conclude that she was a witch, an opinion not mine alone.

So there was a lot going on in New Haven that could have enormous significance for our proposed new setting. The social air and scene were beginning to change. And then chance entered the stage. The daughter of two of our dear friends in New Haven, William and Esther Post, was getting married. I knew that Sviridoff was one of their friends. So guess who was sitting next to me at the wedding dinner? Sviridoff and I started talking, and within the next few weeks the school doors were opened to us, and so were the new neighborhood employment centers in the ghettos, the Skill Center, and the prevocational "work crews," comprised largely of school dropouts and unemployed and unemployable black youth. It says a lot about Mike Sviridoff that it presented no problem to him that we were in the business of learning, we were not sure how we could be helpful, but we would sure as hell try. It took me some time to figure out that

Mike was in the same boat as we were. As he said to me some years later, ''You didn't come across as academics and arrogant experts. You seemed worth taking a gamble on. You were willing to dirty your hands.''

Here is a final example of the importance of context for understanding what happened at the clinic. Within a few years after World War II, the powers that be in the State capitol finally were made to understand that the Southbury Training School, opened in late 1941, was not only a fiscal disaster but also a well-intentioned but misguided institution that was developing a long waiting list, among its other problems. There was no way that the state would build another large institution. It was the dawning of the concept of deinstitutionalization. What the state proposed was a series of small regional centers in or very near population centers. Each would have a small number of beds, which could be used to serve children and families in a variety of ways that would maximize the chances that the children could return to the community. The major aim was to encourage communities to develop their own services and programs that would make residential care unnecessary in many cases. The budget for each center was not only for beds but also for community outreach and new community programs. The centers would be in and of the community, not, like Southbury, in the middle of nowhere. The first regional center to be built would be in New Haven. I, of course, knew the people in Hartford and New Haven who were planning the new center. During its planning and building phase, which overlapped with our planning and start-up phases, we were working out the basis for a cooperative relationship.

My interest in the new regional center was not primarily in its mission, albeit that was important. What fascinated me was the fact that I could participate in and observe the creation of a new setting. Indeed, the clinic, the regional center, and CPI were all instances of the creation of new settings. From the day the clinic opened, the phrase ''the creation of settings'' was probably the most frequent one heard, perhaps ad nauseam.*

---

*I defined the creation of settings as when *two* or more people *get together* in new and sustained relationships to attain agreed-upon goals. Where

I knew that I was on to something that was important, unstudied, indeed unformulated. As federal legislation exponentially increased to deal with poverty, racism, and education, I became aware that more new settings were being created more quickly than in the entire previous history of the human race. I do not believe that to be hyperbole. For example, consider the fact that the Head Start legislation alone mandated the speedy creation of several thousand new settings. And Head Start was one of hundreds (perhaps thousands) of similar legislative acts of the sixties.

      The clinic bore the imprint of me and my times. I created the clinic, but the clinic was not understandable only in terms of my personality, my style of action, my ideas. There was a context: local, state, and national. It was a fast-changing context. I was caught up in it. The clinic was not a consequence of a predetermined script. I acted upon and was acted on. There were times when I knew exactly what we should do and where. As often, I felt like a snowflake in a storm. I wanted to feel that I was captain of my fate and master of my soul. But the world around me frequently made a mockery of that desire. I did not want to be an opportunist, but I found that there were times when I had to be. I did not want to compromise, but I did. I learned the truth of President Truman's remark that "If it is too hot in the kitchen, get the hell out." I learned a lot, and quickly, about the "real world" and in the process saw all too clearly how unprepared I had been for that world by my education and psychological training. American psychology, even *social* psychology, was about individuals, not about individuals in culture and context. At its root, American psychology was ahis-

---

did that phrase come from? If this were only a personal autobiography I would devote a chapter to the purely psychological or private origins of the phrase. Chronologically, the answer begins with my curiosity about and utter conscious ignorance of how babies are created and born. Even now hardly a night passes without a dream containing visual themes of winding passages and the pursuit of exits. I did not connect the coining of the phrase until several months after the Psycho-Educational Clinic was created and I "heard" myself using the phrase somewhat repetitively. We live our lives. We are also lived by them. Freud was no fool.

torical and asocial. You could not understand America and Americans by American psychology, at least not that part of psychology that purported to seek to explain the social behavior of people. There were only two psychologists with whom I felt kinship: the early John Dollard and Roger Barker, neither of whom was (or is) anywhere near mainstream psychology.

My emerging attitude toward American psychology can be illustrated by the following story. When I was in graduate school, I came across a book in a secondhand bookstore with the intriguing title *Know Your Mind*. The author was Dr. Charles P. Psycho. I bought the book. The first chapter began with, "As a child I was very young." Dr. Psycho, my memory says, went on in this way: "If you want to understand human behavior, you picked up the right book. I will teach you how to understand people. But first you have to know something about the human brain. So, please look at Figure I, which is a drawing of the human brain." The drawing showed and labeled the different lobes. And in the center was a small circle in which was one word: Poland. To me, psychology became Poland. My emerging attitude had nothing to do with social action, values, justice, equity, and the like. It was simply that American psychology had never been able seriously to confront the possibility that its axioms, theories, methodologies, and institutional bases were quintessentially American in origin and world view; that is, that American psychology was a product of the American experience, which was both distinctive and constraining, an asset and a deficit, a source of illumination and error in understanding and generalization. American psychology has never been interested in America! It was Poland in the middle of America. (I loaned Dr. Psycho's book to my thesis adviser, Saul Rosenzweig, who never returned it to me. I put searches on for that book, but they were all unsuccessful. If I had been Saul, I would not have returned it either.)

The clinic was started by Murray Levine, Esther, Anita Miller, and me. By the end of the third year, the three-story brownstone on Crown Street housed about twenty people: faculty, nonfaculty, graduate students, staff who were planning regional centers, and others hard to label. They were a remarkable and sparkling assortment of people, each of whom was as at home in the world of ideas as in the arena of intervention and action. Each developed his or her own focus. Each was in more than one community setting. As I said earlier, up to a point, each was in a similar role in similar settings. Albeit dramatically heterogeneous in personal style, talents, and goals, they had one thing in common: the desire to learn and to organize and conceptualize that learning, and to publish it for the critical scrutinizing of others. We did go on forward financing, we were able to support summer salaries, and everyone had equal call on research support. What was amazing, indeed incomprehensible, to the many clinic visitors was the fact that the faculty members there (Murray, Ira Goldenberg, Francis Kaplan, Ed Trickett, Dick Reppucci, Dennis Cherlin, me) were essentially "full time" at the same time that we were discharging our teaching and related responsibilities in our department. We did that willingly, enthusiastically, ungrudgingly. I was grateful for the support we received from the department, I wanted more, but I knew that it would not be forthcoming. The Yales of this world are superb in providing individual faculty members time, means, and space to do their work. Supporting programs or a facility like the clinic is another matter. I knew from the beginning that the clinic would have to garner most of the resources it needed from contracts with agencies; for example, schools, CPI, the Regional Center. The basic attitude of the department could be put this way: "As a professor, Seymour, you can do what you want. You want a clinic? Fine. It sounds like a good idea—we'll throw in a couple of positions. The rest of what you need is your responsibility to garner." I knew and accepted that position. I made it clear to everyone who joined the clinic how dependent we would have to be on ourselves. The good news was that we were responsible for our independence. The bad news was that we had to avoid contractual arrangements that would allow us to survive but not at the expense of doing what we wanted to do in the way we wanted to do it. To each prospective faculty person, I said, "In your first year, you will have to give some of your time to some community setting with which we have a contract but which may not be central to your interests. That is, so to speak, your dues. After the first year, you can do whatever you want wherever you want to do it, and you will have call on any of our resources: graduate students, money for research, summer salary.'' No one whom we selected ever objected. They sensed what I hoped they would sense: the clinic was a strange but interesting joint composed of an assortment of people eager to enlarge their experience and further their intellectual development. The world of action had to serve the world of ideas.

I have been asked countless times to characterize life at the clinic. Two things stand out in my mind. The first is the ''Friday phenomenon.'' We (everybody) met as a group on Friday from nine in the morning until three in the afternoon. That was the one day everyone had to be at the clinic. No other responsibility took precedence over being at that meeting. That was the time that everyone had an opportunity to report on or listen to what others were thinking and doing, and to subject their/our plans, actions, ideas, and problems to critical scrutiny. It was not show-and-tell. Given the assertive, verbal, articulate, intellectual, curious, passionate cast of characters, show-and-tell was not in the cards. The meeting really consisted of two or three intellectual, no-holds-barred discussions, each having a different but inevitably related focus. They were sometimes stormy meetings. I treasured and loved each of these people. I had trouble confronting the fact that they did not always feel that way about each other. But they respected each other. They were my family. Inevitably, there was sibling rivalry. But they knew they were part of a family to which they owed allegiance. The substance of the many books and articles that came from the clinic was the grist from the mill that these meetings were. By the end of the meeting, we were weary, excited, and changed in some way.

The second thing that stands out is a type of two-day meeting we held once or twice a year. We would invite two or three people from around the country whose work or writings we respected highly. Each meeting had a theme. The visitors were told that each would have no more than fifteen minutes to make a presentation when the meeting began. They could not read a paper. Following that, discussion would begin, interrupted only by lunch and dinner on each day. They were, for us and the visitors, among the most memorable of our experiences. They were meetings intended to dilute whatever parochialism from which we suffered.

I do not know whether the following story derives from this type of meeting or from one of our Friday meetings, to which we sometimes invited an outsider. But the story says a good deal about what went on at the clinic. Walking around Yale, I ran into Warren Bennis, whom I knew slightly and whose writings on group dynamics and organizational behavior I valued highly. When I asked him how life was at MIT, he told me he was leaving to become provost for the social sciences at SUNY in Buffalo. That surprised me, and I asked him how come? Warren replied (paraphrased): "I am known as an organizational theorist. I spend a lot of my time as a consultant to some of the largest corporations. I dispense advice, and I get paid handsomely. The fact is that I have never held a position of administrative leadership. I have never had to practice what I preach. The Buffalo position will allow me to do just that." I congratulated him and wished him well, no end impressed with his courage. A couple of months before, Murray Levine had left Yale and the clinic to take up a professorship at Buffalo. I told Warren to get in touch with Murray. A year later, I was invited to give a colloquium there. At the reception in Murray's house, in walked Warren. I reminded him of our conversation of the previous year and asked, "How has it been? What have you learned about organizational theory?" He was startled for a moment and then said, "It is a very long story." I asked him whether he would be willing to spend a day at the clinic discussing confidentially what he had experienced or learned. He agreed, and we set a date. (It had to be a special meeting, because we never had "confidential" meetings, and I distinctly remember telling Warren that it would be a confidential meeting in light of his telling me that what he had learned was not going to be easy to relate.) That clinic meeting was the most memorable of all meetings for me and, I think, for all others who were there. What Warren did in the most candid, illuminating, concrete fashion was to present the phenomenology of a leader who had to unlearn his theories; who in the cauldron of action, power, and pressure found himself thinking and acting contrary to what he had previously preached; who came to understand as he never had before the bedrock importance of understanding the culture of the organization, that is, the university. Theory and practice, thought and action, intervention and change, personal values and social realities—that meeting touched on everything central to the clinic. Those were the only things we ever talked about.

It was not all sweetness and light. There were several things I expected, privately predicted, about life at the clinic. The first had to do with continuity and death. From my youngest days, I have always thought about my death. In a postclinic book, *Work, Aging, and Social Change: Professionals and the One-Life, One-Career Imperative* (New York: Free Press, 1977), I state that the sense of aging revolves around one's experience of the passage of time, and, therefore, what we ordinarily call aging starts very early in life. My sense of aging began very early, and getting married and having a child increased dramatically thoughts about the consequences of my death and the death of those I loved. How would I handle the death of someone I loved? I did a lot of rehearsal in fantasy. When the clinic started and I felt a poignant sense of responsibility for those in it, the question became, what would happen if I or someone else crucial to the clinic died? That question was one of the reasons that I insisted that up to a point, everyone in the clinic had to be doing what everyone else was doing; that is, if there was a death, it should be relatively easy to take up that person's responsibilities. There were other reasons for that insistence, but ensuring continuity was for me personally crucial. So, one day in 1968, I received a telephone call telling me that Dennis Cherlin had just been killed in an auto accident. Dennis had been a graduate student in our department; when he received his doctorate, he was appointed to the faculty, and before and after that, he played an important role at the clinic. When I received the news of his death, I immediately let everyone know and called for a meeting later that day. The purpose of the meeting was to ensure that different people would discharge Dennis's different responsibilities. My behavior at the meeting shocked some people, because I conducted it as a business meeting. Dennis was perceived as a "favorite" of mine, someone with whom I had a special relationship, which was true. How could I, someone later asked, conduct the meeting the way I did? I sidestepped the question. The answer, of course, was that when I received the telephone call and hung up, what flashed through my mind was, "This is it. The moment of truth I had expected and feared is now. The rehearsal for the play is over. I know what I have to do." When I eulogized Dennis at the funeral, I could not control the tears.

There was another moment of truth. I predicted that someone, and it could be me, would do something egregiously stupid that would jeopardize the status or survival of the clinic. Given my imagination, the possibilities were many and frightening. So one night I received a call from a clinic member telling me of an action she had taken involving aversive punishment of a child in one of the community settings. The action was, to say the least, ill advised and the consequences for the clinic potentially quite scary. Here again, I found myself saying, "This is it. This is the moment of truth. Don't stonewall. Put all the cards on the table." The next few days were as anxious a time as I have ever experienced. As in the case of Dennis's death, I appeared calm and possessed, as if I were acting out a detailed script I had long rehearsed. There had been rehearsals. Inside I was peeing in my pants. I know what stage fright on opening night is.

The third thing I knew when the clinic started was that the time would come when I would no longer want to be director of the clinic, that I would have got out of the experience what I had wanted and I would move on to something else. When that would be, the circumstances that would bring it about, I could not predict. But that such a time would come I had no doubt. I was at the clinic for somewhat less than a decade. At the midpoint, the outline of the circumstances that would propel me to leave began to emerge. What began to be clear was that the faculty at the clinic were not highly regarded by our department, they would not get tenure, and they would have to leave. That they were not highly regarded did not surprise me. They did not fit the mold of the empirical researcher who does discrete, quantitatively analyzed studies that derive from and are related to "mainstream" theoretical issues. Psychology, like any other field, has dominating traditions rooted in institutional-professional history and structure. Within those traditions, there are fads and fashions, but undergirding them are shared judgments about how one goes about making a contribution to knowledge. They are judgments about what is good or bad methodology, what is acceptable as evidence, what makes for scientific progress. Substantively and methodologically, the clinic presented problems to these traditions and judgments. We were focused not on individuals but on organized entities. We did not, except infrequently, systematically collect data that we aggregated and analyzed quantitatively. We scanned, participated, and observed, organizing our experiences in a descriptive or narrative way. We were also interveners and advocates, describing in detail what had gone before and what came after our efforts. We never "proved" anything. We sought to identify and describe problems and processes. We were learners more than we were formal researchers. We were interested not in how individuals differed but in how and why communities differed. And everything in which we were interested was in some way powered by our need to better understand America. We were interested in the past as well as the present. Yes, we were caught up in the moment, we "seized the day," but both had prologue and epilogue. We were psychologists seeking to go beyond our field. We were critical but not nihilistic about psychology. We were not proponents of action for the sake of action. We were striving for new conceptualizations of new and old problems, not for putting old wine in new bottles or old wine in old bottles. If we were moving in new directions and forging new identities, we fully accepted the judgment that our obligation was to make public through writing what we did and why and with what consequences. We were more than willing to be judged by what other people thought, fully aware that to some people what we were doing was not psychology.

Though it did not surprise me when it became apparent that no faculty member at the clinic would receive tenure, I never took it personally, of course I was angry and disappointed. It was to me like classic tragedy: the end is known at the beginning. Although I had allowed myself to hope that at least one person would receive tenure, it became obvious that that would not happen. What was upsetting to me was the realization that I was again in the situation where I would encounter one separation after another from close friends. I have never taken separations easily, my overt mien notwithstanding. You get to know and love somebody—a graduate student, a younger faculty member, a secretary, a colleague at your level and age—and then he or she leaves, usually unwillingly. The university is marked by the transiency of its members. I started the clinic to start a family, not to become the sole source of continuity there. The end of my stay in the clinic was foreseeable. It took a handful of years and several separations for me to leave the clinic. But it was not only my difficulty with separations that propelled me to leave. I left when I did because I had done what I had wanted to do, I had learned what I wanted to learn, there were books I wanted to write as ways of organizing the experience of the most stimulating decade of my life. I knew that when I left, the chances that the clinic would continue were minimal. For one year, Dick Reppucci tried valiantly to keep it going, but he soon realized that, as a nontenured member of the department, he would not get academic "brownie points" for keeping it going. From the standpoint of the department, the clinic was "mine," it was not theirs. I thought, of course, that the department was making a mistake, a grievous one, but I also knew that they had no way of comprehending what we had been about and what we had accomplished.

And what had we accomplished? That question is a trap, because it suggests that the criterion for judgment should be what we did for others, what we helped other people do and become, what we changed in ways appropriate to the values of those who pass judgment. And it is a trap also because it assumes that everyone at the clinic had the same goals and wanted their accomplishments to be judged in identical ways. To the question of accomplishment I shall speak largely for myself, although I would be very much surprised if anyone else from the clinic would part company with how I answer the question.

I accomplished my goal of starting and administering a setting in which I and others could learn, change, and grow. The clinic existed for *us* as a place to foster our intellectual development. Of course we wanted to make a difference in the world outside the clinic, but we could not do that if the clinic did not stimulate us to become different from what we had been. And it was a matter not only of becoming different but of sustaining the conditions that avoided the pitfalls of self-satisfaction and parochialism. Our stance could not be "Look, Ma, I'm dancing" but rather "Look, Ma, I'm thinking." The clinic was based on what should be, but too often is not, the basic mission of the university: to create those conditions in which faculty learn, change, and grow. You can have a university without students. The assumption is that unless you create the conditions in which faculty learn, change, and grow, you cannot create and sustain those conditions for students. What I learned via the clinic was that human services settings, including schools, justify their existence by what they do for "others," not what these settings do for the development of their staffs. Because the conditions for their own development are minimal or absent, the quality of their services is mammothly diluted. The clinic was an intellectual enterprise that allowed us to explore the world in what for us were new ways in new roles. The clinic accomplished that goal.

The clinic sought to test our conclusion that American psychology had little or nothing to contribute to understanding social and institutional change. In regard to these matters, American psychology was indeed "Poland." It was more serious than that, because in regard to these matters American psychology was based on a flawed conception of the "basic versus applied" dichotomy. For example, there is much in American psychology that is considered *basic* to the understanding and improvement of learning by school children. To these researchers, the next step is to *apply* the basic findings in our schools. You have *basic* findings "here," you have people "there" who need them, so in order to *apply* them, you have to get the findings to them in a usable way. You "deliver" the basic findings. From the outset, we regarded that way of thinking as the source of confusion, because it ignored another "basic" problem: comprehending the traditions and culture of the setting in which the findings were to be applied. If you did not comprehend the setting in its own terms, you were courting failure. And if anything was disheartening in the years of the clinic, it was our observing, recording, and reporting instance after instance of "applied solutions" that got ground up in settings about the culture of which the basic researcher was ignorant. It was disheartening at the same time that we took perverse satisfaction in the fact that we were learning something important about intervention and change in the quotidian world. We became experts in understanding and predicting failures of application.

Let me give one concrete example, because it also bears on the question of accomplishments. After Russia orbited the first *Sputnik* in 1957, America found a ready scapegoat: our public schools. A few years before, a number of university researchers had begun to articulate criticisms of our schools: our schools were doing a good job of extinguishing student interest in math and science. By the early sixties, they had developed new curricula in math, biology, physics, and social studies that would make learning these subject matters enjoyable and productive. They had done their basic research and began to apply it in schools, all of this getting big play in the mass media. We were going to produce generations of scientifically sophisticated students. And these students would eat it all up. Joy would no longer be an absent commodity in the classroom. For personal-family and intellectual reasons, Esther had to learn the new math. She then decided that she wanted to observe the teaching of the new math, and she arranged to do so in a number of classrooms. She and I wrote up and published her observations ("Some Observations on the Introduction and Teaching of the New Math." In *The Psycho-Educational Clinic Papers and Research Studies.* Boston: State Department of Mental Health). (It was the first and *only* observational study of the teaching of the new math ever done.) Let me just say that the word *joy* is the last word that would occur to anybody sitting in these classrooms. At the same time that Esther was observing, I had been investigating in another school system the steps by which the new math had been brought in and applied, a tale of insensitivity to the needs, phenomenology, and lowly status of teachers—a classic case of blaming the victim. The new math was introduced into schools in ways so ignorant of the culture of schools as to guarantee disaster. (It was no different in regard to other new curricula.) Was it an accomplishment to have predicted validly that these new curricula would fail miserably of their purposes? Was it an accomplishment to have predicted that the many well-heeled efforts in the sixties to reform our schools—efforts frequently carried out by well-known basic researchers in psychology— would have minimal impact? Nobody listened to us or took us seriously. We would have been surprised if it had been otherwise. But to everyone at the clinic, working in schools and other community settings, it was obvious that the cascade of federal programs that characterized the sixties would fall far short of their mark, either because they were put into settings that were poorly comprehended or because they required the creation of new settings, a process about which ignorance was profound.

Let me now answer the traditional question about accomplishments in a traditional way. At least seven books, one monograph, several dissertations, and scores of articles derived directly from the clinic experience. Though quantity is not quality, if the opinion of others is a guide, the clinic was an important shaper of the new field of community psychology. By what we did and wrote, we not only influenced and encouraged psychologists who sought to move in new directions but we also added force to those who were critical of the narrowness and aridity of American psychology. We were certainly not the first to criticize psychology's narrow conception of science, of methodology, and of the criteria for judging a contribution to knowledge. And we were far from the first to point out how the ahistorical stance of American psychology guaranteed that it could not understand its past and present. And before us there were seminal thinkers who looked askance at the failure of American psychology to take social contexts seriously, to observe and study people in ongoing, naturally occurring, culture-bound settings. For many people, the clinic was a fount of intellectual criticism and social analysis. As someone once said to me long after the clinic went out of existence, "To us in the boondocks you were not a bunch of do-gooders and social partisans caught up in the maelstrom of the sixties, having just discovered evil, injustice, and inequity. You were the thinkers and doers trying to make sense of American society. What we had trouble comprehending was that this was going on at Yale, of all places!" I tried to explain to him that his comment about Yale was a comment about the workings of the dialectic in American society. In American society generally, and at Yale in particular, the high value placed on rugged individualism occasionally makes it possible for an individual to forge and sustain for a time a collectivity in which interdependence is the governing value.

Two goals of the clinic were not achieved; that is, we failed of our purposes. We wanted the new field of community psychology truly to focus on *community* and *communities*. We wanted the field to be occupied with more than mental health. Because all of us (that is, faculty) were formally trained clinical psychologists, there was the danger that our pasts would subtly but powerfully keep us in or near the mental health arena: we would, so to speak, play to our strengths. That turned out to be no problem. As our writings plainly indicate, mental health was but one window through which one can look at our communities. And it was far from a clean window. In our minds, community psychology was not identical with community mental health. But, as I see it, community psychology has to a large extent become a part of community mental health programs of action and research. That is not cause for criticism. I simply regret that the potentials of a broad community psychology could not withstand the weight of the past, the increasing size and institutional strengths of an already entrenched clinical psychology, and the style and sources of funding agencies; that is, the pressures they feel to give priority to the problems of the moment.

The second failure concerns prevention. Especially in our work in schools, we sought to be in roles that would enable us to be influential in developing programs that would prevent problems, to avoid roles of repair; that is, dispensing Band-Aids. We quickly saw that we had been unrealistic, really ignorant. If *joy* is the last word that would occur to you when you observed the teaching of the new math, the concept of prevention and appropriate efforts are the last things that anyone in the school culture talks about. I am not about to blame the victim. The fact is that the ideology of prevention is simply swamped and buried by the preoccupation with problems. No one, of course, is opposed to prevention. But how can you regard prevention as other than an indulgence of fantasy when you are confronted with problems the frequency and difficulty of which you find overwhelming? Schools, like clinical settings, are deficit, not asset, oriented. If we failed of our purpose in schools, we took comfort in the fact that we were beginning to understand why schools are so frequently self-defeating settings. This has nothing to do with the intellect and motivations of our educators. It has a lot to do with two things: educators are literally not schooled in regard to a preventive orientation, and we cannot face up to the fact (and its implications) that schools are uninteresting places. It was not until fifteen years after I left the clinic that I realized that schooling in America rests on the unverbalized axiom that education should and best does take place in encapsulated classrooms in encapsulated schools. That axiom is largely invalid, and as long as it remains unchallenged, we set drastic limits to any effort at prevention. My argument is set out in my book *Schooling in America: Scapegoat and Salvation* (New York: Free Press, 1983). With the publication of that book, the world changed not at all, but, then again, I did not expect it to change. Ideas are important, but they do not achieve currency unless the twins of social and institutional contexts make them salient in some way. When we say about an idea that "its time has come," we are saying something about these contexts.

I have tried in this chapter to indicate that the creation of the clinic is not understandable only in terms of my personal and professional life, my critique of American psychology in general and clinical psychology in particular, and a changing society. The clinic was conceived before what we call the sizzling sixties. It opened about the same time that the forces unleashed by World War II coalesced to challenge custom and tradition in America. The clinic became part of that social hurricane. We were small potatoes, but potatoes nevertheless. Every major social institution was challenged and transformed. And, it is necessary to emphasize, what happened in America was happening in other countries as well, especially in Western Europe. Social change was in the international air, secular and religious. But in the next chapter, I shall restrict myself to what the sixties signified to me about America, American psychology, and the university.

15

The World Changes Again:
American Psychology
in the Sixties

In earlier chapters, where I discussed the emergence after
World War II of modern clinical psychology and the Age of
Mental Health, I indicated that one of my criticisms of what
was developing was the virtual ignoring of the nature of and
problems in American society. It was not that I had a sophisticated understanding of American society, but rather that there
was absent a tradition in American psychology for understanding
people in terms of the "American experience." In its attempts
to come up with general laws of human behavior—laws valid
for anyone anyplace on this earth—it assumed two things: first,
that the quest for general laws that transcended cultures was
possible and productive by research that ignored culture, and,
second, that once those laws were established, the basis had been
provided for altering or influencing cultures, depending on what
one thought needed altering. I questioned both assumptions.
There was, in fact, a third assumption: American psychology
was not a reflection, for good and bad, of American society.
It was onward and upward, with no clouds on the horizon, no
need to flush out undergirding values and sources of self-deception, no need to question whether the primary site in which
all new knowledge would be obtained, the university, was the

appropriate site to get that knowledge. But if I was clear about anything, if I was correct about anything, it was that World War II had changed the minds and world views of people, and that American psychology was insensitive to these changes.

The more World War II gets buried in societal memory, the less we remember of what began to happen immediately after the war, the less we comprehend how the Great Depression and World War II altered world views of generations, the less able we are to comprehend the sixties. The sixties were not sudden eruptions of a dormant volcano. Long before the sixties, there were lava flows seeping from the base of the volcano.

The end of World War II was greeted and understood as the end of one era and the beginning of a new one. The response can be captured in several sentences. "The old world is dead, and thank God. The new order will and should be different. We will not make the same mistakes we made after World War I, such as the impotent League of Nations. Having won a war against religious and social bigotry, we can no longer justify bigotry in America. Our obligation is to ensure that the world of our children will be different from what ours has been. The new world will be a just world." We saw a future we wanted to see. We allowed ourselves to hope. For many, if not most, of the adults of that time, there was awareness that a dramatic change in their world view had occurred compared to their world view in the thirties. No one said, "My world view has changed." But everyone knew that they were in a new ball game, and they knew what the final score *should* be.

Side by side with hope was a creeping sense of disillusionment. If war is the continuation of politics by other means, then the international scene suggested that the war was not over. The label "cold war" refers to a series of events each of which was frightening, each of which made hope a frail reed upon which to lean. On the national scene, there were conflict and controversy, especially in regard to decaying cities, juvenile crime, inadequate schools, and racial unrest. If you were black, the fruits of victory in World War II were not palatable. If you were a woman and a part of an emerging liberation movement, American society was not about to unfurl the welcome mat. If you were a political liberal or leftist—or a principled advocate of civil liberties—Senator McCarthy represented the specter of an American Fascism. If you were one of the many war veterans who returned to a meager existence, or whose life had been negatively transformed by displacement into and out of the armed services, America was not a land of opportunity. In brief, the air of hope was, for many people, being suffused with disenchantment. I am not trying to paint a picture of national dysphoria. I am suggesting that American society was a mixed bag of possibilities and obstacles, of clashes between the old and the new, of intergroup polarizations.

As has often been the case, rebellion against custom and tradition was most clear in the arts: the visual arts, music, and literature. Abstract expressionism, existentialism, Sartre, Camus, Beckett, Genet, the Theatre of the Absurd—these and other labels and names stood for and reflected a new world view at the core of which was the search for meaning in life. More correctly, they suggested that meaning was no longer a given, that humans were alone in a meaningless world. It was, of course, not fortuitious that such a view took hold in a Europe that was in a political, economic, and psychological shambles. But such a view did not remain there; it began to find a receptive audience in America, especially in our universities. We were, we were told, at the end of an era of ideology; there was a moral, religious, political vacuum side by side with the end of the industrial era.

Presixties America was composed of myriad groups who, for similar and different reasons, sought to redefine themselves as persons, to seek a new ''center'' for their lives, to put new meaning into their individual and collective existence. Redefinition was a troublesome process, because it required rejecting a past in an ambiguous present for a very clouded future. And for many people, the gnawing question was, What is the point of moving to a future in which war (Korea, the Berlin Blockade, the Hungarian uprising, an atomic holocaust) seemed all too possible?

The sixties are viewed as, among other things, an intergenerational conflict, a rejection of what the parental generations stood for. That is true, but it is misleading in that it totally ignores the crisis in belief in those generations. It was not an articulated crisis. Its relatively silent character hid a cauldron of doubt, perplexity, and the sense of personal drift. On the surface, America seemed to be what it had been in the past; that is, the belief in progress seemed to undergird the striving for individual and material goals. But that belief collided daily with two facts. First, as a country, America was embroiled in a world from which it could not insulate itself and which it could not control. Second, in the lives of many individuals, there was a growing sense of personal and vocational entrapment, of disenchantment with familial and vocational interests that were too confining and unsatisfying, too restricting of new experience.

I am painting in broad strokes an America that was truly dynamic in the sense that world views were being challenged and changed at the same time that on the surface Americans seemed to be whatever they had been. The internal realities were not isomorphic with external ones. In an inchoate way, the adults of the presixties were ready for that decade; they contributed to it in ways we have hardly studied, especially in regard to what they were communicating to their children, who were not passive recipients of parental and societal messages.

And where was American psychology in that interval between the end of World War II and President Kennedy's election? Is it unreasonable to suggest that somewhere near the center of the diverse focuses of American psychology there should have been a serious interest in how Americans were experiencing their world and what they were absorbing, digesting, and concluding? Psychological and social change: are these two intertwined types of changes of peripheral significance for a social psychology? Are not their study and delineation a test of the power and scope of a general psychology? If it is unreasonable and dangerous to require that American psychology should seek to change the world, is it unreasonable to ask that it seek at least to understand how a changing world changes psyches and vice versa? Or should these questions be directed to sociologists and anthropologists, in which case, what is psychology all about?

The fact is that American psychology was proceeding as it always had: concentrating, in research or clinical treatment, on individuals. The social context, the social order, the substance and force of culture, the ongoing formulation and implementation of public policies intended to foster social and institutional change, social and intellectual history—in regard to these issues, problems, and processes, American psychology had little or nothing to say. And the reasons became clear when one examined the formal theories of psychology, be they behavioral or psychoanalytical. They were theories of the workings of the mind independent of time, place, and era. No one denied that the physical and social world had structure and salience, or that the hard-to-define concept of culture was both crucial and omnipresent, or that society had structure and an ideology, or that we are in and of history, or even that the "old" order was changing. But little or none of this was part of psychological theory—and this during a period when American psychology was concerned, if not obsessed, with theory. Let me give two examples of what I mean. Although neither example is from the presixties, they nevertheless illustrate American psychology's riveting on the individual organism.

The first example is from the end of the sixties. At the clinic, Dick Reppucci was engaged in a truly heroic effort to salvage and transform a scandal-ridden state institution for juvenile offenders. He was wrestling with the problems of describing and explaining how the diverse actors in the drama affected and were affected by the structure, history, and ambience of an institution that was embedded in a state legislative, executive, judicial system. It was at this time that I saw the film *One Flew over the Cuckoo's Nest*. I had two reactions to the film. The first was that as a work of art, the film was compelling, upsetting, and excellent. The second reaction was a mixture of anger and disappointment because the film conveyed the message that if anti-hero MacMurphy and nurse Ratchett had been different kinds of individuals, the tragedy could have been avoided. What was not conveyed in the film was precisely what Dick was wrestling with: you could not understand the behavior of the actors in it at the state hospital unless you saw them in terms of the history of that institution, why it was organized the way it was, how personnel were selected, the role of status and professional-

ism, and how all of this was part of a complicated state administrative system. It was an interpersonal drama taking place on
a stage much of which was not in the film. I spoke to many people about that film, and, as I expected, they saw it primarily
as a tragic clash between two individuals and had concluded
that people like nurse Ratchett should not be working in such
places. It was the second conclusion that stirred Dick and me,
because it was another example of proposals for reform that
guaranteed failure because they are based on a psychology of
individuals.

So Dick and I wrote a paper the central themes of which
were that public policies aimed at institutional and social change
that derived from an individual psychology would fail, and that
American psychology could no longer afford to be peripheral
to the arena of public policy and to those fields—the so-called
policy sciences, such as political science and economics—for
which that arena was central. We sent the paper to the *American
Psychologist,* the house organ of the American Psychological Association. We got back a letter of rejection from the editor, a
former colleague who was also the executive director of the association. The letter floored us. For one thing, he expressed a
kind of amused puzzlement at our use of terms such as "policy
fields" and "policy sciences." What were we talking about,
referring to? It is as if we were arrogating to ourselves the creation of new arenas of intellectual, conceptual endeavor. Besides,
he went on, he thought our critique of American psychology
was misplaced and unwarranted. I am sorry that his letter is
not available for reprinting here, because it was as clear an example as I have seen of insensitivity to and ignorance of the
concept of *social systems.* We wrote back and said that across the
street from our offices was a nationally respected social scientist who was editor of a highly respected journal devoted to public
policy, and that there were several other comparable journals
edited by political scientists and economists. And, we said, we
were sorry that he could not comprehend what to us, and others
who were not psychologists, was a glimpse of the obvious.

The second example was a paper I wrote a decade or so
later with the title "The Lack of an Overarching Conception

in American Psychology." I submitted it to the same journal, with the same result. The paper centered around the writings of two people: John Dollard and Alexis de Tocqueville. In the case of Dollard, I asked, Why was the Dollard who wrote *Caste and Class in a Southern Town* and *Criteria for the Life History* so uninfluential in American psychology even though the two books were so prodromal and explanatory of America and Americans? In regard to de Tocqueville, I asked, How was it possible in the early nineteenth century for a young Frenchman to spend less than a year in this country and write a book that is so penetratingly valid and illuminating of Americans and America? What "psychology" was he employing that enabled him to paint a picture that is like a mirror in which we can see ourselves today? The answer to both questions was that they had an overarching not-spelled-out conception of human behavior as a function of local, national, racial, religious, geographical, political contexts on a historical continuum. It is that kind of a conception that was and is lacking in American psychology. My reaction to the rejection is contained in one of my favorite jokes. It is about the journalist who was assigned to the Jerusalem bureau of his newspaper. His apartment overlooked the Wailing Wall. After several weeks, he became aware that, regardless of time of day, he always saw an old Jew praying vigorously before the wall. There must be a story there, the journalist concluded, and so he went down one day and told the old Jew of his curiosity about such daily praying. "What do you pray for each and every day, all day?" he asked. The old Jew replied, "Every morning I pray for world peace, I go home for a little snack, and in the afternoon I pray that illness and disease should be eradicated from the earth. I go home for a glass of tea with two lumps of sugar, and than I come back and pray for the brotherhood of man." The journalist was flabbergasted. "You pray for these things every day, week in, week out?" The old Jew nodded. The journalist asked, "How many years have you been praying for these things?" The old Jew reflected a bit and replied, "How long? Twenty, maybe twenty-five years." The journalist was dumbfounded and finally asked, "How does it feel to be praying for these things all these years?" To which the old Jew replied, "How does it feel? It feels like talking to a wall."

American psychology was utterly unprepared for what unfolded in the sixties. So were other disciplines and people generally. But if psychology was not alone, the fact remains that the substantive core of the field gave a very impoverished picture of the complex transactions among human behavior, social contexts, world views, and societal change. This is not to say, I should hasten to add, that psychology had not enlarged our understanding of human behavior but rather to say that its contributions were within such narrow conceptual limits as to justify saying that it was missing the trees for the forest. I do not want to convey the impression that I predicted the sixties in any detailed way. I was, more than most psychologists, prepared for the sixties only in the sense that I was certain that American psychology had no formal way of dealing with two sides of the same coin: individual and social change. And I was no less certain that those two indissolubly connected changes were taking place in America and the rest of the post–World War II world. In starting the clinic, I was explicitly embarked on an effort to understand better the phenomena and phenomenology of change, both by creating new settings and by trying to observe or alter existing ones.

From one standpoint, psychology was quite prepared for the unfolding of the sixties. By and large, psychologists are politically liberal in the sense that as citizens they favor public policies that seek to decrease economic disparities, increase educational opportunities, eliminate racial and gender discrimination, and bulwark civil liberties. Put briefly, they tend to favor strong federal initiatives that enlarge the rights and the opportunities of individuals and groups in need of some kind of legislative support and protection. They are proponents of the welfare state, a label that to them carries no pejorative connotations. And they advocate as citizens, not psychologists. But, not infrequently, they buttress their advocacy as citizens by their use of psychological theory and research that they regard as relevant to a particular problem or issue. The most notable example, of course, was the use of psychological research findings in the

1954 desegregation decision. But the most revealing example is contained in Skinner's *Walden Two*, where it is obvious that undergirding his research on the behavior of organisms is a conception of what human development can and should be. Skinner makes it plain that in his mind the existing social order obscures the potentialities of the human organism. It is not that Skinner did research on rats and pigeons and *then* developed a conception of human potential. It is rather that he started with the conception that existing theories and the research derived from them vastly underestimated what people could be. Whereas theory, research, and practice led European Freud to a pessimistic view of human potential, in the case of American Skinner we are given a most optimistic view of what people can and should be. If many psychologists, and people generally, did not cotton to Skinner's radical behaviorism, they nevertheless were sympathetic to the belief, clearly expressed in *Walden Two*, that American society contained many inequities and was in need of an overhaul. In contrast to John B. Watson, Skinner was a far more sophisticated critic of American society, far more of a moralist in regard to individual fulfillment and social justice. Skinner was a modern Rousseau. And Skinner's *Walden Two* struck a very responsive chord among many graduate students in psychology. I remember well how that book was a focus for discussion among students at Yale and elsewhere. Initially, that book did not have much of an audience, but as the forties ended and we entered the fifties, it almost had the status of a best seller. Skinner became a household name. If you read that book not as an exemplar of a particular psychological approach or theory but as a call for societal reconstruction, for freeing individuals from imprisoning custom, you will find attitudes and beliefs that are precursors of many of those that became more explicit in the sixties.

Mention should also be made of the research after World War II on the authoritarian personality. It is hard to read that literature and to miss the degree to which it is pervaded by, indeed derived from, judgments about the political and social order in America. That research, of course, derived directly from the European experience with fascism, and it was intended to illuminate how the seeds of fascism were not foreign to this country.

Few psychologists quarreled with the social and political values implicit in that research or with its implications for how children should be reared; that is, how important it was to avoid indoctrinating children with a narrow, rigid outlook that was counterproductive for the individual and society. Indeed, that research was but one example of a burgeoning literature on the optimal ways of rearing children. And *optimal* meant nurturing the child's potentialities for intellectual, social growth and expression. It is not happenstance that Dr. Spock's book on child care rivaled the Bible as a best seller. The fantastic sales of that book said as much about the anxieties of parents as it did about their goal of what they wanted their children to become. It is not an exaggeration to say that many parents wanted their children to experience other than what they had experienced. To a degree they did not fathom, parents were creating the conditions for a generation gap. In intended and unintended ways, American psychology contributed to the changing zeitgeist.

If American psychology was ideologically prepared for what unfolded in the sixties, it was not prepared for the arena of social action. More specifically, it was not prepared critically to examine how one goes from strongly held values to social actions and public policies in a non-self-defeating way. Psychologists were quite sophisticated about the booby traps you encounter when you seek in research to test this or that theory. It isn't easy, to put it mildly. It is very easy to do it mindlessly, as your critics will soon point out. But *mindless* is the term I use to describe how so many psychologists were in their attempts to understand what was going on in the sixties and to influence the course of events. Their hearts were in the right place, but their minds were not. Should there be a war on poverty? Should we desegregate our schools? Should we eradicate racism and sexism? Should we improve our schools? Should we seek to dilute intergroup tensions and conflict? Should those who are affected by the decision makers stand in some relationship to the decision-making process? Should our colleges and universities seek to be more "relevant" to the society of which they are a part? Should inequities in regard to the availability of health care services be eliminated? These and other questions were the easy ones to answer in the affirmative for most psychologists. The hard questions were not asked. Why was all of this coming together *now*? In regard to each of these questions, what were the alternatives for action, and how do we judge them in terms of efficacy and social consequences? Should not passionate advocacy, in ourselves or others, alert us to the possibility that we may not be thinking straight? What did it signify that the major spurs for social change were coming from our courts far more than from the general population? Was explaining and excusing violence in terms of past history justified? Was there not a means-end problem? What were the credentials of American psychology—its theories, research, and applications—in regard to the formulation and implementation of public policy? Was it the case that these questions were not and should not be a central concern of a general *science* of psychology? Can you have a viable science of human behavior that is not centrally concerned with individual and social change? Almost from the time the clinic started, which was before the sixties became *the* sixties, I became increasingly certain that the myriad programs being enacted and implemented would be relative failures. Let me give some examples.

The signing of the initial Head Start legislation by President Johnson was a media event. The legislation was enthusiastically supported by psychologists and the American Psychological Association on grounds of existing research and a moral imperative for equality of opportunity. Much was promised as to outcomes. Shortly after its passage, I gave a public lecture at Boston University in which I stated my opposition to the legislation. I made it clear, of course, that if I had been in Congress, I would have supported its passage on political grounds, as a symbolic gesture testifying to my social outlook. I would not have supported it because it would produce the desired consequences. (Bear in mind that initially Head Start was a summer program.) My reservations were of two kinds. The first was that Head Start was based on a theory of contagion, known to but not verbalized by the professional proponents of the program. What that theory says is that when poor children enter public schools, they catch the viruses of failure, disinterest, and frustration; that is, our schools are unhealthy places for these children. What these children need is an inoculation against those viruses, and that is what Head Start will give them. With that inoculation they are less likely to become "ill." Given my experience in schools, I considered that theory wildly invalid. The second criticism, derived from the first, was that the chances were too great that society would end up "blaming the victim," concluding that most of these children simply did not have the ability to benefit from Head Start.

I had the highest respect for those psychologists who were instrumental in the enactment of that legislation and, more important, willingly gave time and energy to its implementation. I refer specifically to my colleague Edward Zigler, who has devoted so much of his life to protecting Head Start in the corridors of power in Washington. Ed was uncomfortable with the promises made for Head Start, but, given his role in Washington, he was in no position publicly to express his doubts and reservations. The powers that be want to hear about a rosy future, not about a problematic one. But what about psychologists generally? Why were they not alert to and critical of some of the assumptions undergirding Head Start? Why did they expect Head Start to be a resounding success? As psychologists, not as citizens, should they not have voiced reservations about the nature and strength of the intervention? The answer, of course, to these questions is that psychologists had no interest in and understanding of schools. They could not be sensitive to the process and force of the acculturation process that takes place when a child begins school, especially one in our ghetto areas. As psychologists, they were ignorant about the culture of schools. In principle, they were like foreign policy consultants recommending technical aid programs for societies of which they had little understanding—until the programs failed. Head Start did not fail, but it surely fell far short of the promised goals proclaimed at its inception.

The second example is far more complicated and controversial, although, like the first example, it raises questions about the productiveness of American psychology for understanding individual and social change in a historical context. You cannot

write about the sixties—you cannot have lived through them—
without coming to grips with the nature and future of the black
experience in America. There were few problems that occupied
us more at the clinic. In each of the many settings in which the
clinic was involved, the black-white problem was there. I need
not recount the different ways in which the problem became
manifest. And it goes without saying that we at the clinic, like
a lot of other people, strongly supported any effort that might
begin to redress the grievances that were the legacy of slavery.
To me, the troubling question was how to maintain conceptual
clarity at a time marked by unrealistic expectations, black militancy, open civil strife, and challenges to every major institution
in the society. That was a question hard to avoid at Yale in New
Haven. Yale was surrounded by a black ghetto; blacks and
Italians were the two largest groups in New Haven, and that
was like mixing oil and water; and Yale was deservedly viewed
as in but not of New Haven, a well-heeled entity insensitive to
the needs of a dying city and a changing society. It was a view
of Yale that many faculty members came to share, and, it goes
without saying, a large fraction of the students, caught up in
the fight for social justice, were critical of Yale's "irrelevance."
Yale, like America, needed to change. This was the time when
so many psychologists labeled themselves as "change agents,"
as facilitators of institutional change. The word *relevant* became
fashionable, a badge of honor, and psychologists (among others)
who had never engaged in social action sought to become helpful
and relevant in one or another setting where social explosions
were taking place. Some became instant consultants, others
changed the direction of their research, and others applied their
skills in group dynamics to dilute racial, ethnic, or generational
conflicts.

The hotter the social scene became, the more the clinic
became part of it in New Haven, the more personally and intellectually troubled I became. On purely personal grounds, I
was aghast at the anti-Semitism that began to be displayed in
parts of the black community. I read the weekly publication of
the Black Panthers, which blatantly targeted Jews as one of the
groups contributing to the plight of blacks. Today we hear little

of the Black Panthers, but during the sixties they were a potent, hostile, semimilitaristic force symbolic of the rage and frustration in the black community. If they were not representative of that community, they were at the time regarded sympathetically by many in it. To a Jew like me, scapegoating Jews is no trivial matter. I could explain the anti-Semitism as one of the irrational manifestations of more than a century of degradation. I could neither excuse nor gloss over it. Like blacks', my radar for detecting discrimination is quite sensitive.

What was far more troubling to me, because it made me feel so apart from most psychologists, was the fact that the myriad efforts to respond to the needs and rights of blacks—to enable them to take advantage of equality of opportunity—were based on the invalid assumption that equality of outcome would be, could be, realizable in the foreseeable future. What psychological conception of individual and social change permitted one to expect that the attitudinal, intellectual, social consequences of slavery for blacks could be altered in one or two generations? That one had to begin *now* went without saying. That the programs that were enacted were hastily drawn up, that they too frequently were mindlessly implemented, and that their positive consequences were exaggerated and unevaluated were facts submerged by the passions of advocacy. Immersed as the clinic was in so many of these programs, I could not maintain an optimistic stance. But even if these programs had been better conceived and implemented, on what theoretical or research grounds could we expect dramatic or even discernible improvement? In the climate of the sixties, that question did not get raised, nor could it be unless you wanted to be perceived as a fool or a racist, or both. My greatest concern was precisely that which I had raised in regard to the unrealistic expectations proclaimed for Head Start. What would happen when it became obvious that these efforts were falling far short of their mark? And one of the things that happened, predictably, was the publication of A. R. Jensen's monograph in which he notes the failure of compensatory educational programs and amasses evidence indicating that blacks differ genetically from whites in regard to intellectual factors and style ("How Much Can We Boost I.Q. and

Scholastic Achievement?'' *Harvard Educational Review,* 1969, *39,*
1-123). That monograph, again predictably, aroused quite a
controversy. Jensen was called, among other things, a racist,
a misinterpreter of data, and a disturber of the peace. I did not
regard him as a racist. He was asking the question, How do
you explain the failure of the compensatory programs? Is it possible that these programs have had the unintended effect of playing to those intellectual factors in which whites are genetically
superior and not to those factors in which blacks are as good
as and perhaps better than whites?

   Jensen, like many of his critics, was a psychologist. It was
not surprising, therefore, that the controversy centered around
adequacy of data, statistical analyses, methodology, interpretation, and quality of programs. From my perspective, Jensen
and his critics were suffering from the tunnel vision of American
psychology. No one was asking why even under far more favorable circumstances it made no theoretical sense to expect that
blacks would ''catch up'' in respect to whites except over a
very, very long period of time. But that could not be asked,
because American psychology and its theories were ahistorical
and acultural.

   To clarify my own thinking, I wrote the most personal
paper I have ever written. It was entitled ''Jewishness, Black-
ishness, and the Nature-Nurture Controversy'' (*American Psychologist,* 1973, *28,* 962-971). Although I did not mention Jensen,
it was my answer to him. It was also an implicit critique of
American psychology. How, I asked, can you explain the disproportionate contribution of Jews to the arts and sciences in Western society? And the answer was that it was explainable only
in terms of a tradition and experience that covered centuries.
And what was central to the Jewish experience and phenomenology could not be diluted in strength, let alone eradicated, except
over a very long period of time under very unusual circumstances. What gets finely honed over the centuries does not
quickly get blunted. If that is true, why on earth should one
expect blacks to overcome the legacies of slavery except, perhaps,
over a century or more under favorable circumstances? It was
not an easy paper to write. I expected criticism on the grounds

that even if I were right, it would play into the hands of those who sought cutbacks in programs, and it would certainly not be viewed with enthusiasm by blacks, who knew too well what the previous two centuries had been and who would not look favorably on my "long-term" future perspective. I received practically no criticism, perhaps because by the time the paper was published it was clear that the unrealistic expectations of the sixties had been just that: unrealistic.

As the years go by, the sixties have taken on a legendary status. The students of the seventies spoke enviously of those who were part of the sixties. And many adults look back on those days with nostalgia for what they remember as electric, exciting times. Someone once said to me, as criticism, that whereas many people became increasingly radicalized as the sixties proceeded, I became more conservative. That, I told him, was name-calling, and it was also a good example of something that was as characteristic of the sixties as it was overlooked in the community of bleeding hearts: the pressure to conform, to declare where you stand in a Manichean world of good and evil, to suppress doubt, to be part of the movement to refashion a decaying, destructive, insensitive American society. We are told that the fifties were silent and conformist. The sixties were loud and conformist. In the university, at least, the pressures to conform to the prevailing liberalism-radicalism were subtle but potent. Too many faculty and students stopped thinking because they possessed the truth. Too many excused discourtesy, rudeness, and violence as unfortunate side effects of an important crusade. Too many adults, in and out of the university, wanted to be "where the action is," where the youthful avant-garde were laying down their gauntlets. I shall never forget a colleague saying, "The youth of today are the most intelligent, worldly-wise, morally sensitive generation that has ever been on this earth." I could not locate these youthful Platos. Scores of undergraduates and graduate students participated in clinic activities. They were bright, I applauded their activist stance, and I was more than respectful of their moral sensitivities. But I could not overlook their tendency to confuse action with thinking, intention with outcome, facts with truth, and sloganeering with conceptualization. They were a joy, but they were not wise, and I did not expect them to be. For them, their world had been born yesterday, and they wanted a new and better world tomorrow. They tended to be antihistorical and ahistorical, or both, but that I expected, took for granted. After all, were they not in college to comprehend, to some degree at least, where they stood in the sweep of human history? Was college a cafeteria of ideas and areas of knowledge from which one chose those foods for thought that would satisfy appetites for the here and the now? Was it the primary responsibility of the faculty to give students what students wanted? Unfortunately, many professors in our universities caved in to student demands, sometimes unwillingly but frequently willingly, because they agreed that too much in the university was irrelevant to societal reconstruction. Their stance was based on the view that when Rome is being sacked and burned, the world of the human mind and human history takes a back seat, gets put in the trunk.

That brings me to what happened at Yale in the weeks following the Kent State student demonstrations in which several students were killed. That was the time that several Black Panthers in New Haven were indicted and would be standing trial for a murder. Their pictures had been plastered on the front page of the local newspaper, and you can imagine what that front page looked like and what attitudes and fears those rogues-gallery photos engendered. The title of the drama was "The Bobby Seale Trial." Kent State and the Bobby Seale trial came together in the national consciousness. And what began to happen as the day of the trial approached was a steady stream of students from around the country pouring into New Haven. Yale's residential colleges were literally bulging. And student demonstrations began. Kingman Brewster, president of Yale, stated that he doubted that, given the atmosphere, the Black Panthers could receive a fair trial, a statement that endeared him to neither the alumni nor New Haven's Italian community. And he passed the word that Yale's dining halls should feed the incoming students. The National Guard was called out. Downtown New Haven was boarded up. Classes were suspended. Every imaginable type of meeting was going on: "rap" sessions, T-groups, student-faculty "dialogues." And, my counterintelligence in the community told me, there were groups in the Italian community that were buying guns. If you want to get a good idea of what Yale and New Haven were like, although the locale was Paris at that same time, read James Jones's *The Merry Month of May*. He captured it all, the American in Paris.

During the week before the trial, graduate and undergraduate students in psychology asked for a meeting with faculty. It was held at the clinic. A fair number of faculty came, far less, of course, than the number of students. The students passed out a couple of pages of suggestions about curriculum change and requirements. On the surface they were suggestions, but not far below the surface they were demands. I thought some of the suggestions (criticisms) were appropriate, but most were not. I said very little as the meeting went on. Indeed, I think I said nothing. But I became aware that I was getting angry and I was not clear why. And then I had an "aha" experience, and I said the following: "If I were to ask you what is wrong with American television, you would come up with a litany of criticisms about what is shown on our screens. What would happen if we took those criticisms to Sarnoff at NBC, Goldenson at ABC, Paley at CBS, and asked them to justify the crap they put on our screens? Do you know what the answer would be based on *data* they would show us? The answer would be that is what people want. Now, are you saying that it is our job as professors to give you what *you* want? Do you want professors to profess only what you want to hear, to offer only what you want to take?"

That professors should be sensitive to what students think, feel, and want goes without saying. That you should listen to, take account of, student criticism also goes without saying. But there is more than a fine line between such sensitivity and mindless indulgence. And during the sixties too many professors, too many college administrators, shamelessly forgot their profession of professing. I need to repeat that in the sixties too many people were loud and conforming. From one perspective, you could say that the counterculture of the sixties was at its root nonconformist. But there were scads of people eager to conform to what they saw as the wave of the future.

When I started the clinic, I was leaving clinical psychology.

My experiences at the clinic (truly a misnomer) confirmed me in the view that despite its fantastic growth and status in psychology, clinical psychology was hopelessly mired in a stance of repair of individual lives. Such repair needs no defense. When an individual experiences personal misery and unhappiness, there should be people skilled in providing help. In no way am I opposed to the clinical endeavor. What I regret is that the emphasis on individual repair has played into, indeed reflects, the Achilles' heel of American psychology: its ahistorical, acultural view of the human psyche, a view inimical both to the stance of prevention and to an understanding of life in America. The sixties illustrated that all too clearly. When I left the clinic, I was obviously no longer a clinical psychologist. I was unclear about where I belonged in American psychology. American psychology was my house, but it did not feel like a home.

16

Does American Psychology Have a Core?

Given the features of the sixties, the ending of the divisive Vietnam War, inflation, and an economic recession, it would have been surprising if American psychology had been exempt from their influences. One might put it this way: how does one explain why by the mid seventies American psychology manifested some dramatic changes in its substantive focuses and institutional alignment? I do not pretend to have anything like a comprehensive answer to a very complex question. But what I can contribute to an answer stems directly from the fact that when I left the clinic, I was invited to join and be housed in Yale's new Institution for Social and Policy Studies (ISPS). I had the time to view the professional scene unencumbered by administrative responsibilities. And I happily joined ISPS, because it would make it possible for me to reflect on and write about what I had observed and experienced in the previous decade. I did not anticipate that ISPS would become an example, a victim, of what had happened and was happening in America.

ISPS was Yale's conceptual and programmatic response to the local and national turbulence. It was to be housed in a new social science complex intended to foster integration in the social sciences. The main function of ISPS was to bring together faculty interested in current social issues. It was to have three centers: on education, the city, and management. If only because of my age and the years I had been at Yale, I was the only one to note that the rationale for ISPS and the social context from which it arose were very similar to those of Yale's Institute of Human Relations from decades earlier. I was not optimistic that ISPS would be any more successful than IHR in overcoming the rugged individualism and imperialism of faculty and in maintaining financial solvency in the face of the yo-yo features of the American economy. Unfortunately, I was right on both scores. When I joined ISPS, it was already apparent that Yale would not have a new social science building. And it was also apparent that the economic recession and inflation would mightily affect ISPS's already limited resources. The important point, however, is not that there was economic stringency but rather that the downturn made it clear that the programmatic goals of ISPS would take a back seat, so to speak, to the traditions and needs of university departments. Tradition reasserted itself. But there was more than tradition at work. What I began to sense was a strong undercurrent of disillusionment with the substance and consequences of the myriad attempts by social scientists in the sixties to participate in and inform social action. What had been gained from the legislation, the movements, the upheavals of the sixties? Had we not been misled, had we not misled ourselves, did we not forget that our primary task was to contribute to knowledge and not to the manufacture of Band-Aids? The disillusionment was more than an undercurrent. It showed itself in an aversion to anything resembling an activist stance. And it also showed itself in a reluctance to take stock, to try to understand, other than in a superficial way, what had happened and why.

The disillusionment was by no means peculiar to university faculty. It was far more general, far more in the consciousness of people. *Disillusionment* is a word that may not capture the complex mood of that time. Nor does a word like *reaction*. *Bewilderment* may be more appropriate. Life-styles had changed, institutions had changed, but the major social problems had not changed despite the efforts to "solve" them. Indeed, many people concluded that these problems were not solvable by the usual criteria of "solution." If these problems required some kind of action, if what we had done was inadequate or ineffective or both, what should that action be in a time of limited resources and rising inflation? President Carter was criticized for labeling the mood as a "malaise," but he, like most other people, was giving voice to what I termed as disillusionment or reaction or a dysphoric mood.

The most telling example of what I sensed is what happened in psychiatry. During the sixties, American psychiatry was plunged into the social arena by virtue of legislation creating community mental health centers. Within departments of psychiatry, the centers of power changed as the weight of federal and state funding steered interest and programs to a broader and deeper community involvement. "Social psychiatry," "community psychiatry" achieved an institutional power as never before. The psychoanalytical influence began noticeably to wane, and so did the biological orientation (except for the development and use of drugs). The task for psychiatry was to apply its knowledge and techniques to populations heretofore unserved. It was immediately apparent—and I do mean immediately— that psychiatry had mammothly overestimated its knowledge of these populations: their problems in daily existence, their skepticism about what was being offered them, and their militancy. In dealing with the real world—poverty, race, ethnicity, and political constituencies—the parochialism of psychiatry was laid bare. There was turmoil in the community, the community mental health centers, and departments of psychiatry. There were sit-ins, demonstrations, and overt, direct challenges to professional leadership. That was what was going on at Yale and elsewhere.

As funding for these community programs began to dry up; as the bulk of psychiatrists became disenchanted with their excursions into the social arena; as they became aware of how embroiled they had become in matters of federal and state policy; as they developed an "identity crisis"; as they saw the practice of psychotherapy being taken over by clinical psychologists and clinical social workers (among others); as they saw that their respectability (never secure) was lessening—all of these factors coalesced by the early seventies to make the soil fertile for a wholesale reassertion of the biological-genetic tradition. Psychiatry took to biological reductionism with a vengeance. What I found appalling was the almost total lack of interest to try to understand what had happened and why. The psychoanalytical psychiatrists bemoaned their lessening influence and the extreme degree to which rampant biologisms sought to explain the workings of the mind, not only neglecting but also rejecting Freud's legacies. These psychiatrists were now on the outside looking in on the house of psychiatry, the same position they had been in before World War II and for the same reaons. But they, like those they criticized, had no way of comprehending that fashions in a field derived not only from "within field" factors or dynamics but also from reactions to changes in the larger society. The "new" psychiatry, like the one preceding it, was asocial and ahistorical, characteristics conducive to extreme pendulum swings. And psychiatry had swung from a concentration on the intrapsychic to an enamorment with the neurophysiological and biochemical features of this or that part of the brain. There was no middle ground.

I viewed these developments with amusement and despair. I had lived through the pendulum swing before. The biological orientation in psychiatry before World War II had promised much and contributed little, a rather liberal assessment only if you leave out the harmful side effects of some of its proclaimed contributions. Psychoanalysis promised no less, and with the same consequences. And now we had (and have) the new psychiatry that, in this age of computer technology that facilitates wall-to-wall recording of brain activity, again promises that the "secrets" of the brain *and, therefore, behavior* will be fathomed. On an actuarial basis, I have to predict that this too shall pass. What I am describing is more in the nature of a movement than it is a scientific venture. The research methods used have, of course, all of the trappings of science in the laboratory. What seems totally lacking is the understanding that explanations of human behavior have to be seen from several perspectives and that what you learn from one perspective may be, as it frequently is, incommensurable with what you learn from another perspective. It is not that one perspective is right and the other (or others) wrong. How many thousands of books have been written to explain the French and the American revolutions? If anything is clear from these books, it is that each new perspective from which these revolutions have been explained casts them in a different light, not by disproving another perspective but by assigning new weights and emphases. And when someone has come along proclaiming the one and only true explanation, he or she has been laughed out of court. Human behavior, covert and overt, cannot be understood from one perspective. But that kind of tunnel vision characterizes American psychiatry today, the hallmark of a movement.

I suppose I have to add that I have no doubt that out of this will filter some findings that will represent a sustained contribution to human knowledge and behavior. But these contributions will be from a particular perspective, one of many valid but different perspectives. What price are we willing to pay for tunnel vision? And when I say *we,* I mean the individual in misery, the individual professional, the professional field, and the larger society. To proceed as if we are not paying a price is ignorance to an exponential degree. What is lacking today in American psychiatry is humility—one source of which is the sense of history; that is, the knowledge that human history is replete with examples of passionate tunnel vision that began with a bang and ended up with a whimper.

And what was happening in psychology? What began to emerge was a clear cleavage between psychology as professional practice and as a scientific enterprise. By virtue of its fantastic growth (in the university and private practice), clinical psychology had become a politically potent force within the university and in national and state professional organizations. It had not only won its independence from medicine and psychiatry but it had achieved status in the university. But that achievement was not without its critics. For example, as I have noted in earlier chapters, the emergence of community psychology in the sixties was explicitly a reaction to four obvious and related features

of clinical psychology: its emphasis on the individual, its preoccupation with repair, its lack of a social psychological base, and
its ignoring of the preventive orientation. Almost without exception, all of the people who contributed to the emergence of
community psychology had been clinical psychologists. Although
many university departments recognized community psychology
as an area of research and practice, it was in almost all instances
administratively a part of the clinical psychology program. That
guaranteed a number of things that I have discussed in earlier
chapters. One of them was that the new field would have very
limited resources. If in the sixties community psychology gained
recognition, it was more than acceptance-toleration but less than
embracement. With the petering out of the explosiveness of the
sixties and the onset of an economic recession, community psychology lost some of its momentum, attraction, and fiscal base.
The usual explanation I heard went like this: "The sixties are
over. Students coming into the field now are not all that interested in social issues. Where are there positions for community
psychologists? In a period of economic stringency, psychology
must play to its strengths, must protect its major areas of in-
vestigation and practice. Besides, did not community psychology
lack a distinctive core of theory, a recognizable focus derived
from, or capable of being integrated into, a general psychology,
as in the case of developmental, or social, or cognitive, or physiological, or clinical psychology?" These were not illegitimate
concerns. After all, because a field is new is no warrant to give
it status or resources. To me, what was sad about these articulated concerns was the degree to which they glossed over the
nature of the challenge that community psychology represented
to mainstream American psychology. And that challenge was
to psychology's riveting on the individual psyche, to a social
psychology that was egregiously narrow and acultural, to a psychology minimally interested in social and institutional change,
to a too one-sided emphasis on repair at the expense of the
preventive orientation. In short, community psychology challenged parochialism in outlook. I take encouragement in the fact
that unlike what has happened in psychiatry, community psychology continues to exist as a field, a kind of saving remnant

of a critical tradition. I am obviously not a chauvinist for American psychology, but I do take pride in the fact that, despite its parochialism, and unlike what happened in psychiatry, American psychology remains a part of the world of ideas. I cannot resist saying that any field that has tolerated me, that gave and gives me a platform to say my piece and do my things, cannot be all that bad. Having said that, let me turn to the defects of that virtue.

I said that one of the concerns about community psychology was its lack of a clear focus, its hodgepodge character. In the years since I left the clinic, that is precisely the concern that has been voiced about American psychology. By the year 2000, there will be more than a hundred thousand members of the American Psychological Association, and God only knows how many separate divisions it will have. American psychology has become a conglomeration of narrow specialties and vested interests. It is no longer possible for any psychologist to comprehend other than a miniscule fraction of what is going on in the house of psychology. Indeed, within any one specialty there are specialties. We are used to hearing that one of the most troubling features of American society is the number of people who feel socially-interpersonally "unconnected." Words such as *isolation, loneliness, anomie,* and *alienation* have become part of everyday discourse. That is precisely how psychologists see themselves in regard to American psychology. It makes no difference with which kind of psychologist I talk (and I do get around), they give voice to what I call the universal complaint: the feeling of homelessness in the house of psychology. A very noted psychologist said to me, "Homeless people in this country at least share a common language. I don't envy their plight, but we use the same language. But when I peruse the scores of psychological journals—or better yet, when I go to the national convention—I feel as if I am from a foreign country." Winston Churchill once said that England and America are two countries divided by a common language. The occupants of the rooms in the vast house of American psychology are divided by different languages.

I find it hard to comprehend but it is nevertheless true that there are psychologists who see the current picture as proof positive of the vigor, innovativeness, strength, and productiveness of American psychology. If you have any doubt on that score, read the two house organs of the American Psychological Association: the *American Psychologist* and the *Monitor*. It is hard to read them without concluding that American psychology continues on an onward and upward course, contributing mightily to human knowledge and the public welfare. But if I and the many psychologists with whom I have talked are not grossly atypical, the current picture is like a Tower of Babel—except that the people of Babel had a center: the tower that would reach heaven. *There is no longer a center in American psychology.* Let me hasten to emphasize—if only to counter the impression that I am at best a cynic and at worst a nihilist—that I am aware that far from being a total disaster, American psychology has contributed to human knowledge, albeit far less than it promised after World War II. But these contributions do not derive from and cannot be related to an overarching center. They are reflections of a centrifugal, not a centripetal, dynamic in American psychology. This unconnectedness is not peculiar to psychology. It typifies the university. So, for example, it is rare to find that social science department X seeks to establish meaningful discourse, or seeks to share resources, with social science department Y. They are in different worlds. Each has borders it zealously guards. Each knows in an abstract way that it and the others are blood relations, or should be blood relations. But it is not blood that is thicker than water. This is why from time to time over the years institutes have been created to overcome departmental parochialism. Some were more ambitious in scope than others. Yale's Institute of Human Relations was very broad in scope and goal. Less broad in scope was Harvard's Psychological Clinic under Henry Murray. Without doubt, the most bold attempt was after World War II when Harvard created the Department of Social Relations. Each of these efforts disappeared as entities. The fact is that each had an impact that is with us today, not in the form of nostalgic memories but in the conceptual integration each sought and accomplished while they existed.

     Graduate students today are abysmally ignorant of what

these few efforts signified in the past and, therefore, the present. It is not their fault. They are not exposed to a historical view of American psychology: its origins in and separation from philosophy; its earliest critics (for example, James, Dewey); the substance and consequences of the tensions between what was perceived as basic and what as applied, and the value judgments those tensions reflected; the changing religious and social class composition of American psychology; the myriad ways that psychology was transformed by wars and economics; the cultural significances of the controversies between American and European psychology; how psychology has never been exempt from fads and fashions; how judgments are made about what is worthy from the past. If it is true, as Voltaire said, that history is written by the victors, not the vanquished, is that not a warning about how one should view one's sense of identity with the history of one's field? How does one gain a sense of connectedness with a past and with a present? What should be the goals of education in psychology?—not *training* in a specialty but *education* in psychology; not an education determined primarily by "the market" but one that instills, and over time sustains, some sense of connectedness. Or is it that we have come to the point where we have to recognize that there is no core—or even handful of cores—that every psychologist must comprehend?

Relevant here are two chapters in a recent book, *One Hundred Years of Psychological Research in America: G. Stanley Hall and the Johns Hopkins Tradition,* edited by Stewart H. Hulse and Bert F. Green and published by Johns Hopkins Press in 1986. In his chapter "Dismembering Cognition," George Miller says about a lack of a core in cognitive psychology what I have said about psychology generally. The real eye-opener is Wendell Garner's chapter "Interactions of Stimulus and Organism in Perception." The bulk of his paper is concerned with pattern perception, but in his opening and closing pages Garner makes it clear that the significance of his research on pattern perception is in how it illuminates the core or overarching task of understanding "not only the perceiving organism but also the nature of the stimulus world and the interaction between stimuli and organisms." It is rare indeed for someone with Garner's research credentials to begin a tightly reasoned, data-crammed chapter with these words: "Since those of us who do research on perception are usually psychologists, we do not ordinarily use the term *epistemology* in our writing on this topic. Epistemology—the study of the nature of knowing—is the philosopher's province; yet the issues I want to discuss are indeed epistemological, since we are concerned with how the organism comes to know the stimulus world." How do we come to know our world? The failure to keep that question in the forefront mightily increases the frequency of the tendency to "dismember" problems and fields, to forget that the overall enterprise of psychology should be to perceive pattern, or in Garner's words, "a good pattern."

When I say that psychology seems to have no core, I mean that when I read the research literature I rarely get the feeling that the writer of an article sees his study in a larger context, one that goes beyond the circumscribed problem he has studied, one that makes bridges over phenotypically different problem areas. I am certain that some researchers place their studies in larger contexts, but the pressure to be brief (frequently to the point where the study is rendered unintelligible) makes discussion of those bridges impossible.

I know Garner and I know the conceptual bridges he has erected in his fertile brain. The opening and closing pages of his paper were not happenstance. They were meant to underline what he considers to be a core problem in psychology generally. Let us listen to his concluding remarks:

One last comment has to do with the fact that apparently only people who do perception research seem to be interested in the epistemological issues that pervade this report, and more specially, to be interested in the nature of the stimuli used in their research. Why are not these issues and this approach equally important for people studying learning, for example? What is clear is that they have not been.

Shepard comments on this matter by noting that "Hull . . . , as Skinner, treated the stimulus as an unanalyzed entity." But not just traditional learning theorists have failed to be seriously concerned with the nature of the stimulus. Many psychologists working within an information-processing paradigm have also treated the stimulus with disregard. As I once noted, ''For too long we have considered that a stimulus is a stimulus is a stimulus, whose only function is to elicit behavior.''

Of course, the answer to the question posed is that learning specialists and some kinds of information-processing specialists have been so concerned with the role of the response as the behavior to be modified that the role of the stimulus in modifying this behavior has been neglected. But we in perception cannot afford to neglect the stimulus, it being more important to us than overt behavior. In fact, if we are trying to understand perception, the role of the response is simply as an indicant to an internal process; the response itself is not the process in which we are interested. It allows communication between the observing subject in our experiments and the experimenter, but the process being studied is truly perception. So we pay less attention to the nature of the response and more to the nature of the stimulus.

And so to conclude, those of us who study perception must try to understand not only the perceiving organism but also the nature of the stimulus world and the interactions between stimuli and organisms.

Although Garner's words refer to perception research, he is, as I know, in no doubt that he is talking about the core of psychology: how the nature and structure of the ''outside'' transacts with the ''inside.'' How does that ''outside'' get structured at different points in development in different contexts? How should we think of that ''stimulus world''? How do we respond to and absorb its features? Garner is asking the same questions about the role of the configurated stimulus in perception that I have tried to ask in regard to the configurated ''social stimulus,'' the characteristics of which we as observers cannot comprehend apart from its embeddedness in history, culture, and place. Central to Garner's work is the stimulus as *configuration*. Our social world is no less configurated. If we cannot study it with the precision and manipulability of visual patterns, if it requires a different kind of conceptualization, that is no excuse for ignoring the fact that our goals are identical. The bases for my friendship with Garner are many; one of them is agreement about what is the core problem.

So let me turn to what started at Yale in the early seventies and will end in May 1988. When I came to Yale, the department had a proseminar: a vehicle for educating first-year students about the major areas of psychology. Those were still the days when it was expected that a student would indeed know psychology, not only this or that specialty. It was, so to speak, in the tradition of the liberal arts in that it attempted to give a broad overview of what psychology had been and was—a "liberating" exposure, an antidote to tunnel vision. Most of the faculty, and all of the senior professors, had responsibility for segments of the proseminar. Within a few years after the war, the proseminar was dropped from the curriculum. Some members of the faculty felt that their segments were too brief and made for unacceptable superficiality. In addition, some felt that it was wasteful of the time of students and faculty, because the ground covered in a segment of the proseminar would then have to be gone over in greater detail in subsequent advanced courses relevant to that segment. There was another factor: the perception that there was an explosion of knowledge in the different areas that required giving more special courses and that students would be better off taking them than taking the time-consuming, superficial proseminar. If a student really wanted to know something about a specialty, he or she should take a "real" course. It is also fair to say that many faculty members believed that taking courses was less valuable for learning about and doing research than active engagement in an ongoing research project. Courses had their functions, but they were poor substitutes for learning by doing. The quality of a student's research (more than a thesis was required) was weighted more in judging a student than were grades in courses. What dropping the proseminar signified was a devaluation of education in psychology in favor of training in a specialty. There is a difference between education and training, albeit there is always some overlap.

What happened, of course, as the years rolled on was that students took fewer courses and relatively infrequently took one outside of their area of concentration. It was not unusual to sit for an entire faculty meeting devoted to evaluation of students and for a faculty member not to have had any contact with or knowledge of at least half of the students. And those meetings would usually last an entire day! One could count on there being one or two students each of whom would be discussed for an hour or more; that is, the faculty meeting would be transformed into a clinical case conference. And for those who did not know the student, it was one big bore. If the student was in your area, it could be very interesting.

It was at one of these meetings in the early seventies that two concerns became a focus for discussion. The first was that our students were poorly educated in psychology. That concern had been voiced before, but this time it had special force, because several of our problem students had taken amazingly few courses. The second concern was that in a shrinking job market (for university positions), it was important that a student have a semblance of familiarity with more than one area in psychology. The decision was made to have a new proseminar. It would be a year-long seminar divided into five segments, one for each of the five major areas: developmental, clinical, psychobiology, social, and cognitive-perception. Each segment would meet twice a week for an hour and a half, and each segment would be taught by a senior professor. In essence, the proseminar consisted of five courses that all incoming students would take. Each year, one senior professor would attend *all* meetings, serving as a coordinator of sorts. I served as coordinator the first year and one other time.

Sitting in on all of the meetings was an educational experience for me. I was no end stimulated and enriched. To watch and listen to Robert Rescorla and Allan Wagner in psychobiology, Robert Abelson and Irving Janis in social psychology, William Kessen in developmental psychology, and Wendell Garner and Robert Crowder in cognitive psychology was no less than to experience first-class minds at work. (I taught the clinical-community segment, and I judged my colleagues more favorably than I did myself, an old story but a valid one.) The proseminar was a demanding experience for the students, intellectually and in terms of time. Within a few years, two problems began to surface. The first was that enrollment in other seminars decreased noticeably, a fact not viewed favorably by those who taught these seminars. The explanation given was that the proseminar took too much of students' time, which, together with the pressure on students to get started in research, left little time and motivation to take other than a very small number of "regular" seminars. The second problem, related to the first, was that students began to articulate resentment that they had to take segments in which they had no interest. Why, a student would say, should I have to sit through a clinical segment when what I am interested in is cognitive psychology? Or why should I as a clinical student have to learn psychobiology?

My irritation in regard to these concerns had two sources. The first was what I thought was undue departmental sensitivity to the possibility that the students were being overworked. Indeed, it was explicitly stated that we should plan our requirements on the basis of an eighty-hour work week. The second source was what I saw as an anti-intellectual stance in many of the students, a lack of intellectual curiosity, an intellectual laziness and passivity, a stultifying lack of interest in both psychology generally and its history in particular. There were, to be sure, some students for whom this description did not hold. But they were very few in number. Students were, again to be sure, very bright and in their own ways ambitious, but their tunnel vision was, to me, frightening.

What to do? Various adjustments were made. For example, each student was graded in each segment of the proseminar. To reduce pressure on them, it was decided that the segment in which the student had the lowest grade would not be counted in the overall grade. I regarded that as at best a misguided overprotectiveness and at worst an inexcusable caving in to "public opinion." Of course you should be sensitive to student interest and attitude. Of course you should not run them into the ground physically. But at what point do you draw the line and say, "You came here to become psychologists, not narrow specialists. You have a responsibility to yourself and your field to try to comprehend as much of it as possible. You cannot, must not, play only to your here-and-now interests. To become a psychologist is no easy matter. It is demanding of your time and energies. Graduate school is your last chance to experience a general education in your field. Try as hard as you can, you still will have only a glimpse of the overall picture. To attempt less is to consign yourself to the category of the uneducated. If this does not suit your purposes, maybe you should go elsewhere.'' To some readers, I will sound like an old fogey, someone who foists his values on powerless students, someone who would like to go back to the good old days when professors professed and students listened and took notes in a dutiful, conforming way, when students had voices but no power. The world has changed; my values have not. To be a psychologist, to consider yourself expert in matters of human mind and behavior, in any major aspect of them, requires a strange mixture of arrogance and humility, arrogance because of the complexity you seek to understand and humility before the knowledge that understanding is inevitably partial at best.

I think it is the lack of intellectual curiosity of present-day students that bothers me most, if only because of what it portends for the future of the field. As I have indicated, it is a feature of the current scene that there is a compliance factor in many of those who have the responsibility to educate these students. It is interesting that when the Yale department decided to terminate the proseminar at the end of the 1987–88 academic year, several of the senior faculty who taught segments in it felt remorse. This is not to say that they had not been ambivalent about the seminar, because they had been. But they felt that in giving it up, something important was being lost. As one said to me, ''Don't fret, Seymour, in fifteen years the proseminar will be again instituted.''

What I have described at Yale is by no means peculiar to it. Among psychologists of my and the subsequent cohort— those who came into psychology before and immediately after World War II—many are voicing experiences and doubts identical to mine. Some are making an effort to stimulate the national society to focus on graduate education in a field that is increasingly and disturbingly composed of scores of specialties. In the last decade, we have been witness to another one of those debates about how to improve our public schools. As I have discussed in several of my writings, there is no reason in theory or research to expect that what is being recommended will have its intended effects. When a problem has been intractable to change, it is the hallmark of a failure to flush out and examine axioms that undergird our thinking and actions. To flush out those axioms is a dangerous affair, because if those axioms are in part or in whole invalid, it makes the problem of action far more difficult at the same time that it clarifies what has been puzzling. We are in the same boat in regard to graduate education in psychology. If graduate education becomes a focus, the first task is to examine the axioms without which the current scene is incomprehensible and with which we will continue unsuccessfully to withstand the centrifugal force of narrow specialization. The question is not whether there are two cultures in psychology, the hard and the soft. The question is not how to deal with the basic-applied dichotomy. Those are important but not the decisive questions. The important questions are: Are we justified in assuming that graduate education reflects an agreed-upon core of substantive knowledge and skills without which no one should be called a psychologist? If agreement about a core is not possible, if the surface differences among programs go far below the surface, how do we justify the existence of the field? If there is one obvious skill that all students in all programs must acquire, namely statistics, does that mean that at its core the field is nonpsychological? If the overarching goal of a field is to integrate knowledge, to seek commonalities among disparate bodies of knowledge, to explain more and more in a parsimonious way, to make bridges, not islands, why is this not occurring in psychology? Psychology is proceeding as if education for the field were based on axioms about overarching goals. That may be true on the level of rhetoric, but that rhetoric is mocked by educational practice.

Fields, especially the social sciences, change relatively little because of their internal structure and substantial concerns. Psychology, like the other social sciences, has undergone change when there have been cataclysmic changes in the world; for example, wars, the Great Depression, and social movements centering around race and gender. That is another way of saying that fields change when the regnant world views in the society change. I am not advocating, of course, that we sit back and wait for the next upheaval. I would be content if attention began to be given to how and why American psychology grew and changed. Such attention might bring to the fore what to me is a glimpse of the obvious: just as changes in each of us as individuals are consequences of transactions between "inside and outside," the same is true for fields. That is no less true for psychology than it has been for physics; both fields were transformed by war, substantively and methodologically. Of course, changes occur because of the ideas or work of unusual individuals. But those changes are relatively modest compared to those produced by social catastrophe. In an earlier chapter, I said that for me the core problem in psychology is how individuals absorb culture and a world view. Someone said to me that I belonged in anthropology, not psychology. That remark signifies that the unconnectedness among the social sciences is but a variant of the unconnectedness among the diverse fields in psychology. Fences do not neighbors make.

In the years since I left the clinic, I have spent my time observing, thinking, and writing. In a chaotic field and world, writing is the only way I can bring some order to what I have experienced. For me, writing is a way I can reconstruct and construct myself, with the inevitable consequence that I see myself and the world differently from before. I have become aware that my greatest kicks come from trying to fathom the axioms that undergird my thinking and actions. Once those axioms illuminate me to myself, I make the leap that what is true for me is true for most other people. I check it out in one or another way. Let me give but one example. I had long been aware that after a few years of immersion in a particular problem or activity, I want to move on to something else. It is not that I am bored or that I have solved the problem or milked what I could from the activity. I could and did explain my moving on in rational terms; more specifically, in terms of intellectual curiosity and a need to meet new challenges—a very self-congratulatory explanation. Why, then, did I find myself re-examining my usual explanation when I left the clinic to become part of

ISPS? ISPS was then like an inkblot, and I had no idea what I would be getting into. That was not a new problem for me except that now there was a dysphoric poignancy I had never experienced before. A part of the answer, which I struggled to gloss over, was my omnipresent concern with my mortality. I was in my early fifties. Time was growing short. Was I more concerned than I liked to believe that my best years were behind me? Another part of the answer was that Esther and I were then dealing with four dying parents, requiring us to commute for several years from New Haven to New Jersey to Brooklyn. If my mortality had always been salient in my phenomenology, it was now mightily strengthened. Why was it now so much more important for me to get into something new? The answer came one day—one of those "aha" experiences—when I realized that what I sought was *rejuvenation*, literally to experience the juvenile stance of a limitless future. In the past, whenever I had started something new, it had served the function of pushing the future farther ahead, so that tomorrow was only the beginning of something that erased time. It also dawned on me that I was in an atypical role in our society in that as a university professor I could change directions, I could get into something new if I so desired, I could experience rejuvenation. How many people have that kind of freedom? Those kinds of thoughts got quickly connected with a social phenomenon that was getting a good deal of play in the public media and, to a lesser extent, in the professional community: the need for and the frequency of career change. Why was there so much attention being given to the desire for career change among highly educated professional people? Job dissatisfaction among blue-collar workers had long been studied. Why was it now a presumably increasing source of unhappiness among those who, on the surface, had it made? Why did so many of them feel in a rut, that their best days were over?

It all came together in my mind, as it usually does, in a series of statements or conclusions:

1.   Ours is a society that says to us, "Here is a smorgasbord of roles you can be in in life. Choose the one role that you

will be in. You can be *A* or *B* or *C*. Choose *either A* or *B* or *C*. You cannot be in more than one." It is what I called the one-life, one-career imperative.

2. With increasing frequency in the post–World War II period, the message to young people has been that they can and should be many things in life, they should experience as much as life has to offer. Our travel agent captured the sense of the message in his logo: "See the world before you leave it." That message was on a collision course with the one-life, one-career imperative.

3. Our society has made it easier to change marriage partners than to change careers, but their dynamics are identical.

Once these statements got formulated, I was rejuvenated. I knew what I wanted to study and write about. I embraced a limitless future. Of course I would be around to complete the project! It culminated several years later in a book that is one of my favorites: *Work, Aging, and Social Change: Professionals and the One-Life, One-Career Imperative* (New York: Free Press, 1977). The title was an unfortunate one, because it suggested that the book was about chronologically "old" people. There is nothing about old people in the book. It is about young, highly educated people, and the fact that we are at the beginning of an era in which America will have the largest, most highly educated aged population in human history. As a group, they will be dramatically different from those we now call senior citizens. And for that group, as well as for our society, what will be fateful is how individual, institutional, and social arrangements will adjust to "great expectations" and the very problematic one-life, one-career imperative.

As earlier chapters made apparent, there were three people in my professional development who very much influenced my thinking and outlook: Tom Gladwin, Henry Schaefer-Simmern, and Burt Blatt. None was a psychologist. This is not to say that I have not been discernibly enriched by psychologists past or present. But these three people had the greatest and most sustained impact on me. When I left the clinic and went to ISPS to think and write, I did not expect that there would be another person who would mightily influence me. And I never could have imagined that if there would be another influence, it would be someone neither in the university nor in any other conventional intellectual arena. And so Elizabeth Lorentz entered my life. I met her via Don Davies, a former associate commissioner of education in Washington, who came to ISPS for a couple of years to recuperate from his experiences and to develop what later became the Institute for Responsive Education, now at Boston University. Before our initial meeting, Don told me that Elizabeth was a private citizen, a member of a family important in the history of twentieth-century America, and that over the course of her life she had been a participant in scores of public activities. Don thought that Elizabeth and I had a lot in common and we should meet.

I find it hard to describe Elizabeth, and I shall not try except to say that there is in her an oppositional streak that permits her to challenge the conventional wisdom. She went to Vassar but never graduated, and I suspect that she found Vassar, perhaps especially in those long-ago days, as too confining and unstimulating. The fact is that Elizabeth possesses an independence of mind and outlook rare in any group of people. You could say that she has an untutored mind only if you used *untutored* nonpejoratively. She is an omnivorous reader of books and scores of professional journals. But she reads for a purpose defined by some clear, strongly held convictions. She has an integrating mind, although that is not immediately apparent, especially to "professional thinkers," whose prepotent reaction to her is that she is a meddlesome do-gooder. She is in all respects inner directed, appearances to the contrary notwithstanding. Let me state briefly some of her convictions:

1. American medicine, the health professions generally, would not recognize a patient's assets if they hit them in their faces. These professions are so egregiously deficit oriented that they foster dependence and infantilization, at the expense of personal initiative and capability.
2. This deficit orientation, embedded as it is in our major educational institutions, is the greatest obstacle to an un-

trammeled consideration of the preventive orientation. The preventive orientation is asset-, not deficit-, focused because it asks the question, what are people capable of doing for themselves? Prevention requires empowerment of the individual.

3. We can no longer permit human services agencies to proceed as if their alleged distinctiveness justifies their stance of independence, as if they have nothing to gain from or to give to each other, not only for their welfare but for those they serve. Their major task should be how to exchange resources, how to enlarge their professional and intellectual outlook and networks, how to see that interdependence is liberating, not suffocating, that it adds resources, and does not subtract from what they have.

4. We are schooled, literally and figuratively, to be aware of diversity to such an extent that we are rendered incapable of recognizing the potentials for commonalities. So, for example, if agency A is concerned with child abuse and agency B with aged people, and both have very limited resources, we do not ask how each can use the other in mutually rewarding ways. Just as the health professions cannot recognize the assets of people, agencies cannot see potentialities of mutual help through resource exchange.

5. Everyone is embedded in a social network. The size of these networks, and their porosity, are varied indeed. People differ dramatically in how they perceive their networks and, fatefully, how they use them (1) to learn more about their environment (social and physical) and (2) to exploit that environment for their personal or intellectual development. One of the major functions of education, at any level, is to enlarge the individual's recognition of the nature and uses of networks; that is, networks are royal roads to an ever increasing comprehension of the worlds we live in.

Before I met Elizabeth, I had written about the psychological sense of community; more specifically, how the absence of that sense was destructive in the lives of people in American society. What Elizabeth did for me by her focus on resource exchange and social networks was to enlarge my conception of the psychological sense of community and to provide a basis for action. Could we develop a network that would facilitate resource exchange and the sense of community? Thus was born in the early seventies a network that exists today and in which have participated individuals heterogeneous in the extreme in terms of age, status, agency affiliation, and education. And at the center of this network is Elizabeth: the scanner for possibilities for resource exchange, a human radar for detecting commonalities where most of us see only diversity of needs and assets. What we did, what she stimulated, we described in two books: *Human Services and Resource Networks: Rationale, Possibilities, and Public Policy* (with C. F. Carroll, K. Maton, and S. Cohen, 1977) and *The Challenge of the Resource Exchange Network: From Concept to Action* (1979), both published by Jossey-Bass. If you want to understand the world, try to change it. The wisdom of that I had learned at Southbury; I learned it again at the clinic; and Elizabeth forced me to learn it again as we and others, notably Saul Cohen, engaged in the development and maintenance of the Northern Westchester Resource Exchange Network (which, in terms of geography, is amazingly far-flung).

In my book *The Psychological Sense of Community: Prospects for a Community Psychology* (Jossey-Bass, 1974), I recommend that any social scientist whose work purports to inform public policy should be required, every five years or so, to assume a role in the arena of action that allows him or her to implement or observe or test the appropriateness of that work. Action in itself is not virtuous, and the same is true for ideas, simple or complex. Social scientists overvalue ideas and undervalue actions that will establish the "cash value" of those ideas. Ideas derive in some way from observation of the way things are, but when these observations remain as observations, unleavened by experience in the arena from which they derive, the chances of mischievous irrelevance and of untoward consequences are mightily increased. It is like weaving a theory of psychotherapy without experience as patient or therapist. Elizabeth kept me in the world of action, as a result of which I became more modest about changing the world and more knowledgeable about American society.

I do not view the current scene (in psychology, the social sciences, and American society) with optimism. One of my more candid students asked me whether my lack of optimism, my doubts about the concept of progress, were not frequent reactions of people in my age cohort; that is, whether we looked back nostalgically at what had been and were incapable of seeing the virtues of the present. The student reminded me that on more than one occasion I had said, half facetiously, that I was one of the very few people who believed that one of the worst things that befell Western civilization was the industrial revolution. I told the student that he might well have been right, and I meant it. But why, I asked him, was he incapable of entertaining for a moment the possibility that I might be right?

You do not come to the final years of your life without passing judgment on that life. That can be avoided no better than mortality itself. Despite what I said to the student, I look back over my life with gratitude for living at a time, in a country, and in a field that made it possible for me to use my talents in the service of my interests. And my interests, I found out, were in the nature of seeking a "guide for the perplexed," answers to age-old problems concerning how we should judge our individual and collective existence. That we can live without Maimonides's sense of transcendence is clear enough, but it is no less clear that the lack of that sense in the lives of many people today in America has not been replaced by any other meaning-giving sense they find satisfying in passing judgment on themselves and their world. The hunger for transcendence is peculiarly human. It appears most clearly in our earliest and later years. I have been hungry all of my life. I have been unable to satisfy that hunger. It would be more correct to say that I have been rendered unable to satisfy that hunger because I grew up in an age of disbelief, an age that began several centuries ago. If that peculiar hunger has not been satisfied—there is mystery in this world—my psychological nutrition has been far from inadequate. Somewhere Freud said that the adult should be judged by his or her capacity for working and loving. Those were never problems for me, as is inadequately suggested in the dedication to this book. But Freud left out one other task, which, when not surmounted, insidiously invades and negatively affects well-being. And in leaving it out, he was ignoring the major problem in the modern world: achieving a sense of community, the sense that you are not alone in the world, the only sense that can withstand the loss of the sense of transcendence. Any psychology that does not comprehend that need and fact has the most superficial comprehension of the public welfare. Psychology is the study of psyches, and in America that has meant the study of the individual psyche. That, like love, is not enough.

Index